PAPERS IN
LINGUISTICS
1934–1951

BY

J. R. FIRTH

Professor Emeritus of General Linguistics
University of London

LONDON
OXFORD UNIVERSITY PRESS
NEW YORK   TORONTO
1957

Oxford University Press, Amen House, London E.C.4
GLASGOW   NEW YORK   TORONTO   MELBOURNE   WELLINGTON
BOMBAY   CALCUTTA   MADRAS   KARACHI   LAHORE   DACCA
CAPE TOWN   SALISBURY   NAIROBI   IBADAN   ACCRA
KUALA LUMPUR   HONG KONG

First edition 1957
Reprinted 1958 *and* 1961

PRINTED IN GREAT BRITAIN

PREFACE

THE first Chair of General Linguistics in this country was established in the University of London in 1944, at the School of Oriental and African Studies, with which I had been connected since 1931 and which I had served since 1938. On my appointment to the Chair, coupled with the Headship of the Department of Phonetics and Linguistics, there followed a period of development both of staff and teaching, during which the subject of General Linguistics was firmly established in London.

During the last six or seven years the papers here collected proved useful, both to staff and students, and they are frequently referred to in the published work of other members of the Department, of colleagues, and of former students. A bibliography of these works is given in the Appendix. With two exceptions, only minor alterations have been made. A number of phonetic texts have been omitted from 'Alphabets and Phonology in India and Burma' as originally published in the *Bulletin of the School of Oriental and African Studies*, and owing to the necessity of making new blocks for the article on 'Word Palatograms and Articulation', plates nos. 6 and 7 present a new series of film strips. This in turn required new descriptive material and a restatement of the results.

The proved usefulness of these papers has encouraged me to offer them for publication in the present form, which has been made possible by a subvention from the Publications Fund of the School, on the recommendation of the Publications Committee. In expressing my gratitude to the School, may I hope that readers in their turn may be encouraged to find more than a sum of separate papers by following up the general subjects collected in the Index, which is designed as a key to continuity and development.

J. R. FIRTH

ACKNOWLEDGEMENTS

For permission to reproduce the sixteen papers, grateful acknowledgements are due to three learned Societies and to the Editors of the Proceedings of two International Congresses, as follows:

(i) The Philological Society for 'The Technique of Semantics', 'The English School of Phonetics', 'Sounds and Prosodies', and 'General Linguistics and Descriptive Grammar'.

(ii) The English Association for 'Modes of Meaning'.

(iii) The Royal Anthropological Institute for 'The Principles of Phonetic Notation in Descriptive Grammar'.

(iv) The Editors of the Proceedings of the Second International Congress of Phonetic Sciences and the International Phonetic Association for 'Phonological Features of some Indian Languages' and 'The Word "Phoneme"'

And to the Editors and publishers of the following journals:

(i) The *Bulletin of the School of Oriental and African Studies* for 'Alphabets and Phonology in India and Burma', 'The Structure of the Chinese Monosyllable in a Hunanese Dialect (Changsha)', 'Word-Palatograms and Articulation', and 'Improved Techniques in Palatography and Kymography'.

(ii) *Archivum Linguisticum* for 'Atlantic Linguistics'.

(iii) *English Studies* for 'The Use and Distribution of Certain English Sounds'.

(iv) *Lingua* for 'The Semantics of Linguistic Science'.

(v) The *Sociological Review* for 'Personality and Language in Society'.

J. R. Firth

CONTENTS

1. THE WORD 'PHONEME'. *Le Maître Phonétique*, No. 46, 1934   1
2. THE PRINCIPLES OF PHONETIC NOTATION IN DESCRIPTIVE GRAMMAR. *Congrès International des Sciences anthropologiques et ethnologiques*, 1934   3
3. THE TECHNIQUE OF SEMANTICS. *Transactions of the Philological Society*, 1935   7
4. THE USE AND DISTRIBUTION OF CERTAIN ENGLISH SOUNDS. *English Studies*, xvii. 1, 1935   34
5. PHONOLOGICAL FEATURES OF SOME INDIAN LANGUAGES. *The Proceedings of the Second International Congress of Phonetic Sciences*, 1935   47
6. ALPHABETS AND PHONOLOGY IN INDIA AND BURMA. *Bulletin of the School of Oriental Studies*, viii. 2 and 3, 1936   54
7. THE STRUCTURE OF THE CHINESE MONOSYLLABLE IN A HUNANESE DIALECT (CHANGSHA). *Bulletin of the School of Oriental Studies*, viii. 4, 1937   76
8. THE ENGLISH SCHOOL OF PHONETICS. *Transactions of the Philological Society*, 1946   92
9. SOUNDS AND PROSODIES. *Transactions of the Philological Society*, 1948   121
10. THE SEMANTICS OF LINGUISTIC SCIENCE. *Lingua*, i. 4, 1948   139
11. WORD-PALATOGRAMS AND ARTICULATION. *Bulletin of the School of Oriental and African Studies*, xii. 3 and 4, 1948   148
12. ATLANTIC LINGUISTICS. *Archivum Linguisticum*, i. 2, 1949   156
13. IMPROVED TECHNIQUES IN PALATOGRAPHY AND KYMOGRAPHY. *Bulletin of the School of Oriental and African Studies*, xiii. 3, 1950   173
14. PERSONALITY AND LANGUAGE IN SOCIETY. *The Sociological Review*, xlii. 2, 1950   177
15. MODES OF MEANING. *Essays and Studies* (The English Association), 1951   190
16. GENERAL LINGUISTICS AND DESCRIPTIVE GRAMMAR. *Transactions of the Philological Society*, 1951   216

BIBLIOGRAPHY OF OTHER WORKS BASED ON SIMILAR PRINCIPLES AND METHODS   229

INDEX   231

LIST OF PLATES

1. The Zoning of the Palate and the Palatogram Figure — *facing p.* 148
2. Palatograms showing Retroflexion in the Marathi Word — 150
3. Palatograms showing the Articulation of θ, t and s in English Words — 151
4. Palatograms showing Articulations in Burmese Monosyllables — 152
5. Word Palatograms showing Contrasting Articulations in Chinese — 153
6. First Twenty-one Frames of Film Strip *Black Sheep* — 154
7. Last Twenty Frames of Film Strip *Black Sheep* — 155
8. Kymography with Cellophane — 173
9. Three Examples of Kymograms obtained by the Cellophane Technique — 174
10. The Palatogram Projector — 175
11. Examples of Palatograms obtained by the Projector Method — 176

PUBLICATIONS

by PROFESSOR J. R. FIRTH

1930   1. *Speech*, Benn's Sixpenny Library, London.

1933   2. Notes on the Transcription of Burmese, *Bulletin of the School of Oriental Studies*, vol. vii, pt. 1.

1934   3. A Short Outline of Tamil Pronunciation, Appendix to new and revised edition of *Arden's Grammar of Common Tamil*, Christian Literature Society of India.

  4. *The Principles of Phonetic Notation in Descriptive Grammar, *Congrès International des Sciences anthropologiques et ethnologiques*, London.

  5. Linguistics and the Functional Point of View, *English Studies*, vol. xvi, no. 1.

  6. *The Word 'Phoneme', *Le Maître Phonétique*, No. 46.

1935   7. *The Technique of Semantics, *Transactions of the Philological Society*.

  8. *The Use and Distribution of Certain English Sounds, *English Studies*, vol. xvii, no. 1.

  9. *Phonological Features of some Indian Languages, *The Proceedings of the Second International Congress of Phonetic Sciences*.

1936   10. *Alphabets and Phonology in India and Burma, *B.S.O.S.* (Grierson Volume), vol. viii, pts. 2 and 3.

1937   11. *The Structure of the Chinese Monosyllable in a Hunanese Dialect (Changsha), *B.S.O.S.*, vol. viii, pt. 4.

  12. *The Tongues of Men*, Watts & Co., London.

1944   13. Introduction (29 pp.) on pronunciation and the alphabets to *Colloquial Hindustani*, by A. H. Harley, Kegan Paul, Trench, Trubner & Co., Ltd., London.

1946   14. *The English School of Phonetics, *Transactions of the Philological Society*.

1948   15. Word Palatograms and Articulation, *Bulletin of the School of Oriental and African Studies*, vol. xii, pts. 3 and 4.

  16. *The Semantics of Linguistic Science, *Lingua*, i. 4.

  17. *Sounds and Prosodies, *Transactions of the Philological Society*.

1949   18. *Atlantic Linguistics, *Archivum Linguisticum*, vol. i, fasc. ii.

1950   19. *Improved Techniques in Palatography and Kymography, *B.S.O.A.S.*, vol. xiii, pt. 3.

  20. *Personality and Language in Society, *The Sociological Review*, Journal of the Institute of Sociology, vol. xlii, section Two.

1950 21. Introduction on the spelling and pronunciation to *Teach Yourself Hindustani*, by T. Grahame Bailey, The English Universities Press, Ltd., London.

1951 22. *Modes of Meaning, *Essays and Studies*, The English Association.

23. *General Linguistics and Descriptive Grammar, *Transactions of the Philological Society*.

1955 24. Indian Languages, *Encyclopaedia Britannica*.

25. Structural Linguistics, *Transactions of the Philological Society*.

26. Joseph Wright, the Scholar, *Transactions of the Yorkshire Dialect Society*.

1956 27. Linguistic Analysis and Translation, *Festschrift for Roman Jakobson*, Massachusetts Institute of Technology, Mouton & Co., The Hague.

28. Philology in the Philological Society. Presidential Address, 1956. *Transactions of the Philological Society*.

IN THE PRESS

1. A Synopsis of Linguistic Theory, 1930–1955, in a special volume to be published by the Philological Society of Great Britain.

2. Ethnographic Analysis and Language, *Man and Culture. An Evaluation of the Work of Bronislaw Malinowski*, London.

3. Linguistics in the Laboratory, *Beiheft Nr. 1 zur Zeitschrift für Phonetik und allgemeine Sprachwissenschaft* (Panconcelli-Calzia Festschrift), Akademie-Verlag, Berlin.

4. Hindustani, *Encyclopaedia Britannica*.

* Included in this volume.

INTRODUCTION

THE discipline of general linguistics with its ancillary techniques is ultimately directed towards making multiple statements of the meaning of language and languages. In these selected papers, which have appeared over a period of twenty-five years, a developing linguistic theory is presented, as may be apparent from the entries in the Index. These entries are selected items of the technical language which has grown with the theory.

The basic principle, first stated in the *Technique of Semantics*, is a dispersion of meaning at a series of congruent levels of analysis, at each one of which statements of meaning are made in linguistic terms.

At the phonetic level, the problems of phonetic description and statement including notation are dealt with, and two papers take these problems into the laboratory. Phonetic analysis is related to phonology, including reference to the theory of the phoneme.

Analysis at the phonological level will be found to refer to words, pieces, and sentences as wholes, and considerable attention is given to features of the syllable and the syllable as an element of structure. Attention is drawn to the technical use of the words 'systems', 'alternances', 'terms', and 'units'. It is relevant to notice phonetic diacritica and the study of differential features.

The study of words, pieces, and longer stretches of texts as wholes, leads to the prosodic approach which has been proved fruitful in application. There are a number of references throughout to the notion of distribution in linguistic analysis which is still of interest, though my present view is that the logic of distributional relations has been much overrated in linguistics.

The establishing of formal conditions for grammatical categories is related to the phonological level of analysis and also to the whole technique of contextualization which is basic to my approach. Reference to the Index will show the importance of the context of situation in the contextualization process.

An approach to the meaning of words, pieces, and sentences by the statement of characteristic collocations ensures that the isolate word or piece as such is attested in established texts. The characteristic collocations of 'key' or 'pivotal' words may be supported by reference to contexts of situation, and may constitute the material for syntactical analysis and provide citations in support of dictionary definitions. Words and texts representing current usages can be taken as institutionalized and studied in the situation, when necessary in connexion with other social institutions and structures.

Words stare you in the face from the text, and that is enough; and as Wittgenstein said, a word in company may be said to have a physiognomy. The elements of style can be stated in linguistic terms.

This brief Introduction is related to the main general items of the Index. Such linguistic theory as may appear in the papers is not intended as an attempt to establish universals for general linguistic description, but rather as an approach to general linguistic theory to be applied to the particular description of specific language material, in the hope that it may be useful in renewal of connexion with experience.

Some of the papers refer to the historical and general background of descriptive linguistics, and a selected list of names will be found in the Index.

J. R. FIRTH

London, 1956

1
THE WORD 'PHONEME'

In his article on 'Baudouin de Courtenay and the phoneme idea'[1] Dr. Arend mentioned two works by Baudouin de Courtenay, and as ideas change he naturally quotes from the later one published in 1901, though there was a much later work on phonetics and psycho-phonetics published in 1927.

But it is in the introduction to the earlier work (Cracow, 1893) that Baudouin de Courtenay gives the early history of the term 'phoneme'; he takes it back to an essay published at Kazan in 1879 on the influence of accent on vowel alternations (*guṇa*) in the Rig-Veda, by one of his pupils, Kruszewski.

Kruszewski's work belonged to a time, says Baudouin de Courtenay, when among the linguists at Kazan there was a regular mania for new *termini technici* to constitute a better nomenclature. He especially emphasized two of these as being of great theoretical and methodological importance; first the differentiation of unilingual and interlingual sound alternations, and secondly the terms 'phone' and 'phoneme'. And in connexion with both these distinctions, he singles out for special mention his Kazan pupil, Kruszewski, who, he says, 'put in a sounder and more concise form, what he had learnt from another. The proposal to employ the term "phoneme" as different from "phone" comes from Kruszewski.'

Kruszewski developed his theory in the introduction to his Russian essay published in 1879. This introduction was published separately in Warsaw in 1881, and to make it generally known to other European linguists, a German version, *Über die Lautabwechslung*, was published in the same year. Very little notice was taken of it, however, and it was not until phoneticians of other schools, and especially the English School, and more recently the Prague School, developed unilingual studies that widespread currency was given to the terms 'phone' and 'phoneme'.

Kruszewski distinguished between two main types of sound alternations, acoustico-physiological or anthropophonic, and spontaneous, psychical, or historical changes. In the first category of anthropophonic sound alternances he insisted on four characteristics:

1. The sound alternations are produced by anthropophonic, i.e. physical, causes, and are always directly definable and present.
2. The sound alternance $s:s_1$ takes place generally, under the given conditions, in all words regardless of their category.
3. The alternance $s:s_1$, under the conditions $x:x_1$, is necessary, and

[1] *Le Maître phonétique*, No. 46, 1934.

does not allow of any exception, i.e. the appearance of **s** under the conditions x_1, or s_1 with **x** is impossible.

4. The alternating sounds must be in close anthropophonic relationship—or more exactly, they are modifications of one and the same sound, differentiations of one and the same sound conditioned by place in the word or phonetic context. They may be termed divergents or divergencies.

Sound changes of the second type are not so closely related and are not modifications of one and the same sound, but are entirely different sounds. The conditions or immediate causes may not be present, or may have to be explained historically, and sometimes the sound change is connected with a change of morphological categories.

In the above summary there are many points in which Kruszewski, more than fifty years ago, anticipated the work of some of our contemporaries. There is 'the phoneme idea', and what is even more striking, the corollary notion of the 'assimilation' of divergents to the 'anthropophonic neighbourhood', the conditions of divergence being always present, directly definable, and admitting of no exceptions. This, Professor Jones has termed 'similitude' to distinguish it from other sound assimilations falling into Kruszewski's second and third categories which are connected with morphological and historical processes.

Kruszewski, however, extended the term 'phoneme' to include sound alternances associated with changes of morphological categories. In English, for instance, **-s**, **-z**, **-iz** would be one morphological phoneme, represented naturally enough in orthography by one sign, **s**. He also extended it to include interlingual correspondences between sounds in related words in parallel morphological categories. And here he came near to the concept of what Professor Jones calls the diaphone.

It is, then, to Kruszewski we owe the distinct use of the terms 'sound', 'phone', and 'phoneme', and the special use of divergents and divergencies.

As for 'the phoneme idea', quite simply it must be regarded as implicit in the work of all phoneticians and orthographists who have employed broad transcription. It is implicit in Sweet's Broad Romic which dates back to about the same time as Kruszewski. It is implicit in many orthographies. In Tamil, for instance, the **k** letter represents quite unambiguously the divergents c, ɟ, ɡ, ɣ, ç, x, ɦ, occurring each in its appropriate place. Theoretically it appears *in nuce* in Jespersen's *Lehrbuch*, and also in de Saussure's *Cours de linguistique générale*, where something very like a complete theory appears on pp. 163–9. Similar notions are to be found in the works of Sapir and Bloomfield.

The meaning of any ordinary word is subject to change without notice, but technical terms must not be handled in that way. Notice must be given. A word of warning would appear to be necessary with regard to the word 'phoneme'. What does it mean?

2

THE PRINCIPLES OF PHONETIC NOTATION IN DESCRIPTIVE GRAMMAR

A DESCRIPTIVE grammar of a spoken language or dialect must employ some form of phonetic notation. Now a phonetic notation does not attempt to reproduce on paper an exact record of every detail of sound, stress, and intonation. It is not direct sound-script faithfully caught by an acoustic automaton. Phonetics and common sense both tell you, that is impossible. That sort of record is nowadays best done by machines. Phonetic notation enables you to represent the language, when you know something about the way the native uses his 'sounds'. The observer must have a good ear for sound, tone, and other attributes of speech; but a good ear and a few symbols are not enough for the construction of linguistically valid phonetic notation. The observer must be able to interpret and systematize what he hears. This is where technical training is most valuable. The phonetic amanuensis in striving to set on paper a collection of letters, dots, and other marks to represent exactly what he hears, may often miss the 'sound' the native speaker knows (or feels) he is using for a particular purpose in a particular context.

In a sense, therefore, you should record not what the native says, but what he thinks he says. Any speaker using a particular style of speech determined by the cultural situation, will make use of certain phonetic units which make up his phonetic repertory. And in the flow of speech he uses these units in well-defined phonetic contexts; a certain consonant, for example, may occur in initial, final, or intervocalic positions or preceded or followed by other sounds, or perhaps never finally, or never intervocalically. And if the consonant be a morphological instrument it may possibly be 'influenced' by a whole variety of other sounds preceding or following it; so that what we call a 'speech sound', from this point of view, presents itself to the superficial ear in a variety of 'disguises'.

The 'field grammarian' has to describe and classify the facts of his language. These facts include sentences, words, grammatical formations. The phonetic notation must represent without ambiguity all the differential values resulting from differences between sounds or tones or other attributes of speech, which may be used by the native. These differential values may have morphological, syntactical, or lexical function. The important thing is to recognize functions and represent them without ambiguity.

One of the functional phonetic units of Tamil, for example, is something which is not **p, t,** or **pp**, or **tt**, or even **kk**, but variously **k, ɡ, c, ç, x, ɣ** (I.P.A.), according to context. This kind of functional phonetic unit has been termed a *phoneme*. Six alternant **k**-phones have been selected from a very large number, because they are clearly distinguishable by the most stubborn ear. As an illustration of what is meant by a phoneme, we may take the Tamil **k**-phoneme above. The alternant phones k_1, k_2, k_3, k_4, k_5, k_6 necessarily occur under the conditions x_1, x_2, x_3, x_4, x_5, x_6, which are directly observable and definable in one style of speech of a certain type of speaker from a certain place, and can therefore be represented by the sign **k**. The term 'similitude' may be applied to the relations $k_1:x_{17}$, $k_2:x_{27}$, $k_3:x_{37}$, &c., between the alternant phones and the determining conditions.

In Tamil, therefore, the **k**-sign represents something used habitually in a variety of phonetic contexts, in which other 'sounds' or phonemes may also be used.

Now take the English **s**-phoneme. To some phoneticians the English **s** is merely a hissing sound which has no variants. But the English **s** can occur in a large number of phonetic contexts. It may be initial, intervocalic, and final, preceded and followed by a variety of other phonemes.

Contexts such as **bs**, **ds**, **ġs**, occur in special circumstances and usually mark some sort of word formation. Final **d** followed by initial **s** or final **t** followed by initial **z** are common enough in English, but **ds** or **tz** as final consonant-groups are unusual. This contextualization of **s** and **z** is very important, since the assibilation of final consonants has several grammatical functions in English.

A suitable phonetic notation for a given language will develop as the phonetico-grammatical study of the language proceeds. The identification and contextualization of the phonemes is of the greatest importance both in the study of words and their forms in morphology, and also in connected word-groups in syntax. It will be seen that the values of the phonemes, and of the signs which represent them, are linguistic values—differential values which are put to morphological syntactical and lexical uses.

One absolute pronunciation or independent phonetic value, for each letter by itself, is neither desirable nor practical. Even for pronunciation the value of each letter or sign depends on its context. And the value of the notation for pronunciation depends on the contextual conventions laid down.

No phonetician has yet presented us with anything like a complete array of contexts for the phonemes of any language. This is perhaps because too much attention has been paid to superficial listening. If you limit the alternants to those you can differentiate absolutely by direct hearing, or by the technique of the phonetic amanuensis, you may serve all practical teaching purposes, but not those of systematic linguistic research.

All the common phonetic contexts of each phoneme should be stated, and the contextual spread or 'scatter' of the phonemes compared. This knowledge of the contextual scatter of a phoneme will be found of the greatest importance for the statement of our future sound laws.

It will be obvious by this time that I have abandoned the idea that the phonetic symbol should represent a sort of ideal perfect sound, on the principle of 'one symbol, one sound', one letter one perfect ideal noise made by one ideally perfect posture. What we really want is a repertory or store of good letters, in all founts of type and suitable for script, and draw on this for as many as we need for each language—two or three **p**-letters, **b**-letters, **t**-letters, and so on, would be necessary.

I cannot go into typography or scriptics. From the typographical point of view the I.P.A. characters are, for the most part, on psychological, typographical, and practical grounds, the best.

I have indicated not only the process by which you contextualize your alternants and so arrive at your phoneme-units or functional units, or phonetic 'substitution-counters', but have stated the principle of 'one symbol *per* phoneme' as a basis for a practical linguistic transcription.

By contextualization is here meant, not only the recognition of the various phonetic contexts in which the phonemes occur, but the further identification of phonemes by determining their lexical and grammatical functions. Most of the vowel-phonemes of English, for example, can be established by such lexical and grammatical functions.

Perhaps the most difficult problem of notation is deciding what symbols and conventions are to be used to represent the vowels in languages in which there is what is called vowel-harmony.

In deciding on the final form of a practical phonetic notation, the statistical method should also be applied. Working with Mr. Stewart of the London School of Oriental Studies, I found that in Burmese, what is called the 'low-level tone' occurred in about 50 per cent. of the monosyllables counted. This tone we decided should not be marked, or rather that a 'zero' mark should distinguish it from the two other marked tones.

Thus, by combining contextualization with functional and statistical study, it was found practicable to reduce the tone-marks usually employed in Burmese transcription, from eleven to two, and to eliminate length-marks which did not correspond to any functional category.

In a descriptive grammar, the investigator has to delimit and identify what he will regard as words and forms, and this he does in a variety of ways; one of the best being by substitution, and another by slow dictation, using any feeling for word-units the native may have. I mention the 'word' first, because the theory of the phoneme would appear to be bound up with the theory of the word. The substitution of one phonetic performance or sound for another may produce a different lexical unit, or a different form, or a sentence having a different function. In descriptive grammar therefore we employ our notation to represent words in isolation and in combination—so that the notation follows an analysis of the morphological, syntactical, and lexical instruments. Throughout such a grammar, phonetic notation would follow functional units or patterns as far as possible.

The divisions of the grammar would be Phonetics, Morphology, Syntax, Lexicon, and perhaps semantics would require a separate volume with illustrative texts. I am firmly convinced of the desirability of separating semantics as I understand it, that is, the social contextualization of locutions and habitual speech-sequences, from grammar of the technical and formal kind. The forms presented in morphology will be differentiated by the notation and as many of them as possible should be named simply by the formative sounds or symbols. In this way we get rid of absurd explanatory terminology.

Morphology and syntax have quite distinct sets of categories. Syntactical categories are of many kinds, but obviously no syntactical study is possible without a system of intonation marks. The marking of the relative pitch of every syllable is perhaps not necessary. And I hope that, just as narrow transcription has given way very largely to broad, the narrow intonation marks will be abandoned in favour of a more functional system, something like a punctuation system.

By allowing language to use phonetics instead of phonetics using language, we can get nearer a phonetic technique which will not merely show how a language should be pronounced, but also how the sounds and sound-attributes are used.

In the matter of tone and tone-languages, I suggest that the tone patterns which characterize morphological categories be marked differently from sentence intonations, which differentiate different types of sentence, not different forms of words.

A descriptive grammar of a spoken language must be phonetic or phonological grammar, in morphology and also in syntax. Applied and used in this way, phonetics becomes linguistics.

3

THE TECHNIQUE OF SEMANTICS

THE origins of this paper are: first, practical experience of linguistic problems in India and Africa as well as more recently in England; secondly, the prevailing uncertainty reflected in such titles as 'What is a Phoneme?', 'The Problem of Grammar', 'What is a Sentence?', 'What is Syntax?', 'The Meaning of Meaning', and countless other signs of the overhauling of our apparatus; and lastly and perhaps most important of all, a discussion on linguistic theory held by the Society on 1 December 1933, led by my friend, Dr. Alan Gardiner.

The first and earliest entry for the adjective 'semantic' in the Society's Dictionary is most discouraging. It was used in 1665 in J. Spencer's *Prodigies*: ' "Twere easy to shew how much this Semantic Philosophy was studied.' This related to the signs of the weather, and after all, Semantics is rather like Meteorology, only it has nothing so permanent as the 'depression from Iceland'.

The fundamentals of what is properly, because usually, called 'semantics' can be dealt with in connexion with lexicography, phonetics, and descriptive grammar, and although the most important recent contributions to the study of meaning have been made in such fields as philosophy, general linguistics, psychology, logic, sociology, and criticism, they can be touched upon or implied in the discussion of the branches of linguistic technique above mentioned.

As a first approach, therefore, to this study of the meaning or *use* of words, let us consider the Society's Dictionary, and more especially the bearing of certain canons of lexicography which it lays down on the technique under examination. Before the philological age England had already produced a great lexicographer, and in two of the three main guiding principles laid down for the new work the Dictionary was to follow Dr. Johnson—firstly, in being general and registering all sorts of words, even the commonest; secondly, it was to follow him in making systematic use of quotations or context; but the third principle was new—the Historical Principle.

All three principles have important bearings on semantics. The first principle is that a certain component of the meaning of a word is described when you say what sort of a word it is, that is, when you identify it morphologically, and give it what the Dictionary calls a Grammatical Designation.

Secondly, the complete meaning of a word is always contextual, and no study of meaning apart from a complete context can be taken seriously.

But what made the Society's Dictionary different was the third member of the trinity—the Historical Principle. The application of the historical principle has, until quite recently, been the characteristic of most linguistic techniques, including what is properly called semantics.

By the year 1857 the Golden Age of what was called at the time modern philological science had begun, and Furnivall, Trench, Coleridge, Murray, and their colleagues on the Committees constantly reaffirmed the Historical Principle, and on the fly-leaf of each of the ten volumes there is the guarantee—'On Historical Principles'. That explains the N in *N.E.D.*[1]

From Trench through Mayhew and Skeat, Littré, Darmesteter, Bréal to de Saussure, la sémantique, *semantike techne*, the 'science of significations', as the French describe it, deals with changes of meaning classified in such categories as enlargement, restriction, generalization, specialization, transference, metaphor, radiation, irradiation, and many others of the same kind.[2]

Throughout the nineteenth century, before Bréal's book was published in English in 1900 under the title of *Semantics*, the English word for the historical study of change of meanings was 'Semasiology'.[3]

In German, Bedeutungslehre as a linguistic discipline has also been chiefly concerned with the problems of Bedeutungswandel, Bedeutungsverschiebung, Bedeutungsänderung, Bedeutungsübergang, Bedeutungsvarianten, and so on. There also you will meet 'Spezialisierung', 'Erweiterung', 'pars pro toto', and similar categories.

The main point is that this study of meanings was a study of change. And change implies something permanent which changes, the permanent persisting in and through the change. Usually the change is regarded either as development or decay, and is viewed with reference to some essential or original nature or zenith.

Thus Skeat in stating his canons for Etymology wrote: 'We can sum up the whole matter by saying that our pursuit is Etymology, by which we seek to give an account of the *true* origin of a word. The real object is in due time to arrive at a perfect knowledge of the whole, the living and the eternal truth.'[4]

You may smile at this. You may say the etymology of 'etymology' has nothing to do with its present meaning. That is what Greenough and Kittredge say in their well-known book with the somewhat misleading

---

[1] In a report on the Dictionary to the Philological Society in 1928, Dr. Onions remarked that 'the use of New English as a representative of German *neuenglisch*' had nothing to do with the title. The legitimate abbreviation is *N.E.D.*, 'still the official use with the Oxford University Press itself. Not that there is any quarrel with those who prefer *O.E.D.*, the symbol of the *Oxford English Dictionary*, a style adopted now for many years on the covers and wrappers of our sections and parts and on the binding cases of the quarter-persian edition, but not incorporated in the title page.'

[2] Categories of this kind, supplemented by 'Associationist' categories mentioned on p. 12, are used by Edmond Huguet, in *L'Évolution du sens des Mots depuis le XVIme siècle*, 1934.

[3] The introduction to the first volume of the Dictionary uses 'Sematology', and J. A. H. Murray much later also used it—perhaps rather ignorantly—as the word had been previously used of the study of the use of signs in practice, what Smart called 'Practicology.'

[4] *Principles of English Etymology*, 2nd series (1891), p. 462.

title, *Words and their Ways in English Speech*. 'The word "etymology" has quite changed its sense', they say. And yet in the same chapter[1] they also say: 'We often speak of "the proper or essential meaning" of a word. The term is convenient, and one could not well dispense with it in etymological study.' If you must see permanence in change, at least two categories of meaning are methodologically necessary, as we shall see over and over again. To make this clearer let us turn to one of the fathers of the Dictionary. We find in the writings of Trench,[2] upon which high value was placed in the preface to the 1933 Supplement of the Dictionary, a statement of the principles involved in this study of change. He writes:[3] 'This tracing of that which is common to, and connects, all the many meanings of a word, can of course only be done by getting to its heart, to the *seminal* meaning, from which, as from a fruitful seed, all the others unfold themselves.' That is to say, a word has a sort of true origin and originally one meaning, and 'all the others may be brought back and affiliated upon it'. He adds significantly, and this we must notice later: 'The non-recognition of this is *the* great fault in Johnson's Dictionary.' A further explanation of the N in *N.E.D.*

Trench takes the word 'post' and finds that throughout all its meanings there is an active association with an idea of 'that which is placed', and also that etymology takes it back to the Latin *positus* which has the same meaning. So that what he calls the seminal meaning might be expressed either in the equation 'post = *positus*', or by saying that 'post' both in form and seminal meaning comes from *positus*. In his *English Past and Present*[4] he adds to this concept of central or seminal meaning, which is a sort of greatest common measure of all the uses of a word, supported by a unity of ultimate origin, a second kind of meaning that a word may have, what he calls 'domain of meaning', or as he says later 'range of application'

Similarly, Greenough and Kittredge, after listing ten applied meanings of 'head' as illustrating Darmesteter's principle of radiation, conclude that each meaning proceeds 'in a direct line from the central or primary meaning of head'. Even Meillet, whose work shows him to be something of

---

[1] Chapter xvi.

[2] In addition to covering most of the routine technique to be found in much later works on semasiology, Trench touches on many fundamental questions of linguistic theory. Much has been written in recent years on *Innere Sprachform*, e.g. in Vossler's *The Spirit of Language in Civilization* (Kegan Paul, 1932).

In his *Study of Words* (p. 119) Trench mentions the 'creative energy' of a poet's use of language, and we are all in some sense poets. He emphasizes the connexion between language and national character, and in his *English Past and Present* he says: 'For the genius of a language is the sense and *inner conviction* entertained by the mass of those who speak it.'

He deals with the influence of Christianity on language, a subject which Vossler has also treated. He discusses the force and imposture of words, words evoked by necessity, of meanings dictated by things, by usage. And finally he reminds us that 'a word exists as truly for the eye as for the ear'.

[3] *On the Study of Words*, 6th ed. (1855), p. 194.

[4] Pp. 311–14, 1898 edition.

a sociologist and realist, goes back to the Indo-European reconstructed form *pṛtu- and gives it the primary meaning of 'the place through which or by which you can pass', and then notices local specializations in *portus, porta, porte, port*, and *ford*. This shows the danger of going too far for permanence. You get back to nothing. We have here, then, two uses of the word meaning—first, in the sense of true, original, and essential meaning of a word, and secondly, the many meanings it comes to have in application or use.

No one seems to be able to handle the problem of meaning without splitting it up into components which can then be placed in categories and classified, and brought into relation with one another. Erdmann[1] distinguishes three kinds of meaning: (1) *Begriffsinhalt*, or Hauptbedeutung, roughly our Essential or Central Meaning or Denotation; (2) *Nebensinn* or Applied Meaning or Contextual Meaning; and (3) *Gefühlswert* or Stimmungsgehalt or Feeling-Tone.

Sperber and others who have made use of these categories in historical work have emphasized the great importance of the second sort of meaning, Nebensinn or contextual meaning, in the history of change; you may have noticed, for example, the important influence of context[2] and feeling-tone on public-school cant as a result of its being used by the 'old school tie' comedians, who seem to find great public favour. Research into the detailed contextual distribution of sociologically important words, what one might call *focal* or *pivotal* words, is only just beginning. Mention of the public school and pivotal words reminds me of an interesting monograph[3] by Dr. Krebs on what I would call the contextualization of the word *clerk* in Middle English, which is an excellent example of what can be done in the historical study of meaning from the sociological point of view.

Ogden and Richards in *The Meaning of Meaning* also find themselves forced to abandon the single term 'Meaning' itself, and to resolve it into component terms such as intention, value, referent, emotion. The meaning of words is only appreciated when the symbols are expanded, or as I should say contextualized. Richards in his *Mencius on the Mind* says: 'What may be called the Total Meaning of a word or phrase is a complex function of which Intention, Feeling, Tone, and Sense seem to be the main components.' He sketches a technique of what he calls 'Multiple Definition' by means of which we are to present an ordered systematic schema of ranges of meaning of pivotal words, not studied in isolation as they are in a

---

[1] *Die Bedeutung des Wortes*, 3rd ed., 1922.

[2] A very common colloquial English sentence was used by a well-known American actress in a notorious film. Whether we like it or not, that parasite context finds a place in most of our contexts of experience. The extraordinary influence of such contexts is shown by the following extract from p. 3 of the *Sixty-fourth Annual Report of the Deputy Master and Comptroller of the Royal Mint*, 1933: 'As already admitted, I am no Newton—or, to bring the parallel completely up to date, no Angell either, even though the Gold Standard in this country may have gone West—to show the road up out of our confusions.'

[3] *Der Bedeutungswandel von ME. Clerk und damit zusammenhängende Probleme*, Bonner Studien zur Englischen Philologie, Heft xxi, 1933.

THE TECHNIQUE OF SEMANTICS

dictionary, but in association with one another in a common background of a fairly homogeneous cultural context.

This characteristic study of change involving two or more kinds of meaning is even found in a statistical study, Zipf's *Studies of the Principle of Relative Frequency in Language*.[1] He uses the term 'meaning' for something not defined, but more or less equivalent to essential, primary, common, or usual meaning. He makes use of the terms 'primary' meaning or denotation in the singular, and 'secondary' meanings, 'metaphors,' or 'connotations', all in the plural; and yet this author is very doubtful about primary meaning, except perhaps in a statistical sense, a basic highest-frequency meaning. Secondly, he says there is quality, positive quality, and negative quality, that is 'undesirable for the ego'. Thirdly, emotional intensity; and lastly, and this is interesting, order—order being what our Dictionary calls 'Grammatical Designation', and what I shall regard as the grammatical component of meaning, to be contextualized grammatically and understood grammatically.

Turning back for a moment to the correlative of change, permanence, we find it stated in the first volume of our Dictionary that of the words on record since the twelfth century, three-quarters are still in use, and for the whole ten volumes, of 206,565 main words, 177,970 are listed as current.

In Appendix I of Darmesteter's *La Vie des mots*[2] there is a long list of Latin words which 'have not changed in meaning in passing into French'. In this list are such words as *ami, âme, bain, bête, chou, cercle, cité, famille, femme, fille, glace, honneur*. I prefer Johnson, who wrote in the preface to his Dictionary:[3] 'Words change their manners when they change their country.'

Then there is the question of causes of change. The observations of Greenough and Kittredge in this connexion are typical. Causes there must be: 'Since thought proceeds in obedience to definite laws, language ... must also obey rules which, if we could discover them, would account for every variation.'

We have formulated what we call Sound Laws to help us to follow the permanent word through changes of form. Similarly, German scholars have discussed die Gesetzmäßigkeit des Bedeutungswandels.[4] Bréal had answered this question in the negative in one of the best things he wrote, a review of Darmesteter's *La Vie des mots* in 1888.[5] But a classification and ordering of the facts he believed to be possible.

Three main types of classification of changes of meaning have been common: Logical, Psychological, Sociological. Darmesteter's logical conditions of changes of meaning are enumerated under the well-known headings

---

[1] Harvard University Press, 1932.   [2] 1885.
[3] Dr. Johnson's common sense is quite good medicine after a surfeit of specialist literature. As Boswell notes, 'The Preface furnishes an eminent instance of a double talent, of which Johnson was fully conscious.'
[4] Sperber, *Einführung in die Bedeutungslehre*.
[5] No. 36, *Mémoires et documents scolaires*, 1888.

of the figures of speech. They are dominated by *a priori* conceptions and are little more than a scheme of rhetoric. But they continue to travel round the world and one still meets them in new books fresh from the press.

Bréal was much more psychological in his classification, and also deals with certain social causes of change. Meillet also shows sociological tendencies, but on the whole only in theory. He is best on the purely linguistic conditions of change of meaning. But his oblique view of things comes out in his definition of a 'borrowed word' in French. Any word not established in the earliest French or in Caesar's time is 'borrowed'. Thus almost the whole of semantics comes to be the study of 'borrowed words'. He actually says:[1] 'The greater part of the vocabulary of French is "borrowed".' This and the starred form *pr̥tu-* mentioned above are typical pieces of philological obliquity, but there is directness in his insistence on the importance of the *history of things* in the study of the history of words. He is one of the first historical philologists not to be afraid of things. More recently Dr. Sperber in his *Einführung in die Bedeutungslehre* also emphasizes the importance not so much of *Bedeutungsverschiebung* as of *Sachwandel*, which leads to what Wellander called '*Bedeutungsunterschiebung*'.[2] This is common sense, and it again reminds us of Dr. Johnson who wrote: 'I am not yet so lost in lexicography as to forget that *words are the daughters of earth and that things are the sons of heaven*' (the italics are Johnson's). Wundt's classification of changes of meaning is psychological, chiefly based on the Associationist doctrine: Association by Contiguity, Association by Similarity, by Cause and Effect, &c.

A thoroughgoing sociological classification has not yet been attempted, but many valuable suggestions have been made, vaguely by psychologists and sociologists, and occasionally with more point by linguists.

Reviewing the history of the principles of Semasiology, we have first emphasized the Historical Principle and the study of change; secondly, following from that, the necessity of distributing the problem by analysing meaning into elements which can be placed in categories, such as original or primary meaning, applied or changed meaning (Nebensinn), order, and others above mentioned; and thirdly, the schematic classification of types of change. Next there is the problem of the mechanism of change or the stages or steps of change.

In connexion with the problem of meaning-links between a word base and its derivatives Dr. Johnson has something to say. He found it impossible to suggest the steps by which derivatives of simpler words came to have their specialized meanings. In noticing what he called the 'maze of variations' in the uses of such English phrasal verbs as *come off, set off,*

---

[1] 'Comment les mots changent de sens', in *Linguistique historique et linguistique générale*, Paris, 1926. See especially pp. 241–6 and pp. 252–5. 'Le vocabulaire d'une langue telle que le français se compose pour la plus grande partie de mots empruntés.'

[2] See Wellander, *Studien*, vol. i, pp. 55 sqq., and pp. 70 sqq. Stern in *Meaning and Change of Meaning*, chapter 8, p. 193, uses *substitution* as a 'part translation of Bedeutungsunterschiebung'.

he adds: 'Some being so far distant from the sense of the simple words, that no sagacity will be able to trace the steps by which they arrived at the present use.'

There is, of course, a difference between historical changes of meaning of a word as it continues in use in the same morphological type or category, and differences of meaning a word-base undergoes in derivatives, e.g. *cut—cutter, head—header*. But, as we have seen, eighteenth-century rationalism is not really interested in tracing the steps and progress of change. The first attempt of this kind was made by a German contemporary of Bréal's, Stöcklein,[1] who suggested three stages in a change: first, the particular influential context for the special meaning; second, common quotation of the fixed context; third, the use of the interesting word in free combination. He uses the word *Kreuz* in the gospel context in St. Mark[2] as his example. To this Sperber adds a fourth stage, contexts combining an earlier meaning with the new meaning. In this connexion both Stöcklein and Sperber emphasize the fact that a change of meaning is not brought about in a single word as such, but in a complete functioning context. Contextual factors led to the replacing of the noun *Eurasian* by *Anglo-Indian*. And things have also happened since to *Anglo-Indian*.

While 'old school tie' makes the success of a comic turn, the word *plan* with its derivatives provides some of the magic words of the age. Compounds like *air-minded, traffic-minded*, are fairly common. The other day I saw *beacon-minded* and *flat-minded* in a newspaper. Such compounds have favoured the rather un-English formation *likemindedness* as some sort of equivalent of the German magic word *Gleichschaltung*. Cases of this kind are interesting because they are often sociologically symptomatic.

Even in historical semantics of the traditional kind we are reviewing there is an enormous field of work if we follow a contextual and sociological technique. The study of such words as *work, labour, trade, employ, occupy, play, leisure, time, hours, means, self-respect* in all their derivatives and compounds in sociologically significant contexts during the last twenty years would be quite enlightening. So would the study of words particularly associated with the dress, occupations, and ambitions of women, or the language of advertising, especially of quackery, entertainments, food, drink, or of political movements and propaganda.

In the 1933 Supplement of the Dictionary there are evidences of an appalling recent development of derivatives and compounds of the word *sex*, and a large number of divisions have been added. The frequency of reference to sex had necessarily extended what I term the formal scatter of the word, and we now have *sexed, sexless, sexy, sexiness*, even *sexology*. *Sexy* and *sexiness* occur in print in 1928 in the *Daily Express* and the *Sunday Dispatch*. The more frequent and various the contexts, the greater the tendency to extension of formal scatter. We all appreciate the convenience of a term which will 'conjugate'; e.g. I have found it necessary to conjugate

---

[1] *Bedeutungswandel der Wörter*, Munich, 1898.   [2] St. Mark viii. 34.

14   THE TECHNIQUE OF SEMANTICS

context, and find *contextualize* and *contextualization* indispensable forms in which to use the word *context* in certain unavoidable constructions, though I cannot find excuses for Mr. Palmer of Tokio who conjugates *semantic*. These examples bring out once more the close connexion between morphology and semantics.

Lonely words are also interesting. Almost anything can happen to them. In Greenough and Kittredge's book published in 1902 the following passage occurs: 'In England "*car*" has become, in the main, a poetical word for "*chariot*" or the like, as in Milton's "car of night".' The revival of *coach* is also worth noting in passing. Is this a change of meaning?

From the sociological point of view the history of things and of culture is all important for the study of changes of meaning. The other day I re-read *Pride and Prejudice* for the special purpose of noticing not only great formal changes, but the great change of meaning that has taken place even behind those forms of words and sentences which could still be written today. From the syntactical and sociological point of view it is written in 'Old' English.[1]

In connexion with the historical study of changes in meaning we have noted the subdivision of meaning, the classification of types of changes, the examination of causes and of the mechanisms or stages in change, with special emphasis on actual context, particularly stereotyped contexts, and sociological background. There is also the necessity of a parallel study of changes of form according to proved sound-laws and established philological doctrine. Meillet[2] compresses all the essential principles into the following cardinal paragraph: 'Un mot est défini par l'association d'un sens donné à un ensemble donné de sons susceptible d'un emploi grammatical donné. Pour avoir une valeur, une concordance entre deux mots doit donc porter à la fois sur les sons, sur le sens et, s'il y a lieu, sur l'emploi grammatical. Plus la concordance est parfaite *à la fois* aux trois points de vue et plus l'etymologie a de chances d'être correcte.' Murray said:[3] 'The writing of the Morphology and of Sematology must go hand in hand.' In our Dictionary every main word is treated under four heads, the first two of which are identification in the matter of spelling, pronunciation, and grammatical designation, and further under the heading of morphology which shows formation, form history, and etymology. We have already

[1] In this connexion Mr. C. L. Wrenn, of Oxford, contributes an amusing story. A competent Bengali scholar was asked to translate the first page of *Pride and Prejudice* into his native language. An equally competent Englishman was then asked to produce a translation from the Bengali into present-day English. This version was then compared with the original, with results that can well be imagined.

One reason why Shakespeare can be such a success in a modern translation is the fact that he is brought up to date in the process, put into linguistic modern dress, so to speak. In England we cannot do this, but producers have tried the somewhat vulgar expedient of 'Bedeutungsunterschiebung' by putting Hamlet into a dinner jacket and Macbeth into khaki.

[2] *Linguistique historique et linguistique générale*, p. 30.
[3] *Trans. Phil. Society*, 1882–4, p. 511.

noticed in passing the importance of studying words in association with their derivatives in actual use, or in what I have called their formal scatter. This involves all the morphology of word-bases, stems, affixes, and compounds. This branch of semantics is rather neglected in English.[1]

From the preceding review and analysis it should be clear that the work of Trench and the earlier English Etymologists, many of whom helped to build up the earlier volumes of the Society's Dictionary, was both in principles and method what the French began to call sémantique in the eighties of last century. In England we did not get the name semantics until 1900, when Mrs. Cust's translation of Bréal appeared under that title. But we had the thing. In certain respects Trench is to be preferred to Darmesteter and even to Bréal. Bréal has never had quite the same notice in Germany as in England, partly because in Germany they did not feel the need of words like *sémantique* and *polysémie*. Bréal used the word *sémantique* in 1883 and, quite unjustifiably I think, regarded himself as the godfather of the subject. Bréal is the godfather of the words *sémantique* and *polysémie*. In 1885 Darmesteter coupled the word *sémantique* with the sort of work we have reviewed, and in 1897 Bréal's essay was published, the translation of which gave us the noun *semantics*.

The adjectival form, *semantic*, had, however, been vaguely used by the older American philologist, Bloomfield, in 1895. He referred to 'The semantic value of the older reduplications'. This vague sort of adjectival thinking has been served by *semantic* ever since, especially in America. In Bloomfield's latest book on language[2] published in 1933 'Semantic Change' is the title of a chapter in which *semantic change* occurs about half a dozen times. There you will meet once more all the old scheme of rhetoric and the technique of the eighties of last century amid a highly individual terminology bristling with neologisms.

When the noun semantics first appears on page 74, there is an explanatory note on page 513, which, in the light of what has been said, is at once seen to be, and here I must use a derivative, semantically inaccurate. 'Semantics', it runs, 'from semantic (*sic*), pertaining to meaning. These words are less clumsy than semasiology, semasiological.' He continues: 'Literally, then, semantics is the study of meaning.' The definition he gives on page 138 of the text is not quite the same thing, but it is difficult to say exactly what is meant. Semantics is grammar and lexicon, or grammar and lexicon are semantics.

According to Bloomfield semantics is the study of meaning; and also, the study of meaning is the study of grammar. Nothing could be worse than this. It is precisely this confusion of formal grammar with contextual meaning that has been the downfall of all but the most intelligent students of language. Traditional semantics is really the historical study of changes

---

[1] See *On the History and Use of the Suffixes -ery (-ry), -age, etc., and -ment in English*, by Fredrik Gadde. Lund, 1910.
[2] *Language*, by Leonard Bloomfield. Henry Holt & Co., New York, 1933.

of meaning[1] and as such serves a useful purpose. But, as I hope to show, descriptive grammar is another matter altogether, and as I have often urged in other places,[2] we must separate modern semantics from the purely formal, positional, and other categories of grammatical description, thus facilitating the thorough contextual study of meaning on sociological lines, unobscured by categories serving any other purpose. To this I shall return later.

Ogden and Richards in *The Meaning of Meaning* are quite clear about what semantics is, and devote pages 2 to 4 to Bréal and de Saussure and *sémantique* as I have described it above—an established discipline which is not to be neglected, and which has gone to the making of our great Dictionary. Ogden and Richards do not think that semantics has contributed very much to date to the study of the Science of Symbolism, i.e. the actual use of words in practice, and I think they are probably right.

Up to this point I have kept strictly to semantics of the classical kind, and examined only the application of historical principles to the study of changes of meaning.

In the progressive Victorian age historical evolutionism[3] became the main technique of explanation in many branches of knowledge. The origins of historical evolutionism are to be found in the same soil that nourished the

---

[1] A useful bibliography of works connected with historical semantics up to the year 1900, is to be found in K. Jaberg, 'Pejorative Bedeutungsentwicklung im Französischen, mit Berücksichtigung allgemeiner Fragen der Semasiologie', in *Zeitschrift für Romanische Philologie*, vol. xxv, p. 561. For recent work see *Germanische Philologie, Festschrift für Otto Behagel*, Heidelberg, 1934, especially the article by Jost Trier, 'Deutsche Bedeutungsforschung', pp. 173–200, and the article by Fritz Stroh, 'Allgemeine Sprachwissenschaft und Sprachphilosophie', pp. 229–58, which contains an extensive bibliography, pp. 251–8. See also Jost Trier's *Der deutsche Wortschatz im Sinnbezirk des Verstandes*, vol. i, chapter 1, pp. 1–27, bibliography in footnotes. There is also a comprehensive theoretical work of 456 pages by Dr. Gustaf Stern, 'Meaning and Change of Meaning (with special reference to the English language)', *Göteborgs Högskolas Årsskrift*, xxxviii, 1931, a copy of which I received through the kindness of the author after this paper had been read. It is written in English and also contains a bibliography (pp. 421–32). Dr. Stern's work is reviewed at some length in *English Studies*, Feb. 1933.

[2] See pp. 310–12, 325–30 of *Compte-rendu. Congrès international des Sciences anthropologiques et ethnologiques*, Londres, 1934. Also *Man*, No. 174 (Sept. 1934), p. 151.

[3] The evolutionary and comparative method had been used by philologists in the eighteenth century. Comparative Philology was, in fact, the first science to employ this method, and for a very good reason. Although the Bible may have delayed its application to anatomy, the idea of the unity of mankind and the eleventh chapter of Genesis beginning with 'the whole earth was of one language, and of one speech', followed by the confusion of Babel, actually prepared the ground for its use in the linguistic field. Curiously enough Trench makes this quite explicit in 'affiliating' changes of meaning on the one central meaning, 'just as the races of men . . . despite of all their present diversity and dispersion, have a central point of unity in that one pair from whom they all have descended'. From the little I know of the early Jewish Rabbi Grammarians I believe that it was from these medieval Semitic comparativists that Christian scholars took over the technical idea of linguistic unity; and that eventually towards the end of the eighteenth century in the atmosphere of evolutionism and the Romantic Reaction it became the key principle. This is the 'genesis' of *Ur-* and *gemein-, commun, primitive, common, proto-,* and of the emphatic recurrence in French philology of such phrases as *'une langue une'* and *'unité linguistique'.*

Romantic Reaction. Professor Willoughby has given us an interesting paper on Coleridge as a philologist; two Coleridges[1] served the Dictionary, and as we know, more than one book has been written on the Romance of Words. And as for change and permanence, remember Shelley's 'Cloud', 'I change but I cannot die'.

In this twentieth century evolutionism has lost much of its prestige, and other techniques are being tried. In the social sciences and in such subjects as semantics, which as we said at the outset is rather like meteorology, statistical and behaviouristic methods are widely held to be the only ones likely to take us farther in our efforts to understand how language really works.

It is at this point that we turn to the beginnings of modern linguistics. Many of the features of modern linguistics can be traced to Baudouin de Courtenay and his pupils in Kazan,[2] and to de Saussure and his pupils in Geneva, and also to the sociologists, Durkheim and Tarde.[3]

De Saussure was first in many things. He was the first to make a clear technical distinction between the historical study of changes in meaning and the synchronic study of the use of signs, words, sentences in our daily life. As his predecessor Bréal had introduced the word *sémantique* to describe the historical study of changes in meaning, he suggested a new term, *Sémiologie*, to describe a science not yet developed, which should study the use and function of signs and words in the heart of our everyday life in society. This science would bring into service such results of social psychology, sociology, and anthropology as would enable categories to be determined and used for the marshalling and description of the facts.[4] Perhaps the most striking thing in the whole of de Saussure's great work, the *Cours de linguistique générale*, is his statement on page 33 that linguistics can only find a place among the sciences if it is brought into relations with this *sémiologie*, or to use a phrase which in the French would be a contradiction in terms, with synchronic semantics. There is, of course, nothing new in the idea of a systematic study of the use of all sorts of words in their actual contexts in the heart of everyday life.

The historical principle was the third of the three guiding principles of our dictionary, the first two being the continuation and extension of the common-sense principles of Dr. Johnson, whose dictionary appeared in the middle of the rationalistic eighteenth century (in 1755), and who died in 1784, two years before Sir William Jones read the famous paragraph before the Asiatic Society of Bengal.

[1] Herbert Coleridge, son of Henry Nelson Coleridge, nephew of the poet, and the Rev. Henry J. Coleridge, second son of Sir J. Taylor Coleridge, grandson of the poet's father, grand-nephew of the poet.

[2] The Cercle Linguistique de Prague, represented by such linguists as Trubetzkoy and Jakobson, derives its doctrine from both the Russian and Swiss Schools. Modern French work owes much to de Saussure.

[3] A good review of the Sociology of Durkheim and Tarde is given in Dr. Charles Blondel's *Introduction à la Psychologie collective*, Collection Armand Colin, 1928.

[4] de Saussure, *Cours de linguistique générale*, pp. 32–35.

And now I propose to break with the Historical Tradition and outline a non-historical technique[1] for the study of form and function in language.

Form may be either phonetic (including intonation) or orthographic, but it must be taken to mean pure form and position, to the exclusion of all other logical or grammatical categories.

We have already emphasized the necessity of sound morphology as the guarantee of sound historical semantics. Similarly it must be understood at once that no descriptive semantics of any spoken language can be taken seriously, which does not rest on reliable phonetic and intonational forms. It is impossible to begin morphology without the phonetic and sometimes tonal identification of the elements, and syntax is incomplete without a study of intonational form. By way of illustrating this I would draw your attention to a careful comparative study of the intonational forms of French and English by two of my phonetic colleagues.[2] It is obvious that future work on French syntax cannot afford to neglect such carefully recorded forms. The formal categories are phonetic, intonational, and positional. But there are also categories of a general syntactical nature, such as Emphatic and Unemphatic Sentences, Commands, Assertions, Requests, Specific Interrogatives, Intensity, and Contrast. This work also takes a first small step towards semantics by bracketing implied 'meaning' in ordinary French orthography. Sooner or later, of course, all the correlations between intonational forms and other grammatical forms will have to be worked out. This has never been done.[3]

Dr. Gardiner is almost the only grammarian whose theory fully recognizes the place of intonational form in grammar and semantics. Not that he finds it in ancient Egyptian, but I have no doubt his Egyptian studies have convinced him of the value of purely formal and contextual technique. The sort of purely formal and contextual technique I have been advocating since my little book was published in 1930 is illustrated in a book published in 1935 on *Newspaper Headlines* by my friend Dr. Heinrich Straumann, of Zürich. The facts of Headlinese or Block Language are entirely different from those of normal speech, almost entirely visual. Yet the technique works just as well for printed form as for spoken form. Without morphology, then, no semantics.

Throughout our review of the study of meaning we have seen how it

---

[1] I do not wish the description 'non-historical' to be confused with the Saussurean use of the terms 'static' and 'synchronic' as opposed to 'diachronic'. Such 'opposition' is a fallacy. The static synchronic technique is applied to the study of an *état de langue*, and the result is a sort of schematic systematology, a kind of two-dimensional 'still' in black and white. The central concept of the technique here sketched is the context of situation, in which, in a sense, whole stretches of personal biography and cultural history are involved, and in which past, present, and future all meet. For linguistics the pivotal or 'focal' term of the context of situation is the actual verbal context. In normal speech behaviour all locutions whatsoever can be regarded as terms in some context of situation.

[2] Hélène Coustenoble and Lilias Armstrong, *Studies in French Intonation*. Heffer, 1934.

[3] In her booklet, *The Rôle of Intonation in Spoken English*, Heffer, 1935, Dr. Maria Schubiger shows she has an inkling of what might be done.

has been split up and regarded as a relation or system of relations. That is why so many scholars have preferred to study change, because they saw a relationship between one stage and the next, between original or primary meaning and shifted meaning.

Ogden and Richards resolve situational meaning into the three terms, or triangle, of referent, reference, symbol. But meaning is for them a relation in the mind between the facts and events on the one hand and the symbols or words you use to refer to them. To illustrate the Ogden and Richards technique, I should like to take an example from Dr. Straumann's book.[1] In newspapers there is the common phenomenon of the same event being headlined by various newspapers. The event is the Sentence of Lord X. Let us take the first headline from *The Times*. It runs—R.M.S.P. CASE. The *News Chronicle*—LORD X SENTENCED. The *Daily Herald*—LORD X SENT TO PRISON FOR A YEAR. The *Daily Mirror*—LORD X SENT TO GAOL FOR 12 MONTHS. The *Daily Mail*—LORD X'S SENTENCE SHOCKS THE CITY. And lastly the *Daily Worker*'s serve-him-right streamer—LORD X. GETS 12 MONTHS.

According to the Ogden and Richards technique there is one *referent*, the sentence on Lord X, and quite a number of different symbols for it in the various headlines, the various references being the relations between the two, the headlines and the event. By this technique the reference, or rather the relation between the *referent* (the event) and the *symbol* (the words), is regarded as thought or a mental process.

As we know so little about mind and as our study is essentially social, I shall cease to respect the duality of mind and body, thought and word, and be satisfied with the whole man, thinking and acting as a whole, in association with his fellows. I do not therefore follow Ogden and Richards in regarding meaning as relations in a hidden mental process, but chiefly as situational relations in a context of situation and in that kind of language which disturbs the air and other people's ears, as modes of behaviour in relation to the other elements in the context of situation. A thoroughgoing contextual technique does not emphasize the relation between the terms of an historical process or of a mental process, but the interrelations of the terms of the actual observable context itself. In so far as introspection may be relied on, the headlines above quoted, for example, may be considered also in their relations within my context of experience. What may be called memory-contexts or causal contexts are then linked up with the observable situation.

Like all those we have reviewed, I propose to split up meaning or function into a series of component functions. Each function will be defined as the use of some language form or element in relation to some context. Meaning, that is to say, is to be regarded as a complex of contextual relations, and phonetics, grammar, lexicography, and semantics each handles its own components of the complex in its appropriate context.

'No semantics without morphology'—therefore I must briefly sketch the

[1] Heinrich Straumann, *Newspaper Headlines*, p. 28. Allen & Unwin, 1935.

technique for the description of the forms, and indicate what is meant by phonetic, morphological, and syntactical functions, as component functions of the whole complex of functions which a linguistic form may have. Our knowledge is built up as the result of previous analysis. The study of the living voice of a man in action is a very big job indeed. In order to be able to handle it at all, we must split up the whole integrated behaviour pattern we call speech, and apply specialized techniques to the description and classification of these so-called elements of speech we detach by analysis.

I assume then that what we say and hear can be subdivided into elements and components, that there are, to quote Johnson again, 'primitives' or simple word-bases and derivatives. *Circumvent* is in English a 'primitive' or word-base, while *fishy* or *restless* are derivatives. It follows from this that we recognize such categories as word-base, stem, affix, and other formatives, and eventually what we call sounds.

These elements can usually be delimited and identified by the method of substitution. A word is a lexical substitution-counter, and a 'sound' may be a phonetic or a morphological substitution-counter. In the phonetic context of initial **b** and final **d** we observe that sixteen vowel substitutions are possible: **biːd, bid, bed, bæd, baːd, bɔːd, buːd, bʌd, bəːd, beid, boud, baid, baud, bɔid, biəd, bɛəd.** The phonetic function of each one of the sixteen vowels in that context is its use in contradistinction from fifteen others. Between initial **p** and final **l** eleven vowel substitutions or alternances are possible, between **h** and **d** thirteen. The other symbols represent similar counters, and if we compare them, we shall find a function for **d** in **bɔːd**, for instance. Its function is its use in that context in contradistinction from other possible substitution-counters such as **t, l,** or **n,** in **bɔːt, bɔːl, bɔːn.** These phonetic substitution-counters can be determined in purely phonetic contexts, that is, without complete verbal, grammatical, or situational context. This kind of use for an element of speech is the first little bit of meaning we have dealt with in the purely phonetic context, at the level of phonetic understanding. I have called this 'minor function'.[1]

By an exhaustive study of the distribution of such substitution-counters in all possible contexts, that is, of what I have termed the 'contextual distribution' of the sound, the maximum number of alternances of vowels and of consonants in each type of phonetic context can be counted, the relative frequency of the occurrence of a sound in its various contexts estimated, and the total maximum number of the sounds of the given form of speech may be tabulated and described as a whole phonological system. The phonetic function of a form, of a sound, sound-attribute, or sound-group is then its use in contradistinction from other 'sounds'; the phonetic value or use of any sound is determined by its place in the whole system. The phonetic or minor function of a sound is shown by studying it in relation to the phonetic contexts in which it occurs and in relation to other

---

[1] 'The Use and Distribution of Certain English Sounds. Phonetics from a functional point of view.'

sounds which may replace it in those contexts, or, in other words, in relation to the 'context' of the whole phonological system. A phonetic substitution-counter (as distinct from tone, stress, and length) has been termed a phoneme.[1]

Unfortunately in actual speech the substitution elements are not letters, but all manner of things we may analyse out of the living voice in action, not merely the articulation, but quite a number of general attributes or correlations associated with articulation, such as length, tone, stress, tensity, voice. The phoneme principle enables a transcriptionist to get down formulas for pronunciation, but lengths, tones, and stresses, and such substitution elements present many difficulties, both practical and theoretical. The phoneme principle has been extended to these more general elements, and hence the terms *toneme* and *tonetic*, even *chroneme*, are sometimes to be met with.

In the specialized technique of semantics we have seen how scholars have split up meaning into components or sets of relations in order to describe the facts. I now propose to do the same sort of thing in phonetics, and to split up the whole living voice of man in action into elements, some of which, what we may call 'sounds', are to be again split up.

Sounds may be analysed in several ways. I propose to analyse a 'sound' into (1) articulation or articulations and (2) general attributes or correlations such as length, stress, tone, voice, associated with articulations, and having function. Within the phonological system of a given language the articulations and the correlations make up a complex of phonetic relations which it is the business of phonetics to examine and describe and reduce to writing by means of notation.

It is an elementary fact that several sounds share similar articulation,

[1] There is a fairly extensive literature on this subject, some of it controversial. I refer to my own work, as it is more closely related to the present purpose. See my article 'The Word "Phoneme".' As far as my knowledge goes, I believe '*phoneme*' was first used in English by Dr. R. J. Lloyd in a review of Baudouin de Courtenay's 'Versuch einer Theorie phonetischer Alternationen', in *Neuere Sprachen*, vol. iii, 1896, p. 615. As an example of its present use, study the t sounds in the English contexts **tik, stik, trik, betə, ʌtmoust, biːtn, biːtl, eitθ**. These t sounds are all different and each one is *specifically related to its particular context*; so that, though other sounds, such as l or p, may replace some of them, they cannot replace one another. We have then eight *contextually specific* t variants, or eight alternant t phones. The alternant phones $t_1, t_2, t_3, t_4, t_5, t_6, t_7, t_8$, necessarily occur under the contextual conditions $x_1, x_2, x_3, x_4, x_5, x_6, x_7, x_8$, which are directly observable and definable in one style of speech of a certain type of speaker from a certain place or places, and therefore can be represented by the sign t; the specific value in each case is determined by the contextual conditions which, represented in phonetic transcription, provide contextual conventions which are quite unambiguous for described contextual alternants. That the general theory of the phoneme is in the melting-pot has been shown by W. Freeman Twaddell in his dissertation *On defining the Phoneme* (Language Monograph XVI, pp. 62, Linguistic Society of America, 1935). It is all rather like arranging a baptism before the baby is born. In the end we may have to say that a set of phonemes is a set of letters. If the forms of a language are unambiguously symbolized by a notation scheme of letters and other written signs, then the word 'phoneme' may be used to describe a constituent letter-unit of such a notation scheme. See also Trubetzkoy, *Anleitung zu phonologischen Beschreibungen*, Édition du Cercle Linguistique de Prague, 1935.

e.g. **p, b, m**; and several sounds may share the same sort of general attribute, e.g. presence or absence of voice, which is here termed the voice correlation. In French, **p, t, s, f** are all voiceless or breathed, that is, they all share the negative voice correlation, while **b, d, z, v** are distinguished from them by the positive voice correlation.

The difference between **tɔ:** and **dɔ:** in English is a difference between negative and positive voice correlation, and if we add **nɔ:** we introduce a difference by nasal correlation. The same correlations distinguish **pɔ:, bɔ:,** and **mɔ:**. But the difference between **tɔ:** and **pɔ:** is articulation, and a similar articulation difference separates the other pairs **dɔ:** and **bɔ:, nɔ:** and **mɔ:**. We have also **kɔ:** and **gɔ:**, but do not use the nasal correlation in initial position in such contexts.[1]

A number of theoretical difficulties in phonetics are due to the fact that the analysis of the living voice does not necessarily correspond to the letters of the roman alphabet serially employed to represent it. Philologists of the older school have often been charged with studying letters and typography, not language. And precisely the same charge may be brought against some phoneticians. Only the letters and types are different.

It is a mistake to suppose that the stream of speech is just a string of separate roman letters. The letters usually represent an articulation, possibly with one or two correlations such as breath-voice or nasality, leaving other correlations such as tone or stress to be separately indicated, or not indicated at all. In cases where we have two letters such as **s** and **z**, roughly representing the negative and positive voice correlation, people may also talk of the unvoiced **z** and the voiced **s**, using four categories. But what about **m, n, l**?

The use of the length marks in the broad transcription of English is a practical convenience and works well. But we must not make the mistake of supposing the use of the length marks is based on a scientific classification. The length marks are used in association with the symbols **i, a, ɔ, u,** and **ə**. But it must not be inferred that a two-term length correlation, relatively long and relatively short, gives for these five 'vowel sounds' a ten-term series of vowel substitution-counters in a given type of context. For three of the vowel sounds, **i, ɔ,** and **u**, the relations can be expressed as follows: As **i:/i**, so is **ɔ:/ɔ**, and **u:/u**. But there is no second term for **a:,** and the relation **ə:/ə** involves another factor, the correlation of stress. The term **ə** can only occur in unstressed syllables, whereas all the other terms can occur in stressed or unstressed syllables. In dealing with vowels it is often found convenient to analyse out the length correlation from the articulation, even when it is not completely systematic.

There is no reason why the presence or absence of voice, which may be associated with all manner of articulations, should not be treated in

---

[1] Cf. Jakobson, *Preliminaries to Speech Analysis*, M.I.T., Technical Report XIII, January, 1952, and *Fundamentals of Language*, (Janua Linguarum, No. 1), Mouton & Co., The Hague, 1956.

precisely the same way as length, and regarded as a correlation. In which case there would be one lip-closure articulation with positive and negative voice correlation giving two phonetic substitution-counters, **p** and **b**.

The separation of articulation from the voice correlation is particularly important for my present purpose, which is to provide a sound basis for morphology. No semantics without morphology, no morphology without phonetics. Hence the need for this lengthy phonetic digression.

Phonetic analysis of the actual sounds English people utter has made possible a grammar of the spoken language. But phonetic letters sometimes obscure it. For sometimes we put to grammatical use merely an articulation, sometimes correlations, sometimes a complex of both. The two commonest affixed flexions in English are what may be called the -*s* flexion and the -*d* flexion. The -*s* flexion in itself is neutral or 'multi-valent', being put to several uses—plural and possessive of nouns, and third person singular of verbs. But in all these flexions we make use of articulation, or of what may be termed the 'final' assibilation of the simple form. In the case of all stops and fricatives (except sibilant consonants themselves) this assibilation may be indicated by adding **s**: **rends, rents, bægs, bæks**. This use of **s** is not in contradistinction from **z**, as the two-term voice correlation is not possible in these contexts. Similarly either **t** or **d** could be used for the inflected verbal form, and as we are accustomed to **d**, we might write **bækd, bægd, stɔpd, rɔbd**.

Both the positive and negative voice correlation can be associated with all the English plosive and fricative articulations and *made distinctive use of*, except in the case of **r**.

The semi-vowel **j** is not divided by voice correlation, though in the case of **w** many people distinguish betweeh **hwitʃ** and **witʃ**, **hwɔt** and **wɔt** (Watt). But in English the distinction of positive and negative voice correlation can never be combined with nasalization as it can in Burmese, for instance. So that when the same flexion has to be added to words ending with articulations with which both positive and negative voice correlation can be associated, it naturally employs merely an articulatory flexion, ignoring the voice correlation.

Nasals and liquids (**m, n, ŋ, l**) in English are not further differentiated by the voice–breath correlation, so that *after them*, as after vowels, the voice correlation can have function. After the nasals and liquids (**m, n, ŋ, l**) the same process takes place, namely assibilation; but in these contexts, unlike the previous ones, the negative voice correlation may have lexical function, so that in order to represent this we must either use both **s** and **z**, as in **wins** (wince) and **winz** (wins), **wʌns** (once) and **wʌnz** (ones or one's), or make use of additional orthographic devices which are not merely phonetically but also linguistically or grammatically representative; e.g. as the length correlation in final nasals is not significant, we could write **winn** and **wʌnn** for the simple forms, adding **s** for the assibilation as in all other cases. This would then give **wins** (wince), **winns** (wins), and **sins, sinns**.

This method of writing would indicate that such forms as **winns** consisted of a simple form **winn**+**s**, whereas **sins** would be a simple form without flexion. The same device, though with less phonetic justification, could be used to separate *fined* from *find*, e.g. **fainnd, faind,** or **æds, ædds**. The present orthography *wince, wins, once, ones, adze, adds,* &c., is not altogether absurd. And the use of one sign *s* for the plural is in the vast majority of cases quite unambiguous.

In such nominal and verbal flexions we are making use of an articulation in final position. In other morphological processes we make use of the voice correlation and sometimes the stress correlation. Take the noun **ri:θ** (wreath) and compare it with the related verb **ri:ð**, or the pairs **ju:s** and **ju:z, breθ** and **bri:ð**. In the formation of the ordinals, however, the articulation and the negative voice correlation are essential, e.g. **faiv, fifθ**; **twelv, twelfθ**. In **'prousi:ds** (n.) and **prou'si:ds** (v.), **'tra:nsfə:z** and **tra:ns-'fə:z**, we make grammatical use of the stress-tone correlation.

To recapitulate. The stream of speech is analysed into elements or 'units' by the substitution method. At the phonetic level of understanding phonetic substitution-counters will be studied in their relations to their phonetic contexts and within the phonetic structure or system.

Phonetic substitution-counters may be articulations, correlations, or combinations of these, or complexes of phonetic elements such as **hmw, hmy** in Burmese, or what have been called common consonant groups in other languages, **str, skw, kl** in English, **nkp, ngb** in Yoruba. This study of contextual substitution and contextual distribution establishes phonetic or minor function, and deals with the first small element of meaning at the phonetic level.

Morphological and syntactical functions will account for further components of meaning in grammatical contexts at the grammatical level of understanding. 'I have not seen your father's pen, but I have read the book of your uncle's gardener', like so much in grammar books, is only at the grammatical level. From the semantic point of view it is just nonsense.

The following sentence gives perfectly satisfactory contexts for phonetics, morphology, and syntax, but not for semantics: 'My doctor's great-grandfather will be singeing the cat's wings.' We make regular use of nonsense in phonetics, and so also do most grammarians. Even the anthropological Sapir offers an example like 'The farmer kills the duckling';[1] Jespersen gives us 'A dancing woman charms'[2] and 'A charming woman dances'; and Dr. Gardiner makes shift with 'Pussy is beautiful'; 'Balbus murum aedificavit', and Paul's example of 'The lion roars'.[3]

The categories of morphology, and especially of the parts of speech, tenses, and cases, should be allowed to arise from the formal conditions of the language. Nouns and verbs in Arabic[4] can be formally recognized

---

[1] *Language*, p. 86.　　　　　　　　　[2] *Philosophy of Grammar*, p. 166.
[3] *The Theory of Speech and Language*, pp. 22, 243.
[4] See 'The technique of formal description applied to a Palestinian dialect of Arabic',

at sight or on hearing them, and so they can also in Yoruba. Nouns and demonstratives and invariables are formally distinct in most Bantu languages. Purely formal and positional differentiae should be used wherever possible. Beyond such simple categories very few technical assumptions would be necessary, because the form and order in which these elements are put together in the word or in the sentence are always given in the situation in which they are used.[1]

And now to illustrate this empirical analysis of meaning at the phonetic, morphological, syntactical, and semantic levels by means of examples. Let us begin with an example of the simplest context—a purely phonetic context, such as the English form bɔːd, consisting of an initial b followed by ɔː and then d in final position. What is the function or meaning of bɔːd? At this stage, only to be different from fifteen other forms, like biːd, bid, bed, bæd, baːd, &c., and forms such as bɔːt, pɔːt, pɔːd, dɔːb. The form bɔːd can be used in contradistinction from the other forms and has its phonetic or purely formal place, at the phonetic or formal level of understanding. It is a lexical substitution-counter. As it stands, bɔːd is what is termed a *neutral*. Now, if I ask you to put the form bɔːd in your context of experience, you will produce verbal contexts such as 'which bɔːd, bɔːd əv stʌdiz or bɔːd tə deθ?' Or you will spell the words, knowing that spelling in that case means a good deal more than mere phonetic identification. Incidentally that is the main argument against phonetic spelling; it removes phonetic ambiguity and creates other functional ambiguities.

You can now associate various forms together in what I have called 'formal scatter' and 'paradigm scatter'.

You may place bɔːd in the scatter of—

(1) bɔːd, bɔːds

or (2) bɔːd, bɔːds, bɔːdid, bɔːdiŋ

or (3) bɔː, bɔːz, bɔːd, bɔːriŋ.

By placing your form in series such as these, you identify it in (1) as a noun in the singular, in (2) as the simple form of a verb, and in (3) as the *d*-form of a simpler word-base bɔː. But in the first case both forms are semantic neutrals. We might eliminate some of the 'neutrality' by extending the paradigm scatter to include the complete form scatter, derivatives and compounds. We should then have:

(1) bɔːd, bɔːds, bɔːdrum, bɔːdskuːl, &c.,

and (1*a*) bɔːd, bɔːds, bɔːdi.

All this sort of thing can be arrived at merely by recollection, or by asking the native speaker, or by collecting verbal contexts.

by I. M. Huseini. *Proceedings of the International Congress of Anthropological Sciences*, p. 330, London, 1934.

[1] Dr. Straumann also employs formal and positional technique in his *Newspaper Headlines*. See footnote on pp. 31–32.

The establishing of the three sounds, **b**, **ɔː**, and **d** as three phonetic substitution-counters, as being used in contradistinction from other counters in the same phonetic context, disposes of one component of meaning. But the distinctive use of **d**, for example, in this purely phonetic context has not, in any sense, *semantic* function. Without further contextualization in formal scatter or in verbal contexts we cannot even place **bɔːd** in a morphological category as a part of speech. It is, except on the phonetic level of understanding, a neutral. If now I say to you 'Not on the board', you have it verbally contextualized, and another component of meaning, that is, *morphological meaning* or function, is clear. It is a noun. Even now its semantic function is obscure. The whole sentence is semantically neutral. In a definite context of situation you would have the semantic functions determined (1) *positively* by the use of the words in relation to the rest of the situational context, and (2) *negatively*[1] by what is termed *contextual elimination*. The presence of a chess-board might eliminate a commercial board or a board of studies.

I may say 'Not on the board!' and also 'Not on the board?' without considering semantic function in a context of situation, but in the purely verbal context merely at the grammatical level of understanding. There are two different types of sentence, one a statement and the other a question. These are not semantic but syntactical categories. We now see what is meant by a syntactical component of meaning.

To recapitulate, we have resolved meaning into five principal component functions:

First, phonetic function for a sound as a substitution-counter, e.g. **b**, **ɔː**, and **d**, the sounds having their places in the context and in the system of relations we call the phonetic structure of the language.

Secondly, lexical function of the form or word **bɔːd**, as a lexical substitution-counter, distinct from, say, **pɔːt**, or **bɔːt**, or **kɔːd**. Some sounds have only lexical function: for instance **bɔːd** is distinguished from **pɔːd** chiefly by the voice correlation which in this case has lexical function; **kɔːd** is distinguished from **bɔːd** by different initial articulation as well as by the voice correlation, and **kɔːd** from **bɔːd** by two differences of articulation and two differences of voice correlation with the associated differences

---

[1] We are already accustomed to the use of the negative relation in our functional analysis. We have recognized the use of a phonetic substitution-counter in *contradistinction* from other alternatives, and the use of positive and negative in connexion with correlations. But in all these cases there is a positive contextual element and a complex of positive contextual relations. It was far otherwise with de Saussure, who even went so far as to say, in italics, '*Dans la langue il n'y a que des différences . . . sans termes positifs*' and 'Il n'y a qu'*opposition*'. It might almost be said that the whole of his theory rests on negation. There was nothing new in this, of course. It is just possible that he had learned something of Indian philosophy. Such aspects of the philosophy of language had been discussed by Hindu, Jain, and Buddhist writers. Early Buddhist philosophy regarded meaning as a set of negative relations. According to the Buddhist philosopher, Ratnakīrti, 'The essence of meaning consists in affirmation qualified by the negation of other objects.' (See 'Analysis of Meaning in the Indian Philosophy of Language', by Siddheshwar Varma, M.A., D.Litt., in the *Journal of the Royal Asiatic Society*, January 1925.)

of aspiration and vowel length. It is clear that the differences between lexical substitution-counters or words do not really correspond to differences of alphabetic arrangement. Articulations and correlations and complexes of these can have lexical function.

Thirdly, when you have bɔːd contextualized as the *d*-form of a verb, the complex of articulation and voice correlation which we symbolize as *d* has morphological function, but, be it repeated, not semantic function.

Fourthly, if I pronounced the forms bɔːd! and bɔːd?, you would be in a position to assess the syntactical function of intonation and place the forms in syntactical categories without knowing any semantic function, i.e. apart from any actual situation.

Fifthly, if I now contextualize the word bɔːd and turn to you, on this occasion, with the question 'bɔːd?', you may possibly reply 'not really' or just 'no' with a rising intonation, or 'go on', and in the several cases furnish contextual relations which determine the meaning. In such a context of situation you have what I propose to call *semantic function*.

The central concept of the whole of semantics considered in this way is the context of situation. In that context are the human participant or participants, what they say, and what is going on. The phonetician can find his phonetic context and the grammarian and the lexicographer theirs. And if you want to bring in general cultural background, you have the contexts of experience of the participants. Every man carries his culture and much of his social reality about with him wherever he goes.[1] But even when phonetician, grammarian, and lexicographer have finished, there remains the bigger integration, making use of all their work, in semantic study. And it is for this situational and experiential study that I would reserve the term 'semantics'.[2]

But even when we have arrived at the context of situation, we are not at the end of the 'House that Jack Built'. The rest of the contextualization process is the province of sociological linguistics.

Sociological linguistics is the great field for future research. In this short paper I can only indicate the difficulties and make a few tentative suggestions, first in connexion with the very difficult problem of describing and classifying typical contexts of situation within the context of culture, and secondly of describing and classifying types of linguistic function in such contexts of situation.

Our greatest difficulty at present is the absence of any really well-

[1] An Englishman on 'safari' in the wilds of Africa carries not only many English artefacts about with him, but even if there is no Englishman within a day's journey, he may have reason to exclaim in English when something suddenly goes wrong, or use his language to address animals, refractory Africans, and God, and in writing his own notes and to his friends, enemies, and government, and he will, of course, have a certain amount of reading to do.

[2] Taking advantage of what Coleridge called the 'desynonymizing' process, I would use the term 'semasiology' for the historical study of changes of meaning. Another suggestion is that *phonetics* and *semantics* be regarded as branches of *general* linguistics, the corresponding fields in *special* grammar being *phonology* and *semasiology*.

documented work on how we acquire our speech as we grow up. We cannot lay the blame on psychologists or sociologists, because it is much easier for a student of linguistics to acquire sufficient psychology and sociology for this work than for a psychologist or sociologist to acquire the necessary linguistic technique. After all, we are not aiming at linguistic sociology, but building on the foundations of linguistics. And as we have seen, without phonetics there can be no morphology of a spoken language, without intonation no syntax. And unless these are sound, there can be no semantics.

An example from the Society's Dictionary will raise the problem of categories for types of linguistic function. When the word *set* came to be done, it occupied eighteen pages and a column, and it extends to 154 main divisions; the last of these, *set up*, has so many subdivisions that it exhausts the alphabet and repeats the letters again down to *rr*.

Multiplying illustrative contexts might have gone on indefinitely and filled a whole volume. In practice, however, we find that these contexts can be grouped into types of usage; and even if we only employ the few social categories mentioned in the Dictionary, such as common, colloquial, slang, literary, technical, scientific, conversational, dialectal, and remember the principle of relative frequency however approximately, we shall be getting nearer to a practical handling of the social background of the usage of words in typical contexts.

What we need are more accurately determined linguistic categories for the principal types of sentences and of usage we employ in our various social roles. Every one of us starts life with the two simple roles of sleeping and feeding; but from the time we begin to be socially active at about two months old, we gradually accumulate social roles. Throughout the period of growth we are progressively incorporated into our social organization, and the chief condition and means of that incorporation is learning to say what the other fellow expects us to say under the given circumstances. It is true that just as contexts for a word multiply indefinitely, so also situations are infinitely various. But after all, there is the routine of day and night, week, month, and year. And most of our time is spent in routine service, familial, professional, social, national. Speech is not the 'boundless chaos' Johnson thought it was. For most of us the roles and the lines are there, and that being so, the lines can be classified and correlated with the part and also with the episodes, scenes, and acts. Conversation is much more of a roughly prescribed ritual than most people think. Once someone speaks to you, you are in a relatively determined context and you are not free just to say what you please. We are born individuals. But to satisfy our needs we have to become social persons, and every social person is a bundle of roles or *personae*; so that the situational and linguistic categories would not be unmanageable. Many new categories would arise from a systematic observation of the facts.

We learn speech in the routine action of the daily round. Speech is very largely vocal action in control of things and people including oneself, action in relation or in adjustment to surroundings and situations. We establish ourselves on speaking terms with our environment, and our words serve our familiarity with it. 'The study of words in cultural familiarity' might almost describe this aspect of semantics.

We are born into a vast potential cultural heritage, but we can only hope to succeed to a very small part of the total heritage and then only in stages. There would appear to be a need to emphasize that for each stage of childhood and youth, of each type of child, there are a relevant environment and relevant forms of language.

There is a vast field of research here in what may be called the biographical study of speech. There is material for all the branches of linguistics in the study of all the various components of meaning in this linguistic life-history of the young person as an active member of his age-group as well as a pupil, in his seven ages of childhood and youth.

There are great possibilities for 'biographical semasiology' or the history of changes in meaning of such words as *father, mother, love, child, play, toy, work, money, clothes, drink,* &c. There have been a certain number of rather sketchy works on 'biographical phonetics', and odd fragments of 'biographical grammar'; but we are still without real knowledge on language development.

Connected with this biographical approach is the history of what we have called the accumulation of social roles. The grown man has to play many parts, functioning in many characters, and unless he knows his lines as well as his role he is no use in the play. If you do not know your part and your lines, there are no cues for the other fellow, and therefore no place or excuse for his lines either.

The multiplicity of social roles we have to play as members of a race, nation, class, family, school, club, as sons, brothers, lovers, fathers, workers, churchgoers, golfers, newspaper readers, public speakers, involves also a certain degree of linguistic specialization. Unity is the last concept that should be applied to language. Unity of language is the most fugitive of all unities, whether it be historical, geographical, national, or personal. There is no such thing as *une langue une* and there never has been.

This 'free interlocking' of roles is a great conservative influence, for the 'same' word may be used in many different roles, and may even be specialized in certain uses; but so long as the specialized use does not acquire great intensity by virtue of context, or extend in frequency, other uses do not suffer. The entry of the broadcast voice into the homes of the people will have just so much influence as the context of listening provides. But it is one of many new technical instruments of the age which are breaking down barriers of all sorts and promoting 'free interlocking' of social and linguistic circles, tending to prevent further linguistic subdivision and to strengthen the forces of conservation.[1]

For the adequate description and classification of contexts of situation

[1] See pp. 98–99, 110–13, *The Broadcast Word*, by A. Lloyd-James, 1935.

we need to widen our linguistic outlook. Certain elementary categories are obvious, such as speaking, hearing, writing, reading; familiar, colloquial, and more formal speech; the languages of the Schools, the Law, the Church, and all the specialized forms of speech.

Then one might add such types of situation as those in which there is an 'individual' or 'monologue' use of language, and those in which there is a sort of 'choric' use, as when vocal interchange merely promotes or maintains affective rapport. Malinowski has applied to this kind of linguistic behaviour the very happy phrase 'phatic communion'—'a type of speech in which ties of union are created by a mere exchange of words'.[1]

Malinowski has also insisted on the specially interesting types of situation in which vocal interchange is just part of a job of work in hand, such as fishing, hunting, loading a truck, or the co-operative handling of tools and materials. He says the meaning of such words is 'their pragmatic efficiency'. Most of our contemporary 'eye-language' in notices and directions is of this kind.

A great deal of conversation or discussion may also be in preparation for concerted or socially determined action. All the language of public administration and government may be said to be the language of planning and regulation, the language of public guidance. The subsequent discussion of success or failure may be regarded both as 'phatic communion' and as a situation in which something planned is either accomplished or ends in failure.

In more detail we may notice such common situations as

(a) Address: 'Simpson!' 'Look here, Jones', 'My dear boy', 'Now, my man', 'Excuse me, madam'.

(b) Greetings, farewells, or mutual recognition of status and relationship on contact, adjustment of relations after contact, breaking off relations, renewal of relations, change of relations.

(c) Situations in which words, often conventionally fixed by law or custom, serve to bind people to a line of action or to free them from certain customary duties in order to impose others. In Churches, Law Courts, Offices, such situations are commonplace. Your signature or your word is a very important piece of linguistic behaviour. In passing, we may notice that, when other things fail, judges often have recourse to very rudimentary semantics in their interpretations. There is a great field for practical semantics in the contextualization of crucial words in judicial remarks and judgements, particularly in the lower courts.

Such words are made binding by law, but many other words and phrases are used with a similar binding effect in everyday life, because their use releases overwhelming forces of public opinion, of social custom. 'Be a sport!', 'I know you won't let us down.' One of the magic words of the age is *plan*. The mere use of this word and its derivatives releases certain

---

[1] See Malinowski's supplement, p. 315, in Ogden and Richards's *The Meaning of Meaning*.

forces of opinion and experience and gives the word weight. Its association with certain influential contexts gives it a power over us in this age of uncertainty.

Many more types of situation will occur to the interested student, but there is an obvious need for a more accurate study of our speech situations in order that categories may be found which will enable us to extend such social studies all over the world.

It is perhaps easier to suggest types of linguistic function than to classify situations. Such would be, for instance, the language of agreement, encouragement, endorsement, of disagreement and condemnation. As language is a way of dealing with people and things, a way of behaving and of making others behave, we could add many types of function—wishing, blessing, cursing, boasting, the language of challenge and appeal, or with intent to cold-shoulder, to belittle, to annoy or hurt, even to a declaration of enmity. The use of words to inhibit hostile action, or to delay or modify it, or to conceal one's intention are very interesting and important 'meanings'. Nor must we forget the language of social flattery and love-making, of praise and blame, of propaganda and persuasion.

The valuation or judgement in appraisement or blame of people, nations, books, plays are all of the greatest interest and far more stereotyped or socially conditioned than most people imagine. Most Englishmen will know the various reactions to 'a good man', 'a good chap', 'a good fellow', 'a good sort', 'a good scout'. A study of the jargon of contemporary book reviewers in the press shows how all such routine situations involving public judgement tend to produce stereotyped forms of language. This does not mean that such reviews are become meaningless, but rather that a fairly simple set of stock indications are practically convenient.

A more formal and much broader classification of types of language function would notice various types of narrative—traditional narrative, sacred and profane, and the free narrative of ordinary intercourse. Narrative of this kind would include description, but exposition and argument might be examined also.

Finally it must be repeated that most of the give-and-take of conversation in our everyday life is stereotyped and very narrowly conditioned by our particular type of culture. It is a sort of roughly prescribed social ritual, in which you generally say what the other fellow expects you, one way or the other, to say.[1] The moment a conversation is started, whatever is said

---

[1] It will be agreed that the adequate description of speech-behaviour, viewed in this way, necessitates a highly developed phonetic technique. The close connexion between the practical contextual view of speech and the scrupulous formal technique here described has recently been so well expressed by one of my pupils, Fritz Güttinger, that I take the liberty of quoting it at length. It follows also, of course, that loose linguistic sociology without formal accuracy is of little value. 'Zu den nachhaltigsten Eindrücken, welche man von der programmatischen Schrift J. R. Firths über den Sprechvorgang, wie auch von seiner Lehrtätigkeit am University College London davonträgt, gehört die Einsicht, daß die Spielregeln der Sprache und des Sprechens im Grunde etwas viel Roheres sind, als man zu glauben gewohnt ist. Was für Folgen dies für die allgemeine Sprachtheorie hat,

is a determining condition for what, in any reasonable expectation, may follow. What you say raises the threshold against most of the language of your companion, and leaves only a limited opening for a certain likely range of responses. This sort of thing is an aspect of what I have called contextual elimination. There is a positive force in what you say in a given situation, and there is also the negative force of elimination both in the events and circumstances of the situation and in the words employed, which are of course events in the situation. Neither linguists nor psychologists have begun the study of conversation; but it is here we shall find the key to a better understanding of what language really is and how it works.

On a much wider basis, but none the less a branch of linguistics, is the study of dialects and languages as organs of cultural *élites* or other special social groups, e.g. Medieval Latin, the English 'governing voice', Swahili, Classical Arabic, and also as channels or vehicles of culture contacts, as mechanisms of culture diffusion, e.g. French in Egypt, English and Russian in Asia.

In studies such as these in the past there has been too much vague speculation about 'influences', and not enough accurate investigation into the actual mechanisms and channels of culture contacts and culture 'movements'. Who are the 'culture-makers'? Who are the 'carriers' of the particular cultural tradition, of the particular pronunciation, word, dialect, or form of speech? Is the number of 'carriers' increasing or decreasing, and why? What is the mechanism of 'transmission' from 'carrier' to 'carrier'? Where is a particular culture trait or linguistic habit at its best, in its 'optimum "locale"', and why?

The whole problem of translation is also in the field of semantics, but is much too vast to be entered upon here.

The above review of the wide field of general semantics implies rather a different general philosophical attitude towards speech from that which has set our scale of linguistic values hitherto. But I am convinced that the greatest need of linguistic scholarship at the present time is a new outlook over a much wider field of life in company with others looking through adjacent windows converging on the same scenes. The new philosophy, the new outlook, means new values in scholarship, but not necessarily in conflict with the older values.

The technique I have here sketched is an empirical rather than a theoretical analysis of meaning. It can be described as a serial contextualization of our facts, context within context, each one being a function, an organ of the bigger context and all contexts finding a place in what may be called the context of culture. It avoids many of the difficulties which arise if meaning is regarded chiefly as a mental relation or historical process.

braucht hier nicht ausgeführt zu werden. Daraus, daß das Zweckhafte, Handlungsmäßige der Worte und Sätze zur Betrachtung abgesondert wird, ergibt sich letzten Endes die Notwendigkeit, die Formenwelt nach streng formalen Gesichtspunkten zu beschreiben.' *Neue Schweizer Rundschau*, July 1935, pp. 176–7.

By this time we are accustomed to the subdivision of meaning or function. Meaning, then, we use for the whole complex of functions which a linguistic form may have. The principal components of this whole meaning are phonetic function, which I call a 'minor' function, the major functions—lexical, morphological, and syntactical (to be the province of a reformed system of grammar), and the function of a complete locution in the context of situation, or typical context of situation, the province of semantics.

In conclusion I should like to make two suggestions:

First, that steps should be taken to compile a dictionary of English linguistic terminology, with or without French and German equivalents.

Secondly, that the Society might promote research into Present-Day English by inaugurating a Dictionary of Spoken Usage and Idiom.

4

THE USE AND DISTRIBUTION OF CERTAIN ENGLISH SOUNDS

PHONETICS FROM A FUNCTIONAL POINT OF VIEW

During the last hundred years knowledge has grown into an intricate network of sciences. There has been an ambitious multiplication of specialized techniques. Things are studied from so many special points of view, and with such technical versatility, that wider and more comprehensive views are in danger of being crowded out.

Speech, for example, can be studied by all the -ics and -ologies in the polytechnic catalogue. On the purely linguistic side there is the study of usage, of grammatical forms, isolated word-mongering and all kinds of linguistic antiquarianism.

Then there is phonetics, the most specialized linguistic technique. It makes abstraction of the sounds of speech, and has been described as the science of speech sounds. Even within this already specialized field there is further subdivision and specialization. The experimental phonetician carries the study of 'speech-sounds' (whatever that may mean) into the physicist's world of noiseless motion. The 'pure' phonetician collects, describes, and classifies 'sounds' as such, rather like a stamp-collector. His great thrill is the discovery of a 'new sound'. Or he may be likened to a letter-sorter with a set of pigeon-holes labelled off with symbols, to mark the destination of sounds from all over the world. Then there are the more practical technicians who teach people to recognize and make speech sounds, or who can be relied on as skilled transcriptionists.

The 'broader' phoneticians and the new phonologists have also branched off to develop their own specialized techniques. Though differing in method, and to some extent in general principles, they agree at any rate on one fundamental principle, that the phonetic analysis of a language does not consist in merely 'collecting' the sounds, and placing them in universal descriptive phonetic pigeon-holes with a specially appropriate letter attached to them, but rather in placing them as 'terms', as integral parts of the whole phonological system of the given language. The technique of the new school of phonologists is rather in the nature of systematology—but it is all to the good as a definite move in the direction of integrative studies, more pragmatic, more functional, more 'linguistic'; and in the long run, likely to lead to more valuable scientific results than the narrower and more abstract phonetics. Abstract, because being 'panglossic' it can only place sounds as such in universal categories and attach symbols to them. It is purely descriptive and non-linguistic, since it ignores phonological structure and function.

'Phonology' is what might be called 'systemic' phonetics. The 'phonologist' does not merely collect sounds, he establishes the necessary phonetic distinctions in a given form of speech, and so gives each sound a place in the whole phonetic structure or system. Thus the linguistic value of any sound or sound-attribute is dependent on certain other sounds and indirectly on all the sounds of the given language. In English there is a distinction between **p** and **b**, or, in other words, the phonetic values of **p** and **b** are interdependent. Since the publication of a previous article,[1] I have had several opportunities of exchanging views with colleagues of the Prague School and other European linguists, more especially in the Language section of the 1934 International Congress of Anthropological Sciences,[2] and I now think that this systemic or phonological analysis of the sounds of a language is not inconsistent with my own behaviouristic method of contextualization, but is possibly another way of establishing what I would call 'minor' function.

For his philosophy the linguist need go no farther than the second chapter of Genesis. The reign of Adam began when the rest of God's creation was submitted to him to be named. He was given a voice in the world which continues to work wonders. And every child of Adam ever since has entered into his lordship of Creation by wielding the magic power of his voice. Every baby quickly learns the magic action of his voice, and the answering magic of his fellows. It may make him feel better, it may make him feel worse. A noise, an answering noise, and 'hey presto' he either gets what he wants or what he deserves. This phonetic magic, which makes things happen and which so cogently compels people to do things, is our first and most important initiation in humanity, and the first and most fundamental language lesson we learn. That is what language really means to us—a way of doing things, of getting things done, a way of behaving and making others behave, a way of life. Through all the generations of man this magic is handed on—it continues to work wonders.

We can only arrive at some understanding of *how* it works, if we establish with certainty that the facts of speech we are studying can be observed or regarded in actual patterns of behaviour. We must take our facts from speech sequences, verbally complete in themselves and operating in contexts of situation which are typical, recurrent, and repeatedly observable. Such contexts of situation should themselves be placed in categories of some sort, sociological and linguistic, within the wider context of culture.

The process of contextualization may be suggested by the table overleaf:

[1] 'Linguistics and the Functional Point of View', *English Studies*, February 1934.
[2] See *Proceedings of the International Congress of Anthropological and Ethnological Sciences*, London, 1935, and *Man*, September 1934.

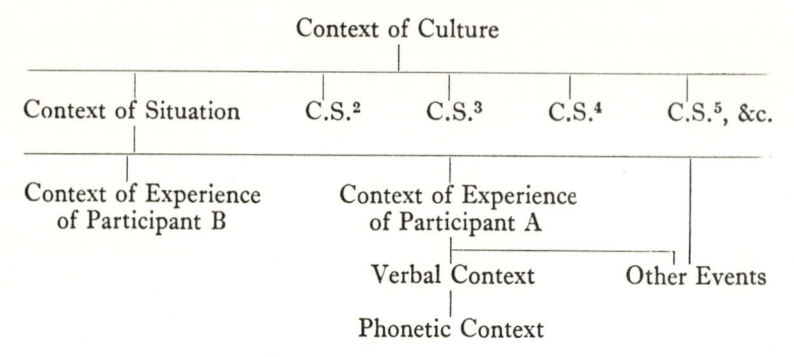

```
                         Context of Culture
                                 |
  ───────┼────────────┼──────────┼──────────┼─────────────
Context of Situation   C.S.²     C.S.³      C.S.⁴    C.S.⁵, &c.
        |                        |
Context of Experience    Context of Experience
  of Participant B         of Participant A
                         ┼──────────────────┼
                    Verbal Context      Other Events
                         |
                    Phonetic Context
```

The progressive contextualization of linguistic facts in this way places them in actual working conditions or use, rather than in systems, and therefore establishes what I would call their 'major' function.

We may admit the value of a purely systematological or structural analysis of the sounds of a given form of speech as a kind of 'systemic' phonetics establishing what I would call the 'minor' functions of sounds.

Nevertheless a pragmatic functionalism seems to me to lead to much clearer definition, and to the statement and explanation of facts, without having to postulate a whole body of doctrine in an elaborate mental structure such as is derived from de Saussure.

The description and explanation of our facts by the simple process of contextualization, the distinction between minor and major functions, and the further subdivision of major functions into morphological, syntactical, lexical, semantic, &c., seem to me fundamentally sound in the present state of our knowledge and for future progress in harmony with prevailing ideas.

To illustrate these contexts and functions let us take the vowels of present-day southern English. It would be possible for a foreign phonetician entirely ignorant of English, and therefore of the major functions of the sounds, to identify all the English vowels and show that each one is a term in a twenty-one-term series; in other words, that the purely phonetic or minor function of each vowel is its use in various similar contexts in contradistinction from twenty others. Taking the phonetic context of initial **b** and final **d**, he would be able to observe bi:d, bid, bed, bæd, ba:d, bɔ:d, bu:d, bʌd, bə:d, beid, boud, baid, baud, bɔid, biəd, bɛəd.

Between **s** and **ks**: si:ks, siks, seks, sæks, sɔks, sʌks, sə:ks, seiks, souks, saiks. Between **p** and **l**: pi:l, pil, pæl, pɔl, pɔ:l, pul, pu:l, pə:l, peil, poul, pail. Between **h** and **d**: hi:d, hid, hed, hæd, ha:d, hɔd, hɔ:d, hud, hə:d, həd (weak form of **hæd**), houd, haid, hɛəd, and also in other purely phonetic contexts, such as initial or final position before or after certain other recognized sounds, e.g. finally after **d** and **m** for certain diphthongs: diə, dɛə, dɔə, duə; miə, mɛə, mɔə, muə.

All this could be done without taking the contextualization process farther than what I have called phonetic context. In other words, you can establish the minor function of a sound merely by noting its use as one of a definite series of phonetic 'substitution-counters' in a given phonetic context.

The number of possible substitution-counters (or possible alternative phonetic terms) varies considerably according to context, so that minor function is not a constant for all contexts, though in some contexts the total maximum number of terms may occur. From the above vowel contexts it will be seen that in the context **bi:d**, **i:** is used as distinct from fifteen other possible substitution-counters, in **pul**, **u** is used in contradistinction from eleven other phonemes, in **hɔd**, the use of **ɔ** is dependent on the potential use of the other twelve alternatives. By comparison a total series of twenty-one terms may be established.

It may also be noted that **ə** can only occur in unstressed syllables, so that we only have a twenty-term potentiality in stressed syllables, and as e, æ, and ɔ do not normally occur finally, only eighteen in that position, and seventeen for those people who use **ɔ:** in place of **ɔə**. As will be seen later, it is of the utmost importance to investigate the distribution of phoneme alternation in various contexts, or what I have termed *contextual distribution*.

If sounds are described, classified, and explained by this statistical contextual technique, most contemporary theories of elision, coalescence, and assimilation will be seen to be confusing and, what is much more to the point, entirely unnecessary.

To establish minor function we have only employed phonetic contexts, and it has not been found necessary to observe our sounds in functionally complete verbal contexts, much less in contexts of situation. But for the elucidation of major functions we must carry the contextualization process much farther.

The major functions of vowels can be classified as follows:

1. Situational.
2. Lexical.
3. Morphological.
4. Phonaesthetic.

First of all, what may be called 'situational' use: **a:, ou, u:** may be functionally complete in themselves as exclamatory sentences in certain contexts of situation. Foreigners speaking English rarely understand the exclamatory use of **ou** in certain very common contexts of situation. The vowels **i:, a:, ɔ:, ei, ou, ai, iə**, and **ɛə** can also be used as one-word sentences functioning by themselves in certain contexts of situation.

The lexical function of the vowels can be shown by referring to the forms in the above series of phonetic contexts (**bi:d, si:ks, pi:l, hi:d,** &c.), and by putting them in verbal contexts, thus establishing these sound-sequences as separate words, distinguished from one another by vowel alternation. This function should not be misnamed *semantic*. The vowel **ɔ:** distinguishes **bɔ:d** as a *lexical* substitution-counter from the fifteen other words with initial **b** and final **d**, but it in no sense determines its function in contexts of situation. **bɔːd** is morphologically and 'semantically' a *neutral*.[1] It may be either *bored, board* (n. and v.) or *bawd*. Other 'semantic' neutrals in the lists are **baːd** (either *bard* or *barred*), **piːl** (*peel* or *peal*), **həːd** (*herd, heard*, or a surname). But they are not neutrals as lexical substitution-counters.

Vowel alternance is also a very important morphological instrument in the strong conjugation of verbs. There are thirty vowel alternances for our babies to learn to use. Both my own children found them very much alive, and produced forms like [brʌŋ] and [θʌŋk]. There is nothing 'dead' about vowel alternance in Modern English. It is, on the contrary, used in a large number (over 100) of the commonest words occurring with great frequency in the speech of quite young children. The alternances are:

1. iː, e	11. əː, uː	21. ai, ʌ
2. iː, əː	12. əː, e	22. ai, au
3. iː, ou	13. uː, ou	23. ai, ou
4. i, æ, ʌ	14. uː, i, ʌ	24. ai, əː
5. i, æ	15. uː, ə	25. ai, ə
6. i, ʌ	16. ʌ, ei	26. ei, u
7. e, ə	17. ʌ, æ	27. ei, ou
8. e, ou	18. ai, ei	28. ou, uː
9. æ, ʌ	19. ai, uː, ou	29. ou, e
10. æ, u	20. ai, i	30. ou, ə
		31. ɛə, ɔː[2]

Vowel alternance has morphological function in nominal forms, particles, and in derivatives (e.g. *strong, strength, steal, stealth*). The vowels **i** and **ə**, used as suffixes, have several morphological functions, e.g. **biːfi, dɔgi** [*doggy* (a.) and *doggie* (n.)], **instrʌktə, blækə**. By adequate contextualization for the establishment of morphological functions alone, we could identify most of the English vowel phonemes. The following have been proved:

iː	i	e	æ	ə	əː	u	uː
1	2	3	4	5	6	7	8

ʌ	ə	ei	ou	ai	au	ɛə	
9	10	11	12	13	14	15	

Then there are very interesting correlations between the occurrence of certain vowels and the characteristic contexts of experience and situation in which they are used.

For example *drip, drop, droop, sweep, swipe, swoop*, and other **uː** verbs like *stoop, scoop, loop, whoop*. There are also the uses of different vowels

---

[1] This is a term I have found very useful, to refer to forms which can only be categorized morphologically and semantically by complete contextualization. (See also *Newspaper Headlines*, by Dr. Heinrich Straumann. Allen and Unwin, 1935.)

[2] See Sweet, *New English Grammar*, Part I, pp. 405 sq.

OF CERTAIN ENGLISH SOUNDS

for near and far demonstratives, for smaller and diminutive things, and for the opposite. And may there not be something more than mere lexical differentiation in such series as:

> stick, stack, stock,
> strip, strap, strop, stripe,
> slippy, and sloppy,
> snip, snap; flick, flake, fluke,

and many others which I have suggested elsewhere.[1] This function I have termed 'phonaesthetic'.

These words also illustrate the phonaesthetic function of initial consonant groups like **st**, **str**, **sl**, **sp**, and **fl**.

The contextualization of consonants illustrates further important theories which appear to me to explain our facts in a simpler and more comprehensive way than any other existing technique.

Let us take for example the series of plosives in the English words *pin*, *bin*, *tin*, *din*, *kin*, *gin*, (*Ginn*). In this phonetic context, namely, initial plosive, the vowel **i**, and final **n**, the total maximum number of 'plosive substitution-counters' or 'plosive terms' may be used, that is to say, **p, b, t, d, k, g**. The glottal stop may also occur under strong stress, ($'^{\text{ʔ}}$**in**), but as the stress correlation is not a factor in determining our phonemes, either for consonants or vowels, we cannot give the glottal stop minor function in initial position; but it has major function for emphasis in certain contexts of situation. If we considered stress as a factor determining the number of our substitution-counters in purely phonetic contexts, we could not place the neutral vowel ə in the same series as the rest of the vowels. And we should have to recognize long **p, b, t, d, k, g** in strongly stressed initial position, which would give us twelve terms. Length of plosives in English under the incidence of stress is best regarded, however, as a major function of the whole context of situation. All six stops can also be used in final and intervocalic position, e.g. kɔp, kɔb, kɔt, kɔd, kɔk, kɔg; and **ræpid, ræbid, rætid, rædiʃ, rækiŋ, rægid**.

Though the place and physiological manner of articulating **p** and **b** or **t** and **d** in similar phonetic contexts, as above, are not identical, they are very similar—so that taking mouth articulation as the principal determinant of our sounds, we should have three pairs of homorganic consonants, the members of each pair being largely, though not altogether, distinguished from one another by differences of laryngeal correlation, or (more simply but more roughly) by the presence or absence of voice. This differentiation of homorganic consonants by 'la corrélation de sonorité',[2] which we may translate 'voice correlation', is very interesting from the functional point of view.

---

[1] See my *Speech*, Benn's Sixpenny Library No. 121, pp. 49–61.
[2] See Trubetzkoy, 'La phonologie actuelle', *Psychologie du langage* (1933), pp. 234 sq. Homorganic sounds can also be differentiated by correlations of tenseness, nasality, length, tone, and so on.

Voice correlation, as we have shown, has minor function in most phonetic contexts, though there are some in which it is not really important; e.g. in such words as *substitution, abstraction*, the voice correlation in the bi-labial consonant is of no importance. Neither is it in the 'd' stop in *width* or *breadth*, or in the labio-dental in *of course*.

The voice correlations of plosives and stops in French, German, and Dutch are so different from one another when we come to contextualize them, that from the functional point of view they have little in common.

A Frenchman who ignores the voice correlation in the velar stop of *black dress*, or the German who always ignores it in final position, are not using the same 'terms', though both of them have six plosives. And those Germans who make no difference between *Peter* and *Bäder* use a three-term plosive system in which voice correlation has no function. In other words, a bi-labial plosive in this latter type of German, whether it sounds like English **p** or **b** or not, is functionally quite different from our **p** and **b** in a six-term system. Compared with the fundamental functional difference, the differences of pronunciation seem negligible.

The plosive and stop systems of the Sanskritic languages of India, Indo-European though they may be, are so utterly different from ours that if we take a Bengali or Delhi Urdu retroflex ṭ and an English t, the superficial similarity of pronunciation is the only thing they have in common. In both minor and major function they are so utterly unlike that no functional comparison is possible, except perhaps in borrowed words.

In Bengali, for the 4 articulations represented by **p**, **t** (dental), **ṭ**, **k**, there is not merely the voice correlation, but the correlation of aspiration; and, in intervocalic position, the correlation of length as well, giving a plosive system of 32 possible substitution-counters or terms; if we include the plosive-like affricates, 8 more, making a round 40 in all. From the functional point of view any comparison of the English **t** in a 6-term system with the Bengali ṭ in a 32-term system is ludicrous except from a rather elementary pedagogical point of view. In Tamil, a Dravidian language, there are 4 rather similar points of articulation for plosives, the retroflex ṭ being more unlike the English t, but the correlations are quite different. There is no voice correlation in pure Tamil, but a combined tenseness-length correlation giving **k**, **kk**, **p**, **pp**, &c., an 8-term system with totally different correlations from either English or any of the Sanskritic dialects. To move still farther East, in Korean there are 3 points of articulation represented by **p**, **t**, **k**, and 3 distinct correlations of tenseness with glottalization, of aspiration, and in intervocalic position of length, within limits, giving a 15-term system different from any so far mentioned.

Now it will be readily appreciated that a **p** in English, German, Bengali, Tamil, and Korean is very different indeed considered from the point of view of minor function alone.

If we contextualize farther to include major function, the functional discrepancy widens to a chasm which completely engulfs any little superficial similarity there may be between the sounds considered from the panglossic phonetic point of view.

If sounds which are so much alike to the ear are so utterly different in function, then Babel is a curse indeed. Is there then no function of any kind which our human noises may share? Is there no general 'm-ness' of m, 'iː-ness' of iː, 'uː-ness' of uː, 'plosivity' of plosives which men speaking different languages feel and use in a very vague and general way in common? I think there is, in varying degrees, and I have called it the 'interlingual phonaesthetic' function.[1]

Now let us return to consider the English plosives in major function. It is obvious from the lists given that in initial, intervocalic, and final position all six have lexical function.

In addition to lexical function, **t** and **d** have morphological functions of two very different kinds, first after **m, n, ŋ**, and **l**, when the voice correlation may have lexical function or morphological functions or a combination of both. For example, if **wɔnd** and **wɔnt** are contextualized as nouns, we have lexical function for the voice correlation. Now take the two neutrals *bend* and *bent*. If contextualized as nouns the function of the voice correlation is lexical, but if as verbs it is morphological.

Other interesting pairs for study are **sent** (neutral), **send; hʌmd, hʌmt; kræmd, kræmt; stʌnd, stʌnt; ʃʌnd, ʃʌnt; bæŋd, bæŋt; wiŋd, wiŋt; bild, bilt; feld, felt; kild, kilt; kould, koult**.

The same is true after vowels: **wiːd, wiːt; fiːd, fiːt; kɔːd, kɔːt**; though in this case the purely morphological function is rare: e.g. **ɡəːd, ɡəːt**.

The case is entirely different when **t** and **d** are used in final position after stops and fricatives in careful speech.

The twin consonant groups **pt, kt, ft, pt, st, ʃt**, are all common enough in final position, but never **pd, kd, fd, θd, sd, ʃd**.[2]

Similarly **bd, ɡd, vd, ðd, zd, ʒd**, occur finally, but not **bt, ɡt, vt, θt, zt, ʒt**.

In such contexts, therefore, no flexion can make use of the voice correlation, as is possible after the liquids. So that if the voice correlation has lexical function in the final consonant of the stem in such contexts, it cannot function in the flexion, and the voice correlation characteristic of the simple form remains throughout the inflected forms, e.g. **bækt, bæɡd, bæks, bæɡz, ript, ribd, slæpt, slæbd**. The ordinary orthography is thus functionally unambiguous.

As a matter of bare statistics, after **b** almost the only stop which can be used in a final twin-consonant group is **d**. Similarly almost the only fricative possible is **z**. It will be realized at once that these facts explain the use and distribution of the two main grammatical inflexions in present-day English **-t, -d**, and **-id**, and **-s, -z**, and **iz**.

[1] See p. 45, footnote.
[2] ʃt and ʃd both occur as weak forms of ʃud, but not in final position.

Other functions of the voice correlation are mentioned in an article previously referred to.[1]

Another interesting feature of the twin consonant groups given above is connected with the identity of the lexical substitution-counter or word in connected speech. Just as the lexical identity of the simple form persists in paradigms, so in certain cases does the word in the sentence. If you hear **pd, kd, fd**, or **bt, gt, vt**, &c., occurring in that order in connected speech, the first is likely to be the 'final' consonant of a word, and the second the initial consonant of the next.

First of all let us take the three phrases **izʃiː?, iʒʃiː,** and **iʃʃiː?**. I use all three myself, but in different contexts of situation and different styles of speech suitable for such situation. In the first style of speech **z** and **ʃ** regularly occur together in that order; but in style two, while the voice correlation still functions in the final consonant of the verb, **z** does not usually occur immediately preceding **ʃ**. In the third style neither **s, z**, nor **ʒ** occurs in such contexts.

Similarly, in the third style of speech above illustrated, final **n** is seldom followed by **p, b, k, g**.

'Final+initial' consonant groups such as **nt, nd, nθ, nð, ns**, &c., occur, but not **np, nb, nk, ng; mp, mb, ŋk, ŋg** are, however, common. Hence in such speech the auxiliary verb *can't* has several forms: **kaːnt, kaːn, kaːm, kaːŋ**.

In this style of speech (which is not recommended to foreigners) syllabic **n** cannot occur after **p** or **b** and not often after **k** and **g**, though syllabic **m** and **ŋ** respectively after such consonants are common.

Then there is the glottal stop. In the speech of many educated people I know, **t** does not occur, in fairly rapid colloquial speech, immediately before **p, b, m, w, ð**, and not often before syllabic **n** and certain other sounds. Contexts such as **pm, ʾm, pp, ʾp** are, however, common; e.g. **nɔʾ mʌtʃ** or **nɔp mʌtʃ, nouʾpeipə, wiðauʾ mʌtʃ trʌbl**.

It may also occur in **mʌʾn** and even in contexts like **senʾts, mæʾtʃ**. It does not usually occur intervocalically in educated speech.

The interpretation to be placed on these facts as I see them is that whereas the number of phonetic substitution-counters or phonemes is likely to be constant in these various styles of speech, the contextual distribution is likely to be very different; and in rapid familiar speech the number of possible contexts for certain sounds will be very much reduced and for others extended, as we have seen. For example, whereas in careful speech 'final+initial' groups such as **vt, zʃ, vk** commonly occur, in rapid familiar speech such contexts are comparatively infrequent; though **ft, fd**, and **vd** are still of common occurrence. The case of the glottal stop is an extension.

There is no need to use the blanket word 'assimilation' at all.

The technique of contextualization, and of explanation by establishing

[1] See p. 35, n. 1.

minor and major functions, is not limited to any one type of linguistic unit. There is no reason to suppose that our only speech units are single phonemes, stems, affixes, words, and sentences.

Consequently I propose to examine English systems of consonant groups just as we have examined the plosives.

Plosives, indeed, seem to be the central sounds round which these groups are built with **s** as the initial on-glide component, and with **r** or **l**, or less frequently **w**, as the off-glide or 'release' component. And, as we might expect from our brief study of the contextual distribution of the plosives, especially of **t** and **d** (and also of the fricatives **s** and **z**), more groups are built round **p**, **t**, **k** than round **b**, **d**, **g**.

Let us take such groups in initial position in common non-derivative English word-bases such as *spray* or *stripe*. In this context there are fifteen very common groups built round the voiceless stops or plosives, and only six in which the stop component is voiced. They can be arranged in a system as follows:

	p	*b*	*t*	*d*	*k*	*g*
with s—	sp	—	st	—	sk	—
with —r	pr	br	tr	dr	kr	gr
with —l	pl	bl	—	—	kl	gl
with —w	—	—	tw	dw	kw	—
with s—r	spr	—	str	—	skr	—
with s—l	spl	—	—	—	—	—
with s—w	—	—	—	—	skw	—

First of all it will be noticed that nine have the **r** off-glide component. It is not surprising that **tl** and **dl** do not occur in initial position in contradistinction from initial **kl** and **gl**, as most people find it extremely difficult to hear any difference, for instance, between **tliːn dlʌvz** and **kliːn glʌvz**. In the north of England thousands of people use **tl** and **dl** in such contexts, instead of **kl** and **gl**, without knowing it.

In addition to these twenty-one groups with 'central' plosives, there are three very common initial assibilations of the liquids **m, n, l (sm, sn, sl)** and five groups using **p, f, s, ʃ**, with one or other of the off-glides **r, l**, or **w**, making twenty-nine common initial consonant groups.

That they have minor function may be shown by such series as the following:

*t*rip, *d*rip, *st*rip, *sk*ip, *cl*ip, *gr*ip, *sn*ip, *sl*ip, *fl*ip;
*st*op, *pr*op, *dr*op, *cr*op, *pl*op, *fl*op, *str*op;
*sp*ank, *st*ank, *pr*ank, *dr*ank, *cr*ank, *pl*ank, *bl*ank, *cl*ank, *fl*ank, *fr*ank, *sw*ank;
*sn*ack, *sm*ack, *sl*ack, &c.;
*spr*ay, *spl*ay (footed), *str*ay;
*dw*ell, *qu*ell, *sw*ell;
*spr*awl, *dr*awl, *cr*awl, *scr*awl, *br*awl.

By multiplying similar series the contextual contradistinctions of the twenty-nine initial consonant groups can easily be established and the test for minor function satisfied.

Many of them have also the major function which I have called phonaesthetic, and which I first described in my little book on *Speech* published in 1930. This phonaesthetic function can be shown by pointing to obvious correlations which exist between alliterative words beginning with these groups, and characteristic common features of the contexts of experience and of situation in which they are used. For example:

stand, stiff, stick, stake, stack, stock, still, stub, stud, stump, stem, stalk, stoke, stuff, stare, stay, stain, &c., &c.

grip, grasp, grab, grope, grapple, gripes, groan, growl, grumb, grouse, grunt, &c.

clay, cloy, clod, clot, clog, clinker, clump, clumsy, cling, clench, clinch, clamp, clasp.

squeeze, squelch, squirm, squirt, squib, squeal, squid, squander, squeamish.

strip, stripe, stroke, strap, string, streak, &c., have 'long, thin, straight, narrow, stretched-out' correlation. The crooked, 'opposite of straight', correlation can be seen in *crank, cross, criss-cross, crick, crab, cramp, crumple, crag, crook, crib, crate, crazy, crimp, cringe, cripple, crutch,* &c.

Then there are all the pejorative words beginning with *sl*, the nasty nasal words with *sn*, the *smoke, smirch, smirk, smug,* and other *sm* pejorative words.

Of course phonaesthetic function does not begin and end with such initial consonant groups, as we have already seen in connexion with vowel contextualization.

Let us consider the rhyming elements of the following groups of words: *drip, slip, snip, flick, snick, slick, quick,* contrasted with *lump, hump, bump, clump, stump, thump, dump, plump, rump, mumps*! Also *hurl, furl, curl, whirl, twirl, swirl,* and the two series rhyming with *sprawl,* and *swoop* given in an earlier paragraph.

It seems to me fairly obvious that correlations exist between the rhyming elements, and characteristic common features of the contexts of experience and situation in which they are used. Furthermore a comparative study of such words as the following, from this phonaesthetic point of view, will show how these sounds and sound groups are used for combined effects.

snack, snag; snip, snub; slip, slap, slam, slump;

crack, crash; smack, smash; spank, splash, swish, swing, swipe, swoop, swoon.

From such comparisons we can show that such words are composed of substitution-counters which have these rather vague phonaesthetic functions and that consonant groups, short front vowels, back rounded and long vowels, nasals, voiced and voiceless plosives, fricatives, all seem to combine to produce their different and sometimes contrasted effects. But of course all this is only a very small element in the specific meaning of such words in actual verbal contexts. 'Semantic' function can only be understood with reference to the whole context of situation on any specific occasion.

I am far from suggesting that there is anything in all this of Humboldt's inherent sound symbolism, or what Dr. Wolfgang Köhler calls 'Similarities of experiences through different sense organs', 'the qualities of different senses being comparable' and associated, or what Swinburne called 'the mixing of senses in the spirit's cup'.

I merely state what I believe to be a fact—namely, that a definite correlation can be felt and observed between the use and occurrence of certain sounds and sound-patterns (not being words in the ordinary sense) and certain characteristic common features of the contexts of experience and situation in which they function.

I have collected hundreds of examples of such sound-patterns in German, Dutch, and the Scandinavian languages and tested them in consultation with native students. Many more also from Indian and other Asiatic languages collected either during residence in Asia or from students in England. These will be fully dealt with in a future piece of work.

The phonaesthetic function of sounds is not entirely limited, conditioned, or specialized within each speech community. The Germanic languages share very many of these, allowing for national variation of pronunciation of front and back vowels, r-sounds, plosives, and so on. There are, however, certain very widespread correlations between sound and sense in a vague general sort of way throughout the whole world.[1]

To sum up, we have shown how the vowels and plosives of English can be delimited and identified by a comparative study of phonetic contexts. Other sounds—nasals, fricatives, l-sounds—can be studied in a similar way. This process of contextualization establishes our phonetic substitution-counters or phonemes in what we have called minor function.

Secondly, we have analysed our speech sounds into components, into what may be called the 'articulation' component and the 'correlation' components of a general nature, such as voice-breath, length, tone, stress, nasality, tenseness, and so on.

Thirdly, we have shown the importance of the study of the contextual distribution of sounds, both of articulations and correlations.

These are the three fundamental principles of the technique based on what is called the 'phoneme' theory.

Fourthly, we have suggested the contextualization of some of these sounds in verbal contexts and paradigms, to prove their morphological function. The morphological functions of other sounds and of the voice and stress correlations have only been mentioned. Functions for initial ð and θ, for n, l, for the voice and stress correlations, have also been suggested. In addition to those previously referred to,[2] there are the following words suggesting various morphological functions for English sounds:

stiːl, stelθ; strɔŋ, streŋθ; wɔːm, wɔːmθ; waid, widθ; blæk, blæks,

[1] Cf. Dr. Wolfgang Köhler, *Gestalt Psychology*, Bell & Sons, 1930, esp. pp. 186–7.
[2] See p. 42, n. 1.

blækt, blækn, blæki; spiːk, spiːtʃ; breik, briːtʃ; hæŋ, hinʒ, hitʃ; bliŋk, blenʃ; stiŋk, stenʃ; driŋk, drenʃ; &c.

The syntactical functions of intonation also become clear when treated in this way, i.e. by contextualization.

Lexical function has been distinguished from situational function, which can only be proved with reference to an instance of a context of situation on some specific occasion.

This technique in descriptive linguistics is developing, and its application may be tried in other languages.

5

PHONOLOGICAL FEATURES OF SOME INDIAN LANGUAGES

THE study of the speech behaviour of man is no simple task. It must be shared by many sciences. Experimental phonetics, for example, deals with certain aspects of a man's actual utterance. Actual speech events in time can be recorded fairly completely by means of the talking film, less completely by means of the phonographic disk or steel ribbon. The apparatus of experimental phonetics records only certain specific components of the speech act.

Linguistic phonetics and phonology deal with types and classes of events. A transcriptionist makes abstraction of certain features only of typical speech events and records them by means of his letters, the values of which depend on four sets of relations:

(i) The relations of the symbols to the general phonetic categories of sound types and their attributes, categories of similarity and identity, and categories of difference.
(ii) The actual contextual relations in any given transcription.
(iii) The systematic relations between the terms or letters of an alternance.
(iv) The relations between the letters considered as an intralinguistic schematic notation for the symbolization of any given language material.

Thus the transcriptionist does not record actual speech events in any sense. He picks out certain features of a bit of speech, decides what general pigeon-holes they belong to and writes down the pigeon-hole labels in a certain order, according to certain rules. In such acts of symbolism the particular and general meet, but the record is nevertheless in general terms, all individuality of voice, pronunciation, and tone being necessarily ignored.

A transcription aims at symbolizing the essentials from the typological point of view. In order to make or use a transcription considerable technical skill is required. To begin with, the whole system of relations above suggested must be fully understood, and the notation correlated with bodily performances. It would be interesting to have a psychologist's analysis of all the skills required for such work.

From a study of speech events, then, you build up a generalized transcription, and in the process two sets of relations have especially to be studied:
1. The relation of the symbolized element, or letter if you like, to the type of context in which it appears, and
2. The relations of the symbolized element to all other different symbolized elements that may also occur in the given type of context.

Under (1) the types of context in which such letters or symbols will appear can be listed and described. They may be described positionally in general terms, such as initial, final, intervocalic, &c.; or more specifically, for example, by saying 'between initial **k** and final **p**', or say 'in initial position followed by **i:** in a stressed syllable'.

It may be practically convenient to think of a language as having a sound system, or phonetic structure as a whole, but this is little more than a sum of all the possible alternances of sounds in all contexts. This is an 'all-over' list, and not to be confused, for example, with a specific context of maximum alternance for a certain class of sound, e.g. the context in which the maximum number of plosives may alternate in English.[1]

Let us now apply these principles to Indian languages. From the linguistic behaviour of many typical speakers of Hindi we may abstract the five typical articulations of plosives which may be suggested by the symbols **p, t, ṭ, c, k.**

These five plosive articulation differences are shared by forty substitution elements in intervocalic position. Using five common plosive articulations the speaker of Hindi multiplies his substitution-counters by differences of voice, aspiration, and length. The voice difference adds five more terms:

b, d, ḍ, j, g.

The aspiration difference doubles these:

ph, th, &c.
bh, dh, &c.

And the length difference doubles these again, making forty in all.

But it is only in certain general contexts that all forty alternances or substitutions are possible, e.g. medially or intervocalically, so that I should hesitate to make any general statement about the function or value of any one term in the language as a whole apart from a more or less determined context. Whereas **ṭ** in intervocalic position is one of forty plosive terms in that context, in initial position it is one of twenty.

This use of a substitution element in contradistinction from others of a series I call 'minor' function. The minor function of **ṭ** in initial position is quite different from its function in intervocalic position. If you like, initial **ṭ** is a different 'phoneme' from intervocalic **ṭ**, the conventions of position differentiating them in the notation.

Marathi has a maximum number of twenty plosive alternants in initial position followed by **i:** or **y**, but of twenty-four if followed by **a**. Certain dialects of Panjabi present a curious variation of this system. In the Gujranwala dialect, before vowels beginning with a low rising tone the plosive alternance is one of five terms only. The five articulation differences are used, but no voice or aspiration differences. Before other tones the five

---

[1] See Chapter 4, and also Trubetzkoy's *Anleitung*, para. 23, 'Stellung der maximalen Phonemunterscheidung'.

SOME INDIAN LANGUAGES

articulation differences are further differentiated by voice and aspiration, and the plosive alternance is constituted by five sets of three of the type **p, ph, b**—fifteen in all.

The contextual distribution of retroflex sounds in Indian languages is interesting. In Sanskritic languages ṭ, ḍ, ṭh, ḍh may occur in initial, intervocalic, and final position, the ṭ as we have seen being one of a twenty-term series of substitution elements in initial position and one of a forty-term series in intervocalic position. Contrast this with Tamil, a Dravidian language. So far as I have been able to ascertain, retroflex sounds do not occur in initial position in pure Tamil words. Initial and final retroflex ṭ occur in a few borrowed words only, so that in Tamil sequences ṭ is not commonly found as a term in inter-word sound junctions. In the common spoken Tamil of Tinnevelly you would hear in intervocalic position the following retroflex consonants: ṭ (flapped sort of ḍ), ṭṭ, ṇ (flapped), ṇṇ, ḷ (flapped), ḷḷ, and the mid-palatal frictionless continuant ɹ. The point here is the reason why ṭṭ and what sounds like a flapped ḍ are grouped together by the notation ṭṭ and ṭ. There are several reasons for this notation.

First of all because of similarity of articulation, the laterals and nasals being obviously differentiated in pairs by the length difference.

Secondly, because the tense voiceless stop ṭṭ is always longer than the ṭ in similar context.

Thirdly, because the differentiation of tense, fairly long, voiceless stops and shorter homorganic flaps or fricatives only occurs in intervocalic position throughout the language.

Lastly, because such alternances have what I have called 'major function'[1] in cases such as the following:

$$
\begin{aligned}
&\text{paṭu} &&= I\ endure \\
&\text{paṭṭu} &&= enduring \\
&\text{paṭṭeen} &&= I\ endured \\
&\text{paṭeen} &&= I\ did\ not\ endure
\end{aligned}
$$

Another kind of major function, lexical function, is illustrated by:

$$
\begin{aligned}
&\text{paṭam} &&= a\ picture \\
&\text{paṭṭam} &&= a\ kite
\end{aligned}
$$

Quite similarly with **tt**, and **t**:

$$
\begin{aligned}
&\text{maatu} &&= a\ woman \\
&\text{maattu} &&= change
\end{aligned}
$$

and **c**, and **cc**:

$$
\begin{aligned}
&\text{peecu} &&= speak \\
&\text{peeccu} &&= talk
\end{aligned}
$$

[1] See Chapter 4.

The vowels group themselves in pairs differentiated by length correlation. There is no strain about that in Tamil. Compare

<blockquote>
paṭu = <i>to endure</i> paaṭu = <i>sing</i>
paṭṭu = <i>enduring</i> paaṭṭu = <i>a song</i>
</blockquote>

In Tamil, Malayalam, and in Telugu the length difference divides the simple vowels in pairs quite clearly.

It is far otherwise with most of the Sanskritic dialects, including Urdu. Gujerati may possibly turn out to be an exception, but I doubt even that. But for Urdu, Hindi, Bengali, Marathi, I doubt very much whether the simple vowel qualities are further divided by the length difference. This is one of the difficulties, not only of phonology but of typography, **i** and **u** being such wretched letters. In Urdu, for example, between **m** and **l** you have **mil, myl,**[1] **mel, mayl, mal, məl, mol, mwl,**[1] **mul.** In this context at any rate I cannot pair them off by the length difference. The alternance is one of quality differences. Now let us take them in major function.

In normal speech **a** in final position is the sign of the masculine, **i** the feminine, and **e** the plural. These vowels are not long either actually or relatively: **ata, ati, ate, mera, meri, mere.**

Again by yet another major function, I see no system of pairing, i.e. in the 'passives':

<blockquote>
pisna = <i>to grind</i>   chedna = <i>to pierce</i>
pysna = <i>to be ground</i> chydna = <i>to be pierced</i>
</blockquote>

Here you will notice two alternances with **y:i** and **y**, and **e** and **y**, and just as **y** alternates in this function with both **i** and **e**, so **w** alternates with **u** and **o**:

<blockquote>
guthna = <i>to plait</i>
ġwthna = <i>to be plaited</i>
kholna = <i>to open</i>
khwlna = <i>to be open</i>
</blockquote>

Compare also
<blockquote>
kaṭna = <i>to cut</i>
kəṭna = <i>to be cut</i>
</blockquote>

I have mentioned the major function of alternances. I suppose in Hindi and Urdu the commonest vowel alternances are those above mentioned, and to them I would add other substitution elements differentiated by nasalization:

<blockquote>
ĩ fem. plural ẽ common plural
ã in particles õ dat. plural
ũ 1st person singular
</blockquote>

There are also other pairs:

<blockquote>ay, aỹ; ə, ə̃.</blockquote>

Other common morphological alternances are the dental **t** and **n** in

---

[1] **y** and **w** are more open than **i** and **u**, and centralized.

verbs, e.g. kərna, kərta, and in initial position in particles y and v, j, and k.

In the matter of the nasalization difference in vowels, Marathi is a special case. It has nothing like the functional importance of nasalization in Urdu, Hindi, or Gujerati.

Nasals and nasalization in the Sanskritic languages raise fundamental questions of phonetic and phonological theory, and also problems for roman transcription. Let us take Marathi, for instance. In initial position only two nasal consonants can be used, **n** and **m**. In final position there is a three-term nasal alternance, but immediately preceding another consonant, especially stops, only one is possible, the nasal homorganic with the following consonant. In these contexts there is no alternance, only a specific and unique nasal, homorganic with the following consonant. Of these I have noted at least eight: alveolar **n** before **ts**, dental **n** before dental **t**, **d**, and similarly retroflex ṇ, palato-alveolar nasal, velar nasal, bilabial, labio-dental, and a sort of nasal w̃. In transcription I should use the letter **n** to symbolize the initial **n** used in contradistinction from **m** only, also for the final **n** which functions in a three-term alternance and again for the specific unique homorganic nasal on-glides before **ts**, **t**, **d**, and perhaps even all the rest. But I should not thereby identify all these **n** sounds as linguistically and functionally the same element or unit. Indeed, they cannot be so identified. The homorganic nasal on-glides to the stops could be represented by a separate nasal symbol such as ~, but that is not really necessary. Surely we are free to use the same letter without being compelled to concoct a rationalized 'derivation' from the letter in the shape of a phoneme theory. Similarity of sound is no safe guide to functional identity, though it may serve as the basis of practical transcription symbols. There are not eight nasal 'phonemes' in Marathi. We might possibly say there are three, though I should prefer to say that the sounds we symbolize by **n** and **m**, for example, constitute the total nasal alternance in initial position, but only two out of three terms in final position, whilst they both serve also as unique homorganic on-glides.

The actual mechanism and act of utterance of **n**, for example, in each of the three cases would be different. They would actually be slightly different sounds, and their minor function would also be different. Though writing them with the same symbol on practical phonetic grounds, I should not identify them in any other way. That they are the same 'phoneme' is the very last thing I should say. In Tamil in initial position three nasals may alternate, in intervocalic position four (some say five) but there are seven contextually specific nasal on-glides. These are unique terms, and do not function in any alternance. That is to say, in the context in which each one occurs the articulation difference does not function. What functions is merely the broad nasalization difference.

There are certain noteworthy phonological differences which function in alternances in certain parts of India only. First of all the characteristic 'implosives' of Sindhi and Western Panjabi and certain dialects of Gujerati. There is also the very strongly marked differentiation of unaspirated and aspirated plosives by a parallel and correlated laryngeal difference in Marathi and also in certain Western Panjabi dialects. The voiceless plosives and even affricates are often ejective in Marathi. There is certainly some glottal and perhaps also pharyngeal difference parallel with the aspiration difference in such languages.

Even more interesting is what may be called the 'phonation difference' which I first noticed in the Nowshera Tahsil of the Shahpur district in 1925. I have since noticed a similar phonation difference in Gujerati as spoken by Indians from Surat. This phonation difference separates pairs of words. That is to say, it differentiates the terms of an alternance. The vowel qualities thus affected are pronounced (i) with breathy phonation, (ii) with what I have called 'tight' phonation. Thus in Surati Gujerati:

Tight phonation		*Breathy phonation*	
kã	= *why*	kãh	= *where*
mel	= *dirt*	mehl	= *palace*
koɖ	= *longing, desire, zest*	kohɖ	= *leprosy*
kəro	= *do*	kəroh	= *wall of a house*
ʃer	= *two pounds weight*	ʃehr	= *city*
kəyũ	= *which*	kəhyũ	= *I said*
avũ?	= *shall I come?*	ahvũ?	= *like this?*

And many others.

Perhaps the most important of all phonological investigations is the study of intonational alternances differentiating otherwise similar sequences of sounds. For example, the following sequence of sounds and words in Gujerati without intonation means very little. It is neutral:

vandro beʈho che.

But if we consider the following intonation alternances, paying special attention to the intonation difference, we make some sort of translation possible.

vandro beʈho che.

1. ——————————————— [statement]
   The monkey is sitting down.

2. ——————————————— [question]
   Is the monkey sitting down?

3. ——————————————— [surprise]
   Is the monkey sitting down?

4. ———————————————
   Is it the monkey that is sitting there?

5. ———————————————
   Is the monkey **sitting** there?

The intonation examples just given serve to remind us what a highly abstract proceeding an alphabetic transcription of speech behaviour really is. And it is only by means of a thorough theoretical understanding of the principles and methods of the technique that we can make scientific use of such records.

In conclusion, may I say that the features and examples selected for comment are intended to raise questions of general theoretical interest and to establish certain general principles for Indian phonology.

6

ALPHABETS AND PHONOLOGY IN INDIA AND BURMA

FOR 300 years after Vasco da Gama touched Calicut generations of traders, merchants, missionaries, soldiers, and other emissaries from at least five different nations of Europe took their turn in India, pursuing their interests at a respectful distance, making no obtrusive efforts to scrape acquaintance with Sanskrit culture.[1] Such advances were socially difficult, and would not have been welcomed. Moreover, our early associations were with Dravidian India, and very few cultured Brahmins sought membership of Christian Churches.[2]

As late as 1771 Amaduzzi, the head of the Typographia Sacrae Congregationis de Propaganda Fide, writing of the *Alphabetum Brammhanicum seu Indostanum Universitatis Kasi*, remarks: 'Cui etiam Historiae, Fabula, Scientiae, ceteraque μυσήεια commendantur ne ceteris de plebe, ac peregrinis quinetiam arcana huiusmodi patere possint. Quare Idioma hoc ab ipsis संकृत Samscrit appellatur . . . Eadem Lingua Samscritica, seu litterali Brammhanica pro sacris, et arcanis rebus singulae hae gentes religiose, constanterque utuntur.'

The Capuchin missionaries,[3] upon whose work the *Alphabetum* is chiefly based, report: 'Brammhanes tamen, ut iam innuimus, maximo studio, tum zelo servandi Religionis arcana, tum metu punitionis subeundae, non solum alienigenis, sed terrigenis etiam, qui de eorum tribubus non sunt geniti, abscondere solent huius Alphabeti institutiones.' The knowledge of the 'Bedpurana' is the secret of the few 'ceteris autem perpetuis in tenebris delitescat'. And so it was with the excellent Capuchin friar, Beligatti, as with so many generations of Europeans in India. Besides, had not the worthy Magister Balgobinda of Patna told him that he himself found difficulties with Sanskrit every day and there was no end to learning it? And so, like many both before and after him to this day, he says: '. . . At cum nobis concessum non fuerit talia penetrasse secreta, ut aliis ad ulteriora perscrutanda planam viam panderemus.'

---

[1] The Italian students of Sanskrit, Sassetti (1581–8) and de Nobili (d. 1656) were the exceptions proving the rule.

[2] The Tamil teacher and interpreter employed by Ziegenbalg in 1706–7 was, we are told, expelled from Tranquebar and subsequently kept in irons in a Tanjore prison, accused 'd'avoir trahi la Religion, et d'en avoir révélé les Mystères le plus secrets aux deux Missionaires de Tranquebar!' La Croze, *Histoire de Christianisme des Indes*, tome ii, p. 391.

[3] Especially Cassiano Beligatti di Macerata, also joint author of the *Alphabetum Tangutanum sive Tibetanum* (1773). Worked in the Tibet–Nepal Mission. In Lhasa 1741–2, then twelve years in Nepal and occasionally in Patna. Died in Macerata 1785.

Alphabets with all their implicit phonetics, phonology, and grammar have a background of at least 2,000 years of history in India, and to this day they remain the totems of the peoples, marks of brotherhood, and against the stranger graven shibboleths. Alphabets divide and rule. We English, following the opinion of Lord Macaulay, pressed our A B C and the rest of our literary arcana on our Indian fellow subjects. The interesting thing is, however, that English continues to serve the best interests of India as an Indian language in the terms of the present constitution.

Contact with the vernacular languages was different. Even in the earliest days, of course, Europeans on arrival in India had, as we say, 'to learn the language', and superficial knowledge of certain vernacular languages necessarily started with the first systematic relations between Europe and India. More scholarly acquaintance was especially necessary for the great missions, and so we find that a study of the vernacular languages long antedates what we are pleased to call the discovery of Sanskrit, following Sir William Jones's epoch-making address in 1786.

In spite of the early neglect and ignorance of Sanskrit, in spite of Lord Macaulay's appalling judgement, European scholars and especially Englishmen have during the last 150 years served Indian scholarship well, and none better than Sir George Grierson. Just as Macaulay's minute, in establishing the use of English in India, inaugurated the biggest Imperial language and culture undertaking the world has ever seen, so this monumental linguistic survey of a vast sub-continent is the biggest thing of its kind in history. Both in devoted labour of direction and in the piety of its collaborators it holds perhaps the highest place in the long history of such work in India.

This is a fitting occasion to recall the work of the earliest students of Indian languages, Portuguese, Italians, Dutch, Danes, Germans, Frenchmen—especially of the missionaries, Catholic and Protestant, and also the pioneer publications of the press of the Sacra Congregatio de Propaganda Fide in Rome and the Tranquebar Mission.[1] In 1771 it was probably justly claimed that: 'Ceterum nullus forte locus Brammhanicis, et aliis quinetiam exoticarum linguarumCodicibus magis abundat, quam Bibliotheca Collegii Urbani de Propaganda Fide. . . .'

If we suspend for a moment all theological notions of linguistic unity, the noises of the human race are indeed a chattering Babel, a confusion of tongues. Such abounding diversity is at once a challenge to those minds which seek ordered simplicity in the world, and at the same time a collectors' paradise. There will always be those who seek an underlying unity, and both theology and historical philology have immensely strengthened this way of regarding the languages of the world. But, in spite of the 'philological revolution', the traditions of plain description and the enthusiasm of the field collector have continued unbroken, from Gesner's *Mithridates* in 1555

---

[1] Most of these earlier works are mentioned in the *Linguistic Survey of India*. See vol. iv, pp. 302, 350; vol. v, p. 18; vol. ix, pp. 6, 7, &c.

to the collections of the International Phonetic Association and the recent Internationale Arbeitsgemeinschaft für Phonologie. In 1592 Hieronymus Megiser of Stuttgart printed *Specimens of Forty Languages*, increased to fifty in the second edition of 1603. But it was not until the eighteenth century that the systematic collection of material was undertaken in earnest. Leibniz stimulated his many correspondents and interested Peter the Great. And it was, in fact, in a letter[1] of Theophilus Siegfried Bayer, one of the founders of the Imperial Academy at St. Petersburg, that the first words intended for Hindustani were published in Europe. In another (1729) we learn of records of the Sanskrit alphabet.

The first really comprehensive compilation was the *Orientalisch- und Occidentalischer Sprachmeister*, by Johann Friedrich Fritz and Benjamin Schulze, published in Leipzig in 1748. It presented 200 translations of the Lord's Prayer and 100 alphabets, including the Bengali, and the Modi alphabet for Marathi, Gujarati, and Tamil, Telugu, and Canarese. It was the first collection of *Alphabeta* in which Indian vernacular words were printed in their own character in movable type. From the phonetic point of view it falls far short of the later *Alphabeta* of the press of the Sacra Congregatio de Propaganda Fide. No notice is taken, for instance, of cerebral or retroflex consonants. But it held the field till 1771, when the *Alphabetum Brammhanicum* was published, marking a new epoch in Indian studies.

The linguistic employment of the parable of the Prodigal Son and the fable of the North Wind and the Sun follows directly in the tradition of the *Sprachmeister*.

At this point perhaps we should notice the very early work of individual students of Indian languages, and mention the career of Maturin Veyssière La Croze.

The first real account of *Hindostani* was not published till 1743, though the work was done much earlier by J. J. Ketelaar, a Dutch envoy to Bahadur Shah, who was in Lahore in 1711 and moved to Delhi with the Emperor. Later he became Dutch director of trade at Surat.[2] There are also several early Dutch accounts of Tamil, but the first systematic grammar, published in 1716, was the work of Bartholomew Ziegenbalg, a German member of the Danish Mission at Tranquebar, 'admiré des Indiens pour la connaissance et l'usage de leur Langue'.[3]

[1] 1 June 1726.
[2] The *Alphabetum Brammhanicum* mentions a 'MS. Lexicon, Linguae Indostanicæ in Bibliotheca Collegii Urbani de Propaganda Fide, quod Auctorem habet Franciscum M. Turonensem ex Capuccinorum Familia, qui ipsum in Suratensi Missione, quae eidem erat concredita, concinnavit, ac dein dono dedit Sacrae huic nostrae Congregationi a.d. III Nonas Quinctiles anni cIɔIɔccIV (1704)'. This manuscript is said to contain 489 pages in pt. i and 423 in pt. ii, giving Latin words in alphabetical order in the first column, 'altera Indostanicas Nagaricis apicibus exaratas'. On the opposite page the Latin words are said to be written and explained in French in the first column, and in the second the 'voces Indostanas' are, 'quantum potis est', also written and explained in French.
[3] b. 1683, d. 1719. For further details of his life and work see La Croze, *Histoire du Christianisme des Indes*, a La Haye aux depens de la Compagnie, 3rd ed. (1758), vol. ii, pp. 384 ff.

La Croze gives an amusing account of how Ziegenbalg and Plutschau learnt 'Damul'. 'Comme la langue Portugaise est depuis plus de deux siècles fort commune dans les Indes, ils jugèrent à propos de l'apprendre la première....' With the aid of Portuguese they applied themselves to the study of Tamil, but found the books 'écrits en cette Langue sur des feuilles de Palmier. C'était là tout le secours sur lequel ils pouvaient compter, y comprenant la vive voix des gens du pays, qui n'ont ni grammaire ni dictionnaire, ni aucun art qui facilite l'intelligence de leur Langue.' They made little progress so they engaged a Tamil schoolmaster, who brought his school of small children with him and the two missionaries began 'à écrire comme eux avec les doigts sur le sable les lettres Malabares, et à les joindre selon que le Maître d'École les dictoit'. Unfortunately the master knew no Portuguese, so they were left in the dark as to the meanings of most of the words they learned to write and pronounce. But eventually they found a Tamil who spoke Portuguese, Danish, Dutch, and German! 'Cet homme leur fut d'un grand secours, aussi bien qu'un petit abbrégé de la Langue Malabare qui leur tomba entre les mains, et qui étoit de la composition d'un Missionaire Portugais.... Ils se formèrent en peu de temps à la prononciation qui est extrêmement difficile.' I suspect that in other parts of India and Burma also the works of earlier missionaries, even manuscript notes, 'fell into the hands' of those who eventually wrote the first real grammars and dictionaries, and established traditions.

In 1716, after completing his grammar on the voyage to Europe, Ziegenbalg preached before the King of Denmark at the siege of Stralsund, and afterwards one of his Indian converts had the honour of being presented to His Majesty. He was received by the King and the Prince of Wales during his visit to England, where he had received the liberal support of the Archbishop of Canterbury and the S.P.G. since 1709.[1] The S.P.C.K. had given him a printing press, which had been set up in Tranquebar in 1711.

His phonetic observations follow the Tamil syllabary, and though sound enough in their way, are not especially interesting. The *D* in *Grammatica Damulica* is good German and not really bad Tamil. He noticed the palatal nasal which he transcribed *yn* and the prepalatal affricate for which he used five roman letters, *ytsch*. He counted eighteen consonants, five long vowels and five short, and two diphthongs.[2] Like many others who followed, even after the publication of the *Alphabetum Malabaricum* in 1772, he wrongly described Tamil as the Malabar language.[3] We even find Pope[4] saying Malayalam 'seems to be but a corrupt Tamil'. The Jesuit Beschi arrived in India about 1700 and produced a new Tamil Grammar (1728–39), which seems to have been used by most of his successors. He had the reputa-

---
[1] Of this support La Croze, who was an admirer of England, remarks 'Rien n'est plus édifiant que la charité de la Nation Angloise, qui se signala en cette occasion', loc. cit., 2nd ed., vol. ii, p. 416.
[2] Cf. my 'Short Outline of Tamil Pronunciation' in *Arden's Grammar*, p. vi.
[3] See *Alphabetum Grandonico-Malabaricum*, 1772, p. xxi.
[4] *A Handbook of the Tamil Language*, 5th ed. (1895), p. 2.

tion of being a good Telugu and Sanskrit scholar as well. He died about 1746.

One of the most interesting personalities in the history of Oriental scholarship during the early years of the eighteenth century is Maturin Veyssière La Croze. He was born at Nantes in 1661 and was educated by Benedictines, taking a great interest in the writings of the early Fathers. In 1682 he went to Paris and soon became known on account of his independence of character and unorthodox views. In 1696 he had to leave France, and went to Berlin, following the example of many exiled French Protestants, who had been welcomed there by 'The Great Elector' (1640–88). In 1697 he became Librarian and Antiquary to Frederick, Elector of Brandenburg, afterwards, in 1701, the first King of Prussia. In 1725 he was given the chair of Philosophy in the French College in Berlin, and he died there in 1739. He wrote histories of Christianity in India and in Ethiopia, and from Berlin carried on a voluminous correspondence with most of the linguists of his time, including Leibniz, Bayer, and Ziegenbalg, mentioned above, and, among many others, with John Chamberlain and David Wilkins in England. After his death this correspondence was published in Leipzig in 1742 as *Thesauri Epistolici La Croziani*. This collection may be regarded as the focus and index of most of the Oriental linguistic work of the early eighteenth century. Though he was no friend of the Roman Church his letters are constantly quoted in the publications of the press of the Sacra Congregatio in the last thirty years of the century from the *Alphabetum Brammhanicum* of 1771 to the revised edition of the *Alphabetum Barmanorum* of 1787.

In view of the discovery of the Tell el Duweir Vase in 1933 and the still more recent researches of Mr. Starkey at Lachish in Palestine, which have furnished the missing link in the evolution of the Semitic and other alphabets from Ancient Egyptian, it is interesting to quote the La Croze letters. In his letters to La Croze, Ziegenbalg expressed the opinion that all the alphabets used on the Malabar and Coromandel coasts, in Ceylon, and other parts of India were derived from the Sanskrit alphabet used by the Brahmans. La Croze himself in letters to Bayer and John Chamberlain suggested a common origin of the Phoenician, Syrian, Arabic, Persian, and Brahman alphabets, and also hazarded a guess that they all derived from Egyptian hieratics and hieroglyphics.[1]

Giovanni Cristofano Amaduzzi, who presided over the press of the Sacra Congregatio, in his preface to the *Alphabetum Brammhanicum* of 1771, was well acquainted with these views, and expressing some doubt continues: 'Nisi etiam dicere velimus Indostanum Alphabetum profluxisse ab alio

---

[1] See tom. i, letter xiii, p. 16; tom. iii, letter ix, pp. 22, 23; letter xlii, p. 85; and letter cccxix, pp. 381 sq. 'J'ai entre les mains les Alphabets Tartares de Tangut, et des Manchous, ceux de Bengale, de Ceylan, de Malabar, de Siam, &c., en partie manuscrits, et en partie imprimés; et je n'ai point eu de peine à me convaincre, que tous ces alphabets n'ont eu autrefois qu'une seule et même origine.' La Croze, loc. cit., tome ii, p. 246. See also ibid., p. 353.

antiquiore Brammhanico non admodum absimili; siquidem, teste Cassiano[1] nostro, extant nunc in Indostanicis Regionibus *antiqui Codices apicibus quibusdam exarati, quos et ipsi peritiores Brammhanes se ignorare ingenue fatentur,* dum interim apud ipsos traditio est, neque eorum maiores, a quibus eos acceperant, huiusmodi litterarum, et nexuum praesertim, qui frequentes sunt, potestatem calluisse.'[2]

The various *Alphabeta* of the press of the Sacra Congregatio de Propaganda Fide are abiding testimony to the work of the Capuchin Friars and other regular clergy working in India and Burma. Some of them contain phonetic and phonological observations quite similar to more recent ones which have brought faint thrills of discovery to observers even in our own time.

The *Alphabetum Brammhanicum* of 1771 presents notes on three alphabets, and below are a few which are of general interest, showing that these early observations had some phonetic and even phonological value—largely because the alphabet, though interpreted to Europeans in Latin or Italian terms, was presented also from the Indian point of view.

There is, for example, a clear separation of the unaspirated from the aspirated consonants, which though transcribed as at present by means of digraphs, **ph**, **bh**, &c., are classed as simple and not two sounds. Aspiration would be at once apparent as the observer notes: 'Quod apud Latinos non in usu habetur.' The mention of 'in interiore gutture' is especially suggestive of some glottal correlation; thus: 'Alios vero obscure in interiori gutture formant, et voce tenui ac quasi dimidiata proferunt. Alios quadam vi, et aliqua aspiratione exhalant.'

Two other prominent phonological characteristics are noted, the cerebral or retroflex consonants and the use of nasalization. 'Alios insuper medio palato, scilicet ad palatum ipsum linguam inflectentes emittunt. Alios tandem narium ministerio pronunciant.'

The dental **t** and **d** are, of course, at once recognized:

'a nostro t non differt'
'd, est nostrum d Latinum.'

Of the retroflex ṭ, 'Aliter quam per *t*, haec a nobis Latinis explicari nequit, nec describi potest; quamvis longe sit diversa, eiusque pronunciationem assequi necessarium sit. *Profertur lingua paullulum inversa, et palatum leniter percutiente,* quo blese pronunciatur.' 'Leniter percutiente' of 1771 shows much more feeling than 'the tip must be pressed firmly against the highest part of the roof to form the obstruction and kept in this position for the greater part stop' [sic] of 1915.[3]

Remembering Beligatti's source of information and probable acquaintance with the dialects of Bihar as well as Nepali, the following note on

---

[1] Cassiano Beligatti, mainly responsible for the *Alphabetum*.
[2] *Alph. Brammh.*, pp. xii, xiii.
[3] Noël-Armfield (on retroflex consonants) in *General Phonetics*, pp. 98–100.

retroflex *ḍ* is interesting. It is given as '*da* vel *ra*', with the remark: 'duplicem huius litterae pronunciationem habes; nunc enim, ut *d* blesum, nunc ut *r* itidem blesum, sed palatum similiter leniter percutiendo pronunciatur. Initio quidem dictionis semper ut *d* blesum pronunciabis, sed in medio, et in fine certa non habetur regula, modo *da*, modo *ra* dices.'

On the affricate च (c), transcribed *cia*, the note is discriminating. Unlike many less scrupulous writers of later centuries, he rejects the Italian *cia*. 'Neque haec ulli ex nostris litteris rite potest assimilari.' Of the voiced correlate of this, transcribed *gia*, the note runs: 'Nostro *gi* et *z* simul arridet haec littera.'

What is said of ब (*Ba*) is also interesting: 'Latinum *b*, de quo adnotes velim quod sicut in nostra Europa apud varias nationes *b* in *u*, and *v* consonans in *b* immutatur, et unum pro alio usurpatur, ita apud Indos invenies dicentes *vap-h* pro *bap-h*, (*vapor*) et *vavo* pro *bavo*.' It is pointed out, however, that '*bha* non convertitur in *v*'.

Of *m* there is the curious note: 'quod debet aperto ore pronunciari ... et obtuso effertur ore.'

He distinguishes long and short vowels of the three types *a*, *i*, and *u*, and on the basis of the alphabet, groups what he transcribes as *e*, *ei*, and *o*, *au*, as similar pairs.

Of 'Bisarkà' he says: 'nullum proprium habet sonum, sed tantum indicio est litteram, cui iunctum est Bisarkà, proferre debere fortiter, *ac si traheretur e pectore*, sono tamen *minime in longum protracto*.'

In 1772 the press published its *Alphabetum Grandonico-Malabaricum sive Samscrudonicum*, largely the work of 'Clemens Peanius Alexandrinus', a Discalced Carmelite of the Verapoly Mission in Cochin. His title was intended to distinguish the literary alphabet from what he calls Malean-Tamuza or Malabarico-Tamulicam—but he was under no misapprehension as to the language represented, 'quae proprie Maleáima vocatur, ... lingua nova et incognita'. He protested against the confusion of Malayalam with Tamil by Ziegenbalg, La Croze, and others, though apparently without effect on Pope, who described it as a sort of corrupt Tamil in the fifth edition of his Tamil grammar, published in 1895. 'Quasi idem prorsus esset Idioma Malabaricum atque Tamulicum; quo sane nihil absurdius hac in re comminisci potest. Asserere enim Tamulicam Linguam Malabaricam esse, aut Malabaricam esse Tamulicam, idem prorsus esset, ac si Gallicam diceres, et Italicam Linguam invicem non differre. Licet autem utriusque Linguae, Malabaricae, et Tamulicae radices communes sint.'

Peanius recognizes five long and five short vowels and two diphthongs. He presents various types of syllable such as those 'quibus copulatur *ja*, seu *jota*', which we may describe as 'yotized'.

Then there are combinations with '*r*', '*l*' *Latinorum*, *v*, and also the characteristic doubling of consonants. Of a common final '*l*' he writes: '*linguae inflexione pronunciatur*'. Of another, which we sometimes think of as an *r* sound, he says it is rather like '*z* finali Latinorum; sed pronunciatur cum aliquo sibilo, clauso ferme ore, ac retrorsum attracta lingua; idem tamen sonat in medio, ac in fine dictionis'. Not at all a bad description of one of the most difficult sounds of Tamil and Malayalam.

The homorganic nasal on-glides to the voiced stops are noticed, which we may represent by ~k, ~p, ~t, &c., in the Indian way.

The author notices several characteristic features of the language, especially the contrast between the lax pronunciation of single **p, t, k**, as *b, d, g*,[1] in intervocalic position, and the energetically articulated voiceless stops usually termed 'double' **pp, tt, kk**.

'*Ka* in principio dictionis aequivalet nostro *k*; in medio autem pronunciatur ut *ga*.

'*kka* est idem duplex maiori vi prolatum, . . . profertur cum aliquo conatu . . . maiori tamen vi, quod in litteris duplicibus semper est observandum.'

A second prominent characteristic of Malayalam is the palatalization of consonants. Peanius appears to have noticed this in distinguishing the two *r* sounds (in addition, of course, to the retracted *r* or *l* sound previously mentioned, which he described as a sort of *z*). The first is 'ut *r*; dulciter tamen, et tenerrime profertur prope dentes, iisdem quasi compressis.' This is a good enough description of what we now recognize as a palatalized *r*. The second *r* is 'ut *r* Latinorum, asperum valde et durum'. He also notes the interesting fact that 'si vero haec littera duplicetur, efformatur duplex *tt*, quod effertur compressis quasi dentibus, lingua ipsos impellente'. This pronunciation is also clearly what we now recognize as palatalized, and, moreover, it is obviously quite a different sort of *t* from the dental and retroflex *t*'s which he also describes. It is the palatalized alveolar *t*, giving three different places of articulation for *t* sounds in intervocalic position in Malayalam: dental, alveolar, and retroflex.

Of the retroflex *t* he says: 'est autem Europeis admodum difficilis, ac pronunciatur inversa omnino retrorsum lingua, adeo ut interiorem palati summitatem attingat'—doubled intervocalically 'cum maiori tamen *impetu*'.

The dental *t* and similar sounds were, of course, easily recognized as Latin. Bearing in mind Peanius's observations on *vis, conatus,* and *impetus,* and *aspiratio,* it is interesting to find he regards all the aspirated voiceless consonants as tense and transcribes them as double consonants aspirated. Aspirated dental *t* is romanized as *tth* 'quasi duplex *tt* cum maiori impetu'. Similarly aspirated *p* is 'duplex *p* cum impetu et aspiratione'.

The author's notes on the aspirated voiced stop **bh** and the dental **dh** show he was not merely a slave of the spelling and that he really had a pretty good idea of the sort of bodily actions that produced these strange sounds. Of **bh** he says: '*ut duplex b*; efformatur ex intimis,[2] atque cum vi et aspira-

---

[1] My own observations of the pronunciation of a native of Trivandrum made some years ago seemed to indicate that the lax intervocalic consonants here referred to were only feebly voiced and often fricative.

[2] 'Ex intimis' is a very good guess at the motor background of the aspirated consonants, which are single-stroke efforts, the release of the stop synchronizing with a 'kick' of the diaphragm, &c. Cf. 'ex pectore' above.

tione profertur'. Of ḍh: 'profertur ex intimis cum conatu et aspiratione'. So very few Europeans succeed in understanding the single-stroke effort *ex intimis*, required for an Indian **bh**, that one feels this insight must have been based on personal knowledge *ex intimis*.

Of the dental **dh**, however, he says: 'quasi duplex *dd, cum aliquo leni impetu*', and does not mention aspiration. But for **ddh** occurring medially he says: 'idem cum maiori vi, et aspiratione'.

He lists most of the nasals including an *n* 'ut *n* Latinorum clare'; and another 'ut *n*, cum aliquo tamen narium ministerio'; that was the best he could do about the retroflex *n*.

He describes the palatal nasal as being like the *gn* of Italian, but not identical with it; 'efformatur prope dentes cum aliquo narium ministerio'. This is also in accordance with modern observations.

Other consonants noted are:

va, ut *u* consonans Latinorum, aliquando ut *b*.

Scia, 'ut *c* gallico ore prolatum', and different from this,

Sza 'inter *s* et *z* pronuntiatur, inflexa ad palatum lingua'.

Sa, 'ut *s* Latinorum formatur prope dentes, quasi sibilando'.

Kcia, 'retracta lingua et ad palatum inversa cum impetu, et aspiratione profertur'.

ha ut Germanico ore prolatum.

la—single and double—'est quoddam genus *l*, quod inflexa omnino ad palatum lingua crassiori sono efformatur'.

za 'quasi *z* Latinorum, dentibus labiisque vix apertis pronuntiatur, retracta tantillum lingua'. He clearly distinguishes s, ɕ, and ʂ—three sibilants.

After all this excellent phonetic description, he concludes: 'genuinus enim ipsarum sonus non scriptis, sed voce est aquirendus'.

In the transcriptions at the end he makes use of grave and acute signs as some sort of indication of accent. Any detailed phonological study of Malayalam would have to pay special attention to accent and intonation.

The *Alphabetum Barmanorum seu Regni Avensis* was first published in 1776, but it was much improved in the revised edition published in 1787. It represents the joint labours of Carpani and Mantegazza of the Catholic Mission.[1]

---

[1] My attention was first drawn to the *Alphabetum Barmanorum* by my friend Mr. G. E. Harvey, who also very kindly wrote the note on the Mission, quoted below. Carpani knew both Ava and Pegu, spending seven years in Rangoon. Bishop Percoto sent him to Rome with 'accurate information' about the mission, Burma, and the language. There is a short note on the *Alphabetum* by E. Luce in the *Journal of the Burma Research Society*, August 1914, p. 144.

'The Catholic mission was small but already old when the first Protestant missionary landed in 1813. Indeed, there had always been a couple of Goanese priests in Burma from the sixteenth century onwards, under the Portuguese hierarchy in India, but they confined themselves to the feringhi colony and were, in addition, only semi-literate. The first mission, that of the Missions Étrangères de Paris (now the dominant Catholic mission in Burma), lasted only four years, 1689–1693, and ended in martyrdom, but it was followed

The *Alphabetum Barmanorum* notices most of the outstanding features of the phonetics of Burmese in presenting the syllabaries of the Burmese writing lesson. To begin with it points out the special roles of aspiration, glottalization, and nasalization. 'Plures Barmana lingua habet aspirationes, nasales, gutturales, aliasque, quibus ea locutio nobis perdifficilis est.'

Carpani not only notices the aspiration of plosives but also of the four nasals and of *l* and *w*. 'Quatuor priores nasali afficit aspiratione: qua nempe aër in pronuncianda littera per nares exploditur.' Of **hl** and **hw** he says: 'quasi pronuncietur *fla, fua*.' Moreover, he draws attention to the morphology in this connexion 'In hac denique lingua per solam saepe aspirationem significatio activa tribuitur verbo neutro aut passivo. Sic, *kià* (**ca**) *cadere*, vel *decidere*; *khià* (**cha**) *deponere* vel *deiicere*; [*hlut*] *dimittere*; [*lut*] *liberum esse*.'

In addition to noticing the antithesis of aspirated and unaspirated consonants, he fully appreciated similar qualities in the vowels or syllables. A certain sign, for example, 'postspirandae syllabae adhibetur', which we now call breathy voice and correlate with length and falling tone. Another is 'signum producendae syllabae'. While of the opposite kind are the signs which mark short checked syllables, e.g. 'syllabam corripit'. 'Punctum suppositum syllabam brevissimi reddit soni, et quasi truncat.' In describing vowels he notices an *i* which is long and an *i*, 'breve ac quasi truncum', and also the opposite kind of syllable which he transcribes *kæh*, 'cum e aperta et postspirata'.[1]

by an unbroken succession of Italian Barnabites, 1721–1832, and it is to these that we owe our first studies of the language. There can be little doubt that both Judson, the founder of the American Baptist Mission in 1813, who wrote the first great dictionary, and the American Baptists whose studies thereafter held the field, were indebted, if only indirectly, to early Catholic MSS. which no longer survive, the bulk perishing in the fire of 1840 which burned down the headquarters mission station at Chanthayua in Shwebo district. Within four years of their arrival in 1721 the Barnabite Fathers had compiled a small dictionary, and in the next few decades they wrote MS. grammars and bilingual devotional works, but the first printed work was the *Alphabetum*. Its author, Melchior Carpani, who arrived in 1767 and does not seem to have returned after leaving for Rome in 1774, was stabbed by one of the Goanese priests, who persistently resented the intrusion of the Barnabites, men of a high type, whose mere presence inevitably invited comparisons; his first edition, 1776, was doubtless based on the work of his colleagues, and the second, 1787, was revised by Mantegazza. Fr. Caejetan Mantegazza, arriving in 1772, died as bishop in 1794 at Amarapura, the then capital where his tombstone still exists; when sailing for Rome in 1784 he took with him two Burmese converts, one of whom, an ex-Buddhist monk and hence a scholar, assisted in the printing, at Rome, not only of the *Alphabetum* but also of a Burmese prayer book, catechism, and dialogues. Fr. Johannes Maria Percoto, who, mourned by the author of the *Alphabetum* as a better scholar than himself, arrived in 1761 and died as bishop in 1776 at Ava the then capital—the Burmese periodically changed their capitals—left translations of epistles and gospels, Genesis, Daniel, Tobias St. Matthew, prayers, catechism, etc., and a Burmese–Latin–Portuguese dictionary, some of which seem to survive in the Library of the College of the Propaganda at Rome. See Bishop Bigandet, *Outline of the History of the Catholic Mission, 1720–1887*, Rangoon, Hanthawaddy Press, 1887; Hosten and Luce, *Bibliotheca Catholica Birmanica*, Rangoon, British Burma Press, 1916; G. E. Harvey, *History of Burma* (Longmans, 1925), pp. 214, 230, 253, 278, 345, 349.'

[1] See my 'Notes on the Transcription of Burmese', *B.S.O.S.*, vol. vii, part i, 1933, also the remarks thereon of Professor Trubetzkoy in his *Anleitung zu phonologischen Beschreibungen*, 1935, p. 29.

His account of the pronunciation of syllables written with final *p*, *t*, *k*, and the check mark is quite in accordance with modern observations, so that the final glottal stop in such short syllables was usual in the late eighteenth century, e.g. on a syllable which he transcribes *kæk* he remarks: 'ita tamen, ut posterius *k* vix audiatur: nempe vix enunciari coeptum supprimitur; quod quidem in qualibet muta finali observandum est'.[1]

He describes nasalized vowels by comparing Burmese syllables with French words. Burmese syllables transcribed with final **n** as *kæñ*, and *kòuñ* he likens to French *vin, pain, bon, baton*. But he realized they were really different from these, for he adds a remark which modern observation confirms: '*n* vix coepta supprimitur.' On the syllable transcribed *kòuñ* his remark is also in accordance with modern observations: '*ñ*, nasalis, diphthongus vix percipitur.' He also noticed that such nasalizations when followed immediately by the initial consonant of the next syllable usually formed a homorganic junction, heard as **m**+**b**, **n**+**d**, **ŋ**+**g**, &c.

Carpani noticed the behaviour of the stops in various contexts: 'saepius vero *t, p*, aliasque fortes, duplicesve in *d, b*, et in alias simplices, seu tenues. Sed quasdam hac in re licuit regulas animadvertere, quas in alphabeto notavimus.' And later he observes that after certain nasals and other syllables 'consonantes immediate sequentes, quae valide, seu durae sunt ut *p, t, k*, pronunciantur *b, d, g*, paucae admodum exceptiones hac in re obtinent'.

In phonological terms we should now say that the presence or absence of aspiration or 'breathiness' is used far more, has more linguistic weight, than the presence or absence of voice, or the voice correlation. Whereas the correlation of aspiration differentiates most articulation types in pairs, and this in most of the typical contexts, there is one very common context in which the voice correlation does not function, and a second context in which it is doubtful.

The first is the context immediately after very short syllables ending with a sharp glottal check, where the only unaspirated plosives to occur in familiar speech are of the **p**, **t**, **k** type. Taking the bilabial class of stops, **p**, **py**, **pw**, and **ph**, **phy**, **phw** are all possible, giving six alternants of the bilabial stop class in this context—and no further differentiation by voice. Here we have what I have termed uncorrelated **p**, **t**, **k**.

Something very like the opposite would appear to be the case in the context immediately after long syllables with closing nasalization, where in most cases, but apparently not in all, the sounds heard are like **b**, **d**, **g̣**, and are not used in contradistinction from **p**, **t**, **k**. These I should term uncorrelated **b**, **d**, **g̣**.

It seems to me quite unnecessary and probably erroneous to postulate relations between the stops in these two utterly different contexts. The question of notation or what letters we shall use in Romanic orthography is another matter altogether.

---

[1] In Modern Korean the final voiceless stops *p, t, k* are held, and quietly released. There is no audible plosion. But they do not seem to have given place to the glottal stop.

Another feature of the *Alphabetum* which deserves notice is the classification of the different types of syllable to be met with in this so-called monosyllabic language. It seems to me more enlightening than a mere catalogue of so-called individual sounds, perhaps because it follows the Burmese traditional writing lesson, and also because it agrees in some measure with the modern contextual approach.

He gives six classes of syllable in the orthography, but naturally some of these classes correlate also with phonetic habit and morphological structure. There is, of course, the distinction between the short sharply checked syllables and the long breathy ones, which we have already noticed as two characteristic contexts in which immediately following consonants should also be studied. He also notices those which begin with aspirated consonants, as well as the breathy ones which fade out, 'postspirandae'. Then there are the diphthong-syllables. 'Diphthongi autem, atque etiam triphthongi in tota lingua Barmana frequentes admodum sunt.' He notices **ei** with '*e* praestricta', **ou** with '*o* medium', and also **ai** and **au**.

There is another characteristic contrast of syllables in Burmese between those which begin with a yotized consonant group and those beginning with a labio-velarized group: e.g. **py, phy, my, hmy, ly, hly**, &c., against **pw, phw, mw, hmw, lw, hlw**, &c. These form classes five and four in the *Alphabetum*. Of the yotization of syllables, it says: 'Hoc igitur signum brevissimi sonum *i* syllabæ intrudit, ut est in gh*i*accio, p*i*anta apud Italos.' The 'w' sound in the other class is given as the *u* of the Italians or the *ou* of the French.

The sixth class is really only due to orthographic superfluities, the Burmese letter 'r', for instance, being pronounced 'y'.

Carpani's description of the vowels holds good today. 'Barmani septem habent sonos, seu vocales Italorum: duas *e*; apertam nempe, et praestrictam: duo *o*; medium, et largum, seu apertum: atque a, i, u.' Failing ordinary letters for the two extra vowels he employs æ and the Greek ω in his transcriptions of the open *e* and *o*.

The close *e* 'ut in *née, portée* apud gallos'.

The open æ 'ut *è* in *après*, or *chaîne, grêle* apud Gallos'.

For the open *o* he suggests 'apertum ut in v*o*to seu vu*o*to apud Italos'.

For the two letters corresponding to *y* and *r* he gives the same pronunciation. His note on *r* being 'quam multi in pronunciatione in precedentem mutant'.

For the Burmese characters which may be transliterated *hy, hðy,* and *hr* he gives the Italian indication *scia* or French *chi*en. This, too, accords with modern observation. In Romanic orthography this element could be written *hy*, as it was probably an aspirated yotized group originally, **and is now pronounced ʃ**, rather like a certain very fronted pronunciation of the *ich*-laut.

Carpani shows acquaintance with French, but not with Spanish or English. He found the velar nasal ŋ difficult to describe. He says of this letter:

'quam per ng̃ utcumque expressimus, simplicis est soni, nullisque nostris litteris exprimi potest'. And the best he can do for the sound θ is to suggest it is a lisped *s*, 'absque sibilo; uti apud nos quoque in nonnullis auditur vitio linguæ vel educationis.'

He heard a *g*, 'iuxta Germanorum pronunciationem', and the affricates **c** and **j** he transcribes as *ts* and *tzh*. On the whole, it will be agreed this *Alphabetum* was an excellent piece of work for that time, and was not surpassed or equalled until our own day.

The following table of letters is appended as an example of a schematic Romanic alphabet for Burmese:

EXAMPLE OF ONE ARTICULATION TYPE
Initial alternance only

Basic type of articulation	Bilabial articulation involving lip closure			Alveolar	Velar
	Voiceless [p]	Aspiration	Voice correlation		
	p	ph	b	t, &c.	k
Yotization . .	py	phy	by	*nil*	*nil*
Labio-velarization .	pw	phw	bw	tw, &c.	kw, &c.
Nasalization . .	hm		m	hn, &c.	hŋ, &c.
Nasalization and yotization	hmy		my	*nil*	ny or specialized palatal ɲ
Nasalization and labio-velarization	hmw		mw	hnw, &c.	ŋw
Total	9	6		10	9
	Total of 15 substitution-counters or terms having basic lip closure or bilabial articulation occurring in initial position.				Total of 34 for plosives and nasals in initial position.

Schematic Alphabet for Burmese in World Orthography

Initial alternance only

	Bilabial articulation	Alveolar articulation	Pre-palatal articulation	Palatal articulation	Velar articulation	Glottal articulation
	p ph b	t th d	c ch j		k kh g	
Yotization .	py phy by				(see c, ch, j)	—
Labio-velarization .	pw phw bw	tw thw dw	cw chw jw		kw khw gw	
Nasals .	hm m	hn n		Palatal hny ny	hŋ ŋ	
Yotized nasals .	hmy my	(see hny, ny)				
Labio-velarized nasals .	hmw mw	hnw nw			ŋw	
	w					
	Dentals	hl l	⎱			
	θ ð	hly ly	⎰ Laterals similarly treated.			h
	θw ðw	hlw lw				
		s sh ʃ				
		shw z zw			y	
	w				yw	
					(hy = ʃ)	

Vowels

Low level tone, long, greatest frequency of occurrence	i iŋ	e eiŋ	ɛ	a aŋ	ə	o ouŋ	u uŋ	aiŋ	auŋ
Falling tone, long, breathy	ˋi ˋiŋ	ˋe ˋeiŋ	ˋɛ	ˋa ˋaŋ	ˋə	ˋo ˋouŋ	ˋu ˋuŋ	ˋaiŋ	ˋauŋ
Slightly falling, medium length, creaky voice, weak closure	iˡ iŋˡ	eˡ eiŋˡ	ɛˡ	aˡ aŋˡ	əˡ	oˡ ouŋˡ	uˡ uŋˡ	aiŋˡ	auŋˡ
Very short, 'bright' voice, abrupt closure, slightly falling	iˀ	eiˀ	ɛˀ	aˀ		ouˀ	uˀ	aiˀ	auˀ
Neutral					ə				

The first thing to be said about the roman alphabet is, that it has been found to work well from the days of greater Rome to the present time, when Western civilization is become a world civilization. Hence the phrase 'world orthography'. The roman alphabet has proved practical in all kinds of printing, both by hand and machines. In education in its widest sense, in all manner of notation, popular and scientific, it serves us well. We have evolved a variety of founts of type and spacing for effective layout in all sorts of printed language. We have developed new letters in harmony with the alphabet, also accents and punctuative signs. No nation, no people, need hesitate to adopt it. Those who have will not go back.

On the general advantages of the roman alphabet, Professor Otto Jespersen has written a useful article which serves as the introduction to a report published in 1934 by the League of Nations *Co-opération Intellectuelle*, entitled 'L'adoption universelle des caractères latins'.[1]

Of the practical advantages, one or two forceful illustrations may be given. The technical results of romanization in Turkey are: with Arabic characters a compositor could handle 4,500 in six hours; with roman 7,000 in the same time. The cost of production has been reduced from 25 to 50 per cent. according to the size of the work. The number of 'touches' on the typewriter keyboard has been reduced from 90 to 37, and the employment of machines and typists enormously increased.[2]

Professor van Ronkel, of the University of Leyden, writes:[3] 'L'écriture javanaise est belle, mais compliquée et peu économique: un text y occupe trois fois plus de place qu'en écriture latine. Les livres sont donc trois fois plus gros qu'il n'est nécessaire.'

Furthermore, the Turks have proved the great advantages of the new alphabet in schools, and a rapid multiplication of books and libraries has followed the adoption of an alphabet at once simpler and better suited to

---

[1] Afterwards referred to as A.U.C.L.
[2] See A.U.C.L., pp. 126–9, by Professor Caferoğlu, of Constantinople. And p. 136, by Professor Rossi, of Rome.
[3] Ibid. p. 92.

represent the forms of the language, and also much cheaper in production costs.

In addition to practical advantages of this kind, the roman alphabet has definite merits as the framework of a scientific linguistic notation. It lends itself to analysis and synthesis. It does not build syllabaries. It is analytic, using a comparatively small number of signs which can be arranged and employed to suit the phonology and morphology of almost any language. Moreover, the synthesis of the letters produces easily recognizable differentiated word-forms as wholes, the differential elements suitably symbolized by letters or signs having their places in the word and also in an ordered series of alternants established by analysis. Having analysed the language into a number of ordered series of letter-units, you put the 'pieces' together again and find you have differentiated word-forms. When you put together your 'pieces' and find the result corresponds with the facts you have a scientific or 'organic' alphabet. It is not surprising, therefore, to find Professor Caferoğlu reporting that the adoption of Roman characters 'a conduit également à une *simplification* de la langue', that it has had some influence 'sur la grammaire turque', and that it has opened 'de nouveaux horizons aux *recherches philologiques* concernant la langue turque'.[1]

The alphabetic revolution in Turkey is, in fact, the most significant movement in the recent history of the world alphabet. It was at the epoch-making Turcological Congress, held at Baku in 1926, that representatives of the Turkish republic, of the Turco-Tartar peoples of Russia and of Russian and other European universities, proclaimed the necessity and the opportunity of abandoning the Arabic alphabet in favour of the roman character. Within two years the alphabetic revolution affected about 25,000,000 Turco-Tartars in the U.S.S.R., which has been carrying out a great romanization programme ever since among the Asiatic daughter republics.[2] Turkey herself followed, and what is called the N.A.T. ('nouvel alphabet turc') came into force partially on 1 January 1929, and completely on 1 June 1930.

In Russia it is true that earlier moves towards romanization had been made by several local governments, in particular by Azerbaijan, but the Congress of 1926 marked the beginning of comprehensive 'alphabetization' on a vast scale. In 1922 only two languages of the Russian Union had adopted a new alphabet, but the number given for 1933 is seventy!

The Russians attach great importance to the unification of the many Roman orthographies which had been independently devised in pre-Soviet days, and they report: 'Actuellement l'unification se poursuit; elle se manifeste par la progression de la fusion phonétique et graphique des alphabets nationaux, la simplification de la forme des lettres et la réduction de leur nombre.'

[1] See A.U.C.L., pp. 124–5. Italics Professor Caferoğlu's.
[2] See ibid. pp. 133–4, by Professor Rossi, the official Soviet report on p. 161, and a report on romanization in the U.S.S.R. by Professor Braun, of Leipzig, pp. 142 sq.

That leads us to the elements of the whole technique of symbolizing the forms of a language by the use of roman letters. It may be described as alphabetical economy. To make the most economical use of letters it is essential that the fullest advantage be taken of contextual conventions, thus reducing the number of signs required not only for the symbolization of the terms of an ordered series of possible alternants in any given context but for the particular orthography as a whole. To achieve this, thorough phonological and morphological analysis is necessary. 'Si toutes ces questions ne sont pas suffisament examinées et résolues d'une manière uniforme, l'orthographe reste maladroite, lourde, difficile à lire, et elle a peu d'attrait pour les indigènes, qui doivent d'abord s'habituer à la lecture. Sous ce point de vue les orthographes déjà existantes ne sont certainement pas toutes très satisfaisantes.'[1]

To a nucleus of thirty-three roman letters the Soviet linguists have added fifty-eight new ones, making a total of ninety-one letters in a sort of unified alphabet which they think will serve all the languages of the Union. There is a great danger of swamping the characteristics of the alphabet if too many new letters are employed. This may quite well result if the letters are based on universal phonetic categories instead of on a phonological analysis of each language *ad hoc*. The Arabic and Indian alphabets are such that they have developed either initial, medial, and final forms or special compound letters. Such specialization of form may even be justified by abstract general phonetic theory, but very little can be said for them from the point of view of alphabetical economy. An orthography can be too phonetic. The value of a roman letter depends on its position and the context.

A certain number of new letters such as those devised by the International Phonetic Association are undoubtedly necessary. But, as Professor Troubetzkoy quite rightly points out, 'Souvent ces caractères modifiés sont très nombreux de sorte que l'aspect général d'un texte écrit dans un tel alphabet est tout à fait "exotique". En raison de cette circonstance un des principaux arguments cité d'ordinaire en faveur de l'adoption des caractères latins pour toutes les langues du monde se trouve presque réduit à néant.'[2] Most spelling is phonologically, not phonetically, representative.

A schematic system of spelling or regular alphabet which enables us to symbolize the forms of a language by means of combinations of letters and other signs without redundancy and yet without ambiguity must be based on linguistic analysis and involves the consideration of word formation and sentence structure as well as of pronunciation. From the Saussurean point of view, which has been applied and developed in English by Dr. Alan Gardiner,[3] orthography is representative of language, not speech.

That is a striking way of saying half the truth, and perhaps the half that

---

[1] A.U.C.L., p. 34. Professor D. Westermann reporting on Africa.
[2] Ibid. p. 48, reporting on the peoples of the Caucasus.
[3] In his *Theory of Speech and Language*, Oxford, 1932.

has too often been obscured. But there is quite obviously a danger in following Baudouin de Courtenay, de Saussure, and Durkheim to the extent of the abstract integration of 'sounds' or 'phonemes' or letters and signs in a mental scheme of ideas or in 'the language as a whole'. This kind of abstraction goes farther than is at present either necessary or desirable for the handling of our facts. In the symbolization of the forms of a language by means of an ordered system of letters and signs, the first principle should be the recognition of characteristic recurrent contexts in which an ordered series of phonological substitutions may take place.

If we take an ordered series of English words or forms such as *biːd, bid, bed, bæd, baːd, bɔːd, buːd, bad, bəːd, beid, boud, baid, baud, bɔid, biəd, bɛəd*, we have sixteen vowel alternants in what may be considered the same context. Between **d** and **g**, however, only three are possible.

In final position the number of possible vowel alternances is two, sometimes three less than in the medial position. In initial position in isolated words the nasal alternances are **m, n,** in intervocalic and final positions **m, n, ŋ**. But immediately before a final *k* only **ŋ** is possible, before final *p* only **m** is possible, though before final *t* and *d*, which have morphological function, all three are again possible, **m, n, ŋ**.

In the application of World Orthography to Indian languages the letters **m, n, ɲ, ɳ, ŋ** have been used to represent the unique homorganic nasals preceding certain stops, as well as for the series of nasals which may occur in initial position. But we refrain from any functional identification, for example, of a specific or unique *m* on-glide to a homorganic stop, and an *m* as a term in a three-, four-, or five-term alternation in initial position.

The initial medial, intervocalic, and final positions in Tamil agglutinations give contexts in each of which various series of alternances may take place. These must be studied in close connexion with the morphology, each series of terms in each context independently, at any rate in the first instance. Similar considerations apply to Malayalam. In that language the consonantal alternation in initial position includes, for example, two homorganic plosives differentiated by the voice correlation which we may symbolize by **k** and **g**. In intervocalic position, however, the consonantal alternation includes two homorganic sounds differentiated by the tensity-laxity correlation which appears to affect the whole manner of articulation, involving also length, and a parallel laryngeal correlation of some sort; both these are again differentiated from a third sound by the voice correlation. This gives us a three-term alternation which we may symbolize by means of **kk, k,** and **g**. It so happens that intervocalic **kk** sounds rather like initial **k**, and intervocalic **k** rather like **g**, except that it is feebly voiced and often fricative. It will be seen at once that from the logical and functional point of view it is impossible to identify the terms of the first series with the second series. It is practically convenient to use the same letters over again both from the point of view of pronunciation and alphabetic economy. We may write **tɔːkt** and **sips**, using **t** and **s** both initially and finally, and they may correspond to similar sounds, but the two *t*'s and the two *s*'s are phonologically and morphologically different. Or take the English word *stick*, which may be transcribed **stik** or **sdik**, according to the nature of the contextual conventions laid down. Discussions have taken place on the further and quite gratuitous question of whether 'the sound' after the *s* is to be identified with *t*'s or *d*'s in other contexts.

In other words, the value of any letter is determined by its place in the context and by its place in the alternance functioning in that type of context. This I have called its *minor* function, but grammatical and semantic function must also be considered. These I have termed major functions.[1]

These ordered series of alternants vary from context to context, so that minor function is not a constant for the language as a whole. The number and nature of the terms of such series also vary from context to context, and it is useful to note the range from contexts of maximum alternance to those of minimum alternance.[1] It follows, therefore, that the differential function of the signs or letters varies from context to context. The same letter may be used to symbolize terms in several different ordered series of alternances. Its phonetic value categorized by perception or physiological phonetics may or may not be similar. A balance must be struck between the convenience of using the same letter for terms which are roughly similar phonetically and the great alphabetic economies rendered possible if the same letter can be used for a variety of purposes according to context.

The most uneconomical, I almost said extravagant, alphabets are those of an abstract schematic order, universal, purely logical and symmetrical but extra-linguistic. Such alphabets are sometimes necessary for dialect and comparative work and in the earlier stages of phonetic research. But they are quite unsuitable for descriptive grammar or as a basis of a practical orthography.

The great advantage of this alphabetic economy based on the fullest use of contextual conventions is what may be described as free letters. Such redundant letters not required in any particular context may be used in all manner of ways. For example, in the Burmese orthography here suggested it would be possible to eliminate the mark which distinguishes the long falling tone with breathy voice, now written, for example, **`la**, and use a final letter **h**, thus **lah**, but this would have the inconvenience that many syllables would have to be separated either by spaces or joined by means of hyphens. Otherwise in compounds printed together there would be confusion with such terms as **hl**, **hm**, &c.

Other common redundancies arise in contexts where certain differentiations do not occur, such as the absence of voice correlation or of distinctions between *f* and *h*, *r* and *l*, *w* and *v*. Sometimes a redundant letter may be used with the purely lexical function of separating homophones. For

---

[1] See 'The Use and Distribution of Certain English Sounds', Chapter 4, and 'The Technique of Semantics', Chapter 3.

example, in Cambodian, which employs an alphabet of Indian origin, the final aspirated consonant is really redundant from the phonological point of view. But it serves a useful purpose in separating, for instance, '*duk* conserver, de *dukh* malheur'.[1] Something of the same sort would probably be necessary in a reformed spelling of English.

It is probably true that there are no qualities in any letter taken by itself which make it inherently superior to any other. What matters is again the clearness and distinctness of the differential features. ɡ is probably better than g, if q is used in similar contexts.

Another important question affecting alphabetic economy and phonological theory is that of consonant groups and consonant junctions, which must be clearly distinguished in all phonological analysis.

Both digraphs and trigraphs are used in my Burmese orthography, but these compound letters are to be understood to represent not two or three substitution elements in the forms of the language, but single substitution-counters or terms belonging to an alternance occurring in initial position. The bodily actions corresponding to these units are all, so to speak, single-stroke efforts. Many of the theoretical difficulties of phonetics have been due to the mistaken notion that the events of a phonetic sequence correspond to the string of roman letters used to symbolize the linguistic forms in the sequence.

Some people are of the opinion that one element should be represented by one letter, not a group of three. As things are I prefer the ordinary world alphabet as far as possible. But I am convinced that we must not allow the characteristics of the roman alphabet to dictate the course of linguistic thought.

Consonant groups, such as **st**, **str**, **sp**, **spl**, **sk**, **skr**, in initial position in English, are best regarded as group substituents, and no attempt should be made to identify the function of the letter 't' (here part of a digraph or trigraph) with that of a similar letter used in another context. It is important, however, to distinguish such groups from consonant junctions, cf. ... *missed riding*, ... *Miss tried*, ... *in my stride*.

The contextual study of such consonant groups and consonant junctions is likely to produce interesting results from several points of view, phonetic, morphological, syntactical, and also what I have termed phonaesthetic.[2] There are also obvious historical advantages in this way of regarding groups like **sp**, **st**, **sk**. I have presented a table of such initial consonant groups in English in the article referred to.

From the foregoing summary of a technique of contextualization it will be clear that no attempt is made to establish psychological or phonological relations between terms of different series. The contexts can be systematically analysed and various alternances constituted, but it does not follow that all these alternances or systems should be forced into a single theoretical

[1] A.U.C.L., p. 43, by M. Martini, of Paris.
[2] See 'The Use and Distribution of Certain English Sounds', Chapter 4.

architectonic scheme.[1] What letters are practically convenient in orthography is a different question and involves additional criteria. In the contextual technique I advocate, the statistical method is the one to be followed, and this allows discontinuity and change of measure and value from context to context.

If the ultimate units of linguistic material be treated in this way context by context, there is no fun left in the notorious question 'Are ŋ and h the same phoneme in English?'[2]

Further progress in phonology will depend on the constitution of alternances the terms of which have differential values in the characteristic and significant contexts of a given language. Up to the present no such exhaustive study has been completed, so that we are not really in a position to examine what relations, if any, there may be between phonetically similar terms of different alternances. We are, of course, accustomed to refer to the influence one 'sound' is said to have on another, to inter-syllabic relations such as vowel harmony, inter-word relations such as assimilation, and at first sight it would seem that these facts are overlooked in a narrow contextual technique. They are approached in a different way, and will be more fully understood when exhaustively examined context by context.

The minor function of an alternant, that is, of one term of an alternance, is determined by the constitution of the alternance as a series of terms having differential values in a certain type of context. Other facts are irrelevant. A term is to be considered first in relation to its context and secondly to the relevant linked alternance. What relations it may have to the language as a whole is difficult to guess. To treat a language as a sort of unity does not mean that every element is to be regarded as in equal relation to every other element. The phonological description of a language will reveal not just one architectonic system, but a series of systems which taken together give a complete and unambiguous account of the facts.

In the translator's preface to Holger Pedersen's *Linguistic Science in the Nineteenth Century*, Professor Spargo calls the reader's attention to one important feature of the book—'the striking role assigned to the study of phonetics in increasing our knowledge of linguistics. It is shown clearly that every important advance during the last century and a quarter was made by a scholar who attacked the problem from the phonetic side.' During the last twenty years phonetics has been applied in all sorts of practical ways. One of these has been the establishment of orthographies for hitherto unwritten

---

[1] In the *Alphabetum Barmanorum* it is obvious from the way various types of syllables are presented in the traditional Burmese way, that the number and nature of the terms or possible 'substituents' varies from context to context, and that a set of letters is not being set up as a functioning system *in vacuo* apart from context. Nevertheless, Carpani finds it necessary to issue the following warning: 'Observandum tamen est non omnia quidem haec signa cum qualibet littera, aut syllaba coniungi vel solere, vel etiam posse.' That he should have gone out of his way to say this shows that he realized the common mistake of regarding a set of letters as a whole as free units or terms in a sort of mathematical relationship.

[2] See Twaddell, 'On defining the Phoneme', *Language Monograph No. XVI*, pp. 10 sq. and 25 sq.

languages, and of simple, readable, unambiguous transcriptions of languages having either an unfamiliar script or one which does not correlate with the forms in actual use even from the native point of view. Considerations which help us to establish such a notation are technical and practical, and cannot fail to have a profound influence on the future of linguistics.

Further, and perhaps most important of all, those of us whose daily business it is to study the speech behaviour of our neighbours without either envy or scorn, and also that of strangers without breach of courtesy, realize as no one else can how narrowly conditioned our speech habits are by the daily round, the common task. Within the framework of social routine and the ritualistic give-and-take of conversation there are great ranges of possibility, but few are unexpected. If you disturb the air and other people's ears by using your speech apparatus in ways both unexpected and highly individual, you run grave social risks.

Such behaviour, to say the least, is felt to be unusual. It is generally tactless, though sometimes it is merely eccentric. Occasionally we condemn such behaviour by saying it is uncalled for, or more strongly by saying it is not done. We usually have a cue for what we say; the lines too, are there, and though there may be a choice our fellow countrymen know them and know what to expect.

To stretch the metaphor, what we say is usually 'called for'. With the linguistic stranger things are different. If you are wise you will be prepared for anything, do what is practically convenient from moment to moment, and avoid strain or weariness, by reducing the necessity of vocal interchange to a minimum within the bounds of international courtesy.

For some years now I have stressed what a friend and former student calls the *Handlungscharakter der Sprache*,[1] and also the very fine distinctions in speech behaviour, determined by typical recurrent social situations for which these locutions are specialized and of which they are organs or functions. It follows from this, of course, that a great deal is demanded of our notation and descriptive technique. Without it accurate morphology is impossible, and without scrupulously identified forms and well-established texts Semantics is apt to be just gossip.

It is the first duty of a describer of language, as it is of a classical philologist, to establish his forms and his texts with a scrupulous exactitude. For what is the semantic value of a corrupt text?

The purpose of this digression into general linguistics is to show that not even the broadest explorations in sociological linguistics are likely to lead to solid results without the pedestrian technique of the A B C as the principal means of linguistic description.

And of all A B C's the roman is the best. Perhaps Lenin was right when he said to the President of the Pan-Soviet Committee for National Alphabets: 'La latinisation, voilà la grande révolution de l'Orient.'[2]

---

[1] In *Neue Schweizer Rundschau*, July 1935, pp. 176-8, by Fritz Güttinger. See 'The Technique of Semantics', Chapter 3, p. 31, n. 1. [2] A.U.C.L., p. 174.

7

THE STRUCTURE OF THE CHINESE MONOSYLLABLE IN A HUNANESE DIALECT (CHANGSHA)

[WITH B. B. ROGERS]

THE only kind of speech behaviour with which the present study is directly connected is the oral naming of Chinese characters. Chinese characters have been prominent cultural objects for thousands of years. Even the sketchiest description of what they have been called by countless millions over a vast area of Asia would be a colossal task. All that is here attempted is a systematic analysis of what a certain number of selected characters were called by Mr. K. H. Hu, of Changsha.

If a precedent must be given, let it be Adam in the Garden. Created things were brought before him to see what he would call them. They did not come into his world until he had called their names. And the names by which he called them were a new creation, henceforth part and parcel of his world. It might even be said that they did not exist until he had called their names. A great deal of grammatical phonetics is concerned with the description of the spoken names of written words and tells the uninitiated what to call them when they are faced with them or when they want them. Such information can, of course, be used indirectly in continuous speech. But we would emphasize once more that the analysis here presented is not directly concerned with what is properly called general speech behaviour.

Consequently no connected text is given. The notation, however, could be used as a simple roman orthography, and lends itself to all modern printing devices. The ordinary typewriter keyboard could be used, and for telegrams, in this dialect at any rate, the ordinary telewriter could be used and the sending of such messages very much simplified as compared with the present numerical code method. A sample telegram is given at the end.

Lastly, the use of the word monosyllable in the title and in the text does not imply that Chinese is to be classed as a monosyllabic language. In actual speech reduplicative and dissyllabic elements are quite common.

The description of the pronunciation to be associated with the notation employed is also sufficient for practical purposes. The principle followed is that the main diacritica of the various types of syllable should be described and simply recorded. These diacritica may be regarded as occurring in two places, first place or initial position, and second place or final position. The tonal diacritica need not be 'placed', although the notation employs

THE CHINESE MONOSYLLABLE IN A HUNANESE DIALECT 77

letters in final position. These are not, therefore, counted as being in a 'place'.[1]

TONES

The technique indicated above was also applied to tones. The analysis and orthographic representation of these is based on observations of the tones used by Mr. Hu when called upon to name the selected characters placed before him. The tonal behaviour of such syllables in connected speech was not investigated, except for the low falling variant of tone 4 often used in certain syllables in connected speech. The nature and function of the so-called 'tones' of Chinese cannot be understood or economically represented in orthography until a thorough study of types of sentences in general speech behaviour has been completed by enlisting a number of workers.

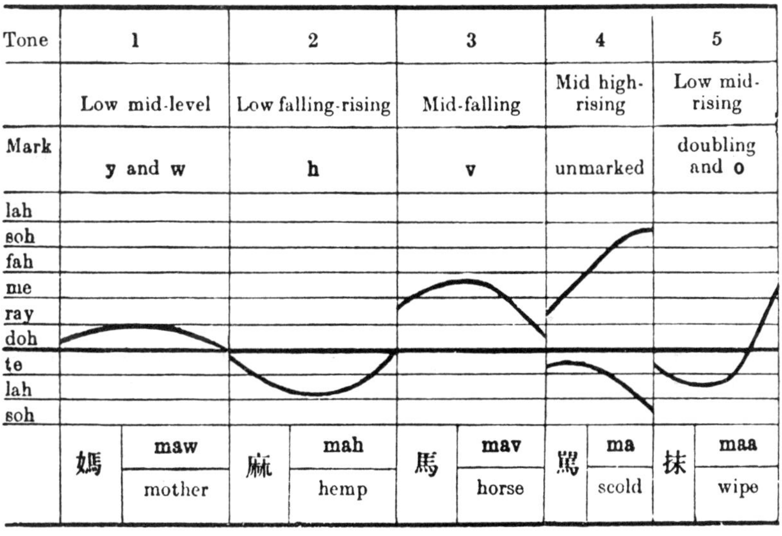

Tone	1	2	3	4	5
	Low mid-level	Low falling-rising	Mid-falling	Mid high-rising	Low mid-rising
Mark	y and w	h	v	unmarked	doubling and o

媽	maw	麻	mah	馬	mav	罵	ma	抹	maa
	mother		hemp		horse		scold		wipe

FIG. 1. *Relative pitch and length of tones*

RELATIVE FREQUENCY OF TONES

Three types of count for frequency were made, the first from a normal personal letter of 802 words (A); the second from a classified list of the 1,013 possible syllables in Changsha dialect (B); and the third from a national 'thousand-character' list (C). The resulting figures are shown in the table and graph overleaf.

[1] See Fu Liu, *Les Mouvements de la langue nationale en Chine*, 1925, paras. 125-7, p. 35, and also paras. 171-7, pp. 49-50.

Tone	(A)	(B)	(C)
1st	143	227	229
2nd	128	168	219
3rd	199	248	200
4th	225	257	334
5th	107	113	189
	802	1,013	1,171

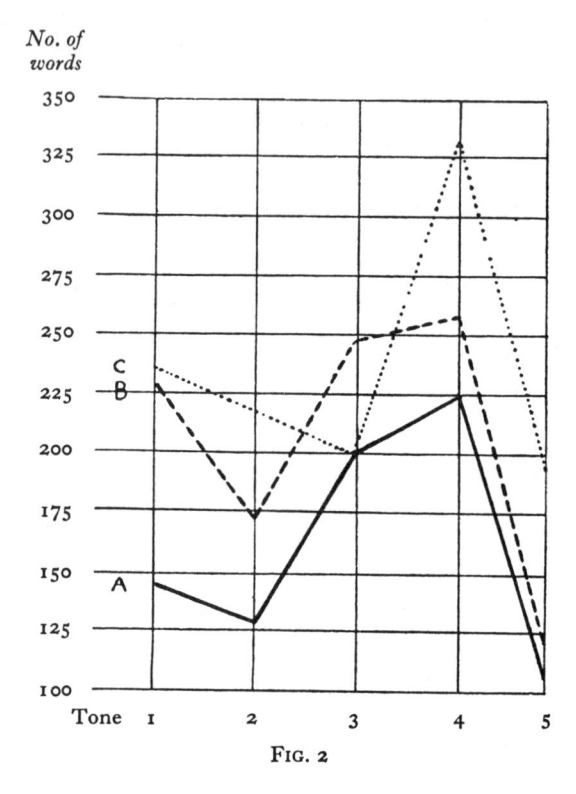

FIG. 2

From the graph it will be seen that there are reasons for thinking that the fourth tone occurs most frequently. Therefore this tone is left unmarked, the final letters, y, w, h, v, o, and the doubling of the final vowel letter, being used to mark the other tones.

In the marking of the first tone y is used with i, e, ei, ae, en, eun, and w with a, o, eu, u, ao, ou, on, aon, an, un. In the marking of the fifth tone the doubling of the final vowel letter is satisfactory for all letters except u. To avoid ambiguity with n in writing, final o is used instead of doubling the u.

In conjunctive spelling which would link syllables together to form words it would sometimes be necessary to use a hyphen after syllables in tones one and two to distinguish the final w, y, and h, which are tone letters, from the initial w, y, h, which represent differences of pronunciation. The hyphen might also be necessary occasionally after tone five.

Table I

Tones—with Vowels and Correlative Attributes

Tone 1, marked with **y** and **w**.	iy, ey, aw, ow, euw, uw, eiy, aey, aow, ouw, eny, euny,* onw, aonw, iny, anw, unw.	Long—longer than 3. Normal voice quality. Sometimes ends with slight creak.
Tone 2, marked with **h**.	ih, eh, ah, oh, euh, uh, eih, aeh, aoh, ouh, enh, eunh,* aonh, onh, inh, anh, unh.	Long—often longer than 1. Voice quality breathy, hollow, 'chesty' with slight initial friction.
Tone 3, marked with **v**.	iv, ev, av, ov, euv, uv, eiv, aev, aov, ouv, env, eunv,* onv, aonv, inv, anv, unv.	Medium length—shorter than 1 and 2. Clear 'head' voice—vowels usually closer and clearer. Slight final creak. Closing nasalization slight.
Tone 4, unmarked.	i, e, a, o, eu, u, ei, ae, ao, ou, en, eun,* on, aon, in, an, un.	Short. Clear 'head' voice. Ends with check. Closing nasalization very slight. Final n very short and checked.
Tone 5, marked with doubled **i, e, a, o,** and final **o**.	ii, ee, aa, oo, euo, uo, ouo.	Medium length—with the a-vowel, longer than 3. Slight initial breathiness. Checked. No closing nasalization.

* See notes on Table VI, p. 84.

Notation

Vowels

The number of letters required for the symbolization of vowels is five, as follows: **i, e, a, o, u**. This is not to say that there are only five vowels, as will be clear from the tables.

Consonants

The number of letters required for the symbolizing of consonants is seventeen, as follows (in alphabetical order): **b, c, d, f, g, h, j, k, l, m, n, p, s, t, w, y, z**.

Tones

Only one letter in addition to the above is found to be necessary to mark 'tones', namely **v** in final position. The other devices for representing the prosodic diacritica include the use of **y, w, h,** and **o** in final position, and the doubling of the final vowel letter. In contradistinction from the above positive marks, the fourth tone, which occurs most frequently, has zero mark.

Phonetic Analysis

As speech behaviour, the naming of the characters is just one complete act, a configuration of bodily postures and movements not easily dissected.

But the differences between these oral names can be systematically described, classified, and represented in notation. To do this it will be found convenient to regard the Hunanese monosyllable as having one, two, or perhaps three places in which the phonetic diacritica may be said to occur. In these places various alternances have differential function. (See alternance tables.) The tonal diacritica and possibly also what we have called yotization and labio-velarization may be considered as syllabic features.

The following vowels constitute a single-term alternance in one-place syllables (tones apart):

i, o, eu, u.

Two-place syllables are by far the most numerous, the initial alternance being consonantal and the final alternance vocalic, including closing nasalization. In syllables with final nasal, only three differentiations of vowel quality occur—fairly close front, mid-neutral, and open central. That is to say, the differences between **i, e, ei** which operate in other contexts are here neutralized. Similarly with **o, eu,** and **u**. When therefore we symbolize these three syllabic elements thus—**in, an, un,** we do not imply that the three vowels are variants of vowels No. 1, No. 3, and No. 6 respectively. We do not so regard them.[1]

In addition to the classification of Hunanese monosyllables according to the number of 'places', it is convenient to distinguish them also according to certain phonetic characteristics as follows:

Syllables (i) with final nasal
         (ii) with closing nasalization
         (iii) with yotization
         (iv) with labio-velarization
         (v) with yotization and nasalization
         (vi) with labio-velarization and nasalization and negatively
         (vii) without the above diacritica.

Syllables with final nasal only show three differences of vowel quality, I-like, a-like, and ə-like, whereas closing nasalization is associated with four qualities, the nasalization in **en** and **eun** being of a front quality, and in **on** and **aon** of a back quality.

The distinction between yotized and velarized syllables is a striking contrast of resonance following the initial consonants, one front, rather like **i** with slight spreading of the lips, and the other back, rather like an unrounded **o** or **u** with neutral lips or slight inner rounding. There must be no pouting. This contrast is a broad distinction of front and back resonance made use of in a similar way by many diverse languages. In the dialect we are considering, the yotization and labio-velarization differences may be regarded as syllabic diacritica and not as being 'placed'.[2]

---

[1] See Table VII and notes.
[2] See p. 91.

Vowel Alternances

Simple

The simple vowel qualities may be suggested by the following symbols and diagram:

Table II

Number of vowel	1	2	3	4	5	6
Phonetic notation	i	e	ɨa, a, aɨ	o,	y ə	ɯ, ʋ, ʐ, ʒ, &c.
Orthographic notation	i	e	a	o	eu	u

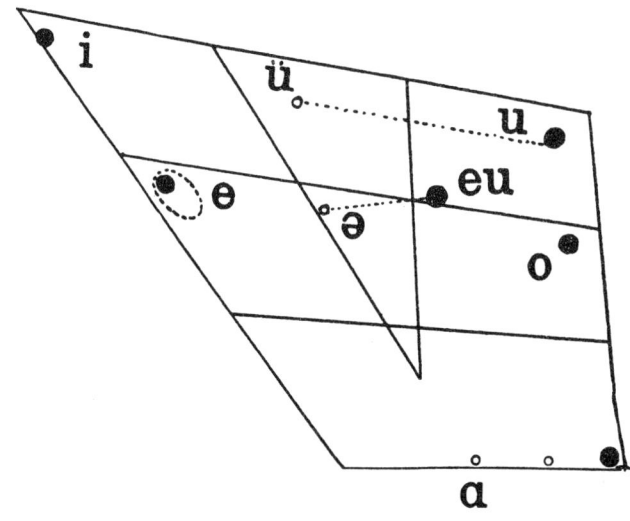

Fig. 3

Notes

General: Vowel quality, diphthongization, voice quality, length, and final 'check' or creak vary with the tones; that is to say, they are correlative attributes. See Table I.

Vowel No. 1—i—close and not diphthongized.

Vowel No. 2—e—varies in quality; sometimes starts with an i-like glide, and sometimes shows slight closing diphthongization, chiefly with the 3rd tone.

Vowel No. 3—a—three variants are shown in Table III.

Vowel No. 4—o—generally of constant quality, except with the second, third, and fifth tones, when there is slight closing diphthongization. In yotized syllables in which this vowel occurs the y is more than usually i-like.

Vowel No. 5—**eu**—a more centralized variant is used in labialized syllables.

Vowel No. 6—**u**—varies considerably according to context. See Table IV.

TABLE III

a

Back[1]		Mid[2]		Forward[3]	
怕	pa / fear	下	hya / under	鴉	yaw / raven
八	baa / eight	恰	cyaa / fitting	牙	yah / tooth
他	taw / he	家	jyaw / family	雅	yav / elegant
大	da / large			亞	ya / second
馬	mav / horse			壓	yaa / repress
刷	shwaa / brush				

Vowel No. 3 (**a**): *Notes*

1. The commonest quality of **a** is back, fairly near cardinal [ɑ], after the consonants given in the column below, and also after the following consonants: **k, f, w, l, s, ts, dz, kw, gw,** and **jw**.

2. After (the consonants) **hy, cy,** and **jy** the position of the vowel **a** is slightly advanced.

3. After initial **y** the position of **a** is further advanced to one approximating English [a]. It will be noted that the five examples given in this column vary in tone only.

Vowel No. 6 (**u**) (Table IV, opposite): *Notes*

1. This common syllabic element is usually produced with friction. After **p, b, k, g, f,** and **w** the 'vocalic' component is back, half close, unrounded, accompanied by bilabial friction, especially at the sides of the mouth. After **p** and **b** there is sometimes a short bilabial trill.

2. After **y,** and in yotized syllables, a close centralized vowel with slight friction.

3. After **s, ts, dz, c, j, sh,** and **z,** the syllabic element is the voiced homorganic continuant, *velarized*, with reduction of friction.

TABLE IV
The Syllabic Element u

	ɯ and ʋ¹ With slight bilabial friction		ü² Fronted unrounded		ẓ³ Alveolar syllabic velarized		ǯ³ Post alveolar syllabic velarized		ʐ³ Retroflex syllabic velarized	
鋪	phɯ	puɯ spread								
入			jü	yuo enter						
四					sẓ	su four				
尺							tʃǯ	cuo foot		
是									sʐ	shu be
不	bɯ	buo not								
女			njü	nyuv woman						
此					tsẓ	tsuv this				
至							dʒǯ	ju arrive		
日									ʐ	zuo sun
枯	khɯ	kuɯ dry								
書			sjü	shyuw book						
調					dzẓ	dzuh style				
古	ġɯ	guʋ ancient								
去			tʃü	cyu go						
富	fʋ̣	fu rich								
除			dʒü	jyuh exclude						
無	wɯ	wuh without								

84   STRUCTURE OF THE CHINESE MONOSYLLABLE

DIPHTHONGS

The diphthongs may be suggested by the following symbols and diagram:

TABLE V

Number of vowel	7	8	9	10
Phonetic notation	əe	aɛ	ɑɣ	ʌɣ
Orthographic notation	ei	ae	ao	ou

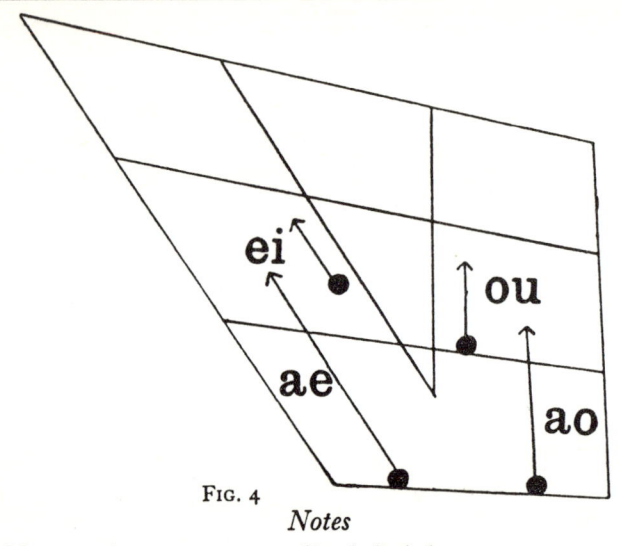

FIG. 4

Notes

Vowel No. 7—**ei**—narrow centralized diphthong.

Vowel No. 8—**ae**—after **sh** and **c** often begins with a **y**-like glide.

Vowel No. 9—**ao**—. No lip-rounding; this vowel occurs in all types of syllable except those with initial **w**, (**hw**) **f**, and [ç] **hy**, though not with the fifth tone. See note on maximum consonant alternance, page 91.

Vowel No. 10—**ou**—. No lip-rounding. Back unrounded glide from advanced half-open position to slightly less advanced half-close position. In yotized syllables the **y** element is **i**-like, and the variant of **ou** used is rather like ɣ.

TABLE VI
Closing Nasalization

	2*		4*		5*		9†
些	e	娑	o	色	ɣ	騷	ɑɣ
sey	e	sow	o	seuo	eu	saow	ao

	11		12		13		14
先	eẽ	酸	oõ	善	əi	送	əɣ
seny	en	sonw	on	sheun	eun	saon	aon

* See Table II.   † See Table V.

Notes

The simple vowels **e, o, eu**, and the diphthong **ao** have nasalized correlates. The nasalization difference in the case of **en, on, eun**, affects the end of the vowel, and gives the impression of a closing diphthong with a nasalized ending. This differentiation may therefore be termed *closing nasalization*, firstly because in **en** and **on** the lowering of the velum appears to be associated with a closer vowel quality and secondly the nasalization is only associated with the end-phase of the vowel. In the case of **eun** the vowel quality is not only fronted at the beginning, but moves in the direction of **i** in the closing nasalization. The end phase of the diphthong **ao** is not rounded, but is back, somewhat centralized. This diphthong has its nasalized correlate **aon**. The latter moves within a similar tamber range though it begins and ends somewhat closer than the unnasalized correlate **ao**. In yotized syllables the beginning of the diphthong in **aon** may be centralized.

It would be possible in orthography to dispense with **eun** as it represents a specific closing nasalization which occurs only after **sh, j**, and **c**. In these syllables the difference between **eun** and **en** is immaterial or neutralized, so the notation **en** would be unambiguous.

Syllables with Final n

Only three vowel differences occur in syllables with final **n**:

Table VII

Number of vowel	15	16	17
Phonetic notation	ɪn	an æn	ən
Orthographic notation	in	an	un

Notes

Syllables with final clear alveolar **n**, with no vocalic off-glide. In syllables with a final **n** there are only three tamber differences: (1) an ɪ-like vowel lowered and retracted; (2) an **a**-like vowel, more front than vowel No. 3 and in yotized syllables rather æ-like and centralized; and (3) a neutral vowel half-open. Our use of **i, a**, and **u** in the orthography **in, an, un** is not to be taken as identifying these elements with Vowels Nos. 1, 3, and 6 in other contexts.

Initial Consonant Alternance

It is convenient to classify the initial alternances first of all according to the number of essential articulation differences for each of the three types of consonant: (*a*) plosives and nasals; (*b*) fricatives, and (*c*) affricates.

Secondly, consonant terms are then multiplied by the following differences: (*a*) the aspiration-tensity difference, and (*b*) the voice difference.

Thirdly, the syllable pattern is further differentiated by diacritica which are here termed yotization and labio-velarization. Hitherto most scholars have regarded these differentiations as part of the vowel system, but analogous phenomena in Burmese suggested it might make for clearer analysis to treat this differentiation of the monosyllable by grouping the contrasted **y**-like and **w**-like elements with the consonantal terms of the initial alternance. It should be noted, however, that in some contexts the **y**-element is more vowel-like in quality, in others more consonantal.[1]

Plosives and Nasals

For plosives and nasals there are three essential articulation differences (not including variations consequent or dependent on the yotization and labialization differences), bilabial, dental, and velar. As a practical convenience in the table a separate column shows the pre-velar articulation of **n** and **ny** and the palatal articulation of **ǥy** and **ky**, which in the plosives correlates with *another* difference, the yotization difference.

As basic terms for this alternance we take **b, d, ǥ**. These three consonants are rather like whispered **b, d, ǥ**—that is to say, they are *not* really voiced although there is obviously some associated laryngeal and infra-glottal behaviour contrasting with the different chest and larynx behaviour associated with the aspirated correlates.

These three basic articulations are differentiated by four further differences, which we now associate with the initial consonantal alternance, in continuation of the above classification of syllables.

(i) The aspiration difference.
(ii) The yotization difference.
(iii) The velarization difference.
(iv) The nasalization difference.

i. *The Aspiration Difference*

The three voiceless stops written **p, t, k** are released with fairly strong aspiration, more than would be heard in southern English in the case of initial **p, t, k** followed by a vowel in a stressed syllable, but not so strong as in Indian languages. So far, then, we have six stops.

ii. *The Yotization Difference*

To the above six stops, six more are added by the yotization difference, viz. **by, py, dy, ty, ǥy, ky.**

Notes on **ky, ǥy, c, j, cy,** *and* **jy**

1. Before **ao, ou,** and **an** the difference between **ky** and **c**, **ǥy** and **j**, is significant; also before **o** and **aon** in the case of **ǥy** and **j**.

[1] See pp. 81, 89.

IN A HUNANESE DIALECT

2. Before **i, in, e, en**, the pronunciation of **k** is palatal, and the difference between **k, ky,** and **c** is immaterial. In many syllables either the aspirated palatal plosive or the aspirated affricate may be used. The use of **gy** and **j** as alternative pronunciations in similar contexts is not quite so common, but it does occur.

TABLE VIII

The Differentiation of Velar and Palatal Plosives and the Palato-alveolar Affricates

	k	c	ky	cy	g	j	gy	jy
i	kiy 欺	..	(kyiy)	..	giy 雞	..	(gyiy)	..
e	(kee)	..	kyee 朅	..	(gee)	..	gyee 結	..
a	kav 卡	..	kyaa 恰	..	..	..	gyaw 家	..
o	kow 科	..	kyoo 却	..	gow 歌	joo 卓	gyoo 脚	..
eu	keuo 客	ceuo 轍	..	..	geuo 隔	jeuo 摺	..	..
u	kuw 枯	cuw 癡	..	cyuw 驅	guw 姑	juw 之	..	jyuw 居
ae	kaey 開	..	..	..	gaey 街	..	..	..
ao	kaow 敲	caow 超	kyaov 巧	..	gaow 高	jaow 招	gyaov 絞	..
ou	kouv 口	couv 醜	kyouo 曲	..	gouv 狗	jouw 洲	gyouw 鳩	..
en	..	..	kyeny 謙	..	..	..	gyeny 堅	..
on	konw 寬	..	..	..	gonw 官	..	..	..
eun	..	ceunv* 諂	..	..	..	jeunv* 展	..	..
aon	kaonw 空	caonw 充	..	..	gaonw 工	jaonw 中	gyaonh 窮	..
in	..	(ciny)	kyiny 輕	..	..	(jiny)	gyiny 巾	..
an	kanw 刊	canw 昌	kyanw 彊	..	ganw 乾	janw 張	gyanw 姜	..
un	kunw 坑	cunw 稱	..	..	gunw 根	junw 眞	..	..

* See notes on Table VI, p. 85.

3. In syllables containing the syllabic element **u**, **ky** and **ġy** do not occur, but the difference between **c** and **cy** is significant. From this fact and other variant pronunciations of **ky** it would seem that the difference between **ky** and **cy**, **ġy** and **jy** is likely to be immaterial.

The difference between **ky** and **cy**, **ġy** and **jy** is immaterial and may be regarded as alternative pronunciations. As will be seen from Table IV, a feature of certain syllables is the use of a syllabic continuant often homorganic with the initial consonant, when that is fricative or affricative. This element is here symbolized by **u**. Before this element it is necessary to distinguish between **c** and **cy**, **j** and **jy**, but of course **ky** and **ġy** would be unambiguous provided that an affricative pronunciation was understood.

iii. *The Labio-Velarization Difference*

To the above twelve stops two more are added by the labio-velarization difference, **kw** and **ġw**, making fourteen stops in all, alternating in initial position.

In these group-plosives (**py**, **kw**, &c.) the combination of aspiration and yotization, and of aspiration and velarization, produce characteristic qualities in the release of the stops. These contextual variations are noted below:

Notes on the Aspirated Plosives

1. Palatalized and ç-like aspiration when followed by **i**.
2. x-like aspiration when followed by **a**.
3. Back resonance of aspiration when followed by **o**, and more so in the case of **kw**.
4. The aspiration of **py**, **ty**, **ky**, is ç-like followed by i-like yotization before **ao** and also sometimes before **e** and **en**.

Table IX

Consonants. Plosives and Nasals

(*Initial Alternance only*)

	Bilabial		Dental		Palatal and pre-velar		Velar	
	Orth.	Phon.	Orth.	Phon.	Orth.	Phon.	Orth.	Phon.
Voiceless lax	b	ḅ	d	ḍ	..	..	g	g̣
Aspiration difference	p	ph	t	th	..	..	k	kh
Yotization difference	by py	bj phj	dy ty	dj thj	gy ky	jj cj	..	..
Labio-velarization difference	..	..	..	..	..	..	gw kw	g̣w khw
Nasal difference and yotized nasals	m my	m mj	l ly	naso- lateral	n ny	ṇ ṇj	[n]	[ŋ]

iv. *The Nasal Difference*

It will be seen from the table that the nasal difference, with yotization, adds six more terms to the initial alternance on the basis of the three articulations noted at the outset.

Notes

1. l—The tongue tip articulation is dental, the sides of the tongue are not completely closed against the teeth and the soft palate not completely raised, so that the acoustic effect is slightly nasal. It may be described as a naso-lateral.

ly—Similar observations apply, the articulation being palatalized.

2. n—In the initial alternance **n** is pronounced as a pre-velar nasal [ŋ]. In the group **ny** it is nearer the palatal position, but never sounds like [ɲ]. It must be noted that the *letter* **n** in final position is used to indicate closing nasalization in **en, on, eun, aon**, and a clear dental nasal in the syllabic elements **in, an, un**. No functional identification of these various nasals is suggested.

FRICATIVES AND AFFRICATES

The plosive and nasal alternance, as we have seen, is based on three articulations, that is, if we classify the pre-velars with the velars. For fricatives and affricates, however, there are six articulations, as set forth in Table X.

TABLE X
Consonants; Fricatives and Affricates
(*Initial Alternance only*)

	Labio-dental	Alveolar	Retroflex and post-alveolar	Palatal	Velar or post-velar
Voiced	..	..	z [ʐ]	..	..
Breathed	f	s	sh [ʂ]	(hy) [ç or ɕ]	h [x]
Yotized	..	sy	shy	hy [ç or ɕ]	..
Labialized	(hw)	..	shw	..	..
Voiced lax	..	dz	j	..	..
Aspirated tense	..	ts	c	..	..
Yotized	..	dzy tsy	jy cy	..	..
Labialized	..	..	jw cw	..	..

Notes

1. The alveolar sibilant is differentiated by yotization only, giving two terms: **s** and **sy**.

2. The alveolar affricates are differentiated by the voice-aspiration

difference and the yotization difference, giving in all four terms: **dz, ts, dzy,** and **tsy.**

3. The retroflex articulation is the base for four terms: (1) voiced **z**, (2) breathed **sh**, (3) breathed velarized **shw**, and (4) breathed yotized **shy** occurring only before the syllabic element **u**.

Initial **z** is much more like a retroflex voiced sibilant than the corresponding sound in the dialect of Peiping which is sometimes described as a sort of post-alveolar **r**-sound.

4. The palato-alveolar affricate articulation is the base for a complete series of six terms differentiated by:

(i) Voice-aspiration difference   **j**   **c**
(ii) Yotization   **jy**   **cy**
(iii) Labio-velarization   **jw**   **cw**

TABLE XI

Semi-Vowels and Fricative Correlates

Vowels	w back semi-vowel without lip-rounding	f (hw) labio-dental or bilabial breathed fricative	y semi-vowel	hy [ç or ɕ] breathed palatal fricative	yw [jɤ] semi-vowel group
i	..	..	yi	hyi	..
e	..	..	ye	hyee	..
a	waw	fa	ya	hya	..
o	..	..	yoo	hyoo	..
eu	..	..	..	..	yweuo
u	wu [ʮ]	fu [fʮ]	yu	..	..
ei	wei	fei	..	..	ywei
ae	wae	fae	..	..	..
ao	..	..	yao	hyao	..
ou	..	..	you	hyou	..
en	..	..	yen	hyen	ywen
aon	..	..	yaon	hyaonw	..
in	..	..	yin	hyin	..
an	wan	fan	yan	hyan	..
un	wun	fun	..	..	ywun

Notes

The digraph **hy** is used for the breathed fricative correlate of **y**. **hw** might also be used for the similar correlate of **w**, and indeed it may be so pronounced. But usually it is pronounced by making a light contact of the inner part of the lower lip with the front of the upper teeth, and sounds rather like **f**. For this reason and for other alphabetic reasons the letter **f** is used. A bilabial pronunciation is also possible. We may bear in mind that there is no surviving **pw** or **bw**.

N.B. In the above table most of the examples given are pronounced with the fourth tone, which has zero mark. This does not mean that similar syllables do not occur in other tones.

Conclusion

Finally, the following single-place consonant and vowel alternances in otherwise identical contexts should be taken as some justification of the notation employed and of the suggestion that it might be used as the basis of a practical roman orthography.

1. The maximum consonantal alternance in initial position consists of thirty-two terms preceding the syllabic element **an**, as follows:
b, p, d, t, ġ, ġy, ġw, k, ky, kw, m, l, ly, n, ny, s, sy, sh, shw, dz, dzy, ts, tsy, j, jw, c, cw, y, hy, w, f (hw), h.

2. The proxime consonant alternance consists of thirty-one terms preceding **ao** as follows: **b, by, p, py, d, dy, t, ty, ġ, k, ky, m, my, l, ly, n, ny, s, sy, z, sh, dz, dzy, ts, tsy, j, jy, c, y, hy, h.** This proxime alternance adds **by, py, dy, ty, my, z** to the thirty-two terms given in (1), making a total of thirty-eight before **an** and **ao**.

3. It will be noticed that in the two longest alternances given, **jy** and **cy** do not occur. It is probable that the difference between **ky** and **cy**, **ġy** and **jy**, is immaterial. Nevertheless, **j, jy, c, cy,** all occur before **u**. (See Tables IV and VIII.) So to our list of thirty-eight, **jy, cy,** and **shy** must be added, making a total of forty-one consonantal terms.

4. The minimum consonantal alternance consists of the three terms **sh, j,** and **c**, before **eun**. The next shortest alternance is of twelve terms before **on**.

This latter would become the minimum alternance if **eun** is for purposes of orthography amalgamated with **en**. (See note on Table VI.)

5. The maximum vowel alternance is in second place after **p, s, dz, ts,** and consists of sixteen terms as follows: **i, e, a, o, eu, u, ei, ae, ao, ou, en, on, aon, in, an, un,** the seventeenth, **eun,** occurring after **sh, j,** and **c**. The proxime is fifteen after **d, m, l**. The minimum consists of the unique term **ao** after **by, py, my, ty,** there being a two-term alternance of **ao** and **ou** after **dy**.

The diacritica of the Changsha monosyllable may thus be regarded as occurring in two places, in the first place or in initial position, and in the second place or in final position. The prosodic diacritica, and to a certain extent what we have termed yotization and labio-velarization, are characteristic of the syllable as a whole, though they are indicated by differentiations of the final letter, by additional final letters, by zero mark, and by the coupling of **y** and **w** with initial consonants.

Message to be Telegraphed

已 得 學 士 學 位 下 週 往 法 准 欵
寄 巴 黎 兩 週 後 囘 倫　　 平 西

Telegram in Roman Orthography

IV DEUO HYOO SU HYOO WEI HYA JOUW WANV FAA FEI KONV
GI BAW LIY NYANV JOUW HOU FEIH LUNH.

　　　　　　　　　　　　　　　　　　PINH YOUV.

8

THE ENGLISH SCHOOL OF PHONETICS

> 'Take stock of what you have, in the first place, and consider your heritage. You will find, I think—let me put it modestly—some occasion for happiness, a little foundation of confidence, in your nationality. It is not our custom, in Britain, to boast much of our achievements, for though we have played our part in the world's history with a certain spirit, we are ill-educated and have bad memories. We are taught only the smallest fraction of what we have done, and even that we cannot remember.'
>
> From 'Our Words and Books and Ways', by Eric Linklater—in the *Observer* of Sunday, 27 October 1946, being part of his Rectorial Address, called 'The Art of Adventure', delivered the day before at Aberdeen University.

IN 1935[1] I read a paper before the Society on semasiology as understood in England, and of semantics, as it was afterwards called, as a result of later French influence, and I drew attention to the prior importance of the Society's Dictionary. Lexicography is a branch of linguistics in which the English are very much at home. Now I turn to phonetics in this country, and as in the early days of the Society, we are going to look into the background of typically English work in orthoepy, orthography, 'alphabetics', and phonetics. Though we in this country are beginning to use the term 'phonology' for a certain branch of linguistics following continental usage, we do so at some disadvantage to ourselves, since in English 'phonology' is an historical, not a synchronic discipline. As usual we conform to international usage, since we cannot impose the meaning of 'phonetics' on those who use the terms *la phonétique*, *Phonetik*, or *Lautlehre*. If synchronic phonology can be summarily described as the grammar of sounds and letters, our term 'phonetics' covers it, and we have practised the discipline in some form or other for centuries. It would be a good thing if we could put 'the rectification of terms' on the agenda of our future international meetings.

The title 'The English School of Phonetics' is a phrase taken from Sweet's paper to the Philological Society on 'The Practical Study of Language', in 1884. In the preface to his *Handbook of Phonetics*, published in 1877, he had said: 'England may now boast a flourishing phonetic school of its own.'

The purpose of this paper is to go farther, and by giving a brief account of the origins and reaches of our notable work in this branch of linguistics and of the share the Society had in its encouragement and propagation, to show how very English it is, and to emphasize above all things continuity in that quality over a long period. My use of the words 'origins' and 'reaches' is neither historical nor technical, but merely personal and occasional.

---

[1] 'The Technique of Semantics,' Chapter 3.

I dare say you will find my use of the word phonetics very broad, since it will be taken to mean what English people have intended to say when they used it. In other words, I am not considering *la phonétique* or *Lautlehre*. [If I refer to phonetics as an American word, I shall give due warning.]

The first step is to summarize the miscellaneous aims of English workers in phonetics. These aims I will state briefly by selecting my headings from a pamphlet by Professor Daniel Jones, published by the International Phonetic Association in 1938:

1. *To help learners of foreign languages to acquire a good pronunciation.* Under this first heading, Professor Daniel Jones introduces the expressions (*a*) 'phonetic analysis', (*b*) 'phonetic training' [Exercises for the organs of speech and ear training], and (*c*) 'phonetic transcription', 'broad transcription'.

Other headings under which the aims are stated are:

2. *To help the study of the Mother tongue and of standards of pronunciation.*
3. *Speech Defects*—and may I add here the difficulties of the deaf and the blind? These interests are fairly common among phoneticians, especially in England and America.
4. *Orthographies for Oriental and African languages.* Under this heading, such expressions as 'adequate alphabets, good alphabets, phonetic orthography, good orthographies' are used—and the following typical sentence occurs: 'And it is perhaps not too much to hope that in due course we in Europe may realize more clearly some of the defects inherent in our conventional systems of spelling, and may take some steps to remedy them.'

'Spelling Reform' in England is not specifically mentioned, but some English phoneticians of today are interested, like many of their predecessors from Orm onwards. This interest in the spelling of English is one of the main origins of what I have taken the liberty to call the English School.

5. *Other Types of Alphabet.* Shorthand and other codes. Here the origins go back to Dr. Timothy Bright of Yorkshire and London in the time of Elizabeth.
6. *The Comparative Study of Languages.*
7. *The History of Languages.*
8. *Dialectology.* Professor Jones says this is a field of research which is essentially phonetic in character. It is under this head that he introduces the expression 'narrow transcription'.

Again, English work has been outstanding, and we must notice Joseph Wright and his fellow workers.

These eight headings are presented in Professor Jones's order—but for the purpose of my paper the order is not significant. Professor Jones thinks the uses of phonetics under headings 1 to 3 most important, and then 4 and 5. Joseph Wright emphasized 8, Dialectology, and, as you will find in the biography by his wife, thought it the best possible school in *practical phonetics*, of which he claimed some knowledge.

A pamphlet by Paul Passy, similar to the one by Professor Jones, had previously been published in 1929, also by the International Phonetic

Association, but again clearly inspired by the work of the English School. Here, typically enough, there is evidence that we select something English which we find good, and not only regard it ourselves as for the good of mankind, but persuade other people to adopt it. Then, with our usual common sense, we agree to call it international.

Mention of Passy is a reminder of another most important interest of English phoneticians—'English for Foreigners'. This interest is the main origin of the International Phonetic Association, as Professor Jones showed in a report to the Association on 27 July 1935.[1] He says:

> For a year or two preceding 1886, a small group of French teachers had been experimenting with using phonetic transcription in the practical teaching of English. . . . I suspect that they must have got their inspiration from the already famous English phonetician, Henry Sweet.

He goes on to tell us how Passy founded a society with an English name, 'The Phonetic Association of Teachers of English', and started a journal called *Dhe Fonètik Tîtcer*. In 1886, says Professor Jones, the following extract of a letter from Sweet was published in *Dhe Fonètik Tîtcer*:

> Agreement is impossible as long as each nation expects concessions to be made to the traditions of its own spelling. We in England [meaning presumably A. J. Ellis and himself, adds Jones] have made a great step in the direction of internationality by adopting the roman instead of English values, and it would be a good thing if Frenchmen could be got to make a similar concession by abandoning their cumbersome diacritics.

Vietor, Klinghardt, Storm, and Passy all discussed this problem, and at one time it looked as though Sweet's improved version of Bell's Visible Speech might be adopted as the alphabet of the Journal. These quotations serve to show the importance of our interest in English for foreign students, and our labours towards a reasonable practical use of the roman alphabet in transcriptions and orthographies.

Since I propose to trace the origins and reaches of the English School of Phonetics by a regressive method, let it be noted that Jones, Palmer, Ripman, Wyld, Wright, Sweet, and Ellis devoted a great part of their work to English for English people and for foreigners. As in other branches of phonetics in England, there were earlier forerunners and there are many followers. After all, the English—or the Britons, as Alexander Hume would have said—have been something of a success as practical internationalists. Through our interest in English for foreigners, we helped to make the International Phonetic Association, and we must see to it as good internationalists that it continues to prosper.

I think the emphasis on 'practical' is a constant feature of the work of the English School, certainly during the nineteenth century, and we do not take offence when Germans refer to our work with pejorative intent, as *ganz praktisch*, because we know that when they have borrowed its ideas,

[1] *Le Maître Phonétique*, Juillet–Septembre 1935.

the result is *wissenschaftlich*. Typically English also are the contradictions to this emphasis. Professor Daniel Jones has from time to time given us some of the most abstract theory in phonetics. I feel 'guilty' too—though here theory led not to a theoretical treatise but to a successful application of phonetics to operational linguistics during the Second World War. May I conclude this play on 'practical' with a quotation from a letter from Henry Sweet to the Vice-Chancellor of Oxford University in 1902:

> My own subject, Phonetics, is one which is useless by itself, while at the same time it is the foundation of all study of language, whether theoretical or practical.

Perhaps we English phoneticians have ourselves talked too much of the practical value of phonetics. If we had followed Sweet's example, and while insisting on its fundamental nature and high academic value, had freely confessed its uselessness by itself, we might have had more university teachers of the subject by this time in our own country.

The fact that a number of English phoneticians studied in Germany also adds a certain piquancy to their English quality. Professor Jones himself tells us in an article on William Tilly that he first studied phonetics in Germany. Sweet and Joe Wright are among others who studied in Germany, but both went out of their way to claim with pride—some might call it arrogance—that they were largely self-educated. So were the Bells.

This individuality, this independence of academies, this proud status of amateur, is quite common among English scientific workers.

Before I move much farther back, following the regressive method, to look for the origins of these features of the English School, I want to do two things—first, to bring in the Scots with James VI of Scotland and I of England, and secondly, to add to the list of interests occupying our attention in phonetics.

A distinguished Scottish schoolmaster, Alexander Hume, wrote a little tract[1] 'Of the orthographie and congruities of the Britan Tongue; A Treates, noe shorter then necessarie, for the Schooles'. He dedicated it to James I, that wise and scholarly monarch, and is believed to have read an address of welcome when James returned to Scotland in 1617, after fourteen years in England.

He insists that grammar is built on good spelling and that the subject of his Tract is really grammar, and begs His Majesty 'at your first entrie to your Roial Scepter', to reform the grammar. His first chapter is entitled 'Of the Groundes of Orthographie', and there are five good sections:

> 1. To wryte orthographicallie there are to be considered the symbol, the thing symbolized, and their congruence. Geve me leave, gentle reader, in a new art, to borrow termes incident to the purpose, quhilk, being defyned, wil further understanding.
>
> 2. The symbol, then I cal the written letter, quhilk representes to the eie the sound that the mouth sould utter.

[1] E.E.T.S. Reprints, 1865, No. 5. Cf. Section 'Of the Britan Vowels'.

3. The thing symbolized I cal the sound quhilk the mouth utteres quhen the eie sees the symbol.

4. The congruence betueen them [*fol. 7b*] I cal the instrument of the mouth, quhilk, when the eie sees the symbol, utteres the sound.

5. This is the ground of al orthographie, leading the wryter from the sound to the symbol, and the reader from the symbol to the sound.

Hume uses the word *symbol* and the expression 'written letter'—not just 'letter'.[1] The English phoneticians have always interested themselves in symbols, letters, types, type-design, and printing; so did their forebears too from the earliest times. Scotland joins in, bringing us to the very central point, namely that all orthographies, even systems of phonetic spelling, are really within the discipline of grammar. Hume found confusion of letters, spelling, and therefore of grammar, both in England and Scotland. He writes in his dedication to His Majesty:

For the printeres and wryteres of this age, caring for noe more arte then may win the pennie, wil not paen themselfes to knau whither it be orthographie or skaiographie that does the [*fol. 2*] turne: *and* schoolmasteres, quhae's sillie braine will reach no farther then the compas of their cap, . . .

. . . fel sundrie tymes on this subject reproving your courteoures, quha on a new conceat of finnes sum tymes spilt (as they cal it) *the King's language*.

In school materes, the least are not the least, because to erre in them is maest absurd. If the fundation be not sure, the maer gorgiouse the edifice, the grosser the falt.

This bringing in of Scotland with Hume is of some importance, since in all probability there was continuity of interest in Edinburgh in the good spelling and delivery of the King's Language down to the time of that well-known Scots family of elocutionists, the Bells: grandfather Alexander, his two sons David Charles and Alexander Melville, and grandson Alexander Graham, who, between them, were the leading exponents of the elocution of the King's English in the nineteenth century in four capitals and five countries—in Edinburgh, Dublin, London, Washington, and Canada; and the last-named, Alexander Graham Bell, was the inventor of the telephone, and of recording on wax, both on flat disks and on cylinders. The Bells were among the makers of the nineteenth-century English School of Phonetics. When I use the phrase the *English* School of Phonetics, I am only following Sweet, who was fully acquainted with the facts. Moreover he probably had Scottish blood himself.

Hume complained of a confusion of letters and spelling. The confusion was characteristic of the age, it is true—but the English and the Scots, and certainly the Irish, do not break their hearts over such things. They become incurable orthographists, alphabeticians, inventors of shorthand and codes, full of adventure in letters and signs. They have always been so. Judging by the bewildering variety of phonetic transcriptions of English now current, it seems that our phoneticians are as English as ever.

[1] *Litera* or *littera* was always a sound—*vox articulata*. Cf. pp. 99, 100, 101.

I have emphasized the long continuity of English interest in those subjects of study which Professor Jones listed as the province of phonetics, and I now suggest a long look back from modern times through the Revival of Learning to the Conquest and before.

Subject number two was the mother tongue and standards of pronunciation. It is this interest in the spelling and pronunciation of the Mother Tongue, the King's Language as Hume and even earlier writers called it (both these, by English tradition at any rate, being within the province of grammar), which provides ample evidence of the main origin of our School, and the reason for the pre-eminence of the English in these studies.

In emphasizing the long continuity of these features of English grammar, I have been greatly encouraged by the well-known introduction to Harpsfield's *Life of More* by the late Professor R. W. Chambers, entitled 'The Continuity of English Prose from Alfred to More and his School'. First of all, therefore, I propose to quote a few key sentences from that brilliant essay. In the sixteenth century,

What England most needed was a prose style in which contemporary events were recorded in living and dramatic narrative. . . . Although the first of the great European nations to evolve such a style, England had been passed in the race by her Continental rivals, till Sir Thomas More and his disciples gave back to her what she had lost.

The King's English of the South was making itself felt in the North of England, in the eleventh century as it did not do again till the fifteenth—a Standard English Prose is there.

And this King's English, standard over all England, was intelligible over the whole of northern Europe in Saxon times.

There was one speech only in the North, before William the Bastard won England.

says one of the Sagas.

In the remarkable development of an official language, England preceded the nations of Western Europe by some centuries.

In this matter eleventh century England was getting into the fifteenth century —until William the Conqueror put a stop to it.

There you have the main subject. The interest for us is the claim that the English were the first in western Europe to establish respect for a standard form of the Mother Tongue, and this before the Conquest. Wherever there is established respect for official prose, wherever a written standard language is institutionalized, there is grammar. Chambers establishes a continuous tradition between Alfred and More in the writing of the King's English. For future research I suggest we might inquire into the continuity of Latin and English grammar and the teaching of Latin and English, between Ælfric and Ascham.

My first step in suggesting the links of this tradition will be to notice a few sixteenth-century scholars at the More period of our story.[1]

Sir Thomas Smith, Secretary to Queen Elizabeth I, travelled widely on State business and met scholars in Paris, Orleans, and Padua, to discuss problems of spelling and pronunciation—especially of Greek and English. His 'abominable' pronunciation of Greek horrified modern Greeks he met in Paris, but he stoutly maintained the metrical value of his reformed pronunciation in the English style and was responsible for the main features of our present-day pronunciation of classical Greek. Roger Ascham, Sir John Cheke, Provost of King's, Walter Haddon, the Latinist, were all friends of his and formed a coterie which did much to mould the course of the Renaissance in England on its pedagogic side.

Thomas Wilson (LL.D. of Ferrara), the author of the successful *Arte of Rhetoricke*, tutor to the Brandons, courtier, statesman, writer, and scholar, was in touch with the Renaissance, the Reformation, and the Revival of the State under the Tudors—the last-mentioned point, taken with the fact that Sir Thomas Smith was Secretary to the Queen, being to my mind significant.

All the coterie confidently believed in the strength and worth of the native English character menaced from abroad. They wished to make learning accessible in the vernacular to Englishmen, and the use of English accessible to the foreigner. They frequently show that the reading of the Ancients had awakened a new delight in the sound and melody of the Mother Tongue as well as its appearance in the new printed books now multiplying.

Wilson points out 'grammar doeth teach to utter wordes: to speak both apt and plaine', and discusses faults in pronunciation. Notice that grammar is concerned with utterance and speech.

Sir Thomas Smith, while drawing attention to the high place of the Mother Tongue in the life of the nation, was not afraid of spelling reform and had a distinct feeling for bringing English into line with classical or Italian values of Latin, which Sweet mentioned with some pride in his letter to *The Phonetic Teacher* already quoted. The following are examples of Sir Thomas Smith's spellings:

cës	cheese
carite	charity
kac	catch

Here was an Englishman with a truly international outlook in transcription.

The works of William Bullokar, published between 1580 and 1586, are of great interest technically, since they present many features immediately

---

[1] Thomas Wilson, author of the *Art of Rhetoricke*, 1559–60; Sir Thomas Smith, scholar and courtier, and most appropriately for my purpose, Secretary to Queen Elizabeth I, author of *de recta et emendata Anglicae Scriptione* in 1568, and *Alphabetum Anglicum*—a most significant title; Bullokar 1586; and John Hart, the Chester Herald.

recognizable as characteristic of our work. May I just list the topics he discusses:

(i) Description of the Pronunciation.
(ii) Problems of Transcription.
(iii) Type—with notice of the skill of the printer, founder, and graver of his many new letters and sorts.
(iv) Use of superfluous or unnecessary letters.
(v) New Grammar.
(vi) Test of the alphabet in various forms of cursive writing.
(vii) The names of the letters.

But the most interesting work from the point of view of continuity and of common English interest was a book published in 1569 entitled *An Orthographie, conteyning the due Order and Reason, howe to write or paint the Image of Mannes Voice, most like to the Life or Nature,* compiled by John Hart, Chester Heralt.

In his preface he says of this treatise:

Orthography is a Greeke woord signifying true writing, which is when it is framed with reason to make us certayne wyth what letters every member of our speach ought to bee written. By which definition we ought to use an order in writing, which nothing cared for unto this day, our predecessors and we have been (as it were) drowned in a maner of negligence, to bee contented with such maner of writing as they and we now, have found from age to age. Without any regard unto the severall parts of the voice, which the writing ought to represent.

And I touching writers, doe marvaile our predecessors have continued in the disorder and confusion which is in our English writing.

Because we think it better to continue in that we know than to larne the thing wee know not.

With due consideration of what letters are, and thereafter framed their use to be knowen certainly for the members of our speech.

Such an alphabet would:

enable people to read in one quarter of the time,

be:

easier and readier for the printer,

secondly, be a boon:

for other nations, e.g. Welsh and Irish.

With such a spelling, a writer or reader would be able to read aloud years afterwards what he wrote:

And so read it again perfitely, when and wheresoever he may see it, though many years thereafter and though he understood no word thereof.

And last for a helpe for the learned sort which desire to pronounce other tongs aright.

This treatise for the profit of the multitude addressed to the learned sort, whose like have been in times past, causers of our present manner of writing, by turning their penne to adde or diminish, alter or chaunge, as though meete into other letters and *carractes*, much differing from the olde Saxon manner [cf. Bell].

So well a learned gentleman in Greek and Latin and travailed in certain vulgares, Sir Thomas Smith, has written his mind, in hys booke of late set forth in Latin, entitled, 'de recta et emendata linguae Anglicanae scriptione'.

Whereof and of this my treatise, the summe effect, and end is one in which is, to use as many letters in our writing, as we doe voices or breathes in speaking, and no more: And never to abuse one for another, and to write as we speake: which we must needes doe if we will ever have our writing perfite: and for such voices, sounds or breathes, as we have not fit carrects, markes, or letters, we may without offence to God or reasonable man, chuse and use, fit new markes or letters for everye of them, and so we may be duely served at our neede: and not be driven to abuse any one in two or three sounds as we noew doe diverse.

Use, power and sound of every letter, by examples in *diverse languages* (i.e. potestas).

Romans made all the world learn Latin. We English, are the same to the Welsh —in whose manner of writing, peradventure there is better order kept.

Letters are the *figures and colours* wherewith the image of man's voice is painted.[1]

On loan-words he remarks:

For so the French doe terme it, when any foren is so received amongst them, they cal him *naturalized*. And let foreigners borowe from us.

The main point for the thesis of my paper is Hart's claim to have spent twenty years studying the spelling of English for five hundred years back— that is, to the eleventh century.

Hart's pride in his study of five hundred years of English spelling gives me, I think, a valid reason for going back to Ælfric's Latin Grammar,[2] which is the first grammar book in English. It is based on Donatus and Priscian, but quite different from either in its composition. Ælfric says two very important things in his preface:

1. That he is making the book for quite young boys.
2. That he hopes it may be some introduction to both Latin and English grammar, if anyone wants to use it that way.

A careful study of the Grammar shows that he is plainly justified in these claims, for he rearranges the information gathered from Donatus and Priscian, and expands or curtails it to suit his English boys. Throughout the book there is no example which a little Saxon could not be expected to understand.

Grammar is *stæfcræft*, letter skill. All English grammars have been rather like Ælfric's—they are all Latin grammars anyway.[3]

---

[1] See remarks below, p. 101, on *nomen, figura, potestas*.
[2] A recent French work of romantic history, *Ælfric*, by Marguerite Dubois, 1943, adds nothing to the historical valuation of Ælfric, but is amusing reading.
[3] See Lindley Murray's *English Grammar*, 1795, part i, chapter i.

In this paper, I can only mention one or two points in Ælfric's Grammar to illustrate the age-old study of letters, their names, their shapes, their values. In discussing the letters he starts us off with the three Latin categories, *nomen, figura, potestas*—**nama, hiw, miht**—roughly meaning a letter has a name, is a shape or image, has an 'office' or power in grammar, according to its position and use.

From Ælfric's time through the medieval sciences of Grammar and Rhetoricke, renewed during the Enlightenment, and on through modern times, the trinity has been a central principle. These three properties continue to interest us all through our grammatical history, since common practice in spelling built up by tradition and follies of various sorts has been a constant challenge and exercise to grammarians, alphabeticians, orthoepists, orthographists, shorthand writers, and spellers, and speakers of the King's Language. As the use of written and spoken English spread throughout the world, the challenge and the interest grow stronger. It is not a senseless chaotic spelling or it would not repay study, as our President has pointed out.[1] It is rather an accumulation of spellings, the rules of which, like those of the British Constitution, appear never to be complete or systematically written down. If our spelling were really 'chaotic' we should have to confess ourselves idiots in *stæfcræft* and common decency, for over a thousand years. Instead of which, from Orm onwards, and perhaps earlier, a whole long line of scholars, and others more enthusiastic than scholarly, have studied our use and pronunciation of letters and helped to make the English School of Phonetics.

Let us return to Ælfric to emphasize once more the connexion of grammar with speaking rightly. I would like to quote a few lines from Ælfric's Colloquy, which gives us an idea of the importance of the speaking or utterance of Latin, and presumably of English also:

We children beg thee, oh teacher, to teach us to speak because we are ignorant and speak incorrectly.
What do you want to say?
What do we care what we say, provided it is correct speech and useful and not foolish or bad.

The Colloquy is really a set of dialogues or colloquial lessons around such common things as husbandry, hunting, fishing, the life of a merchant or sailor. Nowadays we should use other subjects for colloquial exercises, but there is the idea. I do not know whether the old teachers used a Book of the Seasons with pictures, but they might easily have done so. There is nothing new under the sun. Not even Gaspey Otto Sauer!

John Hart, the Chester Herald, looks back, as he says himself, from 1569 even to the Conquest. Now let us go forward from Hart to the Restoration period and the great scholars of the Royal Society. There is a continuous tradition, well summarized by one Elisha Coles, 'Schoolmaster in Russel

---

[1] See *Trans. Phil. Soc.*, 1943.

Street by Covent Garden, Teacher of the Tongue to Foreigners—Author of *The Complete English Schoolmaster*, based on the pronunciation of London and Oxford, 1674'. It is written for children and foreigners:

[Masters themselves] are so miserably confounded and utterly unable to reconcile their way of spelling with an English pronunciation. . . . Words should be spelled as they are pronounced.

But for men to teach folk to spell a word one way and then to pronounce it another; what pitiful senseless contradiction is this.

Coles also compiled an English Dictionary explaining

The difficult terms that are used in Divinity, Husbandry, Physick, Phylosophy, Law, Navigation, Mathematicks, Other Arts and Sciences—
containing
Many Thousands of Hard Words (and Proper Names of Places) more than are in any other English Dictionary or Expositor.
together with
The Etymological Derivation of them from their proper Fountains, whether Hebrew, Greek, Latin, French, or any other language,—
In a method more comprehensive, than any that is extant.

Though a lesser man than Dr. Wallis, he criticized him with great justice. Hart emphasized his study of five hundred years of English spelling. Elisha Coles maintains the continuity.

Not that I am ignorant of what's already done. I know the whole succession from Dr. Bulloker to Dr. Skinner; from the smallest volume to the largest folio. I know their differences and their defects. Some are too little, some are too big; some are too plain (stufft with obscenity not to be named) and some so obscure that (instead of expounding others) they have need themselves of an expositor.

There is a clear continuity of studies in all the main topics of interest to phonetics, from the Restoration to the time of Sir William Jones and thence to the glorious earlier days of this Society. Before linking up with Sir William Jones, let us turn to another feature of our School—the invention of systems of shorthand.

The Elizabethan shorthand writers were the forerunners of an incredibly large number of systems of shorthand leading eventually to what we all know as Pitman's. The connexion of Pitman and Phonography with our nineteenth-century school of phonetics is well known, but Bell and Sweet were also students and inventors of shorthand. The technique of modern shorthand is an English invention and has been continually fostered and developed since the time of the great Dr. Timothy Bright.[1]

---

[1] Timothe Bright, Doctor of Physicke, born in Yorkshire in 1551. At Ipswich in 1583-4. [In passing it is interesting to note that Cave Beck, Rector of St. Helen's, Ipswich, was the author of *Universal Character* (1657) (see my *Tongues of Men*, p. 71).] Studied medicine in Cambridge and Paris. At Bart's in 1584. Took Holy Orders and became rector of Methley with Barwick-in-Elmet in 1594. Was often absent and suffered from 'lack of curats'. Practised medicine at the same time. Work on medicine published at Frankfort-on-Main. Played the Irish harp and hated 'a false stringed lute' or 'a badly shaped quill'.

John Wilkins, writing in 1668, notes how 'English shorthand writing was much wondered at by foreigners'. And well he might be interested, as the author of *Real Character*, particularly since he reproduces a page of Chinese characters in his famous book. For Bright's first astonishing book on shorthand was entitled: *Characterie,*[1] *An Art of short, swift and secret writing by Character—Invented by Timothe Bright, Doctor of Physicke*, published in London in the year of the Armada.

Upon consideration of the great use of such a kinde of Writing, I have invented the like: of fewer characters, short, and easie, every Character answering a word: *my invention on meere English without precept or imitation of any*. . . .

Verbatim and secret. [Italics mine.]

'Excelling the writing by letters, and Alphabet, in that, Nations of strange languages may hereby communicate their meaning together in writing, though of sundry tongues. It is reported of the people of China, that they have no other kind, and so traffic together many Provinces of that Kingdom ignorant one of another's speech.'

My purpose at this point, with Bright's notice of Chinese character, is to link up the interest in spelling and pronunciation with the new age of printed books, and with what I have discussed in Chapter V of *The Tongues of Men* entitled 'The Expansion of Europe and the Discovery of Babel', and in the following chapter. In that little book I dealt summarily with a vast subject that has interested me for many years. And what I have been able to do today is only a summary of a main branch of that study. It is during the great period from Elizabeth to the time of Sir William Jones that English linguists joined with the rest of the world and made such weighty contributions that we may take heart again as we review them. Our young men and women are coming back from their voyages of discovery and another revival of learning may well be upon us.

In Chapters V and VI of the book just mentioned, I noticed five main topics in the new cultural situation which arose after the great voyages of discovery:

Left a collection of Italian books on the theory of Music. He discovered an English 'Spaw Fountain' on Haregate Head, recommended it, and went there himself every summer. Knew the Cecils. Wrote *A Treatise of Melancholie*, and his name, with Burton's, supposed to conceal Bacon's authorship.

His *charactery* is beautifully produced in Italian calligraphic style by Jane Seager in *Ten Sybils*. This first lady shorthand writer used vertical columns in Chinese style. In 1589 'Stephen Egerton, his lecture', was 'taken by Characterly'. William Congreve was one of Bright's descendants. See also Paul Friedrich, *Studien zur Englischen Stenographie in Zeitalter Shakespeares*, Koehler, Leipzig, 1914.

[1] Bright probably gave currency to the word. John Hart aforementioned uses the medieval word *carrectes* as distinct from letters. There is an interesting study to be made of the words 'carrectes' and 'characterie' in this connexion (see p. 100).

The word 'Charactery' occurs in the *Merry Wives*—Anne Page says:

'Fairies use flowers for their charactery.'

And in *Julius Caesar*, Act II, Brutus, addressing his wife, says:

'All my engagements I will construe to thee,
All the characterie of my sad brows.'

1. The widening of the linguistic horizon—the beginnings of Egyptian, Indian, and Chinese studies. The rise of polyglot studies and the world-wide collection of facts.
2. The study of exotic alphabets and the casting of exotic types for the new printing presses enabling texts and translations to be multiplied.
3. The linguistic endeavours of the missions (partly noted in 2).
4. The movement for a universal international or auxiliary language, to take the place of Latin.
5. World English.

All these five great cultural movements touched our country, our English scholars, and eventually our School of Phonetics. We were in a way prepared to take a leading part. The realization of how great that part has been is perhaps occluded by an over-valuation of the type of work we associate with Germany during a relatively small period of the nineteenth century. Let us remember four centuries of linguistics before Bopp was born, and the inevitable change in the intellectual climate of Europe which must follow the downfall of Germany.

But back to Dr. Timothe Bright. His shorthand, published in 1588, is the beginning of a long tradition touching phonetics, orthography, and general linguistics, coming down to our own day. And he brings into the story the influence of Chinese writing which is mentioned by Beck,[1] the author of one of the earliest universal languages, and later by Dalgarno and Wilkins.[2] I append a note on the earliest vehicle and channel of contact with Chinese character.[3] The first real information came from the Jesuits in Japan and related to Sino-Japanese. These letters from Japan begin in

---

[1] See note on Bright.   [2] See *Tongues of Men*, chapter v.

[3] See: (i) Cartas que os padres e irmãos da Companhia de Jesus escreverão dos Reynos de Japão et China aos da mesma Companhia da India e Europa, des do anno de 1549 até o de 1580. Printed at Evora by order of Theo. de Bragança, Archbishop of Evora, 1598.

In 1550 they report a big university at Miáco, and mention visits to Bugo or Bungo, Yamáguche, Cangoxima, and Vocoxiura.

Carta do Padre Baltesar Gago de Japão, para os Irmãos da Companhia de Jesu da India es Portugal, Sept. de 1555, reproduces badly written characters for sun, moon, man, and after these the same in rapid cursive writing, which he says are the ones to learn. On page 61 of the above volume, in a letter from Gaspar Vilela, 1557, is an excellent reproduction of Sino-Japanese characters. There is no mention of China, but two pages are given to the characters. This is the earliest trace of such characters in any Western document I have yet met with and I believe considerably antedates previous notices.

(ii) Rerum a societate Jesu in oriente gestarum volumen. Coloniae 1574.

Reports Jesuits at Sangium insula and St. Francis Xavier's mission to Cangoxima and Miáci in 1569 aided by a Japanese who spoke Portuguese. On page 451 of this Cologne publication of 1574 there is reproduced 'spec. quoddam litterarum vocumque Japonicarum desumptum e Regis Bungi Diplomate'.

(iii) There was published in 1603, Vocabulario da lingoa de IAPAM com a declaração em Portugues, feito por alguns padres e irmãos da Companhia de JESU.

Com licença do ordinario, et Superiores em Nangasaqui no Collegio de Japam da C°. de Jesus—MDCIII. This book runs into 400 pages since equivalents are given both in Latin and Portuguese. Special attention is drawn to *Cana*, and to the enormous borrowings of 'caracteres da China'.

(iv) In the Bodleian Library there is a native Japanese Gojūon Manual printed in Osaka in the year 1617 of our era.

1550 and were printed and circulated. The climax was the visit of princely ambassadors from three kings of Japan to render homage to Gregory XIII in 1585. Details of their visit make thrilling reading in these days.[1] Of the writing of the Chinese, Bright says:

Their Characters are very long and harde to make, that a dousen of mine may be written as soone as one of theirs. Besides, they wanting an Alphabet, fal into an infinite number, which is a thing that greatlie chargeth the memory, and may discourage the learner. . . .

And this my invention being altoghether of English yield, where your Majestie is the Ladie of the Soyle, it appertayneth of right to you onely. . . .

My invention which wanteth little to equal it, with that old devise of Ciceroes, but your Majestie's allowance and Cicero's name. [The learning of Characterie involved two things:]

(i) Making of the Character.
(ii) Value and signification,

with a pricke at every breathing or pause.

Thou mayest attaine unto it, if thou wilt but one moneth take paines therein and by continuance of another moneth mayest thou attaine to great readinesse.

As a model of good Charactery, Bright published the Epistle to Titus. The characters are written vertically from top to bottom in Chinese fashion. They were grammatically representative in that the plural of a character was by context—2, plus the character for man, meant two men— or the plural could be represented by a dot. 'Tence' was also shown by 'prickes', the time to come was shown by a 'pricke' on the right side. He classified his words in categories like 'Primitives' and 'Derivatives', e.g. vertue and vertuous, and marked the derivative as an adjectival word with a grammatical mark. He used the ordinary character for 'ship', i.e. a sea-going vessel, as a nominal mark to the right of such words as 'friend' and 'neighbour', so that the character for 'neighbour' with the 'ship'-character alongside read 'neighbourhood'.

He was the first to classify his words by sense, in the ideological and Chinese manner, and in this way through Wilkins and the later introduction

---

[1] See: (i) Choses diverses des ambassadeurs de trois Roys de Iapon qui n'agueires venuz à Romme, rendirent obeissance au nom de leurs maistres et seigneurs, à Gregoire XIII souverain Pasteur de l'Église, à Louvain, 23 Mars, 1585.

There were two ambassadors, Mantius and Michel, representing the King of Fiunga, the King of Arima, and the Prince of Omura. Their letters were translated from Japanese into Italian and Latin and were publicly read. Then one Gaspar Gonsalvo made a long speech of welcome and appreciation in which the Japanese were referred to as 'gens d'esprit et adonnés à la guerre'. He referred to their faces, features, strange dress, and 'finalement tant par les yeulx que par les oreilles ils puysoient leur langage non plus ouy'. 'Et ceux qui jamais de nulle memoire d'homme (que je puisse scavoir) n'ont octroyé victoire aux armes de leurs ennemis externes.' Their long journey, which took three years, is fully described. They, no doubt remembering that a Pope Gregory had received the conversion of England, made the very first comparison of the Japanese Islanders at the far end of Asia with the British Islanders at the far end of Europe. 'The first come to render homage to the Holy Father, the others one could only pray for.'

of Sanskrit dictionaries, the tradition gave us Roget's Thesaurus and other things like it in the nineteenth century. I will quote one example of Bright's shorthand sense. In the economy of strokes he suggested pairing words by differences, and said:

Leave the vowel and take that which may make the difference—as *straight* and *strain*.

Since 1588 there has been a continuous traditional interest in Characterie, Universal Alphabets, Spelling Reform, and Shorthand. Dalgarno, one of the seventeenth-century rationalists, tried all these and produced an alphabet for the Deaf and Dumb as well, so he is in several streams at once as it were. Wilkins is the best known of that group but is not necessarily the most important. He was the principal spokesman, perhaps.

Then in the eighteenth century we had Gurney, Byrom, Blanchard, and Taylor, and in the nineteenth century the great Pitman.

I need say very little more about shorthand now that I have mentioned Pitman. He is, by right of genius and work—and as the last great man in a long line of distinguished men beginning with Timothe Bright—one of the makers of the English School of Phonetics. In August 1937 I received the following letter from the Isaac Pitman of today:

Dear Sir,

I am sending you, as a member of the International Phonetic Association, a copy of the Souvenir Booklet which has been brought out in commemoration of the Centenary of the invention by my Grandfather of 'Phonography'.

It is written by Mr. D. Abercrombie, a member of the Association, and contains a preface by Professor Lloyd-James, and is on a subject which is presumably of great interest to you.

I hope you will accept it with my best wishes.

Yours sincerely,
I. J. PITMAN.

Mr. Abercrombie by this time no doubt realizes that the origins and reaches of the English schools of shorthand go far back in our history. It is not true that all modern phonetic transcription derives from the work of Pitman and Ellis, nor that many characters, such as ʒ, ʃ, and ŋ, were original with them.

It is this invention of new letters to serve the needs of new spelling or transcription which I wish next to notice.

In the ancient days there were the runes and letters of Old English, later the devices and inventions of Orm. In my *Tongues of Men* I emphasized the importance of the study of alphabets and letters in the early stages of all linguistic endeavour. This applies always and everywhere. Sir Thomas Smith, aforementioned, Secretary of State, wrote his *Alphabetum Anglicum* in 1568. It consisted of thirty-four letters, including four Greek and three Old English.

Smith's *Alphabetum Anglicum* was published *before the great series of exotic alphabet studies* issued by the Propaganda Fide,[1] and is one more illustration of our common saying that charity begins at home. Sir Thomas Smith's *Alphabetum Anglicum* was a very early expression of the spelling and printing problems of the new age resulting from the spread of literacy and the multiplication of books. As you would expect from the story I have already told, we produced a great scholar and public servant who showed English interest in such practical matters, and set an example widely followed on the Continent. He was the Elizabethan 'Sir William Jones'.

The main things to remember about his attitude to letters are:

1. He devised his alphabet as a systematic spelling of the English Language he used, and gave it the European name of *Alphabetum Anglicum*. He wrote his treatise in Latin to give English to all who could read Latin.

2. He made use of those roman letters which became superfluous when he approached the language phonetically, and thus, as we have seen, used *k* and *c* systematically. His use of *c* was an excellent step forward.

3. He drew on other alphabets well known to him and to others—Greek and Old and Middle English.

4. His reputation and prestige were high and his influence at home and abroad considerable. Was he not Secretary to the Great Queen?

Bullokar (1580) aforementioned was prolific in typography, and invented eighty new sorts, and a multitude of letters with diacritics and marks, including the cedilla. He goes out of his way to seek the advice of his printer and commends the skill of the graver and founder. He gives the new letters names, so with due attention he makes sure of the *nomen* and the *figura*— but it is the *potestas* which weighs most and in this matter we must bend a modest head. So do not let us blame him.

Bullokar touches five main topics of interest to all phoneticians: (i) he gives a description of pronunciation, (ii) discusses problems of transcription, (iii) looks at spelling reform and typographical invention, (iv) connects all these with grammar, and (v) sees the importance of English for foreigners. 'What can be more important than speech?' he asks, and 'what is liker to be of longer continuance than letters, which give knowledge without speech, and yet be a pathway to speech?'

For the *figurae* of Sir Thomas Smith and Bullokar's books, and indeed for all of them to come, reference must be made to the original pages. May I suggest that one of our phoneticians should take up this line of development and devote a special study to it? I should welcome anyone who would offer to do it.[2]

Queen Elizabeth tried Bullokar's spelling in a letter to Lord Burghley.[3] But then, she tried most things.

---

[1] *Alphabetum Ibericum sive Georgianum*, 1629. *Alphabetum Coptum*, 1630. *Alphabetum Aethiopicum sive Abyssinum*, 1631, &c., &c.

[2] Mr. David Abercrombie (see p. 106) is engaged on a history of phonetic transcription, in which I hope there will be reproductions of most of the earlier contributions to typographical experiment.

[3] See Strype's *Annals*, vol. iv, p. 77.

The interest of subsequent grammarians in new letters was continuous down to our time.

Charles Butler, author of *The English Grammar, or the Institution of Letters, Syllables and words in the English Tongue*, Oxford, 1633, linked the studies of grammar, music, and gymnastics, believing that the exercise of the limbs and the ordering of the voice in speech and song were complementary. He quotes Quintilian and the Venerable Bede in support of this view. Hebrew, he says, has preference as the original language, but 'the Teutonick (whereof the English is a dialect) being the language of the unconquered Conquerors hath continued from the confusion till this day'. He quotes Sir Thomas Smith, and is happy that the Welsh are not so cursed with imperfection and uncertainty of writing. He invented several good letters, which are still used in transcription, and he employed upside down and reversed letters: e.g. ꝺ for θ.

William Holder, Doctor of Divinity and Fellow of the Royal Society, invented at least two vowel symbols still in common use. His book, to my mind, is one of the most interesting in the early history of phonetics. It is entitled *The Elements of Speech, an Essay of Enquiry into the natural Production of Letters, with an Appendix concerning persons deaf and dumb*. It was published in 1669, after some delay of the manuscript by interested rivals in the group of scholars who were to become the first Fellows of the Royal Society. Holder's book was reprinted by Pitman in 1850 and 1865. It is surprisingly modern, and it is not to be wondered at that Wallis and others endeavoured to delay and even suppress it. Holder realized the obscurity of the sounds of speech and how 'troublesome and laborious' was the Art of Orthography. He did not think much of existing books on the subject.

I have refrained to look into them, for fear of being led away by other men's fancies; whereas I rather chose to consult Nature at hand.

Holder gives an excellent account of the organs of speech, and the following definition of consonants:

But where there is an appulse[1] of one organ to another, the letters which are so framed are consonants. Again the appulse is either plenary and occluse, so as wholly to preclude all passage of breath or voice through the mouth, or else partial and pervious so as to give them some passage out of the mouth—producing lisping, hissing, or jarring. The nature of consonants being framed by appulse, is much easier to be discerned than that of vowels.

His descriptions of the sounds are quite good even judged by present-day standards, and his instructions for the production of laterals, including Welsh ll, surprisingly accurate. He noticed the stop made 'by closing the larynx', 'of some affinity to *k*', and treated this glottal stop and **h** together.

---

[1] Martianus Capella (flourished about 470 A.D. in Carthage) describes Latin D as follows: *appulsu linguae circa superiores dentes innascitur*, Q, *appulsu palati ore restricto*, and T, *appulsu linguae dentibusque inpulsis extruditur.*

He noted pronunciations of voiced consonants that ended 'spirital' (unvoiced). His attempt to establish a 'series of the vowels according to their degrees of aperture' anticipated work in our own day. He even suggested the notion of the syllable as 'determined by alternation of appulse and aperture'. 'Speech is a mixture of apertures and appulses.' 'The so-called diphthongs are, as I conceive, syllables.' 'Accent and emphasis are much confounded.' 'The sense of hearing is only partly understood.' Whether Wallis and other contemporaries really understood Holder is open to question. They treated him very shabbily.

From Holder through Sir William Jones to the Bells, Ellis, Pitman, Sweet, and men we have known personally, there is continuity of interest in all the aspects of phonetics mentioned, including the need for new letters and all manner of typographical invention. Of them all, I find Ellis and Melville Bell rather self-centred, not to say self-opinionated, and am of the opinion that they have been over-rated. However, Bell was by profession a *performer*, and perhaps his performance was very much better than his script. I do not propose to attempt a closer examination without printed examples, but that, I hope, will be done by someone else. The time has come to put Wallis, Ellis, and Bell in their proper places.

As you have just seen, professors and university dons got hold of our subject about the middle of the seventeenth century. In the words of a contemporary, 'many others of the most inquisitive persons in Oxford met weekly'. Great things came of these meetings, but in our own subject the worst side of university life—petty jealousies and rivalries, plagiarism and forestalling—were such that Dr. John Wallis eventually produced thirty-three closely printed pages to defend himself, to attempt to justify indefensible behaviour, and at the same time to cover Holder with ridicule. Wallis's own work makes a great show of bits of Arabic and Hebrew as well as of Greek and Welsh, and refers somewhat childishly to the Cambro-Britanni, but phonetically he is something of a puzzle. He proudly claims that he was the first to add the nostrils to the organs of speech, and said:

> The difference of *f* and *v* lying, not in the lips or larynx, but in the nostrils.

Unless he really had something there and in similar remarks which are too deep for me, I am of opinion that phonetic observations made by him should be treated with caution.

It took nearly two hundred years for some justice to be done to Dr. Holder, and having seen the records of the Restoration rivals, I am happy that so great a man as Pitman should have honoured an original thinker much in advance of his time, who was so ill-used by Professor Wallis and other 'inquisitive persons' in Oxford.

Another contemporary genius of the group, Dalgarno,[1] was also shabbily

---

[1] 'This enterprise of Mr. Dalgarno (i.e. Universal Character) gave occasion to Dr. Wilkins to pursue the same design.' From a report to the Royal Society. See 'The Real Character of Bishop Wilkins', by E. N. da C. Andrade, F.R.S., *Annals of Science*, vol. i, no. 1, 1936.

treated by the said 'inquisitive persons'. Charles II, however, hearing of this, granted him a pension and honourable mention in the award.

Dalgarno and Holder both interested themselves in teaching the deaf to speak, and this interest continues right through our long line of workers to the Bells. Alexander Graham Bell used his father's Visible Speech in the training of teachers of the deaf at the Volta bureau. This interest in hearing, not forgetting the hard of hearing, is still a major interest of the London School. It is in the seventeenth century and in the Royal Society group that emphasis is first laid on the sensory disciplines, and especially on hearing, training the ear, the eye, and close visual observation and introspective observation of the organs of speech and the mechanism of utterance. Holder is remarkably modern, and I think there are still little points of interest to us in this book with the very modern title *The Elements of Speech*.

Now let us turn to Sir William Jones, usually described in library catalogues as The Orientalist. We cannot add to the greatness of Sir William Jones by including him as one of the makers of the English School of Phonetics. I hope I do him no harm. For his letters and writings leave us in no doubt that he rather despised scholars who were absorbed in languages for their own sake. 'A mere linguist' was a word-mongering bore.

Nevertheless, Sir William Jones had a shot at a phonetic transcription of English which you may see either in his works or in A. J. Ellis. Ellis, another Welshman, seems to have given great attention to Jones's excellent account and transcription of the Devanagari syllabary, and he and Murray and other English pioneers spent hours listening, for example, to Mr. K. G. Gupta and Mr. Mookerjee making Indian sounds, and discussing Indian views on phonetics. There is an atmosphere of discovery in exotic regions in all this part of Ellis's work, and to all of us who value sources it will be of the greatest significance that Jones and Ellis link us up with an eastern source of phonetics, far more competent than anything hitherto produced in the West. Not only that. For the first time in this country the Roman alphabet really meets the Arabic, Persian, and Indian systems of writing, and the age-old trinity of *nomen, figura*, and *potestas* severely tested.

Each of the Arabic characters has a distinctive *nomen*. In Greek some of these survive. In the Roman alphabet, the *nomen* is generally derived from the *potestas*. In the Devanagari character we meet with a syllabary arranged according to phonetic principles in a regular phonetic order and the *nomen* of a character, under certain rules of usage, *is* the *potestas*. The importance of these new facts plainly presented by Sir William Jones was never fully realized by the nineteenth-century phoneticians. Sweet was too near to Ellis and Bell, and too specialized in his outlook to appreciate the epoch-making importance of Sir William Jones in the further development of the English School of Phonetics. Melville Bell was a small man. Ellis was more prolific than profound, or in other words, his standards of accuracy and of ready intelligibility were not adequate for the scale of his experiments in letters and transcriptions.

Ellis, Bell, and the early nineteenth-century workers in phonetics had studied most of the work we have so far noticed. Of John Hart's *Orthographie, conteyning the due Order and Reason, howe to write or paint the Image of Mannes Voice, most like to the Life or Nature*, Ellis remarks: 'a most disappointing book'. He made fun of the great Sir Thomas Smith, and had no great opinion of Holder's *Elements*.

The most epoch-making work between that of the Restoration Royal Society group and Sweet's real foundation of the School was the immense stimulus given to phonetics and general linguistics by Sir William Jones.[1] Without the Indian grammarians and phoneticians whom he introduced and recommended to us, it is difficult to imagine our nineteenth-century school of phonetics.

Ellis links up with another great Orientalist, Whitney, who had translated parts of Sanskrit phonetic treatises, and who had published a Unitary Alphabet in the *Journal* of the American Orthographic Society.[2] It is interesting to find Ellis, often inaccurate himself, noting the phonetic clumsiness of Bopp and correcting descriptions of the so-called cerebral consonants. Several modern books which notice Indian sounds might well have been amended in the light of these very early observations. Ellis devotes quite a number of pages and many footnotes to the Devanagari syllabary, and to Indian sounds, which is only what you would expect of a phonetician who knew what Sir William Jones had opened up.

While Charles Wilkins invented and cast types of the Devanagari, Bengali, and Persian character, Sir William Jones felt the great need of a proper use of the roman alphabet in Oriental studies.[3] He produced a special dissertation as President of the Asiatic Society of Bengal on 'The Orthography of Asiatic Words in Roman Letters'. His chart of suggested symbols for the transliteration of the Devanagari, with the addition of letters for Arabic and Persian, is the first presentation of what may be called a phonetic alphabet on such a scale. He finds the Arabic alphabet almost perfect for Arabic itself:

Not a letter could be added or taken away without manifest inconvenience. The same may indubitably be said of the Dévanágari system, which, as it is more naturally arranged than any other, shall here be the standard of my particular

[1] In September 1946 a conference of British Orientalists was held at University College, Oxford, to commemorate the bicentenary of his birth. All the central problems of present-day Oriental studies were discussed, and Sir William Jones was present in them all, including the session in which spoken language and problems of transcription were discussed. In this modest paper I cannot do full justice to the work of our greatest Orientalist, who gave us an introduction to Indian phonetics. Modern grammar and phonetics are founded on the Indian sciences.
[2] Vol. 8, p. 372.
[3] This subject was discussed at the Sir William Jones Bi-Centenary Conference of British Orientalists in September 1946.

observations on Asiatic letters. Our English alphabet and orthography are disgracefully and almost ridiculously imperfect.

He aims at using diacritics *common in Europe* rather than new letters—and symbols from 'fluxions' or mathematics—so as to equal the Devanagari itself in precision and clearness.

The following are extracts from Sir William Jones's comments on the problem:

1. For the expression of Arabian, Indian and Persian words in characters generally used among *Europeans*—almost every writer in those circumstances has a method of notation peculiar to himself; but none had yet appeared in the form of a complete system; so that each original sound may be rendered invariably by one appropriate symbol, conformably to the natural order of articulation, and with a due regard to the primitive power of the Roman alphabet, which modern Europe has in general adopted.

2. There are *two ways* of exhibiting Asiatic words in our letters, founded on principles nearly opposite—

The first professes to regard chiefly the pronunciation—and this is unquestionably useful, as far as it can be pursued. But new sounds are very inadequately presented to a sense not formed to receive them; and the reader must in the end be left to pronounce many letters and syllables precariously.

Beside, that by this mode or orthography all grammatical analogy is destroyed, simple sounds are represented by double characters, vowels of one denomination stand for those of another; and possibly with all our labour we perpetuate a provincial or inelegant pronunciation.

3. The second system of Asiatic Orthography consists of rendering letter for letter and so long as this mode proceeds by unvaried rules, it seems clearly entitled to preference. (And when the native character is mainly regular in sound, what could be better?)

Then Sir William expresses the following opinion, which will interest all English phoneticians who have faced the practical problems of transcription:

4. If anything dissatisfies me . . . it is the use of double letters for the long vowels (which might, however, be justified) and the frequent intermixture of Italick with Roman letters in the same word; which both in writing and printing must be very inconvenient.

He is very near us in such remarks as:

5. The omission of a long mark denotes the short mark if there are only two kinds.

Writers of theses please note:

6. It is *superfluous to discourse* on the organs of speech, which have been a thousand times dissected, and as often described by musicians or anatomists, and the several *powers* of which every man may perceive either by the touch or by sight—using a mirror.

7. *All things abound with error,* as the old searchers for truth remarked with despondence; but it is really deplorable that our first step from total ignorance, should be into gross inaccuracy, and that we should begin our education in England with learning to read *the five vowels,* two of which, as we are taught to pronounce them, are clearly diphthongs.

After which he attempts to describe ten vowels, and then says:

There are numberless gradations, a hundred diphthongs and a thousand triphthongs.

A perfect system of letters ought to contain one specifick symbol for every sound used in pronouncing the language to which they belonged.

Though we celebrated the bicentenary of the birth of Sir William Jones in 1946, we cannot yet claim to have developed a school of phonetics able to cope with the tongues of Asia and Africa. One would have thought the classical and medieval doctrines of the roman alphabet would have broken down by now, a century and a half after the above sentences were written. But no, disputation continues, especially in America, about *figura* and *potestas,* even about *nomen,* and most of it with reference to the employment of roman letters. The use of the roman alphabet is the principal technical aid in the study and teaching of Oriental languages. But the principles and methods of its employment must not be hampered by medieval philosophy.

The most interesting contribution of Sir William Jones to nineteenth-century phonetics is the following:

Letters by which labials are denoted, represent in most alphabets the curvature of one lip or both; and a *natural character* (italics Jones's) for all articulate sounds might easily be agreed on, if nations would agree on anything generally beneficial, by delineating the several organs of speech in the act of articulation, selecting from each a distinct and elegant outline.

The fact that Ellis was particularly interested in the phonetic observations of Sir William Jones, and that he was closely associated with Alexander Melville Bell, and that Bell studied for three years in the British Museum,[1] suggests to me that Bell got the idea of Visible Speech from Jones.

Sir William Jones's contribution to the study of spelling, transcription, and transliteration, together with his wise observations on phonetics, was

---

[1] *Alexander Melville Bell*: Some Memories, with fragments from a Pupil's notebook. Published by the School of Expression, Boston, 1906, p. 13:

'In answer to one of my letters to Professor Melville Bell, in which I asked him regarding books of Elocution, and especially regarding those in the British Museum, he wrote, among other things:

' "From 1840–1843, when I was preparing for an independent professional career, I sought to supplement the 'family knowledge' which I possessed, by the study of all the books I could find by predecessors in the profession. But so far as I could discover, there did not then exist in print any complete directory on the subject. The processes of articulation did not seem to have been practically treated by any author. I was thus led by original investigation from my own organs and those of my pupils. I cannot, therefore, direct you to any works of earlier date containing more than hints and general observations." '

the inspiration for a great deal of work in England, Germany, and America. Sir Charles Trevelyan did a great deal to help this forward. Two missionary societies of London, members of the Berlin Academy, and other interested persons co-operated to produce the Lepsius Standard Alphabet.[1] The first part of the book gives a full account of the origin and development of this work. The bringing in of continental scholars by the British missions had far-reaching consequences, not all of them good. It also led to the collaboration of British scholars in continental publications, and some work which might have been directed in England became associated with foreign publications.

The influence of the English School was felt in France during the Napoleonic Wars partly through Alexander Hamilton,[2] of the Bengal group, who was caught in France. C. T. Volney, who founded the Prix Volney, saw the importance of transcription and transliteration as a result of the Egyptian expedition and he complained bitterly 'de notre inexpérience, permettez moi de dire nationale, et de notre infériorité, sur ces questions relativement aux étrangers'. In 1818 appeared his treatise *L'Alphabet Européen appliqué aux Langues Asiatiques*. This title expresses much more than the book contains. The French have not been very successful in their transcriptions and it is a pity to have to remind them that the French Academy substituted exercises on comparative philology for Volney's express wish that his legacy should be for the encouragement of 'tout travail tendant à donner suite et exécution à une méthode de transcrire les langues asiatiques en lettres européennes'. Volney invented a few letters which have been adopted by phoneticians since.

The phonetic and alphabetic work of the Americans in the eighteenth and early nineteenth centuries is not to be overlooked. I therefore just mention Franklin and Webster and Whitney in this connexion. But the most interesting American was Samuel Haldeman,[3] a great admirer of Sir William Jones,[4] 'the purest rhymer' known to him.[5] Realizing his natural ability, Haldeman came to London to find colleagues and worked

---

[1] 2nd edition, London, 1863.
[2] R. W. Chambers and F. Norman, 'Alexander Hamilton and the Beginnings of Comparative Philology', *Studies in English Philology*, Univ. of Minnesota Press.
[3] *Samuel Haldeman* (see *Dictionary of American Biography*). Of Swiss descent; great-grandfather in the American Revolution. A great-uncle was in the British Army and was the first Governor-General of Canada. Natural history his main interest. Haldeman's sense of hearing was so acute that he could differentiate the sounds emitted by insects; he wrote on the organs of sound in the lepidoptera. Studied American Indian dialects exhaustively, becoming the recognized authority on this subject, and devoted much labour to English, Chinese, and other languages. First Professor of Comparative Philology at the University of Pennsylvania, after being Professor of Zoology and Natural History. In 1858 he won, in competition with eighteen European scholars, a prize of £100 offered by Sir Walter Calverley Trevelyan, a distinguished naturalist, President of the Phonetic Society of Great Britain, for his essay on Analytical Orthography (*Transactions of American Philosophical Society*). See also 'Atlantic Linguistics', Chapter 12.
[4] An earlier American admirer of Sir William Jones, John Pickering, published *An Essay on a Uniform Orthography for the Indian Languages of N. America* in 1820.
[5] Cf. R. M. Hewitt's *Harmonious Jones*, English Association, 1942.

THE ENGLISH SCHOOL OF PHONETICS

with Ellis and Bell, and afterwards on the Continent. He was one of the founders of modern Amerindian linguistics which would be impossible without phonetics of the kind which developed first in this country, where the leading exponents were extending their influence.[1]

Haldeman severely criticized Ellis's *Essentials of Phonetics*, complaining especially that the alphabetic portion was so corrupt as to be useless. He also discusses the work of Volney, Max Müller, and Lepsius, records a 'dental clack' in an American language, and makes the observation that when linguists commit grave errors in the uses of the speech organs which can be seen and felt, in addition to the sounds being heard, we may well doubt the analysis of sounds formed out of sight, in the depths of the fauces. That reminds one of Dr. John Wallis and the nostrils differentiating **f** and **v**. Haldeman's report makes very good reading, and I imagine Sapir must have known page 6 of the Report well, since he used some of the ideas and one of the examples there given. Haldeman had studied the work of Castrén, Sjögren, Schunjitsch, Lepsius, and other lesser-known phoneticians and alphabeticians, reproducing some very interesting new letters from various sources. Sjögren had devised useful single letters, based on the Russian alphabet, for aspirated plosives. Haldeman recommended the marking of the main accent above and the secondary accent below, and experimented with inverted and reversed letters. He offered sensible criticism of Lepsius, especially of his poor phonetics, and seems to have been of the opinion that the missionaries knew no better, and certainly did not know when Lepsius was compromising science to please them.

Since Haldeman worked in close association with the English School, and had the reputation of being an acute observer, further extracts from his work are of present interest. Wisely he pointed out that ə: and ə 'do not yield in distinctness to any of the vowels'. He saw that good phonetics must recognize the value for certain languages of 'alphabets of a more or less syllabic character', in which 'a consonant position and a vowel position of the organs' are regarded 'as in a manner constituting a unitary element'.

All students of exotic or unwritten languages should ponder the following:

The difficulty of pronouncing, appreciating, locating, explaining, and writing down the various phases of speech is so great, and there are so many sources of error, that we must be more cautious in accepting statements here, than in other sciences of observation, few having as much education in this branch as would be required to make a chemist or a musician; or to enable a singer to write down

---

[1] See especially his *Report on the Present State of our Knowledge of Linguistic Ethnology, Made to the American Association for the Advancement of Science, August, 1856*. Professor S. S. Haldeman, published for the Association by Joseph Lovering, Permanent Secretary, 1856.
After the Report was presented to the Association, the author was commissioned to continue the subject in a further report, 'upon a system of alphabetic notation adapted to American and exotic languages'.

a song properly, even in a notation of his own invention. We cannot even trust an observer who claims for himself a good ear. The Reporter is willing that his assertions be received with similar caution.

He pointed out that most of the simple facts of speech had been *long known in England*, certainly since Dr. Holder's *Elements of Speech*. Among detailed observations of English, he avers that syllabic fricatives were common in such words as **misz̧** and **horsz̧**, comparing their syllabic quality and frequency of occurrence with German **v'r-lass'n** and **v'r-der-b'n**.

His view of Dr. Wallis agrees with my own estimate. Haldeman points out that though Wallis knew Welsh and bits of other languages, he was not nearly so accurate or modern as Holder. Haldeman wrote on Amerindian languages and also a work on the *Elements of Latin Pronunciation* (1851), intended as a move towards a general international alphabet.

Having carried the influence of the English School through Sir William Jones to the Continent and America, the story is almost told. The last chapter is a brief summary of the continuity of the work of the English School from Sir William Jones through Ellis, the Bells, Murray, Prince Bonaparte, Pitman, to Joseph Wright and the great Sweet, and thus ending where I began.

The building up of the English School of Phonetics as Sweet understood the phrase can be followed in the transactions of the Society between 1860 and 1880. This is fairly recent history authentically recorded in our own transactions. Nevertheless, a few reminders of those days is not out of place, if they help us to take our bearings and give us confidence on our course.

For the Bells, the following biographical and bibliographical details are merely listed. They speak for themselves. The grandfather, Alexander Bell (1790–1865), married a daughter of a surgeon in the Navy. Her mother was a musician and painter. Alexander Bell advertised 'the means to effect a complete and permanent removal of all vocal obstructions at moderate charges. No charge till impediment removed.' He also advertised the establishments for similar purposes conducted by his sons in Dublin and Edinburgh. He advertises himself as the author of:

1. Principles of Simultaneous Reading adapted for classes of five hundred or one thousand pupils. London, 1842. Mr. Bell's Elocution System will impart more practical power than can be obtained in thrice that number of lessons from any other mode of instruction.

2. Public Reading, The causes of its defects and the certain means for their removal, dedicated to the Clergy, M.P.'s, and Barristers, and all public speakers.

ALEXANDER MELVILLE BELL: 1819–1905, was a son of the above, and the following notes indicate his career.

American[1] educationist, b. Edinburgh, Scotland, became an American citizen at age of seventy-eight.

[1] *Dictionary of American Biography.*

Educated at home; studied under and became principal assistant to his father, Alexander Bell, an authority on phonetics and defective speech. Family profession: science of correct speech.

1843–65: Lectured on elocution at the University of Edinburgh (elder brother Professor of Elocution in Dublin);

1865–70 at University of London; public readings of Shakespeare and Dickens in London. In 1868, 1870, and 1871 he lectured in the Lowell Institute Course in Boston. In 1870 he became a lecturer on philology at Queen's College, Kingston, Ontario.

In 1881 he moved to Washington, D.C., where he devoted himself to education of deaf mutes by the 'visible speech' method of orthoepy, 'Physiological Phonetics'. Removed mystery in Speech Defect work, and denounced quackery.

Works:
Steno-Phonography, 1852.
Letters and Sounds, 1858.
Principles of Speech and Dictionary of Sounds, 1863.
Visible Speech, the Science of Universal Alphabetics, 1867.[1]
Sounds and Their Relations, 1881.
A Popular Manual of Visible Speech and Vocall Physiology, 1889.
The Science of Speech, 1897.
The Fundamentals of Elocution, 1899.
See John Hitz: *Alexander Melville Bell*, Washington, 1906.

The 'professional card' of Alexander Melville Bell:

Single Lessons, 1 guinea. Twelve Lessons, 10 guineas.

Visible Speech: Six Lessons, 3 guineas.

I. Stammering and Stuttering.

II. Defects of Articulation.

III. Elocution.

IV. Universal Alphabetics.

Modulated Whisper (Scale of Lingual Vowels)

Course of Diagrams and detailed schematic technique with schematic terminology.

[1] A Scottish clergyman, and an intimate friend of Professor Bell, the Rev. David Macrea, has given an account of the great discovery of Visible Speech:
'I happened to be at his house on the memorable night when, busy in his den, there flashed upon him the idea of a physiological alphabet which would furnish to the eye a complete guide to the production of any oral sound by showing in the very forms of the letter the position and action of the organs of speech which its production required. It was the end toward which years of thought and study had been bringing him, but all the same, it came upon him like a sudden revelation, as a landscape might flash upon the vision of a man emerging from a forest. He took me into his den to tell me about it, and all that evening I could detect signs in his eye and voice of the exultation he was trying to suppress.'
This is a different story from the suggestion made on p. 113.

The title-page of

VISIBLE SPEECH
The Science of Universal Alphabetics
or
Self-Interpreting Physiological Letters
for the writing of
All Languages in one alphabet
illustrated by
Tables, Diagrams and Examples

by

ALEXANDER MELVILLE BELL,
Professor of Vocal Physiology,
Lecturer on Elocution in University College, London.
Inaugural Edition.
Simpkins Marshall & Co.,
Tribune NY.
1867.
15/-.

Melville Bell pressed his invention of Visible Speech on the government of the day:

VISIBLE SPEECH
System under Copyright.
An invention.

I wish to put on record here a statement of the facts concerning my offer of the Invention to the British Government, and the reception of that offer.

Even the idea which it realizes is entirely new, the idea, namely, of representing the mechanism of speech sounds in their alphabetical symbols.

He expected a Royal Commission, and appealed to the Prime Minister, receiving the following reply:

10, Downing Street, Whitehall, February 12, 1867.

Sir,

I am directed by Lord Derby to acknowledge the receipt of your letter of the 8th inst., and to inform you that there are no public funds from which he can make you the grant you desire.

I have the honour to be, Sir,
Your obedient Servant,
W. P. TALBOT.

A. Melville Bell, Esq.

At Alphabetic Conferences in London in 1854, under the presidency of Chevalier Bunsen, Prussian Ambassador, it was agreed that:

It would be useless and impossible to attempt to find for each possible variety of sound, a different graphic sign.

Bell's comment was:

Nevertheless these learned men might be mistaken.

He claimed that Visible Speech was completely adequate:

And will probably be found to require no *additions* or alterations however *extended* its uses may become. (Italics Bell's.)

ALEXANDER GRAHAM BELL: 1847-1922.

American[1] inventor and physicist; inventor of the telephone.

Son of Alexander Melville Bell, b. Edinburgh; educated MacLarens Academy and Royal High School, Elgin, matriculated at University College; University of London and University of Edinburgh. Attended courses in Anatomy and Physiology 1868-70. Officiated for his father, and then full partnership in the work in London. Bad health. Canada in 1870; Boston, 1872—training teachers of deaf and teaching mechanics of speech. Professor of vocal physiology in Boston.

From Elgin on 24 November 1865, first piece of scientific work was a letter to his father on resonance pitches of mouth cavities during utterance of vowel sounds.

Spent one year with his grandfather, Alexander Bell. Father sent him to A. J. Ellis, who put him on to Helmholtz and physics. This work was the basis of his telephone and electric communications inventions.

1876. Exhibited in Boston an apparatus embodying the results of his studies in the transmission of sound by electricity, and this invention, with improvements and modifications, constitutes the modern telephone.

Also invented the photophone for transmission of sound by vibrations of light, and phonographic apparatus. He invented an improved recorder and both the flat wax record and wax cylinder record, and reproducer. Patents 1886 sold to the American Gramophone Company.

Like Sweet, was interested in flying. Founded Aerial Experiment Association. Invented a motor boat—speed 75 m.p.h.

1915. Opened the first transcontinental telephone line from New York to San Francisco.

Became an American citizen, but always loved Scotland; had a large estate in Nova Scotia. Died in 1922, Nova Scotia.

There is no need to remind the Society of Sweet's work or of his influence on Continental scholarship. But in view of the revival of learning which appears to be coming in this country, and the renewal of our forces, I would like to conclude with two quotations—firstly from Sweet's letter to the Vice-Chancellor of Oxford University in 1902:

My own subject, Phonetics, is one which is useless by itself, while at the same time it is the foundation of all study of language, whether theoretical or practical.

The general theoretical side of the study of language is at present represented in the University by the Professorship of Comparative Philology. This term is ambiguous. If we identify it with Comparative Aryan Grammar, there ought to be another Professorship of the Science of Language (philosophical grammar, etc.). . . .

[1] *Dictionary of American Biography.*

The Readership deals with pronunciation in general, and with special reference to such languages as English, French, Latin; methods of studying languages from a phonetic point of view; history of sound changes, comparative phonology, and methods of investigation in these subjects; methods of dealing phonetically with dialects and unwritten forms of speech (for missionaries, etc.); phonetic shorthand.

We want (1) A School of Modern Languages in the sense of the practical study of languages in general. (2) Restoration of the Professorship of Modern Languages, with the same extension of scope.

And secondly from his presidential address in 1877:

Our tendency is not so much toward the antiquarian philology and text-criticism in which German scholars have done so much, as towards the observation *of the phenomena of living languages* . . . the real strength and originality of English work lies . . . in phonology and dialectology. Our aim ought clearly to be, while assimilating the methods and results of German work, to concentrate our energies mainly on what may be called 'living philology'. The vastness of our Empire, which brings us in contact with innumerable languages, alone forces us incessantly to grapple with the difficulties of spoken, often also unwritten, languages. We ought to be able to send out yearly hundreds of thoroughly and specially trained young men. . . .

It has often been said that England has excelled in two branches of linguistics, lexicography and phonetics. The Society inaugurated our great Dictionary. The Society was also the centre and focus for the development of the School of Phonetics to which Sweet was rightly proud to belong. Today, general linguistics, lexicography, phonetics, and what Sweet called living philology, are well represented and strongly supported. Sweet mentioned dialectology too, as part of our strength and originality. In Joseph Wright we had, in the words of Lundell, the maker of the greatest of all dialect dictionaries. His work on the Windhill dialect is a model dialect grammar that has never been surpassed anywhere. Wright's own opinion was that the *English Dialect Grammar* was far more important than the Dictionary. He wrote notes on gramophone recording. He would have deprecated any approach to dialect study that could not be described as 'living philology'. The Society has great responsibilities to the English School and its traditions in planning a resumption of dialect studies in this country.

9

SOUNDS AND PROSODIES

THE purpose of this paper is to present some of the main principles of a theory of the phonological structure of the word in the piece or sentence, and to illustrate them by noticing especially sounds and prosodies that are often described as laryngals and pharyngals. I shall not deal with tone and intonation explicitly.

Sweet himself bequeathed to the phoneticians coming after him the problems of synthesis which still continue to vex us. Most phoneticians and even the 'new' phonologists have continued to elaborate the analysis of words, some in general phonetic terms, others in phonological terms based on theories of opposition, alternances, and distinctive differentiations or substitutions. Such studies I should describe as paradigmatic and monosystemic in principle.

Since de Saussure's famous *Cours*, the majority of such studies seem also to have accepted the monosystemic principle so succinctly stated by Meillet: 'Chaque langue forme un système où tout se tient.' I have in recent years taken up some of the neglected problems left to us by Sweet. I now suggest principles for a technique of statement which assumes first of all that the primary linguistic data are pieces, phrases, clauses, and sentences within which the word must be delimited and identified, and secondly that the facts of the phonological structure of such various languages as English, Hindustani, Telugu, Tamil,[1] Maltese,[2] and Nyanja[3] are most economically and most completely stated on a polysystemic hypothesis.

In presenting these views for your consideration, I am aware of the danger of idiosyncrasy on the one hand, and on the other of employing common words which may be current in linguistics but not conventionally scientific. Nevertheless, the dangers are unavoidable since linguistics is reflexive and introvert. That is to say, in linguistics language is turned back upon itself. We have to use language about language, words about words, letters about letters. The authors of a recent American report on education win our sympathetic attention when they say 'we realize that language

---

[1] At one of the 1948 meetings of the Linguistic Society of America, Mr. Kenneth Pike suggested that in certain Mexican Indian languages it would be convenient to hypothecate a second or phonemic sub-system to account for all the facts. Taking part in the discussion which followed, I pointed out my own findings in Tamil and Telugu for both of which languages it is necessary to assume at least three phonological systems: non-brahman Dravidian, Sanskrito-dravidian, and Sanskritic.

[2] See J. Aquilina, *The Structure of Maltese*, A Study in Mixed Grammar and Vocabulary. (Thesis for the Ph.D. degree, 1940. University of London Library.)

[3] See T. Hill, *The Phonetics of a Nyanja Speaker*, With Particular Reference to the Phonological Structure of the Word. (Thesis for the M.A. degree, 1948. University of London Library.)

is ill adapted for talking about itself'. There is no easy escape from the vicious circle, and 'yet', as the report points out, 'we cannot imagine that so many people would have attempted this work of analysis for themselves and others unless they believed that they could reach some measure of success in so difficult a task'. All I can hope for is your indulgence and some measure of success in the confused and difficult fields of phonetics and phonology.

For the purpose of distinguishing prosodic systems from phonematic systems, words will be my principal isolates. In examining these isolates, I shall not overlook the contexts from which they are taken and within which the analyses must be tested. Indeed, I propose to apply some of the principles of word structure to what I term 'pieces' or combinations of words. I shall deal with words and pieces in English, Hindustani, Egyptian Arabic, and Maltese, and refer to word features in German and other languages. It is especially helpful that there *are* things called English words and Arabic words. They are so called by authoritative bodies; indeed, English words and Classical Arabic words are firmly institutionalized. To those undefined terms must be added the words *sound, syllable, letter, vowel, consonant, length, quantity, stress, tone, intonation*, and more of the related vocabulary.

In dealing with these matters, words and expressions have been taken from a variety of sources, even the most ancient, and most of them are familiar. That does not mean that the set of principles or the system of thought here presented are either ancient or familiar. To some they may seem revolutionary. Word analysis is as ancient as writing and as various. We A B C people, as some Chinese have described us, are used to the process of splitting up words into letters, consonants and vowels, and into syllables, and we have attributed to them such several qualities as length, quantity, tone, and stress.

I have purposely avoided the word 'phoneme' in the title of my paper, because not one of the meanings in its present wide range of application suits my purpose and 'sound' will do less harm. One after another, phonologists and phoneticians seem to have said to themselves: '*Your* phonemes are dead, long live *my* phoneme.' For my part, I would restrict the application of the term to certain features only of consonants and vowels systematically stated *ad hoc* for each language. By a further degree of abstraction we may speak of a five-vowel or seven-vowel phonematic system, or of the phonematic system of the concord prefixes of a Bantu language,[1] or of the monosyllable in English.

By using the common symbols **c** and **v** instead of the specific symbols for phonematic consonant and vowel units, we generalize syllabic structure in a new order of abstraction eliminating the specific paradigmatic consonant and vowel systems as such, and enabling the syntagmatic word structure of syllables with all their attributes to be stated systematically. Similarly we may abstract those features which mark word or syllable

[1] See T. Hill, *The Phonetics of a Nyanja Speaker*.

initials and word or syllable finals or word junctions from the word, piece, or sentence, and regard them syntagmatically as prosodies, distinct from the phonematic constituents which are referred to as units of the consonant and vowel systems. The use of spaces between words duly delimited and identified is, like a punctuation mark or 'accent', a prosodic symbol. Compare the orthographic example 'Is she?' with the phonetic transcript iʒʃiy? in the matter of prosodic signs. The interword space of the orthography is replaced by the junction sequence symbolized in general phonetic terms by ʒʃ. Such a sequence is, in modern spoken English, a mark of junction which is here regarded as a prosody. If the symbol *i* is used for word initial and *f* for word final, ʒʃ is *fi*. As in the case of c and v, *i* and *f* generalize beyond the phonematic level.

We are accustomed to positional criteria in classifying phonematic variants or allophones as initial, medial, intervocalic, or final. Such procedure makes abstraction of certain postulated units, *phonemes*, comprising a scatter of distributed variants (allophones). Looking at language material from a syntagmatic point of view, any phonetic features characteristic of and peculiar to such positions or junctions can just as profitably, and perhaps more profitably, be stated as prosodies of the sentence or word. Penultimate stress or junctional geminations are also obvious prosodic features in syntagmatic junction. Thus the phonetic and phonological analysis of the word can be grouped under the two headings which form the title of this paper—sounds and prosodies. I am inclined to the classical view that the correct rendering of the syllabic accent or the syllabic prosodies of the word is *anima vocis*, the soul, the breath, the life of the word. The study of the prosodies in modern linguistics is in a primitive state compared with the techniques for the systematic study of sounds. The study of sounds and the theoretical justification of roman notation have led first to the apotheosis of the sound-letter in the phoneme and later to the extended use of such doubtful derivatives as 'phonemics' and 'phonemicist', especially in America, and the misapplication of the principles of vowel and consonant analysis to the prosodies. There is a tendency to use one magic phoneme principle within a monosystemic hypothesis. I am suggesting alternatives to such a 'monophysite' doctrine.

When first I considered giving this paper, it was to be called 'Further Studies in Semantics'. I had in mind the semantics of my own subject or a critical study of the language being used about language, of the symbols used for other symbols, and especially the new idioms that have grown up around the word 'phoneme'. Instead of a critical review of that kind, I am now submitting a system of ideas on word structure, especially emphasizing the convenience of stating word structure and its musical attributes as distinct orders of abstractions from the total phonological complex. Such abstractions I refer to as prosodies, and again emphasize the plurality of systems within any given language. I think the classical grammarians employed the right emphasis when they referred to the prosodies as *anima vocis*. Whitney, answering the question 'What is articulation?' said: 'Articulation consists not in the mode of production of individual sounds, but in the mode of their combination for the purposes of speech.'[1]

The Romans and the English managed to dispense with those written signs called 'accents' and avoided pepperbox spelling. Not so the more ingenious Greeks. The invention of the written signs for the prosodies of the ancient classical language were not required by a native for reading what was written in ordinary Greek. They were, in the main, the inventions of the great scholars of Alexandria, one of whom, Aristarchus, was described by Jebb as the greatest scholar and the best Homeric critic of antiquity. The final codification of traditional Greek accentuation had to wait nearly four hundred years—some would say much longer—so that we may expect to learn something from such endeavours.[2] It is interesting to notice that the signs used to mark the accents were themselves called προσῳδίαι, prosodies, and they included the marks for the rough and smooth breathings. It is also relevant to my purpose that what was a prosody to the Greeks was treated as a consonant by the Romans, hence the 'h' of hydra. On the relative merits of the Greek and Roman alphabets as the basis of an international phonetic system of notation, Prince Trubetzkoy favoured Greek and, when we talked on this subject, it was clear he was trying to imagine how much better phonetics might have been if it had started from Greek with the Greek alphabet. Phonetics and phonology have their ultimate roots in India. Very little of ancient Hindu theory has been adequately stated in European languages. When it is, we shall know how much was lost when such glimpses as we had were expressed as a theory of the roman alphabet.

More detailed notice of 'h' and the 'glottal stop' in a variety of languages will reveal the scientific convenience of regarding them as belonging to the prosodic systems of certain languages rather than to the sound systems. 'h' has been variously considered as a sort of vowel or a consonant in certain languages, and the glottal stop as a variety of things. Phonetically, the glottal stop, unreleased, is the negation of all sound whether vocalic or consonantal. Is it the perfect minimum or terminus of the syllable, the beginning and the end, the master or maximum consonant? We have a good illustration of that in the American or Tamil exclamation ʔaʔa! Or is it just a necessary metrical pause or rest, a sort of measure of time, a sort of mora or matra? Is it therefore a general syllable maker or marker, part of the syllabic structure? As we shall see later, it may be all or any of these things, or just a member of the consonant system according to the language.

---

[1] Amply illustrated by the patterns to be seen on the Visible Speech Translator produced by the Bell Telephone Laboratories.

[2] See *A Short Guide to the accentuation of Ancient Greek*, by J. P. Postgate, The University Press of Liverpool Ltd., Hodder & Stoughton Ltd., London, 1924.

We have noticed the influence of the Roman and Greek alphabets on notions of sounds and prosodies. The method of writing used for Sanskrit is syllabic, and the Devanagari syllabary as used for that language, and also other forms of it used for the modern Sanskritic dialects of India, are to this day models of phonetic and phonological excellence. The word analysis is syllabic and clearly expressive of thê syllabic structure. Within that structure the pronunciation, even the phonetics of the consonants, can be fully discussed and represented in writing with the help of the prosodic sign for a consonant closing a syllable. For the Sanskritic languages an analysis of the word satisfying the demands of modern phonetics, phonology, and grammar could be presented on a syllabic basis using the Devanagari syllabic notation without the use of the phoneme concept, unless of course syllables and even words can be considered as 'phonemes'.

In our Japanese phonetics courses at the School of Oriental and African Studies during the war, directed to the specialized purposes of operational linguistics, we analysed the Japanese word and piece by a syllabic technique although we employed roman letters. The Roomazi system, as a system, is based on the native Kana syllabary. The syllabic structure of the word—itself a prosody—was treated as the basis of other prosodies perhaps oversimplified, but kept distinct from the syllabary. The syllabary was, so to speak, a paradigmatic system, and the prosodies a syntagmatic system. We never met any unit or part which *had* to be called a phoneme, though a different analysis, in my opinion not so good, has been made on the phoneme principle.

Here may I quote a few of the wiser words of Samuel Haldeman (1856), first Professor of Comparative Philology in the University of Pennsylvania, one of the earlier American phoneticians, contemporary with Ellis and Bell. 'Good phonetics must recognize the value for certain languages "of alphabets of a more or less syllabic character", in which "a consonant position and a vowel position of the organs" are regarded "as in a manner constituting a unitary element".'[1] Sir William Jones was the first to point out the excellence of what he called the Devanagari system, and also of the Arabic alphabet. The Arabic syllabary he found almost perfect for Arabic itself—'Not a letter', he comments, 'could be added or taken away without manifest inconvenience.' He adds the remark, 'Our English alphabet and orthography are disgracefully and almost ridiculously imperfect'. I shall later be using Arabic words in Roman transcription to illustrate the nature of syllabic analysis in that language as the framework for the prosodies. Sir William Jones emphasized the importance of the 'Orthography of Asiatic Words in Roman Letters', as he put it. The development of comparative philology, and especially of phonology, also meant increased attention to transliteration and transcription in roman letters. Sir William Jones was not in any position to understand how all this might contribute to the tendency, both in historical and descriptive linguistics,

[1] Cf. 'The English School of Phonetics', Chapter 8.

to phonetic hypostatization of roman letters, and theories built on such hypostatization.

In introducing my subject I began with sounds and the Roman alphabet which has determined a good deal of our phonetic thinking in western Europe—as a reminder that in the Latin word the letter was regarded as a sound, *vox articulata*. We moved east to Greek, and met the prosodies, i.e. smooth and rough breathings, and the accents. The accents are marks, but they are also musical properties of the word. In Sanskrit we meet a syllabary built on phonetic principles, and each character is **akṣərə**, ultimate, permanent, and indestructible. Any work I have done in the romanization of Oriental languages has been in the spirit of Sir William Jones, and consequently I have not underestimated the grammatical, even phonetic, excellence of the characters and letters of the East where our own alphabet finds it origins. On the contrary, one of the purposes of my paper is to recall the principles of other systems of writing to redress the balance of the West.

And now let us notice the main features of the Arabic alphabet. I suppose it can claim the title 'alphabet' on etymological grounds, but it is really a syllabary.[1] First, each Arabic letter has a name of its own. Secondly, each one is capable of being realized as an art figure in itself. Thirdly, and most important of all, each one has syllabic value, the value or *potestas* in the most general terms being consonant plus vowel, including vowel zero, or zero vowel. The special mark, *sukuun*, for a letter without vowel possibilities, i.e. with zero vowel, or for a letter to end a syllable, not begin it, is the key to the understanding of the syllabic value of the simple letter not so marked, and this is congruent with the essentials of Arabic grammar. Like the **hələnt** in Devanagari, **sukuun** is a prosodic sign. The framework of the language and the etymology of words, including their basic syllabic structure, consist in significant sequences of radicals usually in threes. Hence a letter has the *potestas* of one of these radicals plus one of the three possible vowels **i**, **a**, or **u**, or zero. Each syllabic sign or letter has, in the most general terms, a trivocalic potentiality, or zero vowel, but in any given word placed in an adequate context, the possibilities are so narrowly determined by the grammar that in fact the syllable is, in the majority of words, fully determined and all possibilities except one are excluded. The prosodies of the Arabic word are indicated by the letters if the context is adequate. If the syllabic structure is known, we always know which syllable takes the main prominence. It is, of course, convenient to make the syllabic structure more precise by marking a letter specially, to show what is called zero vowel, or to show it is doubled. Such marks are prosodic. And it is even possible to maintain that in this system of writing the diacritics pointing out the vowels and consonants in detail are added prosodic marks rather than separate vowel signs or separate sounds

[1] Or rather, Arabic writing is syllabic in principle. Professor Edgar Sturtevant has stated this view and recently confirmed it personally in conversation.

in the roman sense; that is to say, generalizing beyond the phonematic level, **fatħa, kasra, ðamma, sukuun, alif, waaw, yaa, taʃdiid,** and **hamza** form a prosodic system.

In China the characters, their figures and arrangement, are designs in their own right. Words in calligraphy are artefacts in themselves of high aesthetic value, for which there is much more general respect than we have in England for the Etonian pronunciation of the King's English. For my purpose Chinese offered excellent material for the study of institutionalized words long since delimited and identified. With the help of Mr. K. H. Hu, of Changsha, I studied the pronunciation and phonology of his dialect of Hunanese.[1] Eventually I sorted out into phonological classes and categories large numbers of characters in accordance with their distinguishing diacritica. Diacritica were of two main types, phonematic and prosodic. The prosodic diacritica included tone, voice quality, and other properties of the sonants, and also yotization and labiovelarization, symbolized by **y** and **w**. Such diacritica of the monosyllable are not considered as successive fractions or segments in any linear sense, or as distributed in separate measures of time.[2] They are stated as systematized abstractions from the primary sensory data, i.e. the uttered instances of monosyllables. We must distinguish between such a conceptual framework, which is a set of relations between categories, and the serial signals we make and hear in any given instance.[3]

Before turning to suggest principles of analysis recognizing other systems of thought and systems of writing outside the western European tradition, let me amplify what has already been said about the prosodies by quoting from a grammarian of the older tradition and by referring to the traditional theory of music.

Lindley Murray's *English Grammar* (1795) is divided in accordance with good European tradition,[4] into four parts, viz. Orthography, Etymology, Syntax, and Prosody. Part IV, Prosody, begins as follows: 'Prosody consists of two parts: the former teaches the true PRONUNCIATION of words, comprising ACCENT, QUANTITY, EMPHASIS, PAUSE, and TONE; and the latter, the laws of versification. Notice the headings in the first part—ACCENT, QUANTITY, EMPHASIS, PAUSE, and TONE.'

In section 1 of ACCENT he uses the expression the *stress of the voice* as distinguishing the accent of English. The stress of the voice on a particular

---

[1] See 'The Chinese Monosyllable in a Hunanese Dialect (Changsha)', Chapter 7.
[2] In the sending of Japanese morse ak = ka, the first signal being the characteristic sonant. (Joos, *Acoustic Phonetics*, L.S.A., pp. 116–26, and conclusions on segmentation.)
[3] See also N. C. Scott, 'A Study in the Phonetics of Fijian', *B.S.O.A.S.*, vol. xii, pts. 3–4 (1948), and J. Carnochan, 'A Study in the Phonology of an Igbo Speaker', ibid., pt. 2 (1948). Eugénie Henderson, 'Prosodies in Siamese', in *Asia Major*, N.S., vol. i, 1949.
[4] Cf. 'Arte de Escribír', by Torquato Torío de la Riva, addressed to the Count of Trastamara, Madrid, 1802. The four parts of grammar are: *etimología ó analogía, syntaxis, prosódia,* and *ortografía*. Prosódia teaches the quantity of syllables in order to pronounce words with their due accent. There are three degrees in Spanish: acute or long, grave or short, and what are termed *común* or *indiferentes*.

syllable of the word enables the number of syllables of the word to be perceived as grouped in the utterance of that word. In other words, the accent is a function of the syllabic structure of the word. He recognizes principal and secondary accent in English. He recognizes two quantities of the syllable in English, long and short, and discusses the syllabic analysis and accentuation of English dissyllables, trisyllables, and polysyllables, and notices intonation and emphasis.

The syntagmatic system of the word-complex, that is to say, the syllabic structure with properties such as initial, final, and medial characteristics, number and nature of syllables, quantity, stress, and tone, invites comparison with theories of melody and rhythm in music. Writers on the theory of music often say that you cannot have melody without rhythm, also that if such a thing were conceivable as a continuous series of notes of equal value, of the same pitch, and without accent, musical rhythm could not be found in it. Hence the musical description of rhythm would be 'the grouping of measures', and a measure 'the grouping of stress and non-stress'. Moreover, a measure or a bar-length is a grouping of pulses which have to each other definite interrelations as to their length, as well as interrelations of strength. Interrelations of pitch and quality also appear to correlate with the sense of stress and enter into the grouping of measures.

We can tentatively adapt this part of the theory of music for the purpose of framing a theory of the prosodies. Let us regard the syllable as a pulse or beat, and a word or piece as a sort of bar length or grouping of pulses which bear to each other definite interrelations of length, stress, tone, quality—including voice quality and nasality. The principle to be emphasized is the *interrelation of the syllables*, what I have previously referred to as the *syntagmatic relations*, as opposed to the *paradigmatic* or *differential relations* of sounds in vowel and consonant systems, and to the paradigmatic aspect of the theory of phonemes, and to the analytic method of regarding contextual characteristics of sounds as allophones of phonematic units.

A good illustration of these principles of word-analysis is provided if we examine full words in the spoken Arabic of Cairo, for which there are corresponding forms in Classical Arabic. Such words (in the case of nouns the article is not included) have from one to five syllables. There are five types of syllable, represented by the formulae given below, and examples of each are given.

Syllabic Structure in Cairo Colloquial[1]

(i) CV: open short. C+i, a, or u.

    (*a*) fíhim   nízil

    (*b*) ẓálamu ʕitláxam ḍárabit

    (*c*) ʕindáhaʃu (*cvc–cv–cv–cv*)

[1] See also Ibrahim Anis, *The Grammatical Characteristics of the Spoken Arabic of Egypt.* (Thesis for the Ph.D. degree, 1941. University of London Library.) t ḍ ṣ ẓ = t d̪ s̪ z̪ (I.P.A.)

(ii) CVV: open medium. C+*i*, *a*, or *u*, and the prosody of vowel length indicated by doubling the vowel, hence VV—the first V may be considered the symbol of one of the three members of the vowel system and the second the mark of the prosody of length. Alternatively y and w may be used instead of the second i or u.

(*a*) fáahim   fúulah   nóobah*
(*b*) muṣíibah   ǵinéenah*   misóoǵar*
(*c*) ʕiʃtaddéenah*   (*cvc–cvc–cvv–cvc*)
(*d*) náahum

(iii) CVC: closed medium. C+*i*, *a*, or *u*.

(*a*) ʕáfham   dúrǵuh
(*b*) yistáfhim   duxúlhum
(*c*) mistalbáxha   (*cvc–cvc–cvc–cv*)

(iv) CVVC: closed long. C+*i*, *a*, or *u* and the prosody of vowel length—see under (ii).

(*a*) naam   ṣuum   ziid
      baat   ʃiil̦   xoof*
(*b*) kitáab   yiʃíil   yiṣúum
(*c*) ʕistafáad   yistafíid   yifhamúuh
(*d*) ʕistalbaxnáah   tistalbaxíih

(v) CVCC: closed long. C+*i*, *a*, or *u* and the prosody of consonant length in final position only, the occurrence of two consecutive consonants in final position.

(*a*) ʃadd   bint
(*b*) ḍarábt   yimúrr
(*c*) ʕistaɣádd   yistaɣídd   (*cvc–cv–cvcc*)

In the above words the prominent is marked by an accent. This is, however, not necessary since prominence can be stated in rules without exception, given the above analysis of syllabic structure.

Though there are five types of syllable, they divide into three quantities: short, medium, and long. When vowel length is referred to, it must be differentiated from syllabic quantity—vowels can be short or long only. The two prosodies for vowels contribute to the three prosodies for syllables.

* *The special case of* **ee** *and* **oo**

In most cases colloquial **ee** and **oo** correspond to classical *ay* and *aw*, often described as diphthongs. There are advantages, however, in regarding *y* and *w* as terms of a prosodic system, functioning as such in the syllabic structure of the word. **xawf** and **xoof** are thus both closed long, though *cvwc* is replaced by *cvvc*. Similarly **ǵináynah** and **ǵinéenah**, **náy** and **née** are both medium, one with *y*-prosody and one with vowel length. Though the syllabic quantities are equivalent, the syllabic structure is different. Two more vowel qualities must be added to the vowel system, e and o, different from the other three in that the vowel quality is prosodically bound and is always long.

There are other interesting cases in which, quite similarly, colloquial C+ee or oo with the prosody of length in the vowel in such words as **geet** or **ʃuum**, correspond to equivalent classical monosyllables **jiʕt, ʃuʕm**. The phonematic constituents of the pairs of corresponding words are different, but the prosody of equipollent quantity is maintained. Many such examples could be quoted including some in which the prosodic function of ʕ (glottal stop) and 'y' are equivalent.

	Classical		Cairo colloquial
	ðiʕb		diib
	qaraʕt	[Cyrenaican: ġarayt]	ʕareet
	faʕs		faas
	daaʕim		daayim
	naaʕim		naayim
	maaʕil		maayil
	ḍaraaʕib		ḍaraayib

The prosodic features of the word in Cairo colloquial are the following:

In any word there is usually such an interrelation of syllables that one of them is more prominent than the rest by nature of its prosodies of strength, quantity, and tone, and this prominent syllable may be regarded as the nucleus of the group of syllables forming the word. The prominent syllable is a function of the whole word or piece structure.

Naturally, therefore, the prosodic features of a word include:

1. The number of syllables.
2. The nature of the syllables—open or closed.
3. The syllabic quantities.
4. The sequence of syllables ⎫
5. The sequence of consonants ⎬ radicals and flexional elements separately treated.
6. The sequence of vowels ⎭
7. The position, nature, and quantity of the prominent.
8. The dark or clear qualities of the syllables.

There is a sort of vowel harmony and perhaps consonant harmony, also involving the so-called emphatic or dark consonants.

I think it will be found that word-analysis in Arabic can be more clearly stated if we emphasize the syntagmatic study of the word-complex as it holds together, rather than the paradigmatic study of ranges of possible sound substitutions upon which a detailed phonematic study would be based. Not that such phonematic studies are to be neglected. On the contrary, they are the basis for the syntagmatic prosodic study I am here suggesting. In stating the structure of Arabic words, the prosodic systems will be found weightier than the phonematic. The same may be true of the Sino-Tibetan languages and the West African tone languages.

Such common phenomena as elision, liaison, anaptyxis, the use of so-called 'cushion' consonants or 'sounds for euphony', are involved in this study of prosodies. These devices of explanation begin to make sense when prosodic structure is approached as a system of syntagmatic relations.

Speaking quite generally of the relations of consonants and vowels to prosodic or syllabic structure, we must first be prepared to enumerate the consonants and vowels of any particular language for that language, and not rely on any general definitions of vowel and consonant universally applicable. Secondly, we must be prepared to find almost any sound having syllabic value. It is not implied that general categories such as vowel, consonant, liquid, are not valid. They are, perhaps, in general linguistics. But since syllabic structure must be studied in particular language systems, and within the words of these systems, the consonants and vowels of the systems must also be particular to that language and determined by its phonological structure.

Let us now turn to certain general categories or types of sound which appear to crop up repeatedly in syllabic analysis. These are the weak, neutral, or 'minimal' vowel, the glottal stop or 'maximum' consonant, aitch, or the pulmonic onset—all of which deserve the general name of laryngals. Next there are such sounds as ħ and ʕ characteristic of the Semitic group of languages which may also be grouped with 'laryngals' and perhaps the back ɣ. Then the liquids and semi-vowels l, r, n (and other nasals), y, and w.

Not that prosodic markers are limited to the above types of 'sound'. Almost any type of 'sound' may have prosodic function, and the same 'sound' may have to be noticed both as a consonant or vowel unit and as a prosody.

First, the neutral vowel in English. It must be remembered that the qualities of this vowel do not yield in distinctness to any other vowel quality. The term neutral suits it in English, since it is in fact neutral to the phonematic system of vowels in southern English. It is closely bound up with the prosodies of English words and word junctions. Unlike the phonematic units, it does not bear any strong stress. Its occurrence marks a weak syllable including weak forms such as wəz, kən, ə.

Owing to the distribution of stress and length in southern English words, it is often final in junction with a following consonant initial. Two of the commonest words in the language, *the* and *a*, require a number of prosodic realizations determined by junction and stress, ðə, ði, 'ðiy, ə, ən, 'ey, æn. In other positions, too, the neutral vowel often, though by no means always, marks an etymological junction or is required by the prosodies of word formation, especially the formation of derivatives. The distribution of the neutral vowel in English from this point of view would make an interesting study. The prosodic nature of ə is further illustrated by the necessity of considering it in connexion with other prosodies such as the so-called 'intrusive' r, the 'linking' r, the glottal stop, aitch, and even w and y. Examples: *vanilla ice, law and order, cre'ation, behind, pa and ma, to earn, to ooze, secretary, behave, without money*. The occurrence of southern English diphthongs in junctions is a good illustration of the value of prosodic treatment, e.g.:

(i) The so-called 'centring' diphthongs, **iə(r), eə(r), ɔə(r), uə(r)**.
(ii) What may be termed the 'y' diphthongs, **iy,**[1] **ey, ay, oy**.
(iii) The 'w' diphthongs **uw, ow, aw**.

It may be noted that **e, æ, ɔ** do not occur finally or in similar junctions, and that **ɔː, aː,** and **əː** all involve prosodic *r*.

Internal junctions are of great importance in this connexion since the verb *bear* must take *-ing* and *-er*, and *run* leads to *runner up*. Can the **r** of *bearing* be said to be 'intrusive' in southern English? As a prosodic feature along with *ə* and in other contexts with the glottal stop, aitch, and prosodic *y* and *w*, it takes its place in the prosodic system of the language. In certain of its prosodic functions the neutral vowel might be described temporarily as a pro-syllable. However obscure or neutral or unstressed, it is essential in *a bitter for me* to distinguish it from *a bit for me*. In contemporary southern English many 'sounds'[2] may be pro-syllabic, e.g. **tsn̩'apl, tstuw'mʌtʃ, sekr̩tri** or **sekətri, s'main, s'truw**. Even if '*s true* and *strew* should happen to be homophonous, the two structures are different: **ç'cvw** and **'cvw**. 'Linking' and 'separating' are both phenomena of junction to be considered as prosodies. In such a German phrase as **ʔin ʔeinem ʔalten 'Buch**, the glottal stop is a junction prosody. I suppose Danish is the best European language in which to study the glottal stop from the prosodic point of view.[3] Unfortunately, I am not on phonetic speaking terms with Danish and can only report. The Danish glottal stop is in a sense parallel with tonal prosodies in other Scandinavian languages. It occurs chiefly with sounds said to be originally long, and in final position only in stressed syllables. If the word in question loses its stress for rhythmical or other reasons, it also loses the glottal stop. It is therefore best considered prosodically as a feature of syllabic structure and word formation. The glottal stop is a feature of monosyllables, but when such elements add flexions or enter compounds, the glottal stop may be lost. In studying the glottal stop in Danish, the phonematic systems are not directly relevant, but rather the syllabic structure of dissyllabic and polysyllabic words and compounds. In Yorkshire dialects interesting forms like **'fɔʔti** occur. Note, however, **'fɔwər** and **'fɔwə'tiyn**. A central vowel unit occurs in stressed positions in these dialects, e.g. **'θəʔti, 'θəʔ'tiyn**.

[1] It is, I think, an advantage from this point of view to regard English so-called long *i*: and *u*: as *y*-closing or *w*-closing diphthongs, and emphasize the closing termination by writing with Sweet *ij* or *iy*, and *uw*.

[2] In the general phonetic sense, not in the phonematic sense.

[3] See Sweet, 'On Danish Pronunciation' (1873), in *Collected Papers*, p. 345, in which he makes a prosodic comparison with Greek accents. (On p. 348 he uses the term 'tonology'.

SOUNDS AND PROSODIES

There may even be traces of a prosodic glottal stop in such phrases as t 'θədʔ'dɛɛ, t 'θədʔ'taym. Junctions of the definite article with stressed words having initial t or d are of interest, e.g. ɔntʔ'tɛɛbl, itʔ'tram, tətʔ'tɛytʃə, fətʔ'dɔktə, witʔ'tawil. These are quite different junctions from those in 'gud 'dɛɛ or 'bad 'taym. Compare also Yorkshire **trɛɛn** (*cvvc*) t'rɛɛn (*c'cvvc*), tət'ʃɔp, tə 't'ʃɔp, and especially **witʔ'tak** (*with the tack*) and **wid 'tak** (*we'd take*), also **witə'tak** (*wilt thou take*). In London one hears 'θə:ʔ'tsiyn and 'θə:t'ʔiyn, where the two glottal stops have somewhat different prosodic functions.

The glottal stop as a release for intervocalic plosives is common in Cockney, and is a medial or internal prosody contrasting with aspiration, affrication, or unreleased glottal stop in initial or final positions. Such pronunciations as 'kɔpʔə, 'sapʔə, 'wintʔə, dʒampʔə are quite common. I would like to submit the following note of an actual bit of conversation between two Cockneys, for prosodic examinations: i 'ʔo:ʔ ʔə 'ʔɛv iʔ 'ʔo:f, baʔ i "waw̃ʔ ʔɛv iʔ o:f.

I have already suggested the *y* and *w* prosodies of English, including their effect on the length prosody of the diphthongs and their function in junctions when final. After all, human beings do not neglect the use of broad simple contrasts when they can combine these with many other differentiations and in that way multiply phonetic means of differentiation. In the Sino-Tibetan group of languages the *y* and *w* element is found in a large number of syllables—there are many more *y* and *w* syllables than, say, *b* or *d* or *a* syllables. In the many roman notations used for Chinese, these two elements are variously represented and are sometimes regarded as members of the paradigm of initials, but generally as members of the paradigm of finals. They can be classified with either, or can be simply regarded as syllabic features. Sounds of the **y** or **w** type, known as semi-vowels or consonantal vowels, often have the syllable-marking function especially in initial and intervocalic position. In Sanskrit and the modern languages affiliated to it, it is clear that prosodic *y* and *v* must be kept distinct from similar 'sounds' in the phonematic systems. The verbal forms **aya, laya, bənaya** in Hindustani are not phonematically irregular, but with the *y*-prosody are regular formations from **a-na, la-na,** and **bəna-na**. In Tamil and other Dravidian languages *y* and *v* prosodies are common, as markers of initials, for example, in such Tamil words as **(y)enna, (y)evan, (y)eetu, (v)oor, (v)oolai, (v)oottu**. However, the prosodies of the Dravidian languages present complicated problems owing to their mixed character.

Other sounds of this semi-vowel nature which lend themselves to prosodic function are **r** and **l**, and these often correspond or interchange with *y* or *w* types of element both in Indo-European and Sino-Tibetan languages. Elements such as these have, in some languages, such pro-syllabic or syllable-marking functions that I think they might be better classified with the syntagmatic prosodies rather than with the overall paradigmatic vowel and consonant systems. Studies of these problems in Indo-European and Sino-Tibetan languages are equally interesting.

The rough and smooth breathings are treated as prosodies or accentual elements in the writing of Greek. It is true that, as with accents in other languages, the rough breathing may imply the omission of a sound, often **s**, or affect the quality and nature of the preceding final consonants in junction. 'h' in French is similarly connected with junction and elision. Even in English, though it has phonematic value in such paradigms as *eating, heating*; *eels, heels*; *ear, hear*; *ill, hill*; *owl, howl*; *art, heart*; *arming, harming*; *anchoring, hankering*; *airy, hairy*; *arrow, Harrow*; and many others, it is an *initial signal* in stressed syllables of full words having no weak forms. English **h** is a special study in weak forms, and in all these respects is perhaps also to be considered as one of the elements having special functions, which I have termed prosodic. In English dialects phonematic 'h' (if there is such a thing) disappears, but prosodic 'h' is sometimes introduced by mixing up its function with the glottal stop. I have long felt that the aitchiness, aitchification, or breathiness of sounds and syllables, and similarly their creakiness or 'glottalization', are more often than not features of the whole syllable or set of syllables. Indeed, in some of the Sino-Tibetan languages, breathiness or creakiness or 'glottalization' are characteristic of prosodic features called tones. In an article published in the *Bulletin* of the School of Oriental and African Studies, Mr. J. Carnochan has a few examples of aspiration and nasalization in Igbo as syntagmatic features of a whole word, rather like vowel harmony, which is prosodic.

Apart from the fact that nasals such as **m, n, ŋ** are often sonants—that is to say, have syllabic function—they are also quite frequently initial or final signals, and in Bantu languages such signals have essentially a syntagmatic or syllable or word-grouping function. In a restricted prosodic sense, they can be compared with the glottal stop in German.

In bringing certain types of speech sound into consideration of the prosodies, I have so far noticed the neutral or weak vowel, the minimal vowel, which often becomes zero; the glottal stop, the maximal consonant which unreleased is zero sound; aitch, the pulmonic onset, and the liquids and nasals. The first two, I suggest, deserve the name of laryngals, and perhaps **h**. There remain such sounds as ħ, ʕ, ɣ, and χ, characteristic of the Semitic group of languages. These sounds are certainly phonematic in classical Arabic. But in the dialects they are often replaced in cognate words by the prosody of length in change of vowel quality, generally more open than that of the measure of comparison.

When words containing these sounds are borrowed from Arabic by speakers of non-Semitic languages, they are usually similarly replaced by elements of a prosodic nature, often with changes of quality in the vowels of the corresponding syllable.

Hindustani and Panjabi provide interesting examples of phonematic

SOUNDS AND PROSODIES

units in one dialect or style being represented in another by prosodies. Instances of interchanges in cognates between phonematic units of the vowel system and units of the consonant system are common, and examples and suggestions have been offered of interchanges and correspondences between phonematic units of both kinds and prosodies. The following table provides broad transcriptions to illustrate these principles.

Table I
h

Hindustani, Eastern, careful	Hindustani, Western, quick	Panjabi (Gujranwala)
pəhyle	pəyhle	pŷlle
bəhwt	bəwht	bŵt
pəhwŋcna	pəwhŋcna	pŵwŋc
bhəi		b̥əi
kər rəha həy	kərrahəyh	
rəhta (ræhta)		rŷnɖa

In **pəhyle** we have a three-syllable word in which **h** is phonematic (*cvcvcv*). In **pəyhle** there are two syllables by a sort of coalescence in which **əyh** indicates an open 'h'-coloured or breathy vowel of the æ-type (*cvhcv*). Similarly in the phrase **bəhwt‿əccha** there are four syllables (*cvcvc‿vccv*), in **bəwht‿əccha** three, the vowel in the first of which is *open* back and 'h'-coloured (*cvhcvccv*).

In Panjabi **pŷlle** the open vowel carries a compound high falling tone and the structure is prosodically quite different (*cv̂ccv*) which, I think, is equipollent with *cvhcv* (**pəyhle**). **bŵt** similarly is *cv̂c*, reduced to a monosyllable with initial and final consonant and a tonal prosody. In Hindustani verbal forms like **rəhna, rəhta; kəhna, kəhta**; the **ə** vowel in the 'h'-coloured syllable immediately followed by a consonant is open with a retracted æ-like quality. **yɪh** is realized as **ye**, **vwh** as **vo**, in both of which there is a similar lowering and potential lengthening in emphasis.

Table II
Arabic ʕ in Urdu Loan-words

Spelling transliterated	Transcription of realization in speech
məʕlum	malum
bəʕd	bad
dəfʕ	dəfa
mənʕ	məna
məʕni	məani, mani
ystʕmal	ystemal

In all these cases the vowel realized is open and fairly long. In Maltese, words which in Arabic have h and which still retain h in the spelling are pronounced long with retracted quality, e.g. he, hi, ho, eh, ehe, as in fehem, fehmu, sehem, sehmek, qalbhom. These long vowels may be unstressed. Similarly all the għ spellings (transliterated ɣ) are realized as long slightly pharyngalized vowels which may also occur in unstressed positions, which is not possible with vowels other than those with the Semitic ħ and għ spellings, e.g. ɣa, aɣ, aɣa, ɣo, oɣ, oɣo, ɣi (ɣey), ɣe, ɣu (ɣəw) in such words as għidt, għúda, magħmul, bálagħ. In the phrase balagħ balgħa (*he swallowed a mouthful*) the two forms are pronounced alike with final long a (for form, cf. ħataf ħatfa, *he snatched*). h and għ are often realized in spoken Maltese as a prosody of length.

In Turkish the Arabic ﻉ in loan-words is often realized as a prosody of length in such pronunciations as fiil (*verb, act*), saat (*hour*), and similarly Arabic ɣ, in iblaa (*communicate*), and Turkish ğ in uultu (*tumult*). We are reminded again of Arabic ʕ which is also realized as a prosody of length in the colloquials, e.g. classical jiʕt is paralleled by geet in Cairo, jɛɛt in Iraqi, and ʒiit in Cyrenaican Saʿadi. In Cairo and Iraqi the prosody of length is applied to a more open vowel than in classical, but this is not always the case.

The study of prosodic structures has bearing on all phonological studies of loan-words, and also on the operation of grammatical processes on basic material in any language. Taking the last-mentioned first, elision or anaptyxis in modern Cairo colloquial are prosodically necessary in such cases as the following: misíkt+ni = misiktíni, where the anaptyctic i is required to avoid the junction of three consonants consecutively which is an impossible pattern. The prominence then falls on the anaptyctic vowel by rule. Pieces such as bint+fariid are realized as bintifaríid. With the vowels i and u, elision is possible within required patterns, e.g. yindíhiʃ+u = yindihʃu, titlíxim+i = titlíxmi, but not with a, ʕitlaxam+it = ʕitlaxamit.

Amusing illustrations of the effect of prosodic patterns on word-borrowing are provided by loan-words from English in Indian and African languages and in Japanese. Prosodic anaptyxis produces səkuul in Panjabi and prothesis iskuul in Hindi or Urdu. By similar processes sət̪eʃən and ist̪eʃən are created for *station*. In Hausa *screw-driver* is naturalized as sukuru direba. Treating skr and dr as initial phonematic units, English *screw-driver* has the structure ˈcvw-cvycə, the prosodies of which Hausa could not realize, hence *cvcvcv-cvcvcv*, a totally different structure which I have carefully expressed in non-phonematic notation, to emphasize the fallacy of saying Hausa speakers cannot pronounce the 'sounds', and to point to the value of studying prosodic structure by a different set of abstractions from those appropriate to phonemic structure. It is not implied that there is one all-over prosodic system for any given language. A loan-word may bring with it a new pattern suited to its class or type, as in English borrowings from French, both nominals and verbals. When completely naturalized the prosodic system of the type or class of word in the borrowing language is dominant. In Japanese strange prosodic transformations take place, e.g. **bisuketto** (*biscuit*), **kiromeetoru, kiroğuramu, supittohwaia, messaasyumitto, arupen-suttoku, biheebiyarisuto, doriburusuru** (*to dribble*).

Linguists have always realized the importance of the general attributes of stress, length, tone, and syllabic structure, and such considerations have frequently been epoch-making in the history of linguistics. Generally speaking, however, the general attributes have been closely associated with the traditional historical study of sound-change, which, in my terminology, has been chiefly phonematic. I suggest that the study of the prosodies by means of *ad hoc* categories and at a different level of abstraction from the systematic phonematic study of vowels and consonants, may enable us to take a big step forward in the understanding of synthesis. This approach has the great merit of building on the piece or sentence as the primary datum. The theory I have put forward may in the future throw light on the subject of Ablaut which, in spite of the scholarship expended on it in the nineteenth century from Grimm to Brugmann, still remains a vexed question and unrelated to spoken language. I venture to hope that some of the notions I have suggested may be of value to those who are discussing laryngals in Indo-European, and even to those engaged in field work on hitherto unwritten languages. The monosystemic analysis based on a paradigmatic technique of oppositions and phonemes with allophones has reached, even overstepped, its limits! The time has come to try fresh hypotheses of a polysystemic character. The suggested approach will not make phonological problems appear easier or oversimplify them. It may make the highly complex patterns of language clearer both in descriptive and historical linguistics. The phonological structure of the sentence and the words which comprise it are to be expressed as a plurality of systems of interrelated phonematic and prosodic categories. Such systems and categories are not necessarily linear and certainly cannot bear direct relations to successive fractions or segments of the time-track of instances of speech. By their very nature they are abstractions from such time-track items. Their order and interrelations are not chronological.

An example is given below of the new approach in sentence phonetics and phonology[1] in which the syntagmatic prosodies are indicated in the upper stave and the phonematic structure in the lower stave, with a combination text between. Stress is marked with the intonation indicated.

It is already clear that in cognate languages what is a phonematic constituent in one may be a prosody in another, and that in the history of any given language sounds and prosodies interchange with one another. In the main, however, the prosodies of the sentence and the word tend to be dominant.

[1] For a fuller illustration of the scope of sentence phonology and its possible applications, see Eugénie Henderson's *Prosodies in Siamese*.

Prosodies	$\Bigg\{$	. ⌐\ . ⌐. . ⌐. ⌐\ . . ‾ cy vcə vcə cəz‿mvtʃ‿bvcə vy cvcc ðy ʌðə[1] ɔfə wəz mʌtʃ betə ay θiŋk
Phonematic structure	$\Bigg\{$	ð—ʌð—ɔf—w-z mʌtʃ bet—a—θiŋk
Prosodies	$\Bigg\{$	⌐ ⌐ ⌐ ⌐ ⌐\ ‾ cvy hvz‿ʃvy əccvccic cvc cvc way hæz ʃiy əkseptɪd ðis wʌn
Phonematic structure	$\Bigg\{$	wa æz ʃi kspet d ðis wʌn

To say the prosodies may be regarded as dominant is to emphasize the phonetics and phonology of synthesis. It accords with the view that syntax is the dominant discipline in grammar and also with the findings of recent American research in acoustics. The interpenetration of consonants and vowels, the overlap of so-called segments, and of such layers as voice, nasalization, and aspiration, in utterance, are commonplaces of phonetics. On the perception side, it is improbable that we listen to auditory fractions corresponding to uni-directional phonematic units in any linear sense.

Whatever units we may find in analysis must be closely related to the whole utterance, and that is achieved by systematic statement of the prosodies. In the perception of speech by the listener whatever units there may be are prosodically reintegrated. We speak prosodies and we listen to them.

[1] The use of ə as a prosodic symbol in such final contexts implies potential **r** or **ʔ** according to the nature of the junction.

10

THE SEMANTICS OF LINGUISTIC SCIENCE

SYNOPSIS

Any new attempt at synthesis in linguistics must consider the origins of our theories and terminology. That necessitates the application of the technique of semantics, both historical and descriptive, to the language used about language. To begin with, such terms as speech and language must be examined. Speech as the expression of language and personality. Semantic links with the biological and social sciences. Outline of a new approach in phonetics and phonology involving a rectification of terms and technique.

ON the first page of the first article in the first number of the international review *Lingua*, Professor Reichling made a summary general statement which all linguists must recognize as a fair description of the situation in general linguistics. The study of linguistics 'has renewed itself. It has looked back on a past of often a thousand years and more; and, retaining and bringing to full development the many good things, has incorporated these old things and many new ones in a new attempt at synthesis'. The purpose of my comment is to supplement what I conceive to be his general intention by adding a little emphasis and an amendment which will serve to introduce the subject of the present chapter.

First the emphasis: it is all to the good that we should look back on a couple of thousand years of linguistics[1] without fear of being turned into pillars of salt. The German comparativists had so harnessed and blinkered Western European linguistics in the nineteenth century that nothing earlier could have much interest for linguistic science. The hold and prestige was such that I once heard it said a certain distinguished scholar gave his lifetime to prove that a Frenchman could be as great a master-philologist as a German.

To dismiss two thousand years of linguistic study in Asia as well as in Europe as negligible except in so far as it contributed to comparative grammar is just plain stupid. The semantics of 'grammar' in English takes us back to Ælfric, which, as they say in '1066 and all that', is 'a good thing'.[2]

Second, the amendment: 'the many good things' old and new have not yet been 'incorporated' in anything that deserves the name of synthesis. The words 'system', 'systematic', and other cognates have been much used, but what is really needed in our present situation is the systematic study of the 'languages' of linguistics from the semantic point of view. With a view especially to the enrichment of our science by the contributions of

[1] See my *Tongues of Men*, pp. 59–83, Watts & Co., 1937.
[2] See 'The English School of Phonetics', Chapter 8, pp. 95–120; and 'What is a Letter?' by David Abercrombie, *Lingua*, i. 4.

Asians and Africans, it is desirable that watch be kept so that an international technical language may be developed in English for the use of linguists all over the world. In this semantic watch and ward journals such as *Lingua* should be of great value.

Let it be borne in mind that language is often not very apt when used about itself, even in technical linguistic studies. If we pause to consider the stylistics of the language of the common sensual life, we can be sure it will not serve as the language for linguistic science. The technical language for the systematic statement of the facts of language cannot, any more than for mathematics, be the language of everyday common sense. Professor Hjelmslev, fully realizing this, has endeavoured to frame a sort of linguistic calculus which might serve the linguistic sciences in the way mathematics has served the physical sciences. Even if the attempt be considered unsuccessful, it has not been sufficiently understood that the work of Professor Hjelmslev in general linguistics has been in the direction of our emancipation from the handicap of the common-sense idiom and 'self-explanatory' nomenclature in half a dozen languages, and from the limitations of the technique of comparative grammar. However much we may disagree with it or dislike it, the terminology is necessitated by a system of thought, which is more than can be said of a certain type of work which adds little to knowledge, bristles with neologisms, and brings nothing but discredit on what some people misrepresent as modern linguistics. It sometimes seems as though such people have to elaborate a jargon either to convince their competitors they have something important to say, or to start a discussion in which the jargon is bound to be operative, probably both. I have from time to time been asked by colleagues to suggest what they call 'a suitable term' for use in teaching or in articles. When it appears that we are using similar logical or scientific syntax, using a similar approach, applying a similar system of thought, I can often help. When we are not, the new term can only be a nuisance to everybody and especially to me.

Questions of terminology inevitably arise when new systems of thought are to be applied to the handling of material or events. The whole conceptual framework, the whole syntax of thought and words, should hold together systematically. I have in my possession an interesting letter addressed to Sir George Grierson (of the Linguistic Survey of India) by Sir Richard Temple in November 1907, on the subject of new theories and terminology. Writing apropos of his *Theory of Universal Grammar, as applied to Savage Languages*, he says:

The question of terminology in my 'Theory' resolves itself thus:—is it a smaller strain on the brain to put *new* definitions on to old words or have new words? I thought the latter was the best, but if the former is the best, it is all one to me. Of course to a man immersed in a set terminology a new one is a trouble—but for the learner at large it may be best to discard what is old and give him something new for new notions. At any rate you avoid confusion in teaching by so doing.

THE SEMANTICS OF LINGUISTIC SCIENCE

It must now be quite clear to all linguists that there is a new awareness everywhere of the powers and problems of speech and language. In England the word 'emergency' is still a familiar word, and most of us realize that a period of emergency is also a period of emergence. There are signs of a revival of learning in this country, not least in languages and linguistics, and the awareness I have referred to inevitably leads to a realization of the narrow limitations of nineteenth-century comparative grammar, however good that may be in itself, and an eagerness to develop linguistic science so that it may get to grips with its subject-matter, which is a good deal wider than historical phonology and etymology. For some the awareness of our need has gone much farther. There are those who feel that in grammar especially there is a distinct danger that the more technically historical it becomes, the less philological[1] its outlook, the less it can contain of the full humanism of speech and language. In other words, the more comparative and more historical it becomes, the less linguistic it is. We must therefore welcome new systems of linguistic thought with their terminology as contributions to the semantics of linguistic science. They may be regarded as radical criticism, if nothing more, of the language we linguists use about language.

What I am emphasizing is not the need for a mere reform of terminology or a dabbling in agreed nomenclature when there is no agreed doctrine, but the necessity for turning the technique of semantics,[2] historical and descriptive, on to our own technical terms and the conceptual framework and systems of ideas within which they function or have functioned in our statements of fact and of theory.

With such views in mind, most of us in the school of linguistics in London are increasingly aware of the problems of vocabulary and syntax in technical statements. We are experimenting with notation, tabulation, and the use of diagrams and other technical and even mechanical aids.[3] Though we are prepared for the development of linguistics as a group of sciences, we are anxious not to lose sight of man. We wish to avoid that kind of linguistics which appears to leave out as much of man and personality as possible.

Speech, both oral and written, is the outcome not of the individual, as Sweet used to insist, but of personality and language. Comparative linguistics has been limited in its scope and its dimensions. Personality and language

---

[1] In the classical sense. The semantic study of the English use of the terms *philology, comparative philology, classical philology, English philology, phonetics, phonology, historical grammar, linguistics, general linguistics* in comparison with similar terms in French and German will show there are not many equations. It is amusing to note that the fourth and concluding meaning Dr. Johnson gives to *humanity* is *philology, grammatical studies*.

[2] See 'The Technique of Semantics', Chapter 3, pp. 32-33.

[3] See 'The Structure of the Chinese Monosyllable in a Hunanese Dialect (Changsha)', Chapter 7; N. C. Scott, 'The Monosyllable in Szechuanese', *B.S.O.A.S.*, vol. xii, part 1, 1947; J. Carnochan, 'A Study in the Phonology of an Igbo Speaker', ibid., part 2, 1948; and Eugénie Henderson, 'Notes on the Syllable Structure of Lushai', ibid., Barnett Number, 1948.

are 'multi-dimensional', and though it is difficult to imagine a mathematical system adequate for the solution of the problems before us, something may be gained by applying the principles of mathematical philosophy.

The coupling of language and personality necessitates a re-examination of those two words. For his first entry of the word *person*, Dr. Johnson uses a citation from Locke. 'A person is a thinking intelligent being that has reason and reflection and can consider itself as itself, the same thinking thing in different times and places.' In defining *personality* he again quotes Locke: 'This personality extends itself beyond present existence to what is past, only by consciousness whereby it imputes to itself past actions just upon the same ground that it does the present.' It is quite obvious if we accept even this most general notion of personality, language must be considered with it. Language, like personality, is a **binder of time**, of the past and future in 'the present'. On the one hand there is habit, custom, tradition, and on the other innovation, creation. Every time you speak you create anew, and what you create is a function of your language and of your personality. From that activity you may make abstraction of the constituents of the context, and consider them in their mutual relations. In the process of speaking there is pattern and structure actively maintained by the body which is itself an organized structure maintaining the pattern of life.

At this point we must secure the foundations by reference to the physical basis of personality and of language. We may summarize the genesis of personality and language under the two general terms *nature* and *nurture*, nature being biological endowment and heredity, and nurture the learning or educative process during which the biological individual is progressively incorporated into his social organization, learns his languages, and acquires personality. You weave *nurture* into *nature*, and language and personality partake of both and are the expression of both.

In support of this basis for a semantic reconsideration of such terms as language, a given language, an author's language, speech, a speech event or speech item, I would refer the reader to the general views of our physiologists, neurologists, and anatomists, especially Sherrington. Professor J. Z. Young, in his inaugural lecture[1] as Professor of Anatomy in University College, London, emphasized 'this continuously maintained pattern of activity which is life' rather than the reflex hypothesis to which the sophisticated more often turn. Through all the active changes we call metabolism, the central fact is 'the maintenance of the general pattern of the system', the power of *self-maintenance* of a *dynamic pattern*. Regarding the pattern of activity within the central nervous system, Professor Young remarks: 'we are only just beginning to know anything about it,' and to explain the absence of any reference to psychology he adds 'because any attempt to include it involves great difficulties in the present primitive state of our language'.

[1] *Patterns of Substance and Activity in the Nervous System*, 28 February 1946. Lewis & Co. Ltd., London, 1946.

The kind of humanism with which general linguistics is most advantageously linked places more emphasis on our activities, drives, needs, desires, and on the tendencies of the body, than on mechanism and reflexes.

The linguistic sciences will find a sure semantic basis in alliance with concepts such as these on the biological side, and the development of proper semantic relationships with the other sciences of man is now vital. Linguists and sociologists have to deal with *systems*, but systems very different from physical systems. Personal systems and social systems[1] are actively maintained (with adaptation and change) in the bodily behaviour of men. Most of the older definitions (and de Saussure's must fall in this category) need overhauling in the light of contemporary science. We need to know a good deal more of the action of the body from within and especially of the nervous and endocrine systems. But from what we already know it is clear that we must expect human knowledge to be a function of that action. Language and personality are built into the body, which is constantly taking part in activities directed to the conservation of the pattern of life. We must expect therefore that linguistic science will also find it necessary to postulate the maintenance of linguistic patterns and systems (including adaptation and change) within which there is order, structure, and function. Such systems are maintained by activity, and in activity they are to be studied. It is on these grounds that linguistics must be systemic. On these grounds the phonetic and also the systematic phonological study of one person at a time is not only scientifically justified, but in fact inevitable.[2] The persons studied may of course be regarded as types. In emphasizing the personal as well as the systemic and typic character of descriptive linguistics, there is no implied neglect of the sociological approach and synthesis.

A great deal of abstract sociology is of doubtful value to the linguist because of the sociological neglect of persons, consequently of language also. Not so, however, Malinowski, who gave us an ethnographer's theory of language. He was a close student of persons and people. In his preface to *Coral Gardens and Their Magic*, he pays handsome tribute to the Trobriand personalities who helped in the study of themselves, and especially to Bagido'u.[3] He made a thorough study of Bagido'u, the leading garden magician, in action.

We may now suggest the systematic use of the expressions *language, a language, the language, languages, a speech event, a speech item, the speech event, speech events, speech.*[4]

---

[1] Analogous views in sociology are expressed in Znaniecki's *The Method of Sociology*, 1934, and *Social Actions*, 1936.
[2] Firth, Scott, Carnochan, Henderson, op. cit., *supra*.
[3] B. Malinowski, *Coral Gardens and Their Magic*, London, 1934, Preface, vol. i, pp. x–xi.
[4] Dr. Johnson's entries under *language* are interesting, and relevant.
I. Human Speech.
'We may define *language*, if we consider it more materially, to be letters, forming and producing words and sentences; but if we consider it according to the design thereof, then language is apt signs for communication of thoughts.' (Holder, 1669.) [*Cont. overleaf*

(a) Language is a natural tendency to use our physical endowment to make meaningful sounds, gestures, signs, and symbols.

(b) This tendency maintains systematic activity which we describe in grammars, dictionaries, and other works of linguistic science. There is a vast field of research in the general study of language.

(c) When we study any given language, we intend to refer to a specific language system or systems, actively maintained by persons carrying and conveying the system or systems.

(d) The comparative study of language systems is a vast field already highly developed historically in Indo-European languages, but only just beginning in descriptive linguistics. In this field, which involves the direct study of persons in action, lies the most promising future development of the linguistic sciences.

(e) A speech occurrence or an utterance may be oral or written and is considered as taking place in a context of situation.

A speech event in *a context of situation* is therefore a technical abstraction from utterances and occurrences. *A speech event* may be subdivided into *speech items*.

(f) Such 'events' are expressions of the language system from which they arise and to which they are referred.

(g) Speech consists in myriads of such events in their contexts, derived from a universe of human sounds in action, and vast masses of ink-spotted paper.

I would point out that the somewhat analogous notions previously coupled with the French words *langage*, *langue*, and *parole* in the work of de Saussure under the influence of Durkheimian sociology are not a satisfactory philosophical basis for the techniques of linguistic analysis I have in mind. They do not accord with the philosophy or general theory of language here put forward. Moreover, in emphasizing the systemic nature of language, I do not propose an *a priori* system of general categories by means of which the facts of all languages may be stated. Various systems are to be found in speech activity and when stated must adequately account for such activity. Science should not impose systems on languages, it should look for systems in speech activity, and, having found them, state the facts in a suitable language.

The basic or most elementary systems are probably phonological systems. The descriptions of pronunciation in phonetic terms at the phonetic level

II. The tongue of one nation as distinct from others.

> 'O! good my lord, no Latin;
> I am not such a truant since my coming,
> As not to know the *language* I have liv'd in.'   (Shakespeare)

III. Style, manner of expression.

> 'Though his *language* should not be refined,
> It must not be obscure and impudent.'   (Roscommon)

only, do not form part of a given language system, since the categories of phonetics are inter-lingual, 'international'. Technically speaking, 'a phonetic system' is a contradiction in terms, unless it be thought that a system of notation such as that of the International Phonetic Association, purporting to represent all the typical language sounds of man, is a 'linguistic' system. Have contemporary theories of Indo-European phonology reached a similar stage? That is, do they constitute a system for a language, or type of language, or for hundreds of languages? There is nothing new in the question. 'Indo-European' is not a language, any more than the I.P.A. alphabet is the alphabet of a language.

Semantic reconsideration of the categories of descriptive phonetics will be forced by the demands of descriptive linguistics, as we have already proved in the development of linguistics in London at the School of Oriental and African Studies. Phonetics as an academic discipline has never been more highly valued than at present when research in many Oriental and African languages begins anew on the formidable task of finding and stating the language systems expressed in the speech of our Asian and African colleagues. We must begin with utterance, so that phonetics is not mainly regarded as the science of pronunciation for European learners, but rather as a group of techniques for the study of utterance with a view to systemic analysis, the statement of linguistic facts, and eventually to the establishing of valid texts. The application of the results in the teaching of pronunciation is clearly indicated, but is not the semantic basis of present-day phonetics. Similar trends are observable in other countries, especially in America.[1]

There would appear to be a need for a semantic reconsideration of the categories employed in the description of articulation, especially for the purposes of phonological tabulation and statement. Though phonetics and phonology are on different scientific levels, they must work in harness and their findings should prove congruent in descriptive linguistics. It is manifestly advantageous for the phonologist to be a competent phonetician. It is also desirable that the requirements of phonological analysis should be considered in any semantic reconsideration of phonetics.

The word *phoneme*[2] appears in both disciplines. The derivatives *phonemic* and *phonemics*, much used in America though not in England, are not phonetic terms. A good deal of 'rectification of terms' is necessary in these cases.

The clear recognition of the two different systems of discourse in phonetics and phonology enables us to employ the terms consonant and vowel to much better purpose in both these related systems of thought. While we may find it necessary in general phonetics to distinguish and classify phones as consonant or vowel sounds on general phonetic grounds,

---

[1] See Chapter 1, also Chapter 3, pp. 20–29 and footnote. There is a good deal of literature awaiting semantic examination on this subject.
[2] See Sweet, *Primer of Phonetics*, pp. 15 and 40.

we cannot employ these on the same terms in the language of phonological statement. What are called 'the vowels' and 'the consonants' of a particular phonological system in a particular language must be determined *ad hoc* for that particular language, and it might well be that a phonological unit phonetically described as having the qualities of 'a vowel' would have to appear in the consonant system, and vice versa. In the phonological analysis of the word, syllable structure is basic, and for a 'syllabic sound' we might use the term *sonant*. Thus in phonology *sonant* and *consonant* would be kept distinct from *vowel sounds* and *consonant sounds* in phonetics.

From this point of view it will be seen that a good deal of semantic reconsideration is required at the phonetic level. The cardinalization of vowels and consonants was first suggested by Sweet,[1] and Daniel Jones has developed a practical method of describing and classifying vowel sounds by using a system of cardinals. For consonant and semi-vowel sounds we still rely in the main on the traditions of the roman alphabet. From the phonological point of view, the elements or constituents of a particular language system are comparatively simple, however complicated they may be in combinations. The mechanism of utterance studied by phonetics with phonological statements in view is not as complicated as some transcriptionists make it appear. The instrumental study of utterance, especially by palatography,[1] suggests a new approach in the description and classification of articulations with the ultimate purposes of phonology in mind. The study of the phonological structure of words in a particular language must be based on the findings of phonetics.

The phonological analysis of the word must take into account the syllabic structure, and that involves the recognition of the constituents of the syllable itself. These constituents are sonants and consonants, and may be termed *phonematic* constituents of the syllable and of the word also.

Syllables as constituents of words can be said to have *features* such as stress, quantity, nasalization, aspiration, tone, and a number of other attributes. These may be termed prosodic features, or just simply prosodies. Such prosodies may be coupled with sonants, consonants, syllables, words, 'pieces', or sentences, and whole sentences. When coupled with consonants they may be termed 'modifications'.

Phonological analysis on the above lines recognizes phonematic and prosodic constituents[2] in the structure of the syllable, the word, and groups of words called 'pieces'. Phonetics provides the necessary techniques for the description, classification, and notation of the phones, and other elements of speech, and it is an advantage to employ a particular fount of type throughout for such notation, to distinguish it from the orthography if there is one, and from the systematic notation or systematic transcription, which should also have its own fount. The most suitable one, perhaps, is italic.

[1] See Chapter 11, in which a tentative 'cardinalization' of consonant articulations is submitted for consideration.
[2] This subject is treated in Chapter 9.

THE SEMANTICS OF LINGUISTIC SCIENCE

The linearity of our written language and the separate letters, words, and sentences into which our lines of print are divided still cause a good deal of confused thinking due to the hypostatization of the symbols and their successive arrangement. The separateness of what some scholars call a phone or an allophone, and even the 'separateness' of the word, must be very carefully scrutinized. In synthesis a good deal of the 'separateness' disappears. What I term separateness in linearity is produced by abstraction in the analysis of utterance. Great care, however, is necessary in delimiting and identifying the isolates which are to be regarded as linear, and the most meticulous phonetic observation is required to decide whether or not they are to be regarded phonologically as 'successive' or 'serial'.[1] The attempts which have been made to prove a one-to-one parallel relation between the segments of oscillograms and kymograms and the letters of a transcription on the phoneme principle have not been convincing. 'It must not be taken that the division of a tracing—which are divisions in time—will correspond point for point with the letters of the systematic transcription placed beneath them; the letters are certainly not divisions in time.'[2]

An utterance happens in time. The stream of speech with all its items integrated unrolls itself, so to speak, on the *time track* of occurrences. But the systemic abstractions which we isolate in language systems are not limited by the time-track dimensions of the utterances from which they are taken. The statement of the systems when we talk or write about them have their own time track, since they are also speech events. The reflexive character of linguistics in which language is turned back upon itself is one of our major problems and the reason for the present chapter on the semantics of linguistics.

[1] Cf. Chapter 3, pp. 22–23.
[2] See Carnochan, 'A Study in the Phonology of an Igbo Speaker', *B.S.O.A.S.*, vol. xii, part 2, 1948, p. 426.

11

WORD-PALATOGRAMS AND ARTICULATION

(PLATES 1-7)

THE purpose of these notes is to suggest a new approach in the study of articulation with the aid of palatography.

The language material studied consists of words in English, Marathi, Burmese, Chinese, and Fijian uttered for the purpose by native speakers of the languages, trained to work with artificial palates.

It must constantly be borne in mind that utterances are events, *not* facts. The finding and the stating of the facts are the business of the phonetician. He attempts this by means of a set of correlated techniques each one of which makes its own specialized abstractions from the utterances. The findings are stated in the technical syntax and idiom of the discipline, employing categories and notations required by the conceptual framework.

Phonetic listening rests on a general psycho-physical basis, and on the nature and nurture (including the technical training) of the individual observer. He is usually aware of the limitations of this technique.

The alphabetic notation employed does not rest mainly on modern acoustic and physiological categories but largely on fictions, some of them very ancient, set up by grammatical theory and adapted for the statement of the findings by listening and looking, and by reference to the sense of posture and movement of the listener.

In the alphabet of the International Phonetic Association the symbols for what are called consonants are arranged in a classification based on the ancient grammatical traditions of the roman alphabet, modified as the result of an ever-widening exploration of Babel and under the influence of Sanskrit phonetics since the end of the eighteenth century.

The technical use of the roman alphabet today is different from what it was even ten years ago. It is now realized by some that:

(i) the units of a phonetic transcription at their best are abstractions from utterances, but often they are merely letters about other letters, quite literally *transcriptions*;

(ii) the use of letters in phonetics is notational and arbitrary and, in any given instance, their values are determined by the contexts in which they are used, and by the systems they express;

(iii) it will become increasingly necessary to specialize the use of roman letters in different founts of type, in order to distinguish different systematic findings at different levels by different abstractions from utterance, in the notational expressions used to state them.[1]

[1] See N. C. Scott, 'The Monosyllable in Szechuanese', *B.S.O.A.S.*, vol. xii, part 1,

PLATE 1

The Palatogram Figure

```
                          .  Zones
                         Left | Right
4th Molar Line......
                              |   7        ....2nd Molar
3rd Molar Line....
                              |   6        ...1st Molar
2nd Molar Line....
1st Molar Line.....           |   5        ....2nd Pre-Molar
Canine Line........           |   4        .....1st Pre-Molar
                              |   3        .......Canine
Lateral Incisor Line..        |   2        .........Lateral Incisor
Incisor Line..........        |   1        .........Frontal Incisor
```

FIG. 1

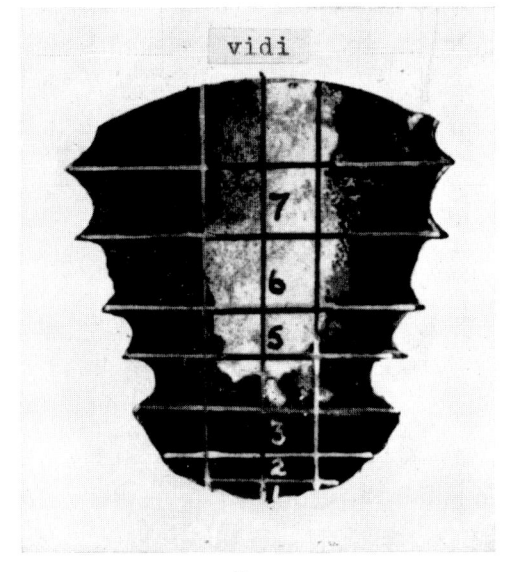

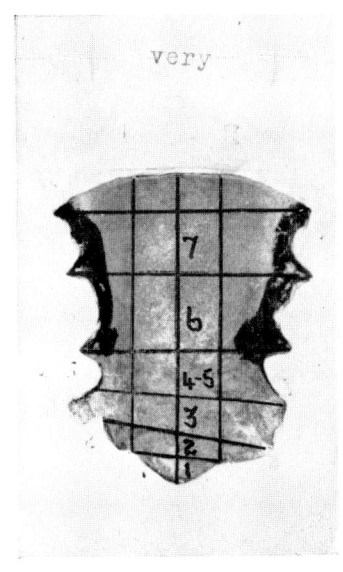

FIG. 2

FIG. 3

THE ZONING OF THE PALATE AND THE PALATOGRAM FIGURE

WORD-PALATOGRAMS AND ARTICULATION

When the trained observer studies an utterance by the perception technique, he employs at least three sensory channels—hearing, sight, and reference to his own kinaesthetic sense. In the nature of things, each of these three senses makes its own 'abstraction' from the utterance, and the observer integrates his findings in stated abstractions of a higher order.

Similarly, each instrumental technique used in investigations of repeated utterances is an extension of bodily equipment, an additional sense, so to speak, able only to make its own specialized 'abstraction' from the utterance, always within the limitations of the instrument. By means of the camera, various types of oscillograph,[1] and the *artificial* palate, specialized *instrumental abstractions* from utterances are obtained, and theoretical integration of the various abstractions from the utterances may then be attempted, leading perhaps to statements of the facts of the utterances in terms of linguistic science. It is encouraging to find from the most recent research that there is a correlation between the acoustic features of utterances as shown by physical analysis and what can be stated in phonetic notation by the perception technique.[2] These processes of abstraction have not been clearly stated before.

Palatography has been used since the pioneer work of Rousselot.[3] Generally speaking, it has been used to justify the traditional descriptions of what are called sounds, and most palatograms have been presented as diagrams of sounds symbolized by single roman letters. That method is misleading. Film strips[4] of words having easily observable articulations show the overlapping and mutual interpenetration of such 'sounds', and the integration of movement for the whole word or phrase. Figs. 22 and 23 show forty-one frames of a film taken at sixty-four frames a second while nursery rhymes were recited. These frames were cut from the film picturing the line 'baa baa *black sheep*, have you any wool?' and they show the two words *black sheep*. The first three frames (starting top left) show postures associated with **b** rather different from the three last (bottom right) for **p**. The fourth, fifth, and sixth show something of **l** but not really separable from the rest of the word since there is overlap, not only in the third frame but also in the sixth and seventh. The tongue is visible through ten frames from the fifth to the fourteenth. It moves forward and down from the fifth to the seventh and it is not possible usefully to correlate any one posture of the

---

1947, and Eugénie Henderson, 'Notes on the Syllable Structure of Lushai', ibid., pp. 713–25.

[1] See J. Carnochan, 'A Study in the Phonology of an Igbo Speaker', *B.S.O.A.S.*, vol. xii, part 2, 1948.

[2] See Potter, Kopp, and Green, *Visible Speech* (Van Nostrand, New York, 1947), an important work for all phoneticians. It is a descendant of Melville Bell's Visible Speech and of the invention of the telephone by his son, Graham Bell. See Chapter 8, pp. 96, 116 ff.

[3] See Panconcelli-Calzia, *Die experimentelle Phonetik in ihrer Anwendung auf die Sprachwissenschaft*, 1924, pp. 69 et seq.

[4] See Fig. 22.

tongue, lips, and oral aperture with a unit written æ. From the first to the eighth, there is lowering of the jaw and it rises from the eighth to a close position in the nineteenth frame with progressive change of lip posture. From the nineteenth to the thirtieth, a close position is held with development of lip-rounding associated with what is written ʃ. There is slight opening in the thirty-first which appears to be maintained with progressive relaxation of rounding, until lip-closure is approached from the thirty-seventh to the end. The difference of lip movements and postures associated with rounding from those in lip-closure are to be noted, as, indeed, are those in frames fifteen and sixteen and thirty-six and thirty-seven. Note the stress falls on ˈblæk.

The stream of an utterance identified in a reading transcription with the two words ˈblæk ʃiːp is 'partitioned' or 'segmented' into forty-one frames, quite arbitrarily, according to the movements of the camera. The reading transcription employs seven letters, two prosodic marks, and three spaces isolating the two words—ten devices in all. It would be difficult to justify even these abstractions, from the time-track pictures, and impossible to set up, let us say, seven time-track segments in which the exponents of seven phonemes could be said to occur. There are obvious prosodic features of the generalized utterance which might be associated with certain postural features common to a series of frames, but these are not represented in the transcription. These pictures illustrate what is merely a peripheral aspect of the articulatory basis of phonetic generalization, but they suggest perplexing problems of the dimensions involved when utterances are segmented or partitioned in analytical references to phonemes and distinctive features or, for that matter, to other phonematic units and prosodies.

Palatograms here presented are reproduced from photographs and are *word-palatograms*. That is to say, they are used for the abstraction of articulatory contact and possibly also of movement (see especially Figs. 4 and 7) from suitably selected words taken as whole utterances. Palatograms are not much use for any velar articulation, but throw light on many articulations forward of the soft palate.

The abstractions obtained from such palatograms cannot be linked directly with the articulation of something that might be called a single separate sound. But by comparison and deduction, bringing in the abstractions obtained by the perception technique, and by orthographic notation based on adequate phonetic conventions, statements can be made about certain articulations. For instance, it can be stated that in the Marathi utterance **paḍ** (Fig. 4) the blade of the tongue is retroflexed with the under edge of the tip opposite the post-palatal zone beyond the third molar line, and that it flaps and sweeps forward again, the tip first touching the post-palatal zone and lightly brushing the pre-palatal zone almost reaching the first molar line, and then, without the slightest touch, passing the alveolar and dental zones. The retroflex flapped articulation in the Marathi word

PLATE 2

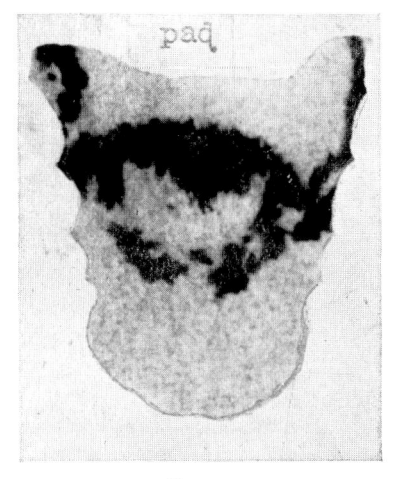

Fig. 4

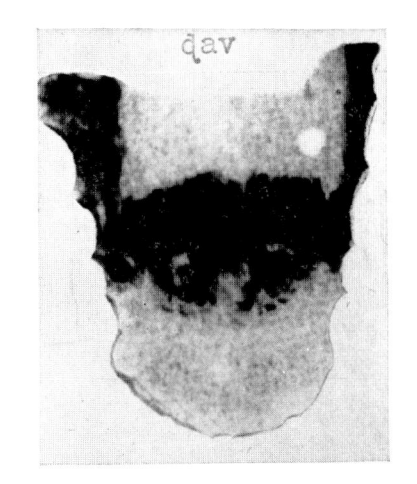

Fig. 5

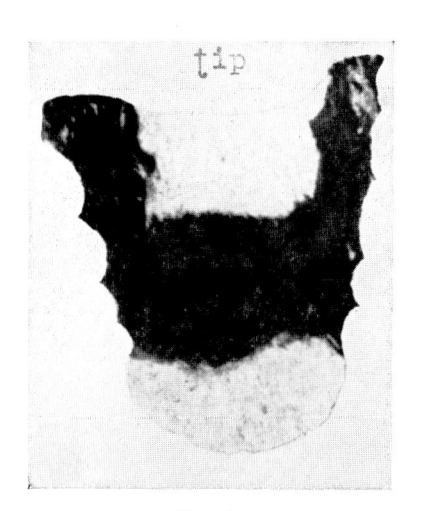

Fig. 6

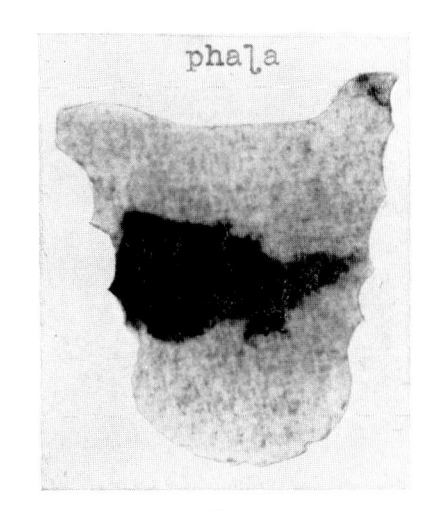

Fig. 7

PALATOGRAMS SHOWING RETROFLEXION IN THE MARATHI WORD

PLATE 3

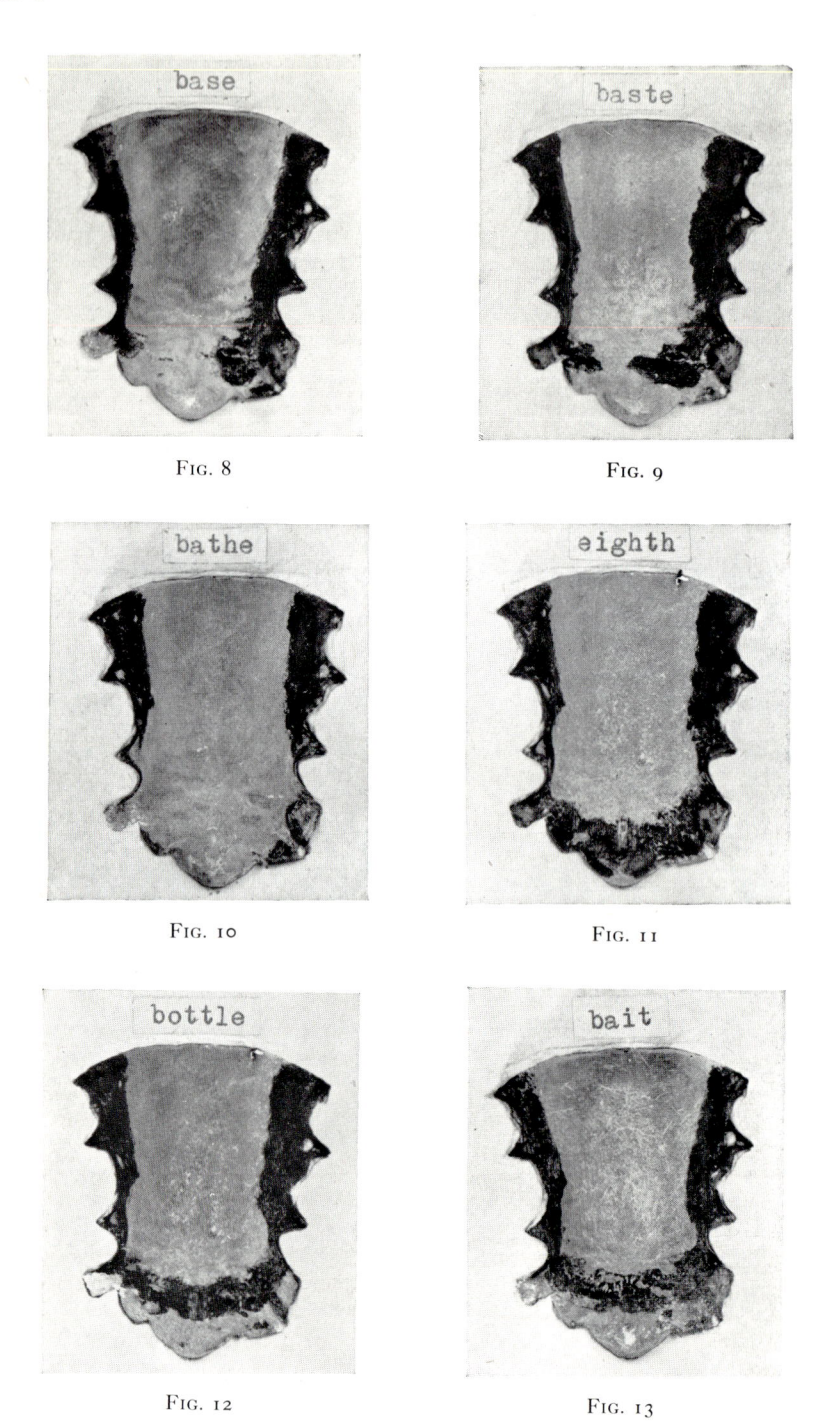

Fig. 8 — base

Fig. 9 — baste

Fig. 10 — bathe

Fig. 11 — eighth

Fig. 12 — bottle

Fig. 13 — bait

PALATOGRAMS SHOWING THE ARTICULATION OF θ, t AND s IN ENGLISH WORDS

paḍ may thus be regarded as entirely in the palatal zone and the first rapid touch made with the under edge of the tip of the tongue as far back as the post-palatal zone. This articulation is typical for Brahmin speakers of the Satāra dialect of Marathi. It does not hold for other so-called 'retroflex consonants' of Northern Indian languages. Measured by this type of retroflexion, such articulations do not function in Hindustani or Urdu. Indeed, it could be maintained that in those languages ṭ, initial ḍ, and also ḍḍ *cannot* be regarded as having retroflex articulation. For the study of articulations in this way the selection of utterances is determined by knowledge that some articulations, bi-labials for example, give no palatogram, and others homorganic or non-interfering articulations.

This approach to palatography suggests that what is often referred to as the organic basis of articulation seldom deserves that description. If reference lines and zones based on dentition are used, a thorough comparative study of individual utterances can be carried on over a long period, even if the teeth move, as they do. The reference lines move with them, when a new palate is necessary. Eventually the cardinalization of articulations by this method may be set off against cardinalization by the acoustic method first systematically suggested by Sweet.[1]

For the present it will be best to use a special terminology to describe articulatory abstractions obtained from palatograms and collate these with such alphabetic terms as are employed, for example, in the I.P.A. alphabet.

TABLE I

The Palatogram Figure

The horizontal lines	The zones	The grouped zones
1. Incisor line	Dental	Dental
2. Lateral incisor line	Denti-alveolar	
3. Canine line	Alveolar	Alveolar
4. First molar line	Post-alveolar	
5. Second molar line	Pre-palatal	
6. Third molar line	Mid-palatal	Palatal
7. Fourth molar line	Post-palatal	

The vertical lines	The vertical zones
The median line	Right and left zones: to speaker's right and left of the median line.
The right line	Right alveolar zone: to the right of the right line.
The left line	Left alveolar zone: to the left of the left line.

The above Table I is a first attempt at zoning the palate on the basis of the dentition plan, adding a natural median line and right and left lines parallel to the median starting from the interstices between the front and

---

[1] See Sweet, *Primer of Phonetics*, p. 40. He also suggested *nine cardinal positions* as a system of reference for the scientific description of vowels. See ibid., p. 15.

lateral incisors. Reference may be made first to Fig. 1, which is based on Fig. 2, an almost perfect palate made for a Fijian assistant, Mr. Bogidrau, who in this instance uttered the Fijian word *vidi*. Secondly, reference should be made to Fig. 3, showing the palate made for Miss Eugénie Henderson, Reader in Phonetics at the School of Oriental and African Studies. This does not show perfect dentition and is therefore interesting. It is the palate used in Figs. 8 to 13, all English words uttered by the lecturer in a normal southern English pronunciation.

First of all, names are required for the ten reference lines, and the zones, in Fig. 1. Each zone is forward of the line opposite which it is entered in Table I. The terms *right* and *left* refer to the speaker wearing the palate. If diagrams are to be drawn from photographs or direct from the palate then the reference lines may perhaps ensure an adequate representation of the significant features of the palatogram.

The Fijian example *vidi* in Fig. 2 shows what happens during a typical utterance of *vidi* [βindi] when every care is taken by the trained assistant and the observer that the demands of the technique are satisfied.

First, the very thin black plastic palate is dusted with fine French chalk[1] by means of a suitable de Vilbiss spray, and carefully inserted. The assistant holds an open mouth and then an easy position for an instant without tongue movement or swallowing, and then makes the utterance. The palate is then carefully removed and photographed. In this case the only articulations giving any palatogram are the two close vowels **i** and the intervocalic **nd**. The only zones left white and untouched by the tongue are the right and left zones as far forward as the middle of the post-alveolar zone. The black area shows the articulation contact made by the tongue during the utterance which wiped off the chalk. The 'wipe-off' is unusually extensive even for dentals between close front vowels. There is a 'wipe-off' of both the right and left alveolar zones and of half the post-alveolar, all the alveolar, the denti-alveolar, and dental zones. Here is evidence of a dental stop preceded by homorganic nasal fully deserving the description. There are dental stops in Indian languages, but not of this type. Such dental stops are not common in the Romance languages either. Compare this Fijian dental with the English **eighth** (Fig. 11) and the Burmese θi (Fig. 16).

The type of tongue contact must be ascertained by perception, and the use of such terms as apical, dorsal, retroflex, sulculized, flat, spread, cupped, retracted, narrowed, is suggested as of some assistance. Others may be invented according to need. The Fijian tongue contact in Fig. 2 is flat or spread.

Marathi

Figs. 4, 5, 6, and 7 show retroflex articulations in Marathi words uttered by a Satāra Brahmin. The articulation of **paḍ** (Fig. 4) has been described above. The tongue contacts are retroflex apical and flapped. In **ṭip** (Fig. 6)

---

[1] See Fig. 3, which shows a palate dusted with French chalk and untouched. The reference lines were added on the photograph.

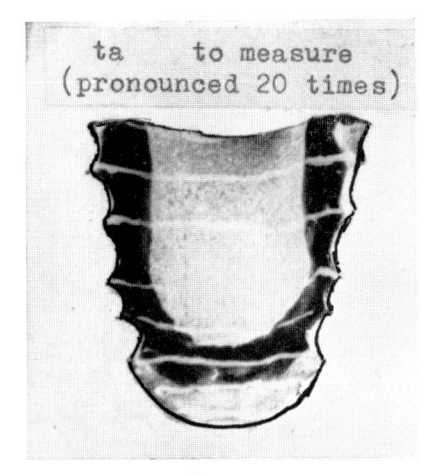

PLATE 4

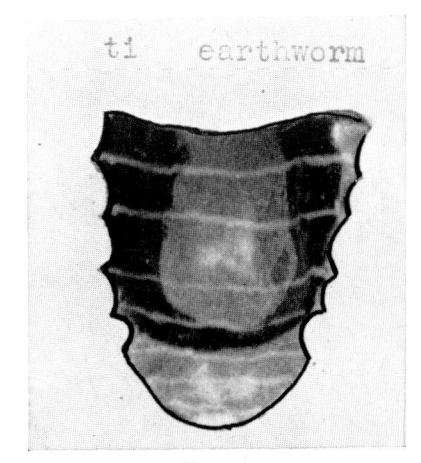

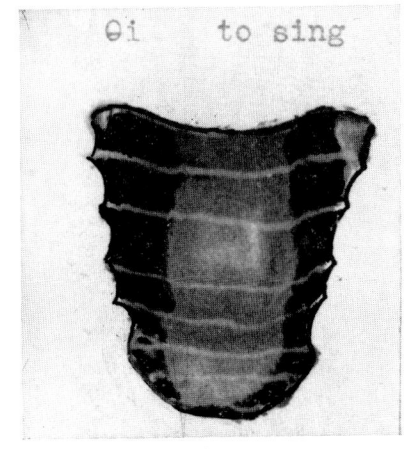

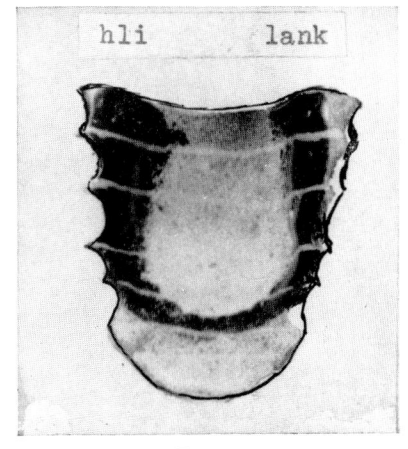

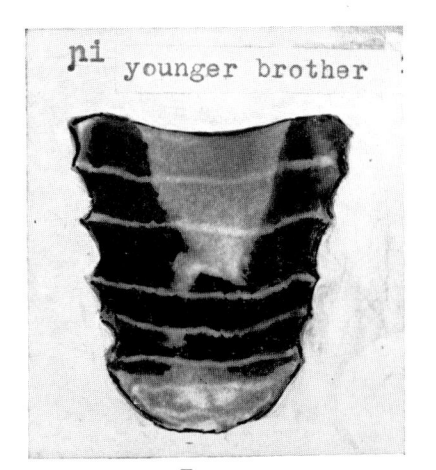

FIG. 14 — ta to measure (pronounced 20 times)

FIG. 15 — ti earthworm

FIG. 16 — θi to sing

FIG. 17 — hli lank

FIG. 18 — ca to delay

FIG. 19 — ɲi younger brother

PALATOGRAMS SHOWING ARTICULATIONS IN BURMESE
MONOSYLLABLES

PLATE 5

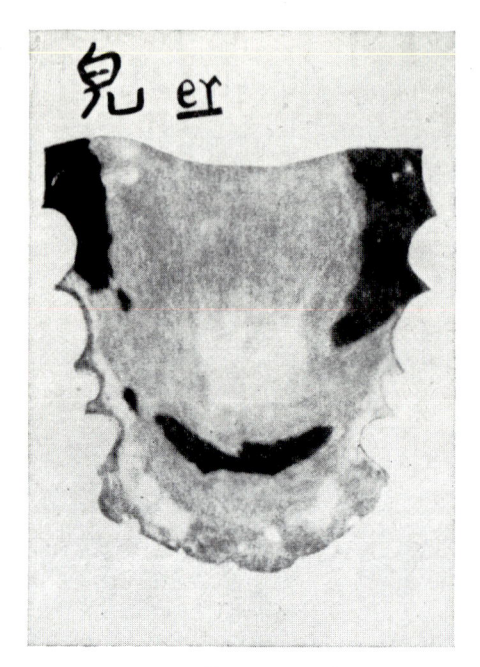

FIG. 20

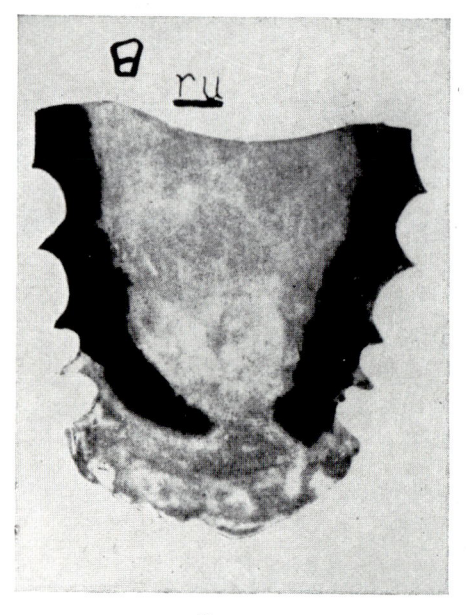

FIG. 21

WORD PALATOGRAMS SHOWING CONTRASTING
ARTICULATIONS IN CHINESE

as in **paḍ**, there is lateral wipe-off which in **paḍ**, at any rate must be part of the retroflex articulation. In **ṭip** (Fig. 6) the first contact is not so far back and only reaches the mid-palatal zone. The wipe-off as the tongue moves forward sweeps away the chalk from three zones, mid-palatal, pre-palatal, and post-alveolar, in which latter the tongue leaves and the three forward zones alveolar, denti-alveolar, and dental are untouched. This last negative feature is important. Here is evidence of a retroflex stop articulation. Such retroflex stops do not usually occur in Hindustani as spoken in polite society in Delhi or Lucknow. In **ḍav** (Fig. 5) the wipe-off is firm in only one zone, the mid-palatal zone, and continues less firmly in the pre-palatal zone. In **phəḷa** (Fig. 7) there is evidence of a unilateral retroflex flap, the lateral quality perceived arising mainly from the open right alveolar zone practically unaffected by the flap. There was obviously a 'curl' in the retroflexed blade of the tongue which lightly touched the palate diagonally across the mid-palatal zone and part of the left pre-palatal zone. Articulations of this type do not occur in Hindustani.

English

Figs. 8 to 13 are English word-palatograms for which reference lines and zones are shown in Fig. 3. The interesting features are:

(i) The normal alveolar articulation of the final stop in *bait*.

(ii) The absence of complete stop closure in *baste* (Fig. 9), though this palatogram records six successive superimposed utterances.

(iii) The articulation differences between *base* (Fig. 8), *baste* (Fig. 9), and *bait* (Fig. 13) are adequate in function.

(iv) The superimposed articulations of **t** and **l** in *bottle*, and **t** and **θ** in *eighth*, showing **t** in junction with **l** and **θ** following; final **t** in *bait*; and final **t** in *baste* in junction with **s** preceding.

(v) The dental zone not completely wiped-off in *eighth* (Fig. 11); cf. Burmese, Fig. 16.

(vi) In *bathe* (Fig. 10) the absence of wipe-off in the dental zone, evidence for either an inter-dental flap or fricative. Again compare Burmese, Fig. 16, in which there is a very light stop contact in the dental zone only, not in the denti-alveolar zone.

Burmese [Figs. 14 to 19]

An experiment was tried with an extra long artificial palate incorporating white reference lines cast in the material. The lines did not come out straight and there is an extra post-palatal line, but this does not seriously interfere with reading the palatograms. The black cupid's bow at the top of each palatogram is the shadow cast when the photographs were taken. The main points of interest are:

(i) The absence of 'wandering' out of the articulation zone in *ta* (Fig. 14) with twenty successive superimposed utterances. Experiments showed that native speakers are so conditioned to articulations that they do not 'wander' in normal utterance. The foreign learner, however good, does not usually achieve such results. He cannot hit the target like this twenty times in succession. This habituation is a justification for taking palatograms, if the typical pattern is recorded. See also Fig. 9, six utterances.

For Burmese **t** in *ta*, the description apico-alveolar stop is suitable, since the wipe-off affects both alveolar zones.

(ii) In **ti** (Fig. 15) the stop is post-alveolar only, and this description also applies to **hl** in **hli** (Fig. 17). The absence of lateral opening in Fig. 17 is due largely to the palatographic effect of **i**.

(iii) **θi** (Fig. 16).

Note the light closure indicated by the wipe-off of the *dental zone only*. This justifies the isolate of this very small zone. The slight stop before the fricative **θ** is commonly heard and distinguishes Burmese **θ** from English **θ**. Cf. Fig. 11.

(iv) **ɲi** (Fig. 19).

This illustrates a *dorsal* tongue contact as distinguished from an *apical* contact. The front hump of the tongue is the contacting surface. There is a lack of outline definition and a wide area of wipe-off of the pre-palatal, post-alveolar, and part of the alveolar zones with the tongue 'front' bunched nicely and squarely forward. Contrast this with the clean, narrow bow-front outline of the apical articulation in **ti**, **hli**, and **ta**.

(v) **ca** (Fig. 18).

Here again the contact is dorsal but probably firmer and more contracted. Cf. Fig. 14.

Chinese

Figs. 20 and 21 give two word-palatograms of two utterances by a cultured Pekin speaker of Mandarin. They are interesting demonstrations of characteristic Pekin articulations. Tongue contact in both is apical, and very light both with the tip and edges in Fig. 20. Moreover, they are the reverse of one another. In Fig. 20 the tip of the tongue lightly touches the post-alveolar zone, but the greater part of the palatal zone and the right and left alveolar zones are open forward of the third molar line. The sound suggests a frictionless continuant of the ɹ/l type—a sort of 'muted' vowel.

In Fig. 21, on the contrary, the sides of the tongue wipe off the right and left alveolar zones and the blade leaves a small opening in the post-alveolar zone. The sound is distinctly ɹ-like, though occasionally there is fricative noise suggesting z.

Palatography isolates the study of articulations in the front of the mouth from the rest of the mechanism of utterance. Of the thirty-seven consonant articulations in Urdu, twenty-two give palatograms. Of the twenty-two

PLATE 6

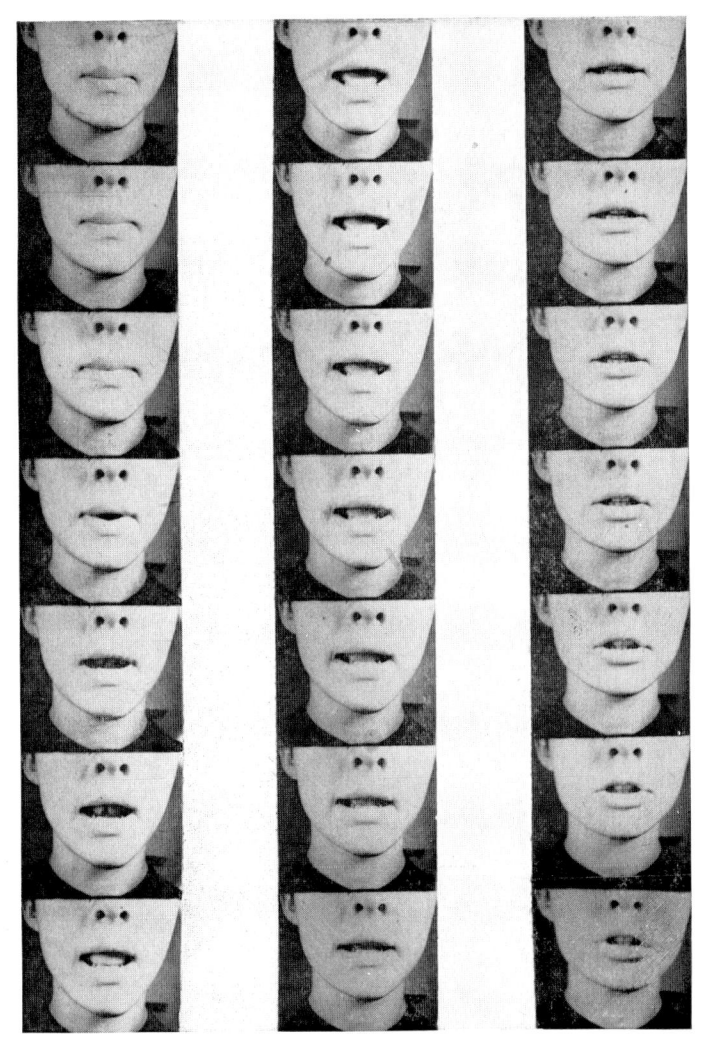

FIG. 22

FIRST TWENTY-ONE FRAMES OF FILM STRIP *BLACK SHEEP*

PLATE 7

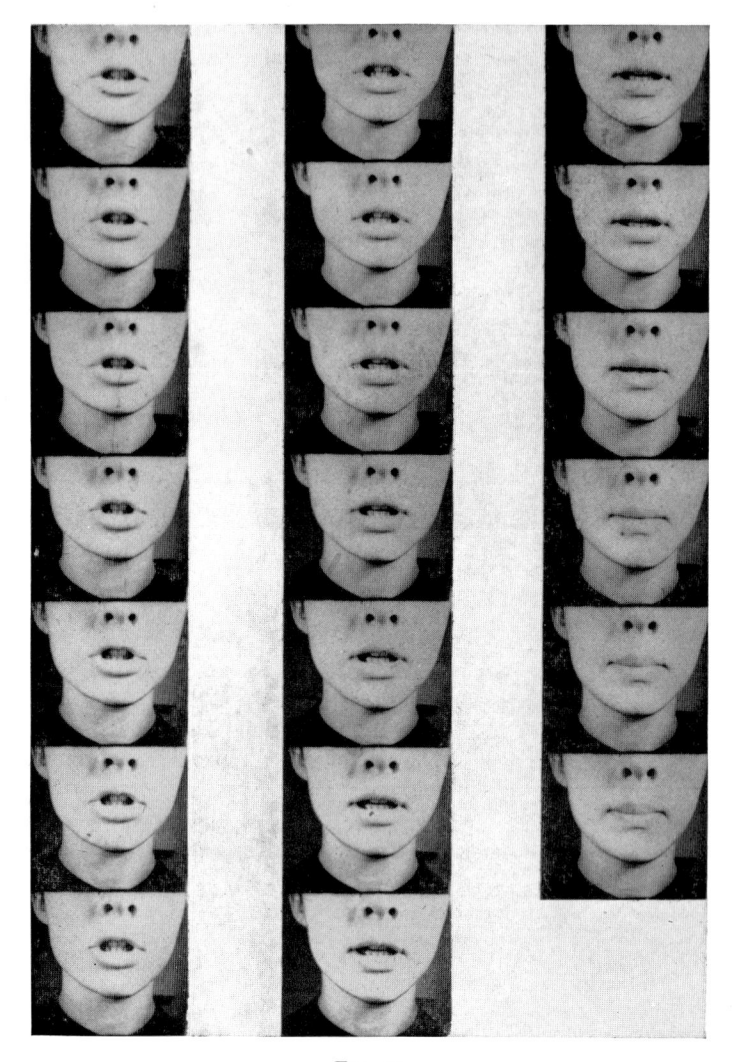

FIG. 23

LAST TWENTY FRAMES OF FILM STRIP *BLACK SHEEP*

in English, twelve at least would give palatograms. But apart from the possibility of a large proportion of palatographic abstractions in any given language, there is the suggestion, fortuitous perhaps, that the other mechanisms outside and below the buccal cavity may usefully be regarded as a general group, to be subdivided into extra-buccal, supra-buccal, and infra-buccal. Even on general grounds, quite apart from the showings of palatography, a simple grouping of types of articulation has proved useful in phonology.

Finally, unlike kymographic abstractions from utterance, these word-palatograms do not emphasize the sequence of sounds in the utterance of a word. They present features abstracted from the whole utterance regardless of 'seriality' or timing. The study of what are called 'features' of syllables and words as wholes, or as systems rather than sequences, promises productive results, both by instrumental and perception techniques.

12

ATLANTIC LINGUISTICS

EUROPEANS of all nations, and the Americans in their turn, have woven a web of crossings over the Atlantic, across the sea, in the air, in war and in peace. The Atlantic is now more than ever a common pool.

Since Columbus first crossed it, the Atlantic has meant communications, and the central linguistic fact is that the main vehicle of cultural communication around it is English. The title and purport of this chapter are to call attention to certain common interests in the study of English, of other languages, and of language in general, shared by all who have written in English both in Europe and America since the middle of the eighteenth century, to the characteristic and highly significant development of American Indian studies, and to the present fact that the centre of gravity of the linguistic sciences is no longer in the heart of the continent of Europe, but appears to be moving westwards. *Archivum Linguisticum*, with its headquarters in Glasgow, is another indication of liveliness in the West.

As the occupant of the first Chair of General Linguistics to be established in Great Britain, and as a contributor to the first volume of *Archivum Linguisticum*, may I be allowed to indulge in personal observations which I think may be relevant to the present situation in linguistics? The Chair of General Linguistics in the University of London is at the School of Oriental and African Studies, now rapidly developing in accordance with the recommendations of the Scarbrough Report. The range and outlook of the School reach far beyond the European scene, and the scholar himself must pursue his quest in distant lands among the peoples he wishes to know and bring nearer to us.

My own academic experience includes India, Egypt, and America, to which I may add study and travel in Europe and Africa. This experience prompts me to recommend *Archivum Linguisticum*—a title which calls to mind *quod semper, quod ubique, quod ab omnibus*—to publish its contributions in the most international idiom of today, English.

Again I would emphasize the weight of the American schools of linguistics and the advantage of the Atlantic grouping, which includes all Western Europe, as the home base. Farther afield, reaching out from the wider base of the English-speaking world, we face all the other civilizations and happily we enjoy such facility for mutual exchanges that we may confidently look forward to a great revival of learning in the languages and cultures of Asia and Africa.

In Britain the politics of the American Revolution have passed into history, and memorials of Washington, Lincoln, and Roosevelt stand in honoured places. In America they may agree with us that Queen Anne is dead, but George III still lives on. There is, however, one memory of the Crown which is perpetuated happily, and that is in New York where there was a King's College seventy years before we had one in London. That College has become one of the richest academic foundations in the world, Columbia University. Europeans are apt to forget the strength of the transatlantic academic tradition since the foundation of Harvard College in 1636. Yale College dates from 1718, Pennsylvania begins in 1740, Princeton in 1746, King's College (Columbia) in 1758, Brown in 1764, North Carolina in 1795. The Yale Graduate School granted the first Ph.D. in America in 1861. The continuity of common traditions of learning and scholarship between England and America is one of the chief points of the present chapter. With this common background in mind, I propose to outline the main features of what I have called Atlantic Linguistics.

I have dealt at length elsewhere[1] with the interest of the English in their old-established standard language, the King's English, which, in the words of the late Professor R. W. Chambers,[2] 'was making itself felt in the north of England in the eleventh century as it did not do again till the fifteenth' ... 'And this King's English, standard over all England, was intelligible over the whole of Northern Europe.' The traditional interest in the orthography and orthoepy of English, and in its usages and grammar, was inevitably transplanted in America. Noah Webster, the educator and lexicographer, wrote an essay on *The Reforming of Spelling*[3] in which he refers to the Elizabethan Sir Thomas Smith and other English orthoepists. Webster was in the tradition and linked it with nationalistic sentiments: 'The question now occurs: ought Americans to retain these faults which produce innumerable inconveniences in the acquisition and use of the language, or ought they at once to reform these abuses, and introduce order and regularity into the orthography of the American Tongue?' He pointed out the usual alleged educational advantages and then added, 'But a capital advantage of this reform in these states would be that it would make a difference between the English orthography and the American. This will startle those who have not attended to the subject, but I am confident that such an event is an object of vast political consequence.' For: 'The alteration, however small, would encourage the publication of books in our own country. It would render it, in some measure, necessary that all books should be printed in America. The English would never copy our orthography for their own use; and consequently the same impressions of books would not answer for both countries. The inhabitants of the present generation would read the English

[1] See Chapter 8, pp. 97–100.
[2] R. W. Chambers, 'The Continuity of English Prose from Alfred to More and his School', pp. lxxv seq., in Harpsfield's *Life of More*, E.E.T.S., o.s., no. 186, 1932. This masterly essay is of central importance in any study of institutionalized English.
[3] Noah Webster, 'The Reforming of Spelling', *Old South Leaflets*, vol. viii, pp. 4–9.

impressions; but posterity being taught in a different spelling, would prefer the American orthography.

'Besides this, a national language is a bond of national union. Every engine should be employed to render the people of this country national; to call their attachments home to their own country, to inspire them to the pride of national character.'

The promoters of a recent amateurish scheme of spelling reform in this country might well ponder the implications of Webster's idea. It would be a colossal stupidity for any exclusively British body to inaugurate any drastic reform. The great majority of the native users of English are outside these islands.

Webster himself had no such drastic plans. 'It is not to be expected that an orthography, perfectly regular and simple, such as would be formed by a "Synod of Grammarians on principles of science", will ever be substituted for the confused mode of spelling which is now established. But it is apprehended that great improvements may be made, and an orthography almost regular, or such as shall obviate most of the present difficulties which occur in learning our language, may be introduced and established with little trouble or opposition.'

He was no hot-head.

Benjamin Franklin did, however, propose an entirely new alphabet and mode of spelling. He was a printer among other things, and devised six new letters including one for the vowel 'in *um, un*; as in umbrage, unto, etc., and as in *er*', and the interesting letter *ŋ* '(ng)ing, in repeating, among'.

Franklin corresponded in his new spelling with an Englishwoman, Miss Mary Stevenson, a resident of Kensington, hoping that the reform might be inaugurated in the Old Country, but Miss Stevenson never quite learnt it or quite approved of the scheme. So Franklin in 1786 turned to Webster and offered to give him the types for experiment. But Webster wished to effect reform without 'a single new character, by means of a few trifling alterations of the present characters and retrenching a few superfluous letters, the most of which are corruptions of the original words'.

The American orthoepists from Franklin in 1768 to Whitney in 1889 deserve fuller notice than they have been given. The American dictionaries from Webster (1783) to the present day have been studied in America, but little noticed in England. It is interesting to note that the work of completing the 'Oxford' Middle English Dictionary is being done at Ann Arbor, Michigan.

The most striking of the early transatlantic contributions to the teaching of the English language is the English grammar[1] of the American Quaker,

---

[1] 'English Grammar, / adapted to the / different classes of learners, / with / an appendix / containing / Rules and Observations, / For Assisting the more Advanced Students / To write with Perspicuity and Accuracy' first published in 1795 and had run into a twenty-sixth edition by 1815.

Lindley Murray,[1] who came to live in Holgate, near York, in 1784. Writing of his Grammar he says:

> I was often solicited to compose and publish a Grammar of the English language, for the use of some teachers who were not perfectly satisfied with any of the existing grammars. I declined, for a considerable time, complying with this request, from a consciousness of my inability to do the subject that justice which would be expected in a new publication of this nature. But being much pressed to undertake the work, I at length turned my attention seriously to it. . . . But the approbation and the sale which the work obtained have given me some reason to believe that I have not altogether failed in my endeavours to elucidate the subject, and to facilitate the labours of both teachers and learners of English Grammar. . . . And the repeated editions through which it passed in a few years, encouraged me, at length, to improve and extend it still further; and, in particular, to support by some critical discussions, the principles upon which many of its positions are founded.[2]

In 1808 a much improved octavo edition in two volumes on fine paper and in a large letter was published as more suitable for libraries. Lindley Murray comments:[3] 'Some positions and discussions, I persuade myself, are not destitute of originality.' In some respects there was no improvement in the basic theoretical approach until Sweet treated the whole subject at a much higher level. Lindley Murray's careful attention to the prosodic features of pronunciation[4] were in the best classical tradition, and his discussion of case and mood in English original.[5] He was the first modern grammarian to treat 'auxiliary' verbs like *have, be, will, do* as sentence operators in the manner of Sweet, Harold Palmer, Jones, and others. Dealing with *do* and *did* he pointed out[6] their use in emphasis, in negative

---

[1] See *Memoirs of the Life and Writings of Lindley Murray*: in a series of letters, written by himself. York, 1826. He had visited England in 1771, but came to live here in 1784. He landed at Lymington, 'after a prosperous voyage of about five weeks'. He had 'strong prepossessions in favour of residence in this country; because I was very partial to its political constitution, and the mildness and wisdom of its general system of laws. I knew that, under this excellent government, life, property, reputation, civil and religious liberty, are happily protected; and that the general character and virtue of its inhabitants, take their complexion from the nature of their constitution and laws. On leaving my native country, there was not, therefore, any land on which I could cast my eyes with so much pleasure; nor is there any which could have afforded me so much real satisfaction as I have found in Great Britain. May its political fabric, which has stood the test of ages, and long attracted the admiration of the world, be supported and perpetuated by Divine Providence. And may the hearts of Britons be grateful for this blessing, and for many others by which they are eminently distinguished.'

[2] 'But my views in writing and publishing were not of a pecuniary nature. My great objects were, as I before observed, to be instrumental in doing good to others, to youth in particular; and to give my mind a rational and salutary employment.'
Lindley Murray applied the profits to charitable purposes, though he did not wish to imply any censure on other authors who could not afford to do the same. When we think of the profits which have since been made on selling English throughout the world, the example of the American Quaker living in the 'bad old days' is all the more to be honoured.

[3] Op cit., pp. 90–100.

[4] Grammar—29th edition, 1817. Part IV. Prosody—Chapter I. Pronunciation, pp. 224, 241. This does *not* refer to the laws of versification which are treated in Chapter II.

[5] Ibid., pp. 54–55, and pp. 78–79.   [6] Ibid., p. 97.

sentences, in asking questions, and also, a characteristic function, that they supply the place of another verb, 'and make the repetition of it, in the same or a subsequent sentence, unnecessary'.

His section on Accent or 'the stress of the voice' is extremely competent for that time. The Grammar is addressed to intelligent users and though built on a Latin model, is of a very different quality from those which began to appear after William Cobbett's *Grammar of the English Language* which appeared in 1820, 'intended more especially for the use of soldiers, sailors, apprentices and ploughboys'. The first introductory letter to James Paul Cobbett is dated 6 December 1817, from North Hempstead, Long Island. The eighteenth-century American writing in York is much to be preferred to the nineteenth-century Englishman writing epistles from Long Island. And during the nineteenth century, especially after the 1870 Act, most grammars for the young were execrable. Many of them still are.

The quality of the leading American scholars in the eighteenth century and the early nineteenth is not surprising. They remind us of the seventeenth-century English rationalists, scientists, philosophers, scholars of all kinds, some of whom eventually formed the Royal Society under Charles II. There were some distinguished Cromwellians, but natural philosophy was also a hobby of Prince Rupert. It was to be expected that some of those free and daring spirits who crossed the Atlantic would do honour to their brethren in England.

In the early days of the Royal Society a great deal of interest was shown in the problems of speech and language,[1] and so it was with the American Philosophical Society founded in 1744 in Philadelphia for promoting useful knowledge. 'Benjamin Franklin Esq., LL.D.' and several Penns were founder members. By February 1774 it had been forced to become political and Benjamin, now a Fellow of the Royal Society, had the following entered in the proceedings: 'The Act of the British Parliament . . . having alarmed the whole of the American Colonies, members partaking with their countrymen in the distress and labors [sic] brought upon their country, were obliged to discontinue their meetings for some months untill [sic] a mode of opposition to the said Acts of Parliament was established, which they hope will restore the former Harmony and maintain a perpetual Union between Great Britain and the American Colonies.' On 16 January 1779, however, it was necessary to report that their proceedings 'had been interrupted by the Calamities of War and the Invasion of this City by the Enemy'. In the annals of our common traditions such entries may be reminders of painful events, but they are of passing moment in our cultural history.

We have seen how Americans contributed to the age-old subjects of the orthography and orthoepy of the common language, to grammar, and to lexicography in Webster's *American Dictionary of the English Language* in 1828.

[1] See J. R. Firth, *Tongues of Men*, pp. 69, 71–74; also Chapter 8, pp. 102, 108, 109.

Sir William Jones, the Orientalist, is, in a very real sense, of transatlantic significance.[1] Hs held uncompromising liberal views in politics which delayed for many years his appointment to any Indian post in the gift of the British Government. In the parliamentary election of 1780, as a candidate for the University of Oxford, his detestation of the American War and of the slave trade were too strongly expressed to be agreeable to the voters, and he was forced to withdraw from the contest. In the same year he failed to secure election as Professor of Arabic in the University for similar reasons. His avowed hostility to the American War, rumours that he was a republican at heart, rumours that he was planning to go to America, were recorded by contemporaries. Finally, in 1783, with the disappearance of Lord North, he was appointed Judge to the Calcutta Court and given a knighthood.

The work of Sir William Jones had an immediate effect on American scholarship. He was the great hero, both as a lawyer and a linguist, of John Pickering,[2] himself lawyer and linguist, and one of the two greatest general linguists of the first half of the nineteenth century in America. Though Sir William Jones was apparently on friendly terms with Benjamin Franklin, I can find only one mention of his name in the early proceedings of the American Philosophical Society, when Benjamin Franklin caused to be read at a meeting on 18 September 1789 Sir William Jones's opinion that the Royal Society could 'sue for arrears due by their members'.

The American learned bodies such as the Philosophical Society and the Oriental Society from the very beginning admitted to honorary membership British and other European scholars and expressed their solidarity with European learning. It is no accident that Professor Franklin Edgerton, when occupying one of the Salisbury chairs at Yale, should contribute his review of American linguistics to the pioneering Philosophical Society and his commemorative tribute to Sir William Jones to the Oriental Society. In August 1842[3] 'a meeting of a few gentlemen interested in Oriental Literature was held at the office of John Pickering, Esq. in Boston to consider the practicability and expediency of forming an American Oriental

[1] See Franklin Edgerton's 'Sir William Jones: 1746–1794' in *J.A.O.S.*, vol. lxvi, no. 3, July–September 1946.
[2] See Franklin Edgerton's 'Notes on Early American Work in Linguistics', *Proceedings of the American Philosophical Society*, vol. lxxxvii, no. 1, 1943.
[3] 1842 is an important year in the history of linguistics on both sides of the Atlantic. In that year was founded the Philological Society of Great Britain. See *Philologists at University College* by R. W. Chambers, being the third of a Series of Centenary Addresses, 2 May 1927, pp. 19–20, University of London Press Ltd. 'The Philological Society had begun as a student society of this College, almost as soon as the College itself began. But a revolution took place. The object of this revolution (as described by the present Secretary of the Society) was the exact reverse of that of most modern revolutions: it was "that the unripe or otherwise undesirable elements might be got rid of". A dictatorship of the professoriate was established. Then in 1842 the Society became a national, instead of a University body.... Three professors of University College—Latham, Key, and Malden—"began the publication of a periodical—the *Proceedings* (later called *Transactions*) which remains today the oldest purely philological periodical still running in England".'

Society'.[1] The officers of the Society, as one would expect, were mostly Bostonians. In the Act of Incorporation the Society was 'for the purpose of the cultivation of learning in the Asiatic, African and Polynesian languages' and it was to sponsor 'the publication of Memoirs, Translations, Vocabularies and other works relating to the Asiatic, African and Polynesian languages'. Much more recently in England we have similarly grouped African and Oceanic as well as general linguistics with Oriental studies in the University of London. The following extracts are taken from the first address in 1843 to the gentlemen of the American Oriental Society by their first president, John Pickering:

'We shall one day have it in our power to co-operate on more advantageous terms with our European brethren. . . . Europe and the United States constitute but one literary community.' Handsome tribute is paid to 'that great country in whose language we shall make our intellectual contributions, and with whose labours foreign nations will naturally compare those of our countrymen, labours of the scholars of England to whom we owe so much—(yet, if the opinions of eminent Englishmen themselves are of any authority in this case, the actual state of philological and ethnographical knowledge among them is far lower than it ought to be)'.[2]

My present comment on the above revealing excerpts is that many English linguists are out of touch with contemporary American work in linguistics and that some branches have become so specialized that far from being written in a language we can readily understand, require considerable preparatory study of the idiom in which they are written. The tables are turned. We must hope that more British scholars may 'one day have it in their power to co-operate on advantageous terms with their *American* brethren'. The development of Oriental, Slavonic, and African studies referred to earlier provides excellent opportunities for collaboration with the new world-wide interests in linguistics which must expand and multiply now that America has accepted her responsibilities. Permit me to repeat the sentence above quoted from the proceedings of the American Oriental Society: 'Europe and the United States constitute but one literary community.'

Further emphasis of the 'Atlantic' conception arises from a study of the leading personalities; John Pickering (1777–1846), Peter Stephen Du Ponceau (1760–1844), and James Smithson, the founder of the Smithsonian Institution which stimulated and fostered linguistic research in American Indian and exotic languages.

Pickering,[3] said to be descended from a Yorkshire carpenter, was Secretary to the United States Minister to Portugal where he studied Turkish and Arabic. He was transferred to London in 1799 and from there he visited Paris, Brussels, and Holland, cultivating the society of scholars and looking into the libraries. After he retired to New England he devoted himself to

---

[1] *J.A.O.S.*, vol. i, 1849, p. ii.   [2] Ibid., p. 53.
[3] See Franklin Edgerton, *Notes on Early American Work in Linguistics*, pp. 27 et seq.

linguistics and learning languages. His *Greek Lexicon* is regarded by some as the best Greek–English dictionary before Liddell and Scott; he was the leading authority of his day on the North American Indians, the first to publish a collection of Americanisms,[1] and yet earned the reputation of writing in the style of the most eminent British reviewers.

Du Ponceau[2] was born a Frenchman of ancient lineage, landed and fought for America in 1777, and became a citizen of Pennsylvania in 1781. He also promoted the study of American Indian languages and in 1838 was awarded the Prix Volney by his native country for his *Mémoire sur le système grammatical des langues de quelques nations indiennes de l'Amérique du Nord.* He it was who invented the term *polysynthetic*.

Perhaps his most interesting work is *A Dissertation on the Nature and Character of the Chinese System of Writing* published for the American Philosophical Society in 1838, in which he establishes that it is not ideographic but *lexigraphic* or *logographic*. He was not so wise in dealing with Father Morrone's *Cochinchinese Vocabulary*, for in spite of all information on Annamese dialects since Father Alexander de Rhodes's *Dictionarium Annamiticum* (1651), he endorses M. de la Palun's[3] comment 'we can hardly believe the Cochinchinese have *six* tones'. 'We have omitted these last signs in copying the Vocabulary.' Du Ponceau therefore agreed that all Father Morrone's accents and tone marks might be omitted.[4]

Modern descriptive linguistics which flourishes today in America also owes a great deal to the Smithsonian Institution[5] which linked linguistics with ethnology and promoted research by issuing questionnaires and by publications. Whitney's *Lectures on Linguistics* were given a wide distribution by the Institution.[6]

The linguistic publications began characteristically enough with an article by Dr. Francis Grieber 'On the Vocal Sounds of Laura Bridgman, the Blind Deaf Mute at Boston, compared with the Elements of Phonetic Language'. Between 1850 and 1876 a large amount of work was done collecting vocabularies in American Indian languages. In 1876 'it was found necessary to enlarge the alphabet to include a wider range of sounds which

---

[1] See Allen Walker Read, 'The Collections for Pickering's "Vocabulary"', *American Speech*, December 1947.

[2] See Franklin Edgerton, *Notes on Early American Work in Linguistics*, pp. 27 et seq.

[3] M. de la Palun was one of those who believe that 'all tones are bunk'. Such people are still about. He comments: 'The missionaries of Pekin had carried to five the number of those of the Chinese language, because they did not examine with sufficient care the assertions of the Chinese grammarians, who have sought differences in intonations which escape the delicate ear of poets and which consequently, if they are real, can only exist for purists, and are of no kind of use.'

[4] See *Vocabulary of the Cochinchinese Language* by the Rev. Joseph Morrone, missionary at Saigon (appended to Du Ponceau's *Chinese Writing*), pp. 134 and 141.

[5] Founded by *James Smithson*, whose mother was a descendant of Charles, Duke of Somerset, and who was himself related to the Percys, Dukes of Northumberland. In his will he prophesies: 'My name shall live in the memory of man when the titles of the Northumberlands and the Percys are extinct and forgotten.'

[6] See *The Smithsonian Institution*, 1846–96, pp. 757–66, for a 'Review of Anthropological Work' by Jesse Walter Fewkes.

have been discovered in the North American languages'. In furthering the collection of material, the suggestion was circulated that 'many simple sentences should be given, so chosen as to bring out the more important characteristics of grammatical structure'. Still good advice! Together with the American Philosophical Society and the Oriental Society the Institution helped forward all this pioneer work in descriptive linguistics which is in America and overseas such a feature of the American contribution to the study of language today.

The close association of missions with the development of linguistics is a constant feature of the history of the subject. 'It is difficult indeed to imagine what our present knowledge of exotic languages would be like without the libraries of books which have grown out of the labours of generations of missionaries, Catholic and Protestant.'[1] First the Propaganda Fide in Europe, and today in America, the work of Dr. Kenneth Pike and his colleagues for the mission fields and for linguistics.

In 1848 the American Oriental Society published a detailed report on American missionaries 'residing beyond the bounds of Christendom not including those among the North American Indians'.[2] A total of 234 is tabulated as follows:

Africa, Western	. 25	West Asia . .	. 33
Southern	. 8	India and Ceylon.	. 66
Greece . . .	. 3	China . .	. 43
Burma, Siam, and Borneo	. 29	Sandwich Islands (Hawaii)	. 27

The large number of American missionaries with competent phonetic training now going out to all the important mission fields in the world is a great advance on the nineteenth-century achievement. Experienced missionaries and ex-civil servants returned to England from overseas are associated with other scholars in the development of such learning in Britain today.

The American Indian work was a good background for field linguistics. The Americans report a Fijian Vocabulary (1811), early work on Berber by Newman (1846), on Yoruba by Bowen (1858) and on the dialects of the Gabun, on Swahili, as well as a first attempt at reducing the Karen dialects to writing. On the last type of work the American Oriental Society report in 1848:[3] 'Scarcely less than a score of languages have been reduced to writing within the last thirty years, by our countrymen engaged in foreign missions; and for the most part on the principles advocated by the late President of the Society, in his well-known "Essay on a Uniform Orthography for the Indian Languages in North America". A remarkable simplicity and uniformity of orthography have thus been secured. This is a subject to which the Society will do well to direct its attention.'

---

[1] J. R. Firth, *Tongues of Men*, pp. 13 and 59–69. Watts, London, 1937.
[2] See *J.A.O.S.*, vol. i, pp. xli–xlvii.
[3] Ibid. p. xlvii. The president referred to was John Pickering.

A great deal of early work suffered because of phonetic incompetence. The linking up of American and English phoneticians was a step forward in Atlantic linguistics. There is no doubt that Sir William Jones and Sanskrit were the active sources of stimulus for new developments in general linguistics and phonetics both in Europe and America. One of the greatest vehicles of this enlightenment was William Dwight Whitney,[1] Professor of Sanskrit in Yale College. In 1861 he presented a highly competent criticism of Lepsius's Standard Alphabet,[2] in which there is some first-rate phonetic theory. It is a great pity more attention could not have been given to phonetics by later Sanskritists so that we might have been spared the *naïveté* of a good deal of 'modern' phonetics. Whitney realized the effect of the roman alphabet on our theories, which suffered in consequence.[3] He objected to 'the division of the spoken alphabet . . . into the two distinct classes of vowels and consonants. This is a convenient practical classification, but it possesses only a superficial correctness. . . . We cannot sanction, then, a theoretical system which makes the distinction of vowel and consonant absolute and fundamental, which holds the two classes apart from one another, and adopts for them two different methods of classification and arrangement.' He came very near to the theory of cardinal vowels. 'On the line of palatal closure, the closest position capable of producing a sound which shall possess a vowel quality gives the vowel *i*. . . . The line of lingual closure produces no vowels. These two vowels *i* and *u*, the farthest removed from *a* in their respective directions, are, with *a*, the most primitive and most universally occurring of all the vowels: in them we are on the very borders of the consonantal territory.' He severely criticizes Lepsius's treatment of vowels. The following sentence has a curiously familiar ring: 'From *a* to *i* is a line of direct progression, a process of gradual approximation of the organs, in which there are theoretically an infinite number of different points, or degrees of closure, each of them giving a different vowel sound.' He is extremely good on **y** and **w**, and on whispering; 'the place of tone being taken by a rustling of the breath through the larynx', thus enabling us 'to make audible the distinction between surd and sonant'. He 'serialized' sibilants followed later by Sweet.[4] He was quite clear that the Indian aspirated plosives, though written with digraphs in roman transcription, were 'simple sounds'. After stressing the need for 'good judgment' and 'enlightened insight' in the makers and users of alphabetic systems, he concludes his masterly review in the following words: 'No slight responsibility, however, rests upon him who first puts into written characters a virgin tongue, since it is impossible to say of how many individuals and generations the convenience depends upon his work. There can be no better

---

[1] See also Franklin Edgerton, *Notes on Early American Work in Linguistics*, p. 33.
[2] See *J.A.O.S.*, vol. ii, 1860–3, pp. 229–332. See also ibid., vol. iii, 1864, for a lively exchange of views. 'On Lepsius's Standard Alphabet—A letter of Explanations from Professor Lepsius, with notes by W. D. Whitney', pp. 335–72.
[3] See Chapter 9, pp. 122–4.
[4] See *Primer of Phonetics*, p. 40.

preparation for this than a thorough physical comprehension of the sounds of one's own native speech, and a correct understanding of the history of the signs with which it is written; and a searching and intelligible analysis of the English spoken alphabet must be the most valuable phonetical assistant to any one who, having the English for his mother tongue, is required to study the phonetic system of another language, whether for description or for reduction to a written form.' Wisdom indeed!

In the following year, 1862, he presented to the Society a text of the *Atharva-veda prātiśākhya* with translation and notes,[1] one of the ancient treatises on phonetic technique, containing more wisdom than many modern manuals of phonetics. The Indians understood the importance of the study of the features of connected utterance, or what nowadays are sometimes called prosodies.[2]

The study of phonetics in all its branches has continued to be a feature of Atlantic linguistics, especially in England, America, and Scandinavia. Lepsius was officially brought into the community by British missionary bodies, and we have just noticed the great interest and important contributions of Whitney. There was an interesting American link with A. J. Ellis and Melville Bell in Samuel Haldeman, who, though crazy as an etymologist, had a sound knowledge of phonetic technique and the right ideas on the recording of phonetic observations.[3]

The Bells[4] are perhaps the best symbol of Atlantic phonetics, since they linked up Scotland, England, Ireland, Canada, and the United States by their own work, and eventually the world by telephone. The *Visible Speech*[5] of the Bell Telephone Laboratories today is a reminder of the *Visible Speech* of 1867 by Melville Bell.

Henry Sweet was undoubtedly the outstanding English general philologist in the nineteenth century, realizing as he did where our strength lay: 'Our tendency is not so much toward the antiquarian philology and text-criticism in which German scholars have done so much, as towards the observation *of the phenomena of living languages.* . . . Our aim ought clearly to be, while assimilating the methods and results of German work, to concentrate our energies mainly, on what may be called "living philology".'[6] Sweet especially appreciated the work of Scandinavian scholars who hold a proud place not only in those branches of linguistics in which the Atlantic communities using English have excelled, but generally in linguistics and philology. A great deal of Scandinavian and Dutch work has been written in English, and among these, the best known is the honoured name of Otto Jespersen.

Sweet is perhaps to be regarded as the real founder of what he himself

[1] *J.A.O.S.*, vol. iii, 1860–3. Article VIII, pp. 331–615.
[2] See Chapter 9.
[3] See Chapter 8, pp. 114–16.
[4] Ibid., pp. 116–19.
[5] See Potter, Kopp, and Green, *Visible Speech*, New York, 1947.
[6] From his presidential address to the Philological Society of Great Britain, in 1877.

called *The English School of Phonetics*. Since his time, Professor Daniel Jones and his colleagues in London have carried its work to all parts of the world. Daniel Jones has built the International Phonetic Association, which is strongly supported in the United States, and has introduced one form of the phoneme theory into the principles which are applied in its work. In the United States the phoneme concept has inspired several groups of scholars who have developed techniques in descriptive linguistics known as *phonemics*. Though descriptive work based on what may be loosely called 'the phoneme principle' is one of the characteristics of Atlantic linguistics, and though it has its real roots in the work of Sweet and Jespersen, it is much indebted to Slavonic sources. The influence of Baudouin de Courtenay, Kruszewski,[1] and indeed of the whole group who worked in Warsaw, Dorpat, and later in Kazan, was strengthened by their close understanding of the Geneva and Paris schools led by de Saussure. The importance of the Slav contribution to modern linguistics is not overlooked but rather emphasized in Atlantic linguistics, not only in phonology but also in other branches of general linguistics, especially perhaps in semantics. In the recent past what was called the 'new phonology' aroused widespread interest largely through the inspired leadership of Trubetzkoy and the work of the Prague Circle. Leading Central European scholars have migrated westward during the last twenty years, and Roman Jakobson, significantly enough, worked in Scandinavia before going to Columbia. It is symbolic too that Jakobson, Martinet (lately of Paris), and others should form a society called *Le Cercle Linguistique de New York*.

The development of American Indian Linguistics[2] from the early beginnings noted above remains the characteristic American contribution. The work of Boas and Sapir, later development by Bloomfield who has schools of American followers at the present time, all contribute to the position now held by American scholarship in linguistics. Sapir and Bloomfield have exerted a world-wide influence on general linguistics in their different ways. Every student of the subject must know their work, for it immediately precedes present-day developments in Atlantic as well as in Slav linguistics, which are certainly post-Saussurean and showing signs even in America of becoming post-Bloomfield.

Bloomfield's approach to linguistics was much influenced by American behaviourism.[3] In the preface to the 1933 edition of his *Language*, he ranges himself with the 'mechanists' against the 'mentalists'. Such an antinomy does not vex Western European scholars today, nor need it be

---

[1] See Chapter 1.
[2] See Zellig S. Harris, 'Developments in American Indian Linguistics', *The American Philological Society, Library Bulletin*, pp. 89–97 (1947). Also the volumes of the *International Journal of American Linguistics*. In vol. xiv, no. 3, July 1948, pp. 209–10, Professor Sebeok, in a brief notice of Harris, says 'considerable development is now to be expected: partly because of methodological advances, partly because of popular application of certain techniques originating in this field'.
[3] See especially A. P. Weiss, *A Theoretical Basis of Human Behaviour*, Columbus, 1929.

regarded really as a vital issue in the United States. Aristotelian logic and metaphysics, psychological conceptualism, Durkheimian sociology, and behaviourism have all ruled linguistics in one way or another.

Today the linguistic disciplines are much surer of their own principles and philosophical outlook. Indeed, it is possible that during the next fifty years general linguistics may supplant a great deal of philosophy. The process has begun.

Referring to my paper on 'The English School of Phonetics', Mr. David Abercrombie[1] pertinently reminds us once more 'that our antecedents are older and better than we think'. In linguistic philosophy, in the study of shorthand, universal languages and nomenclature, in logic and 'logical syntax', in lexicography and in pioneer descriptions of exotic languages, England has maintained a high standard of original work since the days of Elizabeth. Some early Americans have also taken part, and one of them, Alexander Bryan Johnson,[2] author of *The Meaning of Words analysed into Words and Unverbal Things*, has long been known to scholars but not noticed. Similar views were put forward by Sir Graves Chamney Haughton, F.R.S., in *Prodromus*, published in 1839, and also in his 'Short Inquiry into the Nature of Language' prefaced to his *Dictionary of Bengali and Sanskrit Explained in English* (1833).[3] Both Johnson and Haughton were fully aware of what we now refer to as the sociological context, and both saw the danger that linguists might concentrate on languages and words as autonomous organisms or mechanisms. Haughton emphasized that man developed language 'in the infancy of Society, impelled by the pressure of his wants'. It was 'called into existence by the exigencies of his situation, and the circumstances by which he was surrounded ... and consequently in exact relation to the general laws of nature.... In every inquiry which we make into the nature of language, we are bound to ascertain its relation to the other phenomena of nature, and to consider it as something more than a detached and subservient instrument of thought.' In his *Prodromus*, referring to Metaphysics and Morals, he says: 'I found the whole of these topics a perfect chaos, from the deceptive character of language.'

In the preface to the first edition[4] of *The Meaning of Meaning*, the authors

---

[1] 'Forgotten Phoneticians', *Transactions of the Philological Society*, 1948, p. 34. See also ibid., p. 142.

[2] Born in Gosport, England, 1786. Family emigrated to the U.S. in 1797. Went to Utica, N.Y., in 1801. *Treatise on Language*, 1836. *The Meaning of Words Analysed*, 1854. The following pages are worth study for the speculations and suggestions which are well known to us in twentieth-century work. Johnson was an amateur and, though his work may have been read, it was of course rarely quoted by professionals: pp. 18, 38, 47–48, 50–52, 94, 96, 106, 111, 129, 141, 144, 147, 183, 185, 191. The edition I used was published in New York by Appleton & Co. in 1854.
See the recent publication *A Treatise on Language* edited by D. Rynin, Berkeley and Los Angeles, 1947.

[3] Pp. xi–xiii. On page 8 of his note on Bengali grammar he indicates his independence of mind and good phonetics by remarking: 'The cerebrals are denoted by a dot written beneath; though it should rather have been put under the dentals, to mark that they are different from our own letters.' [English, of course.]

[4] 1923.

announce that writing began in 1910, that much of the material appeared in periodicals during the period 1920-2, and that the work arose 'out of an attempt to deal directly with difficulties raised by the influence of Language upon Thought'. They refer somewhat disparagingly to linguistics, linguists, and grammarians. Mention is made of Malinowski, who contributed a Supplement of thirty-nine closely printed pages, a forerunner of his ethnographic theory of language[1] founded on sociological postulates, which bears little relation to the epistemological character of the main work, but which has had far more influence on general linguistic theory.

And yet it is important to note that the work of Ogden and Richards, and of the Vienna Circle of logical positivists and their followers, derives in part from Bentham and from the English rationalists of the seventeenth century. Basic English is in the same tradition.

I have dealt with English work in semantics and phonetics elsewhere.[2] I now draw attention to English interest in general linguistics and problems of meaning lying outside the scope of comparative grammar and 'Indo-Germanism' and 'Aryanism' which held such sway in linguistics focused on German scholarship of the nineteenth century. England was never really good at it, and it is interesting to point out that the select few Master Philologists we have today are not principally grammarians but have wide philological and sociological interests.[3]

In employing the title *Atlantic Linguistics*, I am not excluding or ignoring the great contribution of Russian and other Slav or Central European scholars. Indeed, it is probably true that our approach today, especially in London, has distinct affinities with Slav linguistics. In phonetics, Professor Daniel Jones had a number of Russian colleagues including Professors Ščerba, Trofimov, Boyanus, and Trubetzkoy. The modern phoneme theory is Polish and Russian in origin, although it undoubtedly exists *in nuce* in Sweet's *Broad Romic*, in Jespersen's *Phonetics*, and in the principles and practice of the International Phonetic Association.

The Prague Circle and its many imitators, running in parallel with the Vienna Circle, have been formative influences especially in America, where a few distinguished Central European scholars wield great influence.

Contemporary Russian linguists following Marr, such as Meshtchaninov and Tchemodanov, are critical of the abstractions of phonological and morphological isolationism, indeed of the purism and autonomy of all comparative grammar of the traditional nineteenth-century pattern. Where is the sociological component? Our Russian critics must be told that the advances in linguistics in the twentieth century, and especially in England since the end of the First World War, are in accordance with changes in the intellectual climate and in the contexts of science. I can say of the

---

[1] See also his *Coral Gardens and Their Magic*, 1935, vol. ii, part iv, pp. 3-74.
[2] See Chapters 3 and 8.
[3] So also Professor Benveniste in his lectures in the University of London referred the study of the vocabulary of Indo-European to sociological context.

London group to which I belong, that our work is certainly not Saussurean in the Russian pejorative sense, nor is it 'autonomous' linguistic structuralism, without sociological component. Marr criticized the phonetic and morphological formalism of the comparativists who pushed vocabulary study into a secondary place. More recent criticisms[1] are directed against the formalism of Prague and Copenhagen.

Professor A. V. Isačenko of Bratislava has reviewed the discords among linguists today, in an article in Slovak on the scope and limits of synchronic linguistics. He brings out quite clearly the importance of semantics and the problems of the relations of the word to the sentence. He suggests a preliminary definition of the sentence which may be rendered in English as 'the smallest grammatically organised unit of predication'. I do not like the idea behind 'unit of predication', but most linguists would agree that the study of the sentence as our primary datum is the order of the day.

I have no doubt at all that if some 'Atlantic' work could be disguised in Russian it would pass the censors, and I am equally sure that a good deal of contemporary Eastern European work is 'bad old bourgeois Imperialist race-conscious' linguistics, smelling of Germany in the nineteenth century.

In order to make clear what is meant by isolated phonological and morphological structuralism without any sociological component, I would quote the extreme case of Dr. Eugene Nida's *Morphology*.[2] The phonology is 'nonsense',[3] the word-classes and related morphology are also 'nonsense'. When 'nonsense' is added to 'nonsense', and there is no sociological component or sanction, the result must be superlative nonsense from the Russian sociological point of view. If this sort of book is explained as a necessary mechanism for mass training, the Russians will answer 'bourgeois imperialism'. It is important to understand Russian criticism. We must not ignore it, still less try to laugh it off.

Having attempted to round off this study by bringing in the highly important Slav component, I think I must conclude by a brief statement of the London point of view by reviewing my own contribution, emphasizing its distinctive features.

General linguistics in London has had the advantage of association with two well-known schools—the School of Phonetics founded at University College by Daniel Jones, and the School of Social Anthropology built up by Malinowski at the London School of Economics, and now flourishing under his successor, Professor Raymond Firth. That perhaps accounts for what students have described as my 'spectrum' method of handling linguistic material at a series of levels. 'Spectrum' analysis makes sure of the social

---

[1] N. S. Tchemodanov, *Structuralism and Soviet Linguistics*, 1947.

[2] Eugene A. Nida, 'Morphology: The Descriptive Analysis of Words', *University of Michigan Publications, Linguistics*, vol. ii, 1946.

[3] The language material is concocted to fit the categories and procedures recommended to the student. 'A second and completely new edition based on actual-language materials' has since appeared. Ann Arbor, 1949.

reality of the data at the sociological level,[1] before breaking down the total meaningful intention into the semantic, grammatical, lexical, phonological, and phonetic components each dealt with at the suitable level of abstraction employing specialized techniques. Speech at all levels is regarded as a social and bodily process, not forgetting the biological or physical basis of personality.[2] Indeed, language and personality are coupled as twin factors or twin forces in the complex process.

I first suggested the beginnings of this approach in two articles published in *English Studies*.[3] The notions of *minor* and *major* function were only a beginning in the development analysis at a series of levels.

Professor Isačenko, in the article previously referred to, remarks that in the discords among linguists, the differences of their philosophical point of departure is especially clearly reflected. My own 'philosophical point of departure' was clearly stated in *Speech*,[4] published in 1930 in Benn's Library. It was restated in *The Tongues of Men*[5] in 1937. A preliminary sketch of the 'spectrum' method of analysis at different levels was submitted to the Philological Society of Great Britain in February 1935 and published in the *Transactions* of that year.[6]

The main stream of linguistics during the nineteenth century flowed in the channels of comparative grammar, Indo-European at that, and restricted as it was to historical phonology within the framework of morphology, its limitations were severe. It could not reach the rich fields of creative linguistic action in human society. The linguistic sciences have broadened out to deal with speech and language as processes, bodily and social, maintaining the patterns of life.

The rise of Asia and Africa entails the responsibility of regarding language from a world point of view, and of considering other forms of writing, other systems of grammar, and other philosophies of language than those of Western Europe and America. In London the chair of General Linguistics is tenable at the School of Oriental and African Studies, which is all to the good.

Finally, it should be said that the tendencies noted under the title

[1] Professor A. V. Isačenko of Bratislava, in a recent article in Slovak, expresses agreement with this order of approach, which was first emphasized in this country in my little book *Speech*, first published in 1930. He says we have got used to the 'ascending' course of thinking in linguistics (i.e. 'from the phoneme to the sentence'). The opposite descending procedure is the right one. And so say all of us. In the early thirties, when I was teaching at the Indian Institute in Oxford, I remember Professor F. W. Thomas, Boden Professor of Sanskrit, one of our most senior and highly respected scholars, followed up a reference to similar topics, with an outline plan for a grammar beginning with Syntax and 'descending' to phonetics in an appendix.

[2] See Chapter 10.

[3] 'Linguistics and the Functional Point of View', *English Studies*, February 1934, and Chapter 4.

[4] See especially Chapter I, Chapter II, pp. 14-16, Chapter III, pp. 17-18, Chapter V (The problem of meaning), Chapter VI, pp. 45-47.

[5] See Chapter I, pp. 13-17, Chapter II, Chapters VIII, IX, and X.

[6] See Chapter 3, especially pp. 19-33. This work has been noticed by Sir Philip Hartog, in *Words in Action*; see pp. 68, 83, 256, 260.

'Atlantic Linguistics' are world wide. American linguistics has found its strongest stimulus in American Indian Studies, and Boas, Sapir, Hoijer, and others are as well known in social anthropology as in linguistics. Descriptive linguistics in America ranges over all the language families of the world. Russian linguists have long been at work on the languages of their peoples of Asia, and loudly proclaim their special form of appropriate sociology.

The linguistic sciences are more and more autonomous and the need is for many more workers, including Asians and Africans, a wide circulation of journals and publications, especially in English, and frequent meetings in well-selected centres all over the world.

PLATE 8

(a)

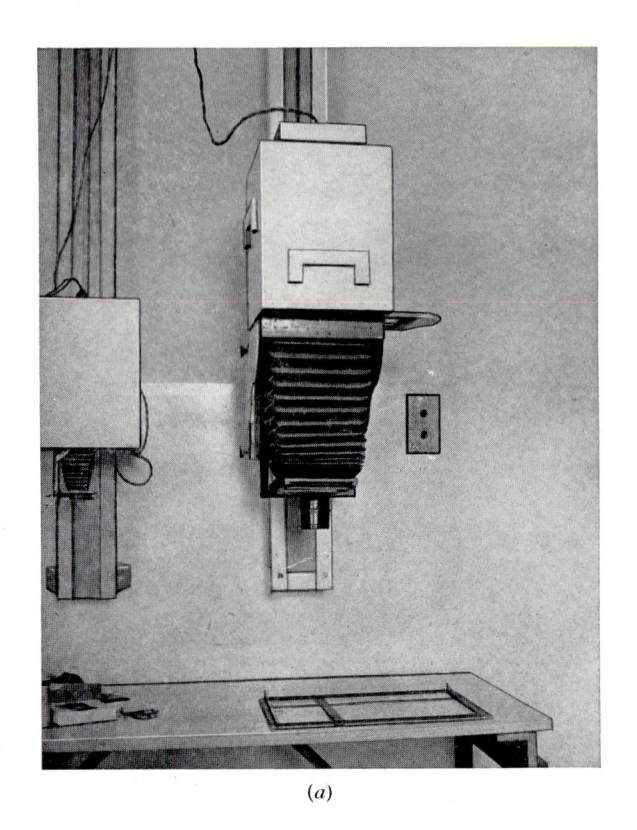

(b)

KYMOGRAPHY WITH CELLOPHANE

13

IMPROVED TECHNIQUES IN PALATOGRAPHY AND KYMOGRAPHY

[WITH H. J. F. ADAM]

(PLATES 8–11)

SINCE the early thirties we have found it necessary constantly and independently to review the sort of abstractions usually made in descriptive linguistics, and in making new ones to refer them to a schematic framework of levels, at each one of which some component of meaning could be handled by a system of constructs and stated.[1]

Professor Panconcelli-Calzia seems only recently to have awakened to the idea that four-fifths of linguistics, including even experimental phonetics, is invention rather than discovery.[2] The work of the English School of Phonetics since the time of the Bells has been rich in invention, and earned the inadequate description of being 'practical'. In the best sense of the word, descriptive linguistics must be practical, since its abstractions, fictions, inventions, call them what you will, are designed to handle *instances* of speech, spoken or written, and make statements of the meaning of what may be called typical speech events. All these fictions, whether made by machines or by direct verbal statement, may perhaps be figuratively described as 'asymptotic'.

If we are constantly mindful of the different levels of abstraction and the nature of the fictions set up, the inventions of kymography and palatography and the inventions of phonology or other branches of linguistics[3] may be brought into relation and used to justify one another mutually.

The purpose of the present article is to give an illustration of the pressure of 'invention' at the levels of phonology and even of general linguistic theory, which has led to ancillary 'inventions' in the laboratory. It is not merely the apparatus for kymography and palatography which are inventions. The kymogram and the palatogram are also inventions. They are not

---

[1] See Chapters 3 and 11.
[2] *Das Als Ob in der Phonetik*, 250 pp., Stromverlag, Hamburg-Bergedorf, 1947.
[3] See footnote on 'Word Palatograms and Articulation' in *Language*, vol. xxv, no. 1 (Fries and Pike, 'Coexistent Phonemic Systems'):
'J. R. Firth, in "Word-palatograms and Articulation", *B.S.O.A.S.* xii, 857–864 (1948), makes a related but experimental abstraction of a phonetic characteristic from a word or syllable by noting the total effect of some one articulator throughout the whole unit; these effects are not Harris's simultaneous components, which affect contiguous sounds, but may be the result of non-contiguous segments.' It will be seen that the theoretical implications of the new approach are much wider than indicated in the above note.

nearer to 'reality' than the fictions of perception phonetics or the abstractions, fictions, or inventions of phonology.

The 'inventions' of the palatogram projector and the inventions of phonological research now going on in a number of languages justify one another. When we measure any features of a kymogram in centiseconds, we must realize what the machine itself abstracts from the single instance and what is abstracted by the employment of the kymogram. We may measure the *duration* of a feature abstracted at another level, say the duration of 'a stop' or 'a vowel' duly identified and delimited, but it is a measure of *duration*, not of *gemination* or *quantity*, which are fictions at a level which cannot be measured in centiseconds. At the lowest level we are really only measuring a section of a tracing.

It will also be readily agreed that the palatograms do not measure or display the articulation of what some call *a sound*, nor do they exhibit anything which could correlate with a phoneme variant or allophone. The new palatogram is a new invention and is justified by its relation to inventions in phonology. These interrelated techniques at different levels are, it is claimed, an advance on previous methods of handling speech events.

DETAILED DESCRIPTION OF KYMOGRAPHIC AND PALATOGRAPHIC TECHNIQUE EMPLOYED

Kymography

The kymographic technique now employed produces a 'black-on-white' wave-form, having the effect of giving a clearer and more striking picture than was previously the case. The practice of varnishing the smoked paper has become unnecessary, thus eliminating one of the more undesirable aspects of kymography by the usual method.

Apparatus

A full-plate ($8\frac{1}{2} \times 6\frac{1}{2}$ in.) camera is mounted on a vertical slide (Plate 8*a*). The plate-holder has been modified, giving it a glass base on which to lay the tracings for projection. (See *Method*, 5.)

A lamp-housing is mounted over the camera to provide the necessary illumination.

For light diffusion a sheet of Perspex 'Opal 020' has been used. This has been found to make the use of condensers unnecessary.

The camera is in effect a photographic enlarger, and by varying the height of the camera and by use of the focusing screw the size of the projected image can be varied as required.

Method

1. The drum of the kymograph is covered with the usual sheet of glazed white paper.

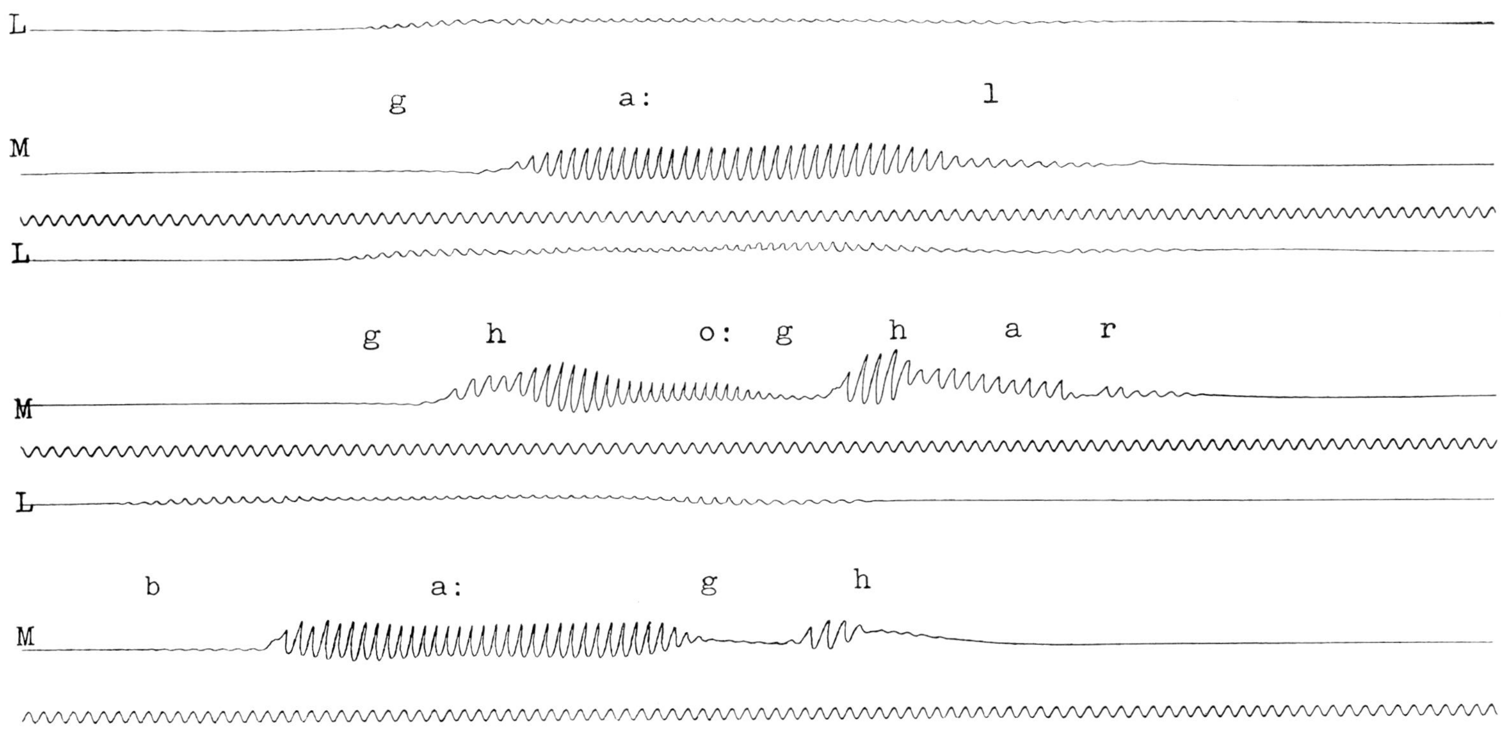

PLATE 9

g   aː   l

g h oː g h a r

b aː g h

THREE EXAMPLES OF KYMOGRAMS OBTAINED BY THE CELLOPHANE TECHNIQUE

PLATE 10

THE PALATOGRAM PROJECTOR

2. A sheet of thick cellophane, previously cut to the correct size, is then mounted *over* the white paper.

3. The cellophane is lightly smoked.

4. Tracings are taken in the usual manner.

5. Using a sharp knife or razor blade the required section of tracing is now cut from the drum (Plate 8b) (this section must not exceed 8 × 6 in. in size) and laid, smoked surface uppermost, in the slide-holder, which is placed in position.

6. Switch on the light in the lamp-house and light is passed through the tracing, which is in effect a photographic negative, and the tracing is then projected on to the paper frame.

7. Adjust the focus to obtain maximum clarity.

8. Place photographic paper in position and expose for a suitable time (taking care to have the lens 'stopped down', that is, using a small aperture, thus preventing 'fogging' at the edges of the tracings).

9. Develop the paper as with normal prints.

10. The resulting black-on-white tracing can now be photostatted and reproduced as often as required.

Plate 9 shows typical tracings obtained by this method.

The Palatogram Projector

This device enables palatograms to be easily, quickly, and accurately traced, thus providing a permanent record of the palatograms of words or phrases. It is also possible to photograph the palatogram without the use of camera or film.

The projector consists of a box having a truncated conical top.

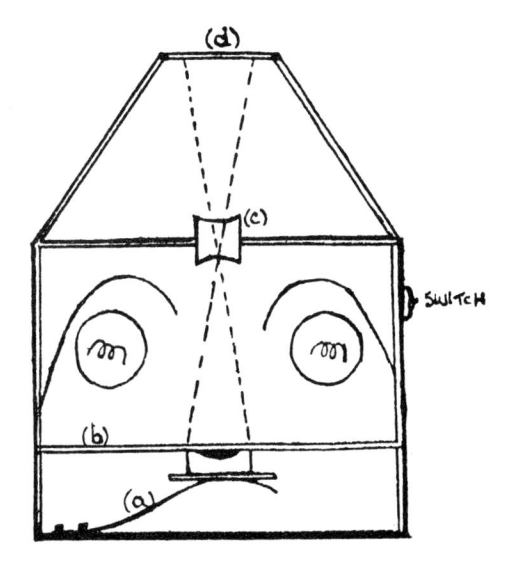

Sectional diagram (not to scale)

In the bottom compartment a platform, mounted on a spring (*a*), is fitted to hold the palate, resting in its cast; the spring presses the palate against a sheet of plate glass (*b*) which is placed at the correct focal distance from the lens (*c*). On the left and right of the lens, and screened from it, are bulbs and reflectors, so arranged as to shine directly on to the palate, the image of which is reflected to the top of the projector, which is fitted with a sheet of plain glass (*d*).

Method for Producing Tracings

The palatogram having been produced, the palate is placed in its cast on the platform (*a*). The lights are switched on and a piece of fine tracing-paper laid over the glass (*d*); this tracing-paper acts as a screen and receives the image of the palatogram projected by the lens. It can now be traced with ease and accuracy. The operation can be conducted at considerable speed, enabling many impressions to be traced in a short time. The possibilities of comparison between utterances are, therefore, obvious, and variations are immediately apparent. So also are the characteristics which persist.

Method for Photographing Palatograms

The operation is the same as for tracing the palate, except that instead of tracing-paper a sheet of photographic paper of suitable size is placed emulsion side down on the glass. The light is then switched on for a suitable exposure period (to ensure constancy in the exposures a 0–60-second time-switch is used), and the paper developed and fixed as with a normal photographic negative. This can then be photostatted or reproduced in other ways as required.

Plate 10 shows an improved projector now in use in the laboratory. Some typical tracings and photographs produced by this technique may be seen in Plate 11. Many tracings of the palatograms produced by instances of utterances repeated on different days were compared before making the present selection of the two characteristic sets taken on separate occasions, one by the tracing method and the other by immediate photographic print.

The kymograms and palatograms illustrated were made in the laboratory in connexion with research in Bhojpuri by Dr. B. N. Prasad of the University of Patna. See his thesis for the Ph.D., 1950, University of London Library.

PLATE 11

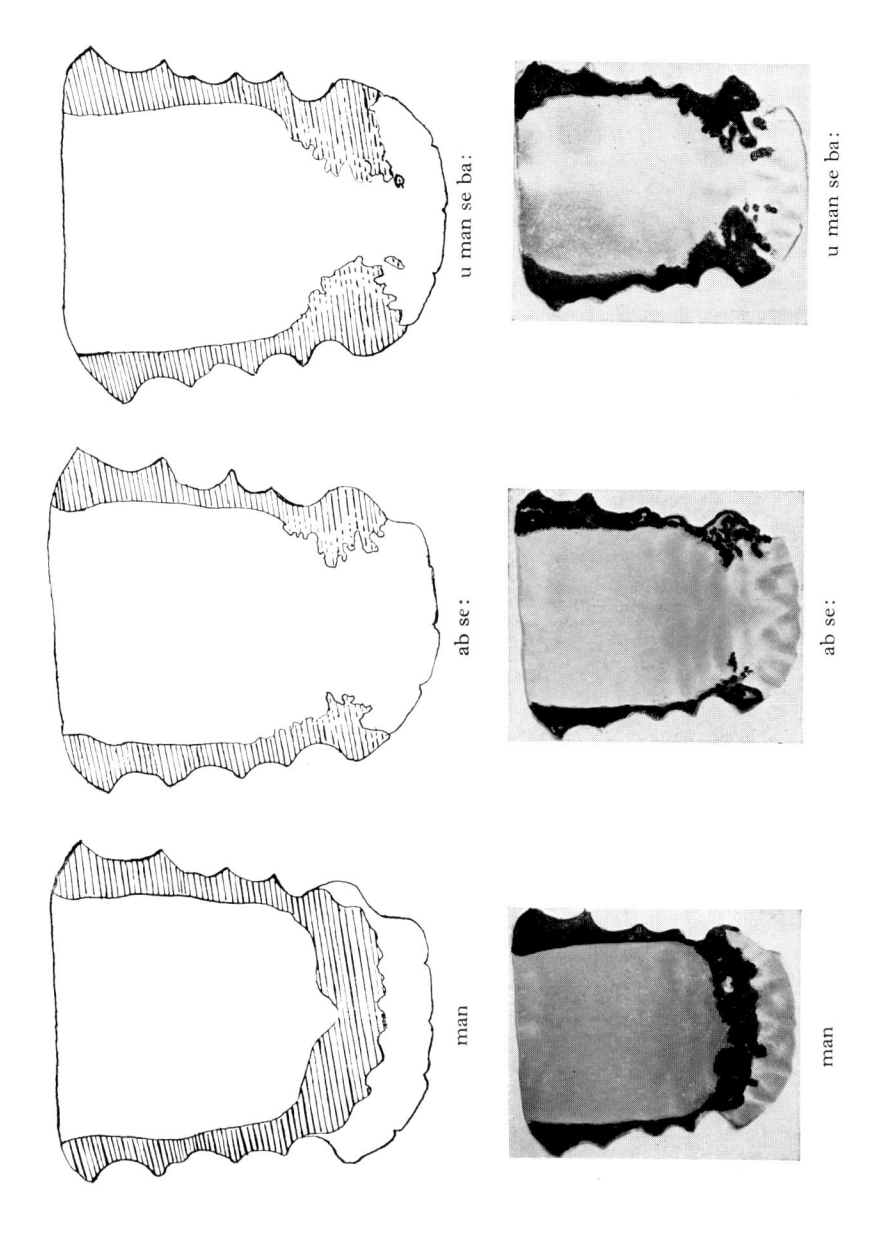

u man se ba:

ab se:

man

u man se ba:

ab se:

man

EXAMPLES OF PALATOGRAMS OBTAINED BY THE PROJECTOR METHOD

14

PERSONALITY AND LANGUAGE IN SOCIETY

THE Belgian sociologist Waxweiler once said it was not the task of sociology to explain what 'society' is. May I venture in the same direction and say it is not the task of linguistics to say what 'language' is. 'Personality' is perhaps more manageable, though I do not propose to say in existential terms what that is either. Some understanding of the relations suggested by the title, however, is attainable in the light of sociology, psychology, biology, and descriptive linguistics.

Descriptive linguistics is deserving its place more and more as an autonomous group of related disciplines—such as phonetics, phonology, grammar, lexicography, semantics, and what may be called the 'sociology of language'. Like the countryman telling you the way, I shall first mention the direction I am *not* taking, by giving an outline sketch of how language and languages have been studied from quite a different point of view, especially in Western Europe during the nineteenth century. That is mainly in the form of what we call comparative linguistics and comparative grammar. We begin, then, with a kind of linguistic science which is not very helpful for our present subject.

In the nineteenth century the only kind of linguistics considered seriously was this comparative and historical study of words in languages known or believed to be *cognate*—say the Semitic languages, or the Indo-European languages. It is significant that the Germans, who really made the subject what it was, used the term *Indo-germanisch*. Those who know the popular works of Otto Jespersen will remember how firmly he declares that linguistic science is historical. And those who have noticed the fly-leaves of the volumes of the *New English Dictionary*—generally referred to as the *Oxford Dictionary*[1]—will remember the guarantee, 'on historical principles', which explains the N. in *N.E.D.*

Everyone knows the name of Sir William Jones and has heard of the famous paragraph in his 1786 lecture in Calcutta on the obvious relationship of Latin, Greek, Persian, and the Germanic languages with one another and with Sanskrit, and the probability of their all being derived from a *common parent language*.

The notion of an original parent language and of an ancient and present underlying linguistic *unity* was as old as the Bible—the Flood, Noah and his sons, the confusion and all that. Indeed, Jewish rabbi grammarians in the tenth and eleventh centuries in North Africa and Spain had compared Aramaic, Arabic, and Hebrew and declared them to be related forms of one language. These Jewish rabbis were the first comparative philologists.

[1] See Chapter 3, p. 8, footnote 2.

When Sanskrit was really discovered in 1786, the parent Hebrew was replaced by a primitive parent rather like Sanskrit, linking the Aryan languages in one great family.... Unity in Babel after all. And unity and universality have always been a basic Christian teaching. The languages, the alphabets and characters, may be many, but the Word *is one*. Jesus Christ is God the Word.

At the end of the eighteenth and the first half of the nineteenth centuries, historical romanticism and evolutionism were part of the intellectual climate. Linguistics was the outstanding example of comparative historical study within the framework of an evolutionary theory remaining entirely acceptable and orthodox to the Churches. Not so anatomy or certain other studies of the human being.

This comparative study of the Indo-European languages, *the* science of language of those days, has become, in its most developed form, mainly a study of isolated comparable words, in accordance with the principles of morphology and phonology. The highest abstractions are the so-called reconstructed or * (starred) forms, which are hypothetical summaries of sets of relations bringing comparable cognate words in scores of languages within one typical system, e.g. $*ek_1vo\text{-}s$ $*p\underset{\circ}{r}tu\text{-}$. They have morphological value only. Such formulas have not in themselves any actual pronunciations, nor do they refer to any recognizable equine animal, or ford, portal, or port.

Now you will see that this kind of linguistics has no direct—indeed, no obvious—connexion with the subject of this paper. In present-day Russia, as elsewhere, such linguistics is still studied for application to textual philology, but it is frequently criticized there as fossilized formalism, without sociological component. Where is the sociological component? The complaint is that intrinsically there cannot be a sociological component where there are no sentences, no real language, functioning in a society. There is found, however, a sociological context for this sort of linguistics as a whole—it is the context of race-conscious Aryanism and imperialism, tempered by bourgeois cosmopolitanism.

These things are said and must not be laughed off. We must meet them in some way. Nowadays a master comparative philologist is not really occupied, as many of the nineteenth-century Germans were, with comparative grammar, but with the establishing and interpretation of texts; in that work the sociological component is very much to the fore. For classical philologists the establishing and interpretation of texts have always been the central task. Classical studies are still the humanities.

A scholar who spends all his time in the formalism of comparative morphology, and in the perilous paths of etymology based thereon, perhaps deserves some of the criticism that has recently fallen on him. But he has stood the test of time. Not so the more romantic theorists who enjoy Indo-European fantasies and from *Ursprache* go on to speculate on the *Urvolk* and the *Urheimat*. Such linguistics cannot throw even the dimmest indirect

PERSONALITY AND LANGUAGE IN SOCIETY

glimmer on personality and language in society, which I submit is a major concern of science. From the present empirical point of view, the origins of speech and language are to be studied in living human beings in contemporary society.

From the point of view indicated by the title of my paper, I am going far out of my way in noticing comparative and historical linguistics at all. I have already given a reason for doing so and will re-emphasize it by quoting the first sentence from Jespersen's book, *Language*, published in 1921: 'The distinctive feature of the science of language as conceived nowadays is its historical character.' The basic assumption for such study is that you can regard any given language, well documented over a long period, and also the words duly recorded in it, as social facts over and above the untold number of individuals who have used the words and the language.

This leads me straight to the sociological bases of modern French linguistics linked with the well-known names of Meillet, Brunot, and Vendryès. And not only French linguistics. The Slav schools grouped round Baudouin de Courtenay and later Trubetzkoy and the *Cercle linguistique de Prague* all shared this philosophical point of departure with the famous Geneva scholar, Ferdinand de Saussure, whose well-known but little understood *Cours de Linguistique Générale* was published in 1916, and was one of the foundation-stones of modern linguistics.

De Saussure's general linguistics is closely linked with the sociology of Durkheim. His theoretical approach may fairly be described as Durkheimian structuralism. The groups of linguists I have mentioned and many more at work today are of the same ideology. Nowadays professional linguists can almost be classified by using the name of de Saussure. There are various possible groupings: Saussureans, anti-Saussureans, post-Saussureans, or non-Saussureans.

Contemporary Russian linguists, in spite of the obvious influence of Marx on Durkheim, and through him on certain types of structural linguistics, use the name of de Saussure to abuse the linguistics of the West, including of course the American behaviourist linguists.[1]

A word or two, therefore, about de Saussure. De Saussure, thinking in Durkheimian terms, regarded social facts as *sui generis* and external to and on a different plane from individual phenomena. The 'collective conscience', though perhaps a psychical entity, is not arrived at by studying the psychology of the individual. The social fact is on a different plane of reality. The group constrains the individual, and the group culture determines a great deal of his humanity.

Consequently de Saussure in terms of his linguistics could only refer to my personal linguistic activity, writing or reading this paper, as emanating

---

[1] Chiefly the late Professor Leonard Bloomfield and his followers. See Bloomfield's *Language*, 1933 edition, preface, p. vii, and pp. 32–39. Bloomfield can be said to follow the behaviourism of A. P. Weiss.

from *un sujet parlant*. And individually each one of you as a listener or reader would be a *sujet parlant*. After bearing with me to the end, he might even express the opinion that I was a *mauvais sujet*. Since the whole idea of a *sujet parlant* is that he should speak a reasonable language suitably constrained by the right group and his thoughts determined by the culture of that group. Our linguistic behaviour as *sujets parlant* he would classify as '*parole*'—the activities of '*sujets parlants*'. *La parole* is a function of *le sujet parlant*.

But *la langue, une langue*, any socially established language, is a function of '*la masse parlante*'. The whole object and purpose of the science of linguistics is the study of *la langue*—'the language', *a* language. The Saussurean trinity is completed by the concept he attaches to the French word '*langage*'—language in general; *le langage* comprises the linguistic tendencies of the general human faculty. Language in general is a power, a part of human nature, social, individual, heterogeneous and multiform—it includes vast masses of ink-spotted paper, the miscellaneous gibberish of dialects. There is no one science of '*le langage*' in this most general sense. It is, he says, *inconnaissable*.

Now if from this generality he calls '*langage*' in any community we subtract all the individual items of speech, all speech-sounds on the air, and all spelling marks on vast masses of paper—that is, if from '*langage*' in general we take '*parole*'—if we take away all the overt individual acts of *sujets parlants* of any given community, we have the all-important residue, the language of the community, a function of *la masse parlante*, stored and residing in the *conscience collective*—a silent, highly organized system of signs existing apart from and over and above the individual as *sujet parlant*. *Langage* minus *parole* gives you *langue*, and now we come to the main conclusion: that it is the study of this *langue* which is the real purpose and object of linguistics synchronic and diachronic, i.e. descriptive and historical.

Such a language in the Saussurean sense is a system of signs placed in categories. It is a system of differential values, not of concrete and positive terms. Actual people do not talk such 'a language'. However systematically you may talk, you do not talk systematics. According to strict Saussurean doctrine, therefore, there are *no sentences* in a language considered as a system. Sentences are used by *sujets parlants* in *parole*. Strictly speaking, in 'a language' there are no real words either, but only examples of phonological and morphological categories. There are no actual phones, though there may be phonemes, between which relations of opposition may be said to obtain. This is structural formalism.

Antoine Meillet stated as a basic principle (in the Saussurean sense of *langue*) that 'chaque langue forme un système où tout se tient'. A language is a system in which all the constituent units are held together in function by the whole. To get at such a language as a system, you must assume it holds together in *a state*. Hence the Russian objection that this theory leads to static structural formalism, to mechanical structure, to mechanical materialism in linguistics, which is according to them clearly superseded by the dialectical materialism given to the world in the name of Marx, Engels, Lenin, and Stalin.

The Russian critics understand de Saussure and represent his theory quite fairly as static mechanical structuralism. Moreover, they are right in believing that true Saussureans, like true Durkheimians, regard the structures formulated by linguistics or sociology as *in rebus*. The structure is existent and is treated as a thing. As Durkheim said, such social facts must be regarded 'comme des choses'. This is structural realism, or social realism.

In this country such theory has not taken root in professional linguistics. Even Malinowski pursued what I call *personality studies* in his ethnographic work.[1] For my own part and for a number of my colleagues, I venture to think linguistics is a group of related techniques for the handling of language events. We regard our group of disciplines as designed for systematic empirical analysis and as autonomous in the sense that they do not necessarily have a point of departure in another science or discipline such as psychology, sociology, or in a school of metaphysics.

In the most general terms we study language as part of the social process, and what we may call the systematics of phonetics and phonology, of grammatical categories or of semantics, are ordered schematic constructs, frames of reference, a sort of scaffolding for the handling of events. The study of the social process and of single human beings is simultaneous and of equal validity, and for both, structural hypotheses are proved by their own social functioning in the scientific process of dealing with events. Our schematic constructs must be judged with reference to their combined tool power in our dealings with linguistic events in the social process. Such constructs have no ontological status and we do not project them as having being or existence. They are neither immanent nor transcendent, but just language turned back on itself. By means of linguistics we hope to state facts systematically, and especially to make *statements of meaning*.

A key concept in the technique of the London group is the concept of the *context of situation*.[2] The phrase 'context of situation' was first used widely in English by Malinowski. In the early thirties, when he was especially interested in discussing problems of languages, I was privileged to work with him. He had also discussed similar problems with Alan Gardiner, now Sir Alan Gardiner, the author of that difficult book, *The Theory of Speech and Language*. Sir Alan Gardiner, by the way, dedicated his book to one of the earliest users of the notion of a situational context for language, Dr. Philipp Wegener, who thought there might be a future for the 'Situa-

[1] See his *Coral Gardens and Their Magic*, preface, vol. i, pp. x and xi, for the central importance of his study of Bagido'u, the garden magician.
[2] See my *Speech*, Benn, 1930, pp. 38–43; 'Linguistics and the Functional Point of View', *English Studies*, xvi, pt. 1, February 1934; Chapter 4, Chapter 3, pp. 27–33; *The Tongues of Men*, Watts & Co., London, 1937, Chapter x.

tionstheorie'.[1] Malinowski's context of situation is a bit of the social process which can be considered apart and in which a speech event is central and makes all the difference, such as a drill sergeant's welcome utterance on the square, '*Stand at—ease!*' The context of situation for Malinowski is an ordered series of events considered as *in rebus*.

My view was, and still is, that 'context of situation' is best used as a suitable schematic construct to apply to language events, and that it is a group of related categories at a different level from grammatical categories but rather of the same abstract nature. A context of situation for linguistic work brings into relation the following categories:

A. The relevant features of participants: persons, personalities.
   (i) The verbal action of the participants.
   (ii) The non-verbal action of the participants.
B. The relevant objects.
C. The effect of the verbal action.

Contexts of situation and types of language function can then be grouped and classified. A very rough parallel to this sort of context can be found in language manuals providing the learner with a picture of a railway station and the operative words for travelling by train. It is very rough. But it is parallel with the grammatical rules, and is based on the repetitive routines of initiated persons in the society under description.

When I was consulted by the Air Ministry on the outbreak of war with Japan, I welcomed the opportunity of service for the Royal Air Force because I saw at once that the operating of reconnaissance and fighter aircraft by the Japanese could be studied by applying the concept of the limited situational contexts of war, the operative language of which we needed to know urgently and quickly. We were not going to meet the Japanese socially, but only in such contexts of fighting as required some form of spoken Japanese. A kind of operational linguistics was the outcome, and from those practical war-time endeavours we learned a good deal about language and personality in society, both British and Japanese.

If I give you one brief sentence with the information that it represents a typical Cockney event, you may even be able to provide a typical context of situation in which it would be the verbal action of one of the participants. The sentence is:

'Ahng gunna gi' wun fer Ber'.'
(I'm going to get one for Bert.)

What is the minimum number of participants? Three? Four? Where might it happen? In a pub? Where is Bert? Outside? Or playing darts? What are the relevant objects? What is the effect of the sentence? 'Obvious!' you say. So is the convenience of the schematic construct called 'context of situation'. It makes sure of the sociological component.

[1] See Dr. Philipp Wegener, *Untersuchungen über die Grundfragen des Sprachlebens,* Halle, 1885, especially pp. 21–27.

The context of situation is a convenient abstraction at the social level of analysis and forms the basis of the hierarchy of techniques for the statement of meanings. The statement of meaning cannot be achieved by one analysis, at one level, in one fell swoop. Having made the first abstraction and having treated the social process of speaking by applying the above-mentioned set of categories grouped in the context of situation, descriptive linguistics then proceeds by a method rather like the dispersion of light of mixed wavelengths into a spectrum.

At this point, linguistics treats the verbal process of a speaking personality by writing down, let us say, a *sentence*. The technique of syntax is concerned with the word process in the sentence. The technique of phonology states the phonematic and prosodic processes within the word and sentence. The phonetician links all this with the processes and features of utterance. The sentence must also have its relations with the processes of the context of situation. Descriptive linguistics is thus a sort of hierarchy of techniques by means of which the meaning of linguistic events may be, as it were, dispersed in a spectrum of specialized statements.

We are now a long way from de Saussure's mechanistic structuralism based on a given language as a function of a speaking mass, stored in the collective conscience, and from the underdog, considered merely as the speaking subject, whose speech was not the 'integral and concrete object of linguistics'. The unique object of Saussurean linguistics is '*la langue*', which exists only in the *collectivité*. Now it is at this point that I wish to stress the importance of the study of persons, even one at a time, and of introducing the notions of personality and language as in some sense vectors of the continuity of repetitions in the social process, and the persistence of personal forces.

The greatest English philologist of the nineteenth century was, I think, the Oxford phonetician, Sweet. He was never weary of asserting that language existed only in the individual. Others would say that all the essentials of linguistics can be studied in language operating between two persons. I am not subscribing to any theories of 'existence', and one must abandon the individual and look to the development and continuity of personality born of nature and developed in nurture. Language is part of the nurture, and part of the personality.

Before making any further use of the word 'personality' and its cognates, I propose briefly to review some of the contexts of its occurrence, and indicate the limitations within which it may be profitably employed in general linguistics.

Let us begin with Johnson's dictionary. For his first entry on *person*, he uses a citation from Locke: 'a person is a thinking intelligent being that has reason and reflection and can consider itself as itself, the same thinking thing in different times and places.' In another entry Johnson emphasizes the idea of being 'present in person', not through a representative. There is also the notion of responsibility which is made explicit in the phrase 'a responsible person'.

The meaning of *person* in the sense of a man or woman represented in fictitious dialogue, or as a character in a play, is relevant if we take a sociological view of the *personae* or parts we are called upon to play in the routine of life. Every social person is a bundle of *personae*, a bundle of parts, each part having its lines. If you do not know your lines, you are no use in the play. It is very good for you and society if you are cast for your parts and remember your lines.

To 'personate' in Johnson's sense is not so good. It is to feign. We must not personate unless it be professionally as a performer. The word 'impersonate' is not entered by Johnson in his dictionary. I have the impression that in England there has been a certain amount of impersonation in the matter of what is called public school pronunciation and what is wrongly described as the Oxford Accent.

In America the Schools of Speech use the dramatic method and presumably train people to produce themselves better, which is useful education. Happily only a few persons need become impersonators.

In defining *personality*, Johnson again quotes Locke: 'this *personality* extends itself beyond present existence to what is past, only by consciousness whereby it imputes to itself past actions just upon the same grounds that it does the present.'

If we accept the view expressed in Johnson's citation of Locke, we must consider language, like personality, as a systematic linking of the past with the present and with the future. Just as life itself is directed towards the maintenance of the general pattern of the bodily system, so also personality and language are usually maintained by the continuous and consistent activity of the bodily system, personality and language through life, language through the generations.

There is the element of habit, custom, tradition, the element of the past, and the element of innovation, of the moment, in which the future is being born. When you speak you fuse these elements in verbal creation, the outcome of your language and of your personality. What you say may be said to have style, and in this connexion a vast field of research in stylistics awaits investigation in literature and speech.

The continuity of the person, the development of personality, are paralleled by the continuity and development of language in a variety of forms. Human beings do vastly more than this. By means of language we can pass on our acquired learning and experience through the generations. We can now see two very different streams linking the generations and linking people.

For the earliest relevant use of *personality*, the *N.E.D.* goes back to Wiclif (1380) for the citation: 'All the personality of man standeth in the spirit of him.' I do not exclude the characteristic *modern* meaning given by the *O.E.D.* 'that quality or assemblage of qualities which makes a person what he is as distinct from other persons—distinctive personal or individual character especially when of a marked kind'. The important words in this definition are 'personal or individual' regarded as alternatives. The earlier view I have put forward does not need and does not use the word 'individual'. In a Penguin book entitled *The Physical Basis of Personality*, Professor Mottram, a physiologist, favours the modern usage and makes the following astonishing comment: 'the word was first used in 1795, though there were *personalities* before that time. The idea is so closely linked with individuality and character that these words can be used almost interchangeably with personality.' They can, of course, but I do not propose to do so. I can quite understand why Professor Mottram preferred to call his book *The Physical Basis of Personality* rather than *The Physical Basis of Individuality* or *The Physical Basis of Character*. Such contexts of the word 'personality' may be relevant for a scholar dealing with language from the point of view of stylistics. The contexts of sociology, however, provide notions of wider applicability, since they establish a close association between personality and social structure. For the significance of this association has long been a feature of sociology, and in that connexion may be quoted the names of Tönnies, Durkheim, and Mead with other American scholars.

Following these lines of thought we see two very different streams linking the generations and linking people. The first is breeding, biological heredity, physical inheritance. This I shall refer to as *nature*. Physical inheritance, and the unification or integration of bodily activity by the nervous system and the endocrine organs, has a great deal to do with *personality*, and sex is a main determinant. In most societies social roles by sex are formally recognized in speech.

The second stream is *nurture*, and this includes the learning of the languages of the community. You weave *nurture* into *nature*, and you do this with the most powerful magic—speech.

In order to live, the young human has to be progressively incorporated into a social organization, and the main condition of that incorporation is sharing the local magic—that is, the language.

Allow me to misapply to speech and language Rousseau's famous sentence, 'Man is born free and is everywhere in chains'. The bonds of family, neighbourhood, class, occupation, country, and religion are knit by speech and language. We take eagerly to the magic of language because only by apprenticeship to it can we be admitted to association, fellowship, and community in our social organization which ministers to our needs and gives us what we want or what we deserve. The emphasis is on society and fellowship, in which a man may find his personality.

The various forms of local and familiar speech may be stated by means of constructs, so-called cultural systems, the elements of which we may regard as values to the people, who by continuing to give utterance to them maintain them or modify them by their activity. They are not to be measured by values in other cultural systems such as those of the A B C. These values do not necessarily conflict and a healthy personality can carry more than one set without developing morbid symptoms. A useful distinction can be drawn between speech fellowship and language community. The speech of those whose sounds, intonation, grammar, idiom, and usage are similar in structure and have similar function is a bond of fellowship based on the sharing of a truly common experience. A speech fellowship sees itself and hears itself as different from those who do not belong. Such speech, besides being a bond among the fellows, is a bar to the outsider. Local dialects, regional and occupational dialects, as well as the accents of the big English public schools, are speech fellowships. Within such speech fellowships a speaker is phonetically and verbally content because when he speaks to one of his fellows he is also speaking to himself. That can be the most deeply satisfying form of self-expression. No wonder the true proletarian despises 'fancy talk' or any form of impersonation, except when it has entertainment value.

Members of various speech fellowships may, however, belong to larger speech or language communities without conflict of values. Both sets of values deserve respect. The vast enterprises of the English-speaking world, operated by English, go on without a standardization of accent. You may estimate the relative values of what is called an Oxford accent, an Aberdonian accent, a Boston, a New York, or an Australian accent, but the main thing is a wider language community with room for diversity of personality. The genesis of correctness deserves study in all the fellowship groups, and not only in what is called a standard language. The genesis of correctness in several forms of speech is possibly part of the social process and part of the personal process. It is true that in everyday life we generally say what the other fellow expects us, one way or the other, to say, but this expectancy is the measure even of our most delightful surprises, and good personal style is highly valued.

Our studies of speech and language, and indeed a good deal of our educational methodology, have been dominated far too much by logic and psychology. Individual psychology tends to emphasize a kind of experience which is incommunicable or at any rate is not usually shared. And logic has given us bad grammar and taken the heart out of language.

My intention is to link language studies with social human nature, to think of persons rather than individuals. Linguistics may learn something from the sciences which treat human beings as separate natural entities in their psycho-biological characters, but it is mainly interested in persons and personalities as active participators in the creation and maintenance of cultural values, among which languages are its main concern.

Language and personality partake of both *nature* and *nurture* and are the expression of both. I am not now using the word 'language' in any Saussurean sense. I use the word 'language' without article, in three principal senses according to context:

1. The urges and drives in our nature which impel us to make use of sounds, gestures, signs, and symbols.

In the first sense, then, *language* is a *natural tendency*.

2. As a result of nurture, traditional systems or habits of speech are learnt and maintained by social activity.

Language in the second sense is everywhere actively maintained by *persons*, that is, by people who are members of society. Language in this sense must be *systemic*, because it owes its genesis and its continuance to human bodily systems living in society.

3. We may apply the word *language* collectively to the myriads of personal uses or the millions of speech events in social life. Or, alternatively, we may use the word—*speech*.

When we use *the article* or *any determining expression* such as *a language, the language, the English language*, we intend to refer to a specific set of language habits, some of which may be inadequately stated in grammars an dictionaries. I have suggested that language is systemic. Most grammars and dictionaries are systematic statements of fact—but quite a number are not. Even when they are systematic, they can sometimes fail to represent the language systems, in the sense in which I have used the expression *systemic*.

We may assume that any social person speaking in his own personality will behave systematically, since experienced language is universally systemic. Therefore, we may study his speech and ask the question, 'What is systemic?' We must not expect to find one closed system. But we may apply systematic categories to the statement of the facts. We must separate from the mush of general goings-on those features of repeated events which appear to be parts of a patterned process, and handle them systematically by stating them by the spectrum of linguistic techniques. The systemic statements of meaning produced by such techniques need not be given existent status.

A few specific language systems are stated in grammars and dictionaries and other works of linguistic science. But the vast majority of languages are not recorded. Such language systems can, however, be regarded as actively and consistently maintained by persons in the social process. Here I feel bound to say that the study *of one person at a time* seems to me amply justified as a scientific method, and the collaboration of informants of suitable personality is fundamental in certain types of research. The word informant is widely current on both sides of the Atlantic for such persons, but I normally use the description 'assistant'. The Department of Phonetics and Linguistics at the School of Oriental and African Studies employs a number of assistants from various parts of Asia and Africa, each one of whom works with a lecturer specializing in his language, and may continue collaborating in linguistic research for two years before the lecturer goes overseas, often with the assistant, to make a fuller study in the field. Such scholars are not merely 'learning the language'. They are aiming at scientific statements of the facts.

The personalities studied are carefully selected and are usually typical of an important speech fellowship in a wider speech community.

There are a number of further applications of the twin notions of language and personality to linguistic studies. While a great deal of linguistic research must abstract the impersonal from the personal by regarding it as typological, the researcher must be fully aware of the nature and degree of the abstractions he is making. The personal features, too, are well worth study and furnish suitable subjects for stylistics. In so far as personality is typical, such studies are of general interest and application.

Individual linguistic biographies should also be attempted through the seven ages of man. There may be such biographical studies of language in existence, based on adequate documentation of the learning of speech and language by children and young persons—but I have not seen them. Some therapists have kept detailed case-history sheets of patients suffering from speech defects and language disorders. Language disorders are of greater interest to us than speech defects. In London I have had some slight experience of what one might term *morbid linguistics*. Most linguists appreciate the light that has been thrown on language by clinical studies of aphasia. In all work in morbid linguistics personality must remain a factor of high relevance.

Physiology, anatomy, neurology, and in fact most of the relevant biological and medical sciences, emphasize the importance of the whole of the nervous system and of the endocrine organs in integrating the personality. So that whatever language system is woven into the bodily framework, personality characteristics are bound to find expression through it. The context of circumstances may lead to rapid changes in the system or to mechanization and stagnation. In these days I seem to meet more unhappiness finding expression in Europe than would suggest a long lease for the tenure of many features of our civilization. But is there anywhere a real desire to halt the forces of dissolution? There are millions of people just watching the march of events. But there is little real vigilance or concern.

The attention that has been given to semantics and to speech training everywhere is an indication of the close connexion that is felt between language and personality. But such superficial tinkering is no real education in language which is a priority need today. An English writer, George Orwell, has tried to frighten us by suggesting it would not be beyond human ingenuity to write books by machinery. The sort of mechanizing process we see at work in the film, in radio, in publicity and propaganda, and in the lower reaches of journalism is greatly to be deplored. A great deal of writing, he says, consists of prefabricated phrases bolted together like the pieces of a child's Meccano set. Too much mechanism, too much totalitarianism, prevents a creative personality from making the most of his language, and there is a prevention of originality. In his recent satire, *1984*, he provides a new language for the new society, Ingsoc. He calls it Newspeak, distinguishing this form of language from Oldspeak or Standard English. There is quite a lot of Newspeak about nowadays, and language education should train people to be aware of it.

In treating personality and language in society as a sort of basis for linguistics with a sociological component, I have preferred the whole man with his fellows, not forgetting the importance of the single human being. That being so, I should like to conclude by quoting two paragraphs from the inaugural lecture[1] given by Professor J. Z. Young, F.R.S., on appointment to the Chair of Anatomy at University College in the University of London:

I have left all direct reference to psychology out of this treatment, not because I feel it unimportant, but because any attempt to include it involves great difficulties in the present primitive state of our language. But it is evident that consideration of our brains as active agents agrees with our subjective knowledge that we are such. The development of a proper relationship between neurology and psychology should be much easier on the basis I am suggesting than on that of the reflex concept.

Indeed, I venture to think that emphasis by biologists on drives as well as reflexes will have wide effects on Society in general. It is interesting to note that the scientific biology which has been the ally of humanism for the past few decades has been mainly concerned with the influence of environment in determining man's activity. There are clear historical reasons for this, but *humanism* and *mechanism* are strange bedfellows, and I believe that much will be gained by clearer recognition of the activities within us, which makes us masters rather than creatures of fate.

[1] *Patterns of Substance and Activity in the Nervous System* (28 February 1946). London, Lewis & Co. Ltd., 1946.

15

MODES OF MEANING

THE study of meaning is a permanent interest of scholarship. It has been pursued in all the languages of the major civilizations and in ancient times, especially in Sanskrit, Greek, and Latin, including the Latin of the Medieval Scholastics—Duns Scotus, Thomas of Erfurt. In English the obvious phrase 'the meaning of meaning' is well known as the title of a work on the definition of knowledge, a matter which is not under examination in the present essay. There are many other ways of applying the word 'meaning' in English, including the usages of logicians, psychologists, sociologists, mathematicians, and lexicographers. The use of the word 'meaning' is subject to the general rule that each word when used in a new context is a new word.[1] The disciplines and techniques are those of general linguistics which are designed for empirical analysis and do not necessarily have a point of departure in other disciplines such as biology, psychology, literary criticism, or in a school of metaphysics. The constructs or schemata of linguistics enable us to handle isolates that may be called language events. These systematic constructs are neither immanent nor transcendent, but just language turned back on itself. The present essay is an attempt to sketch the framework of a language of description in English about English for those who use English, to illustrate what I understand by linguistic analysis, and especially to show the dangers of an over-facile superficial use of the word *stylistics*, without an adequate logical syntax or even without considering the essential prerequisites of linguistics. The disciplines and techniques of linguistics are directed to assist us in making statements of meaning. Indeed, the main concern of descriptive linguistics is to make statements of meaning.[2]

Every scientific worker must mark out his field in accordance with the resources of his disciplines and techniques and develop them in the handling of his chosen material. The linguist studies the speaking person in the social process. It has been said that two persons taking part in the continuity of repetitions in the social process offer material for most branches of linguistics in making statements of meaning. The linguist deals with persons habitually maintaining specific forms of speech or writing which can be referred to dialects or languages operating in close or open social groups.[3]

---

[1] For further contexts see Chapter 14, pp. 181-7, and Chapter 3.
[2] See Chapter 14.
[3] The techniques of linguistics have not been developed to deal with language in general human terms. De Saussure stated his opinion that *le langage*, that is, language in its most general use, was *inconnaissable*. What he really meant was that *linguistique* as he knew it

The study of linguistic institutions is thus more specific and positive and on the whole less speculative than the sociological study of societies. Sociologists and social anthropologists are much bolder than linguists in what they find it possible to state in general human terms. To what lengths sociological abstraction can be extended is well exemplified in Pareto's theory of residues and derivations.[1]

There are, however, indications that students of human biology, neurology, acoustics, and electrical communications are beginning to converge on certain aspects of man as a speaking animal. It is extremely difficult at present to get any detailed picture of the general physiology of utterance which must comprise the whole of the respiratory tract and all the relevant musculature and innervation and, moreover, the processes of the nervous system and especially of the brain. Acousticians are limited to a small fraction of the bodily energy (probably less than 20 per cent.) given to speaking. Any sort of measurement or assessment of speech energy by acoustics principally affects the hearing, and, as the Vedanta philosophy would remind us, mention of the hearing implies the hearer of the hearing of the heard. What is the energy of listening? Of comprehension? Of aesthetic enjoyment? Besides, a man finds nothing worth listening to if he cannot speak to himself. It is easier to analyse what happens in the air when we listen than what goes on in the body when we speak.

If I am to use the word 'language' without article to describe a main characteristic in general human terms, it could be linked with a general physiology of utterance (if one existed) and of its perception and also with the urges and drives in our human nature which impel us to make use of sounds, gestures, signs, and symbols. The only mode of meaning assignable to language in this most general sense might be vaguely called communicativeness, or the word *vox* might be used for it. It may eventually be shown on general musical grounds that human language has a phonetic and phonological mode of meaning. But at present not even music itself can be said to have a general mode of meaning. If mathematics may be said to have general modes of meaning, we are still lacking a general calculus of language.

Let us therefore apply the term linguistics to those disciplines and tech-

in the early years of this century had little or nothing technical to say of language in general human terms. That is still true. What is commonly called general phonetics merely codifies the results of detailed study of personal and social dialects. There are no acceptable definitions of word, sound, or syllable in general human terms. Neither are the various phoneme concepts of universal application to human speech in general, whatever that might mean. Theories of sound symbolism in general human terms are nowhere taken seriously. Phonology, too, in spite of the labours of the Prague School and its followers, is exemplified by systematic studies of particular languages. General or universal grammar has no meaning in any of the recognized branches. Semantics is concerned with studies of the meaning and changes of meaning of specific language forms.

N.B. The term 'General Semantics' was used by the late Alfred Korzybski for a kind of linguistic therapy quite unrelated to technical linguistics.

[1] Vilfredo Pareto, *The Mind and Society*, 4 vols., Jonathan Cape, London, 1935; see especially iii. 990–1119.

niques which deal with institutionalized languages or dialects as such. A statement of the meaning of an isolate of any of these cannot be achieved at one fell swoop by one analysis at one level. Having made the first abstraction by suitably isolating a piece of 'text' or part of the social process of speaking for a listener or of writing for a reader, the suggested procedure for dealing with meaning is its dispersion into modes, rather like the dispersion of light of mixed wave-lengths into a spectrum. First, there is the verbal process in the context of situation.[1] Social and personal commentary is especially relevant at this level. The technique of syntax is concerned with the word process in the sentence. Phonology states the phonematic and prosodic processes within the word and sentence, regarding them as a mode of meaning. The phonetician links all this with the processes and features of utterance. Such processes are characteristic of persons, of social groups, even of nations. Moreover, the general feature of voice quality is part of the phonetic mode of meaning of an English boy, a Frenchman, or a lady from New York. Surely it is part of the meaning of an American to sound like one.

Even in a dictionary, the lexical[2] meaning of any given word is achieved by multiple statements of meaning at different levels. First, at the orthographic level the group of letters, *peer*, is distinguished from the group *pier*, and both of these from *pear*, *pair*, and *pare*. Next, by means of some kind of phonetic notation, the pronunciation is stated, and new identities arise. At least two grammatical designations are possible for *peer*—noun, substantive, or verb—and by making such statements at the grammatical level a further component of meaning is made explicit. Formal and etymological meaning may be added, together with social indications of usage such as *colloquial, slang, nautical, vulgar, poetical*.

To make statements of meaning in terms of linguistics, we may accept the language event as a whole and then deal with it at various levels, sometimes in a descending order, beginning with social context and proceeding through syntax and vocabulary to phonology and even phonetics, and at other times in the opposite order, which will be adopted here since the main purpose is the exposition of linguistics as a discipline and technique for the statement of meanings without reference to such dualisms and dichotomies as word and idea, overt expressions and covert concepts, language and thought, subject and object. In doing this I must not be taken to exclude the concept of mind,[3] or to imply an embracing of materialism to avoid a foolish bogey of mentalism.

At the phonetic level no case has yet been made out for systematic sound symbolism or onomatopoeia in general human terms.[4] I have myself made experiments with speakers of many languages belonging to all the principal

---

[1] See Chapter 14, and *Tongues of Men*, Watts & Co., London, 1937.
[2] See *New English Dictionary*, vol. i, Preface, pp. xxvii–xxxiv.
[3] See Gilbert Ryle's *The Concept of Mind*, 1949.
[4] See Bloomfield, *Language*, 1933.

races and have found, with Koehler, evidence of some correlation of sounds with shapes (sense of feeling them or of drawing them).[1] The experiment consisted in drawing two shapes in line, one of a round bellying shape, 'clumpy', and the other a sharp angular zigzag of points prickling in all directions. Two words were then offered in sound and in roughly phonetic spelling as their names, viz. *kikeriki* and *oombooloo*. The only cases when *kikeriki* was chosen as a suitable name for the clumpy figure occurred when someone wished to enliven the proceedings and provide amusement, which he invariably did.

To begin with, we must apprehend language events in their contexts as shaped by the creative acts of speaking persons. Whenever a man speaks, he speaks in some sense as a poet. Poets have often emphasized that a great deal of the beauty and meaning of the language of poetry is in the sound of it. If that be called the phonological mode of meaning, in poetry, it is a mode impossible of translation from one language into another.

In his dialogue on the critic as artist in *Intentions*, Wilde, who had a fine ear for a phrase, followed the Greeks in the appreciation of the high aesthetic values of language. The test applied by the Greeks, who criticized language more carefully than any other material, 'was always the spoken word in its musical and metrical relations. The voice was the medium and the ear the critic.' The story of Homer's blindness Wilde liked to think of 'as an artistic myth'. And he adds, 'when Milton could no longer write, he began to sing'.

Words have not merely music as sweet as that of viol and lute, colour as rich and vivid as any that makes lovely for us the canvas of the Venetian or the Spaniard, and plastic form no less sure and certain than that which reveals itself in marble or in bronze but thought and passion and spirituality are theirs also, are theirs indeed alone. If the Greeks had criticized nothing but language, they would still have been the great art-critics of the world.

Such was Wilde's figurative realization of a literary approach to language analogous to what with another figure I have called a spectrum of modes of meaning.

The phonological mode of meaning in English is perhaps most easily isolated in nonsense verse such as Jabberwocky:

> 'Twas brillig, and the slithy toves
> Did gyre and gimble in the wabe;
> All mimsy were the borogroves,
> And the mome raths outgrabe.

The prosodies of the stanza and especially the specific rhymes are English enough. So are the word-processes and most of the phonematic and prosodic processes.[2] *Brillig*, placed where it is, sounds and looks a pattern

---

[1] Cf. W. Koehler, *Psychologische Probleme*, Berlin, 1933, p. 153, and *Gestalt Psychology*, London, 1930, pp. 186 f.
[2] See Chapter 9.

foreign to current English. *Slithy*, on the other hand, is familiar and undoubtedly pejorative. *Gimble* could probably be classed as an iterative or frequentative verb perhaps with diminutive and picturesque associations.[1]

These observations must not be interpreted in the sense of sound symbolism or of onomatopoeia. If we apply the test of frequent use, most native English words with initial *sl* seem to have been associated with pejorative contexts. There is, therefore, an association of social and personal attitude in recurrent contexts of situation with certain phonological features. This association is, of course, within the given speech community. In previous discussion of this mode of meaning, I invented a word, *phonaesthetic*,[2] to describe the association of sounds and personal and social attitudes, to avoid the misleading implications of *onomatopoeia* and the fallacy of sound symbolism.

Alliteration, assonance, and the chiming of what are usually called consonants are common prosodic features of speech, and from the phonological point of view can be considered as markers or signals of word-structure or of the word-process in the sentence. Such features can be so distributed by a writer as to form part of artistic prosodies in both prose and verse.

This kind of phonological meaning in a language may be referred to as the prosodic mode. Really good dialogue in contemporary drama or other forms of modern prose literature requires almost unalterable patterns of stress, emphasis, and intonation which are felt to be necessary. Such meaningful features are also in the prosodic mode. Prosodic features extend to the well-known markers and signals, for example, in Edward Lear's limericks. These are so well known that they may serve as an illustration of the phonetic and phonological modes of meaning, including what I have referred to as the prosodic modes. Once started on a limerick, there are modal expectancies for the initiated at all these levels, at the grammatical, stylistic, and indeed at a variety of social levels. At this point in my argument, still confining our references to the language of limericks, I propose to bring forward as a technical term, meaning by 'collocation', and to apply the test of 'collocability'.

The following sentences show that part of the meaning of the word *ass* in modern colloquial English can be by collocation:

---

[1] Mrs. Tillotson tells me that this stanza, which was first 'published' in MS. in a private family magazine in 1854, was then entitled 'Stanza of Anglo-Saxon Poetry'. It was printed in 'gothic' characters and with more archaic spelling. (See S. D. Collingwood, *A Lewis Carroll Picture Book*, 1899, p. 37.) Notes on the made-up words were appended, perhaps in mockery of current edited texts. Some of these explanations resemble Humpty Dumpty's in *Through the Looking-glass*, chapter vi. Examples are:

BRYLLYG (derived from the verb to BRYL or BROIL). 'The time of broiling dinner, i.e. the close of the afternoon.'
SLYTHY (compounded of SLIMY and LITHE). 'Smooth and active.[']
GYMBLE (whence GIMBLET) 'to screw out holes in anything.[']

[2] See *Speech*, Benn, London, 1930, pp. 49–54, and Chapter 4, for word lists illustrating phonaesthetic association.

(i) An ass like Bagson might easily do that.
(ii) He is an ass.
(iii) You silly ass!
(iv) Don't be an ass!

One of the meanings of *ass* is its habitual collocation with an immediately preceding *you silly*, and with other phrases of address or of personal reference. Even if you said 'An ass has been frightfully mauled at the Zoo', a possible retort would be, 'What on earth was he doing?'

There are only limited possibilities of collocation with preceding adjectives, among which the commonest are *silly, obstinate, stupid, awful*, occasionally *egregious*. *Young* is much more frequently found than *old*. The plural form is not very common.

It must be pointed out that meaning by collocation is not at all the same thing as contextual meaning, which is the functional relation of the sentence to the processes of a context of situation in the context of culture.[1]

In the language of Lear's limericks, *man* is generally preceded by *old*, never by *young*. *Person* is collocated with *old* and *young*. There are only four *old ladies*—of Prague, of France, of Winchelsea, and the one 'whose folly' rhymes with 'holly'. There is only one *girl*, 'a young girl of Majorca, Whose aunt was a very fast walker'. One of the 'meanings' of *man* in this language is to be immediately preceded by *old* in collocations of the type, *There was an Old Man of . . ., Who* [or *Whose*] *. . .*, in which names like *Kamschatka* or *Jamaica* or *the East* frequently complete the 'of' phrase. The collocability of *lady* is most frequently with *young*, but *person* with either *old* or *young*. In this amusing language there is no *boy* or *young man* or *woman*, neither are there any plurals for *man, person*, or *lady*.

This kind of study of the distribution of common words may be classified into general or usual collocations and more restricted technical or personal collocations. The commonest sentences in which the words *horse, cow, pig, swine, dog* are used with adjectives in nominal phrases, and also with verbs in the simple present, indicate characteristic distributions in collocability which may be regarded as a level of meaning in describing the English of any particular social group or indeed of one person. The word 'time' can be used in collocations with or without articles, determinatives, or pronouns. And it can be collocated with *saved, spent, wasted, frittered away*, with *presses, flies*, and with a variety of particles, even with *no*. Just as phonetic, phonological, and grammatical forms well established and habitual in any close social group provide a basis for the mutual expectancies of words and sentences at those levels, and also the sharing of these common features, so also the study of the usual collocations of a particular literary form or genre or of a particular author makes possible a clearly defined and precisely stated contribution to what I have termed the spectrum of descriptive linguistics, which handles and states meaning by dispersing it in a range of techniques working at a series of levels.

[1] See Chapter 4.

The statement of meaning by collocation and various collocabilities does not involve the definition of word-meaning by means of further sentences in shifted terms. Meaning by collocation is an abstraction at the syntagmatic level and is not directly concerned with the conceptual or idea approach to the meaning of words. One of the meanings of *night* is its collocability with *dark*, and of *dark*, of course, collocation with *night*. This kind of mutuality may be paralleled in most languages and has resulted in similarities of poetic diction in literatures sharing common classical sources.

Examples may be taken almost at random from any English work at any period. *Gorboduc*, for instance; *The silent night, weary day, tender love, deadly strife, hateful strife, cruel wrath, manly breast, deep repentance, hold life in contempt, Is all the world drowned in blood and sunk in cruelty, learn to live in peace.* Or take Blake's *King Edward the Third*, the following verses of which may be made the basis of the guessing game of filling in blanks:

> Let Liberty, the chartered right of Englishmen,
>   Won by our fathers in many a glorious field,
> And these fair youths, the flower of England,
>   Venturing their lives in my most righteous cause,
> Oh sheathe their hearts with triple[1] steel, that they
>   May emulate their fathers' virtues.

There are many more of the same kind throughout this work, and of course a large number of collocations which have been common property for long periods and are still current even in everyday colloquial. This method of approach makes two branches of stylistics stand out more clearly: (*a*) the stylistics of what persists in and through change, and (*b*) the stylistics of personal idiosyncrasies.

II

The study of collocation in a more generalized way could be used to describe the poetic diction of, say, Swinburne. Throughout his poetry Swinburne lays general constructions alongside each other, syntagmatically parallel collocations are a feature of verse-form and stanza-form, and often carry parallel phonaesthetic and prosodic features. The following examples are taken from 'Before Dawn':

> Delight, the rootless flower,
> And Love, the bloomless bower:
> Delight that lives an hour,
>   And love that lives a day . . .
>
> Sin sweet beyond forgiving
> And brief beyond regret.

---

[1] The residues of collocations do influence one another, as we have seen in the phonaesthetic mode. What is the meaning of 'Triple Shell'?

The meaning of the next stanza can be almost completely stated in the lower modes previously illustrated, but especially in parallel grammatical collocations, parallel phonetic and prosodic meaning, all contributing to the verse prosodies:

> Ah, one thing worth beginning,
> One thread in life worth spinning,
> Ah sweet, one sin worth sinning
> With all the whole soul's will;
> To lull you till one stilled you,
> To kiss you till one killed you,
> To feed you till one filled you,
> Sweet lips, if love could fill.

In 'The Garden of Proserpine' a great deal of the meaning is stated by making use of what I have called the lower or simpler modes at the phonetic, prosodic, grammatical, and collocational levels.

Since Swinburne is the most 'phonetic' of all English poets, let us apply the prism of linguistics to a few of his verses and examine the lower end of the spectrum stating partial meanings at abstracted levels or in certain modes. Opportunities for such experiments are numerous, and a good beginning may be made with 'Quia Multum Amavit' in *Songs before Sunrise*.

> Ah the banner-poles, the stretch of straightening streamers
> Straining their full reach out!

This occurs as the third couplet in a consecutive series of six beginning with *Ah the* and ending with a mark of exclamation. There are repeated Swinburnian patterns of collocation and also of grammatical mode. Normal grammatical markers such as *the, their, -ing, -er-s*, make possible a statement of meaning in the grammatical mode. All six exclamatory units, including the present example, are of nominal type, though three make use of finite verbs in dependent clauses. The prosodies of stress and intonation are fairly fixed and the end-words (*streamers* and *out!*) are linked by rhyme with the next end-words (*dreamers* and *doubt!*). Normal junction prosodies marking initials and finals of words in the sentence are there—for example, the sequence of *straightening . . . streamers . . . straining*. The alliterative use of *str-*, which is to be regarded as one initial unit, has been noticed in the mode of verse prosody as well as in the sentence prosodies. It must also be noticed in the phonaesthetic mode.[1] The words and phrases could be described as in the normal phonological mode of meaning. The *str-* words here can be grouped with many more English words often used in collocations and in contexts of situation referring to *long, lengthening, straight, stretched out* phenomena, involving both strength and stretching and a sort of active linearity, and which are used so often that when accumulated in a collocation such as the one quoted have a meaning which

---

[1] See below, *clogs* and *clings*. Cf. Chapter 4, pp. 34-46.

can be stated in the phonaesthetic mode. The phonaesthetic meaning of a collocation of several *str-* words of this type is to be taken in contrast with collocations of *cr-* words, *cl-* words.[1]

If the verses have the implication of a southern English pronunciation, then normal statements can be made at the phonetic level.

At the level of meaning by word collocation there is the interesting point that, both as a whole and in phrases, the collocations are unique and personal, that is to say, a-normal. In the wider context of the whole poem, even within the context of the six exclamatory units, similar collocations accumulate which must be referred to the personal stylistics of the poet, to what may, indeed, be called Swinburnese. But its English quality is in what I have called the lower modes, and that enables us to understand the common statement that most of Swinburne's poetry is untranslatable into any other language. This is true even of masses of writing inspired by Greek and Latin poetry, and of some writing inspired by French. In a similar way the modes of meaning of the following verses may be dispersed at various levels of abstraction:

    (i)   Ah the noise of horse, the charge and thunder of drumming,
          And swaying and sweep of swords[2]

    (ii) And prince that clogs, and priest that clings[3]

    (iii) As the flash of the flakes of the foam flared lamplike . . .[4]

    (iv) Welling water's winsome word,
          Wind in warm wan weather,[5]

    (v) By the wind that went on the world's waste waters . . .[4]

    (vi) And windy waves of woods[6]

    (vii) What wind soever waft his will
          Across the waves of day and night[7]

    (viii) Sleek supple soul and splendid skin?[8]

The *w-* feature is to be noticed at the phonetic, phonological, and phonaesthetic levels. At the phonological level it is an initial prosody in the word-process within the sentence, and by correlation with the prosodies of stress and intonation is also the alliterative feature of the verse prosody.

It will be clear that no attempt is made in the present analysis to exclude meaning from the consideration of language events or language isolates at any level. The phrase 'lower modes of meaning' has been used to refer chiefly to the handling of meaning at the phonetic, phonological, prosodic, and grammatical levels of abstraction. It is, however, to be understood that though the presentation of the scheme of analysis is in an ascending

---

[1] See below, *clogs* and *clings*. Cf. Chapter 4, pp. 34-46.

[2] 'Quia Multum Amavit.' Phonaesthetic groups of words with *sw-* and certain finals, cf. *swoop, swipe, swagger, swoon, swish*, even *swing, swill, swell*.

[3] Note *cl-* group, alliteration and collocation of *prince* and *priest*, repetition of parallel phrases in the same grammatical phonaesthetic and phonological modes. 'The Eve of Revolution.'

[4] 'Quia Multum Amavit.'   [5] 'A Child's Laughter.'   [6] 'A Song of Italy.'
[7] 'Prelude.'   [8] 'At A Month's End.'

order from phonetics to the context of culture, the total complex, including what may be called the higher levels in the context of situation, is a first postulate. The phonaesthetic mode, for example, correlates more closely than the phonetic mode with features of contexts of situation in which the personal and social attitudes are more easily apprehended in the light of ordinary experience.

Returning to Swinburne's poetic diction, further notions of generalized meaning may be applied to the statement of characteristic features in terms of syntax, word-formation, and the association of synonyms, antonyms, contraries, and complementary couples in one collocation. Analogous features may be found in groups of three or more associated words, and there are numerous instances of reversed and crossed antitheses, for example:

(i) Till life forget and death remember,
Till thou remember and I forget.[1]

(ii) The delight that consumes the desire,
The desire that outruns the delight.[2]

(iii) Change feet for wings or wings for feet.[3]

As an example of multiple word-polarities in one collocation, we could take two lines from stanza 14 of 'The Eve of Revolution' in *Songs before Sunrise*:

... freedom clothed the naked souls of slaves
And stripped the muffled souls of tyrants bare.

Stanza 5 of the poem 'A Match' exemplifies many of the linguistic features previously suggested and provides the prosodic pattern of the stanza-form. It illustrates repeated collocations opening and closing the stanza in which there are three polarities. Parallel collocations with features reversed are illustrated in lines 5 and 6:

If you were April's lady,
And I were lord in May,
We'd throw with leaves for hours
And draw for days with flowers,
Till day like night were shady
And night were bright like day;
If you were April's lady,
And I were lord in May.[4]

A few examples may now be given to illustrate phrase-formation and the association of words above referred to. The poem 'Prelude' introducing *Songs before Sunrise* provides many examples. Throughout Swinburne's writing, nouns in strings of two's and three's or even more occur in the same collocation, and the meaning may largely be studied in the modes already indicated:

[1] 'Itylus.'   [2] 'Dolores.'   [3] 'At A Month's End.'
[4] 'A Match.'

(i) From eyes and tresses flowers and tears,
From heart and spirit hopes and fears.
(ii) With souls that pray and hope and hate....
And dance and wring their hands and laugh,
And weep thin tears and sigh light sighs.

The first eight phrases quoted below illustrate another common feature, the use of derivatives of the same base within the same collocation. The last also shows a common Swinburnian polarity:

(i) ... for a little we live, and life hath mutable wings.[1]
(ii) So long I endure, no longer; and laugh not again, neither weep.[1]
(iii) She sees all past things pass,[2]
(iv) And wings of swift spent hours
Take flight and fly;[2]
(v) Soft as breathless ripples that softly shoreward sweep,[3]
(vi) Landor, once thy lover, a name that love reveres:[3]
(vii) O Garment not golden but gilded,[4]
(viii) And press with new lips where you pressed.
For my heart too springs up at the pressure,[4]
(ix) The life unlived, the unsown seeds,
Suns unbeholden, songs unsung, and undone deeds.[5]

Nominal phrases in which the substantive is preceded and followed by adjectives provide a framework for all the lower modes of meaning. For example:

(i) And dreams of bitter sleep and sweet,[6]
(ii) And die beneath blind skies or blue[6]
(iii) Of barren delights and unclean,[4]

From the point of view of linguistic criticism there is sufficient evidence to show that much of the Swinburnese vocabulary, embedded in his typical collocations with their prosodies, takes its form from his patterns of opposition, requiring such phrases as 'Mis-trust and trust'.[6] He had to use such words as 'miscreate',[6] 'misconceived',[7] 'misbegotten',[8] 'disengirdled',[6] 'discrowned',[6] 'undisbranched',[8] and hundreds of adjectives in '-less',—'With footless joy and wingless grief, And twinborn faith and disbelief',[6] 'red pulseless planet',[9] 'The shameless nameless love',[9] 'flowerless rose',[10] 'plumeless boughs',[10] 'dim green dayless day'.[11]

As a further example of parallel collocations and regular patterns of

---

[1] 'Hymn to Proserpine.'   [2] 'Before the Mirror.'   [3] 'A Ballad of Bath.'
[4] 'Dolores.'   [5] 'Blessed Among Women.'
[6] 'Prelude.'   [7] 'The Triumph of Time.'
[8] 'Tenebrae.'   [9] 'Faustine.'
[10] 'A Vision of Spring in Winter.'   [11] 'Félise.'

repetition in the verse prosodies, the six opening and concluding distichs of the six stanzas of 'A Match' are tabulated below:

Lines 1 and 7

Stanza	First place	Second place	Third place	Fourth place
1	if	love	were	what the {rose is
2		I		what the {words are
3		you		life, my darling
4				thrall to sorrow
5				April's lady
6				queen of pleasure

Twelve pieces for twenty-four places.

Lines 2 and 8

Stanza	First place	Second place	Third place	Fourth place
1	and	I	were	like the {leaf
2		love		like the {tune
3		[I]	your love	[were] death
4		I	were	page to joy
5				lord in May
6				king of pain

Twelve pieces for twenty-four places, twenty-two pieces for forty-eight places.

In stanza 5 there are three pairs of polarities in the opening and concluding distichs.

A detailed study of the words and pieces of Swinburne's poetry would be laborious, and most scholars would be satisfied to guess the probable result. I offer a few examples of (1) pieces employing the participial forms *clothed, clad, girt*: 'Clothed round with the strength of night', 'Clothed with delight, by the might of a dream', 'One warm dream clad about with a fire', 'Clothed with powers', 'Clothed with the wind's wings', 'Clothed about with flame and with tears', 'girt about with', 'Intolerable, not clad with death or life'; and (2) participial compounds:

White-eyed and poisonous-finned, shark-toothed and serpentine-curled.[1]

Commenting on this verse in terms of the lower half of the spectrum, the first item is notice of the two parallel collocations, and then to add the prosodic features marking the two pairs of participial compounds, themselves described at the grammatical level, completing the picture in the phonaesthetic mode and finally stating the congruence of all these in the verse prosody.

All this should be done after the contextual study of the whole poem has been attempted by the methods of linguistics.

Swinburne's verse should also be criticized by those concerned at the higher levels of the spectrum. This would mean its examination within

[1] 'Pan and Thalassius', 'Recollections', 'Hesperia', 'Félise', 'Sapphics', 'A Ballad of Bath', 'Who Hath Given Man Speech', 'Hymn to Proserpine'.

the culture context, which includes what is offered by biography and history. To the scheme already outlined further categories may be added at the levels of grammar, word-formation, or descriptive etymology, and also of collocation or phrasal stylistics, a few of which have been exemplified. Even a casual reader of Swinburne will soon appreciate that he is in a strange world in which contrast and concord are one and contraries divine. *Life* and *death, night* and *day, vices* and *virtues, waves sand sea* and *foam, fire* and *flame, deserts* and *blossoms, seeds* and *flowers, deaths births* and *ghosts, wine poison* and *blood, snakes* and *fangs, kisses* and *hisses, fervent* and *frigid, sterile barren* and *fruitful, heaven* and *hell*, commonly occur together (as grouped by the punctuation) in the same collocation.

I may end these notes on Swinburne by remarking that 'the philosophy of Swinburne's poetry' forms no part of a linguist's technical language. Not that philosophers have a language for this either. The statement of his philosophy by a philosopher would be almost impossible without a previous analysis of Swinburne's language. The philosopher might then agree with the linguist that there was nothing more to be done, for clearly Swinburne had nothing to say as a philosopher in the language of philosophy.

On the basis of half a dozen poems,[1] a sort of poet's philosophy could be expressed in other words and imputed to Swinburne. We might call it a kind of holism supported by pan-humanism and worship of

> The earth-soul Freedom, that only
> Lives, and that only is God.[2]

Before leaving Swinburne the victim of analysis at the lower end of the spectrum, it must be understood that no aesthetic or literary valuation has been attempted. Since I have not employed the language of literary criticism and since I have not even implied any criticism of such language, I should like to quote from the leading article in a well-known weekly[3] to illustrate a quite different type of language about Swinburne. The first quotation applies almost exactly to what has happened to the present writer:

The mind, therefore, which returns to Swinburne in middle life is not entirely unprepared for the discovery that its early doubts about the quality of the master's thought were well founded. A great deal of what he wrote is seen to be nonsense—

---

[1] See, for example, 'Hertha', 'Genesis', 'To Walt Whitman in America', 'Tenebrae', 'Tiresias'.

[2] The poetical languages of English writers on autumn were brought to my attention not long ago by 'The Transit of Autumn', a middle article contributed by Lord Dunsany to the *Observer*. Applying the scheme of analysis exemplified above, I found the results were in general terms similar. You must use the words *spring, summer, autumn,* and *winter,* and a stock of collocabilities. Having announced in the second paragraph that 'Autumn' is 'a queen although not yet crowned', you string out the range of meaning by collocation through the remaining six paragraphs—*robed, glory, crowned, resplendent, no singers go before her, prophets, the old régime, the reign, allegiance to new queen, proclaims, gold, throne, bodyguard, treasure, dynasty, court, the last dance of the leaves.*

[3] 'On Re-reading Swinburne', *The Times Literary Supplement*, 17 November 1950.

and pernicious nonsense at that. Perhaps some part of the blame is to be imputed to the reader, since what is good reading for a man at one age may be fairly poor at another. That is a truth from which critics are apt to shrink.

My second quotation employs a different sort of language about language from that normally used in linguistics, including usages which have the features of value judgements, though here and there such words as *alliterations, inversions, chime, rhyme, couplet, stanza, words, phrases*, necessarily appear:

Swinburne... whose eloquence is so often mere rhetoric, and whose loves and passions have no more reality than that of a deliberately induced mood.... The old magic of words is still, in many passages, there, so that sixty goes about murmuring a couplet or a stanza over and over again a whole day on end, just as did twenty. The foaming torrent of alliterations, double-rhymes, and Greek names may be sheer literary violence—but it still carries the reader away. The juggling with a small group of phrases or rhymes may be a trick—but with what grace and skill the juggler throws and catches them in every conceivable sequence and combination, and how exquisitely balanced and contrasted are his inversions. ... The gloomy magnificence of... can escape the ear no more than the simpler, languorous, melancholy charm of 'Rococo'.... The chime of the words—first read so long ago and since half-forgotten—rings once more incessantly in the mind, soaking through the hide and limbs of middle-age to the heart. Time is cast away, the world is forty years younger, and manhood back at its fresh, unknowing, unreasoning dawn.

It is entirely suitable that the somewhat impersonal experience expressed in the concluding paragraph is expressed anonymously. Can this also, like so much more, be 'mere rhetoric' having 'no more reality than that of a deliberately induced mood'? A linguist, as I have already said, is not at home in such idiom, and though I have raised the question by quoting the article, I have no means of answering it.

The examination of Swinburne's poetic diction has emphasized the idiosyncrasies which make it so personal that it can be called Swinburnese. It has been found possible to do this without reference to the higher levels of the spectrum of meaning, such as those provided by the biographical and cultural contexts.

III

Let us now turn to linguistic material of a very different kind, which requires the application of the categories of the context of situation,[1] in order to complete the statement of meaning by collocation. A cursory examination of certain letters of the eighteenth and early nineteenth

---

[1] See works previously quoted, especially Chapter 14: 'a group of categories forming a schematic construct for application to typical repetitive "events" in the social process. A. The Relevant features of participants: persons, personalities. (i) The Verbal Action of the Participants. (ii) The Non-verbal Action of the Participants. B. The Relevant Objects. C. The Effect of the Verbal Action.'

centuries[1] clearly shows collocations which will be recognized as current for at least two hundred years—that is, as part of the common stock of what we may call recent modern English.

In studying the extracts we note that many collocations are still generally current. In setting them out I have enclosed in brackets 'pieces' which to me seem glaringly obsolete.

The first extract is from Dr. Johnson's letter to the Earl of Chesterfield, dated 7 February 1755:

(i) [To be so distinguished is an honour, which, being very little accustomed to favours from the great, I know not well how to receive, or in what terms to acknowledge.]

(ii) [When, upon some slight encouragement, I first visited your Lordship, I was overpowered, like the rest of mankind, by the enchantment of your address, and could not forbear to wish that I might boast myself *Le vainqueur du vainqueur de la terre*;—that I might obtain that regard for which I saw the world contending;]

Applying the categories of the context of situation and of meaning by collocation, it will be seen that very little survives that could be considered current today.

Applying similar categories it will be agreed that the language used by William Wilberforce to the Earl of Galloway in a letter from the House of Commons on 3 December 1800 is much nearer to contemporary usage:

(iii) Through the medium of the great clubs, Etc., one set of opinions manners, modes of living, Etc., are diffused through a vast mass [of the higher orders.] Domestic restraints, and family economy, and order, [are voted bores,] [while, from the nature of our constitution,] aided by the increasing wealth and the prevailing sentiments of the age, whatever ways of thinking, speaking, and acting become popular [in the higher classes,] soon spread through every other.

What Wilberforce has to say in the above quotation is relevant to one of the purposes of the present essay, which is to draw attention to the stylistics of the letters of upper-class society in the eighteenth century and to similar features in what is today considered good standard English for everyday use in polite society. The great doctor did not belong to the class which developed modern polite colloquial style, as the following extracts from his more familiar letters will illustrate.

(iv) Apologies are seldom of any use. We will delay till your arrival the reasons, good or bad, which have made me [such a sparing and ungrateful] correspondent.

(v) I went away from Lichfield ill, and have had a troublesome time [with my breath;] for some weeks I have been [disordered by a cold,] [of which I could not get the violence abated till I had been let blood three times.]

[1] For convenience I have drawn them from (a) *English Letters of the XVIIIth Century*, edited by James Aitken (Pelican), and (b) *English Letters of the XIXth Century*, edited by James Aitken (Pelican). The study of letters, if it is to be a scientific study, requires an examination of the manuscript—that is, of the material before it has been tampered with by editors and printers.

MODES OF MEANING

(vi) [The usurpation of the nobility, for they apparently usurp all the influence they gain by fraud and misrepresentation,] I think it certainly lawful, perhaps your duty, to resist. What is not their own, [they have only by robbery.]

In the above extracts the English is dated, at almost all levels, and in a systematic study of all Johnson's letters, as well as of similarly dated material, the linguistic features would have to be stated.

The following interesting sentence from a letter to Mrs. Porter in 1782 is almost contemporary at the level of collocation:

(vii) I have, by advertising, found poor Mr. Levett's brothers in Yorkshire, who will take the little he has left;

Since the above has the implication of utterance, we must know whether Mr. Levett is dying or already dead before we read the last clause. If he is still alive, then we may stress both the words *has* and *left*, but if the reference is to a will,[1] then *has* must be unstressed. From the point of view of present-day English 'by advertising' should begin the sentence, or better, be replaced by some reference to the newspapers. In a full statement of the elements of the context of situation, Johnson's method of advertising would have to be known.

The two following sentences make use of the word 'want', which at the grammatical level of meaning is a verb. The meaning by collocation stands, but differs in situations.

(viii) I want every comfort.

(ix) I can only recommend a rule which you do not want; give as little pain as you can.

The first sentence could quite well be used in talking to a reception-clerk at a first-class hotel. But by extending the collocation, and by reference to the situational context, the meaning is seen to be very different.[2]

There are, of course, a large number of collocations in Johnson's letters which are clichés of present-day writing, such as:

(x) Begin again where you left off.

(xi) Let me have a long letter from you as soon as you can.

And it is interesting to notice that an old-established part of the meaning of *neglected* is collocation with *criminally*:

(xii) You are not to think yourself forgotten, or criminally neglected.

[1] He died the following year.
[2] See also *English Synonymes* explained by George Crabb, 3rd edition, 1824:

'{ WANT, *v. Poverty.*
{ To Want, Need, Lack.

To be without is the common idea expressed by these terms; but to WANT is to be without that which contributes to our comfort, or is an object of our desire;

From the close connexion which subsists between desiring and *want*, it is usual to consider what we *want* as artificial, and what we *need* as natural and indispensable:

tender people *want* a fire when others would be glad not to have it;

He who *wants* nothing is a happy man: he who *needs* nothing, may be happy if he *wants* no more than he has; for then he *lacks* that which alone can make him happy, which is contentment.'

Johnson's English in all his prose styles examined objectively and statistically in connexion with a biographical study of his personality would give us a statement of stylistics in a social setting which would mark it off sharply from the English of such letter-writers as Lady Mary Wortley Montagu, Mrs. Delany, Horace Walpole, Fanny Burney, and Lord Byron. A linguistic study of the letters of the upper class seems to show persistent features of what we call the King's English in modern times, and these features have been shared by increasing numbers of writers and speakers in the nineteenth century and up to the present time, largely perhaps as a result of the influence of the big public schools, the older universities, and the snob value of the aristocratic. The Johnsonian styles at a fairly high social level have, of course, been common, and so have other styles suggesting that the speaker or writer had 'swallowed a dictionary', or spoke 'like a school book'. We frequently ask people to say what they mean in words of one syllable, and there is much talk today about plain English.[1] As George Orwell's satire[1] suggests, Oldspeak is perhaps being replaced by Newspeak. Should the snob value of Newspeak establish itself, the spectrum of meaning analysis might then describe the new language at all levels from pronunciation through word distribution in collocation to the study of the processes of the newer contexts of situation.

Turning to the letters of Lady Mary Wortley Montagu to the Countess of Mar, the Countess of Bute, and others of her friends and perhaps equals, we find a number of characteristics of the King's English which are still promoted by a good family upbringing, and by education at a good school. The written use of *don't* and the collocations of the participles in *-ing* are especially to be noted.

(xiii) In my opinion, dear S., I ought rather to quarrel with you for not answering my Nimeguen letter of August till December, *than to excuse my not writing again* till now. I am sure there is on my side a very good excuse for silence, having [gone such tiresome land-journeys,] though I don't find [the conclusion of them] so bad as you seem to imagine.

(xiv) Those dreadful stories you have heard of the *plague* have very little foundation in truth.

(xv) To reconcile myself to the sound of a word which has always given me such terrible ideas, though I am convinced there is little more in it than in a fever. As a proof of this, let me tell you that we passed through two or three towns [most violently infected.]

(xvi) Luckily for me. . . .

(xvii) who are very fond of speaking of what they don't [know].

(xviii) If you don't like my choice of subjects, tell me what you would [have me write upon;]

---

[1] See, for example, Sir Ernest Gowers's *Plain Words*, 1948, and George Orwell's *1984*, 1948.

(xix) which I don't think so bad as you have perhaps heard it represented. I am a very good judge of [their eating,] having lived three weeks in the house of an *effendi* at Belgrade, who gave us very magnificent dinners,

(xx) and I am extremely glad I was so [complaisant.]

(xxi) I am willing to take your word for it,

(xxii) I am satisfied I have been one of the *condemned* ever since I was born; and in submission to the divine justice I don't at all doubt but I deserved it in some pre-existent state. I will still hope that I am only in purgatory; and that after whining [and grunting] a certain number of years, I shall be translated to some more happy sphere, where virtue will be natural, and custom reasonable; that is, in short, where common sense will reign. I grow very devout, as you see, and place all my hopes in the next life, being totally persuaded of the nothingness of this. Don't you remember how miserable we were in the little parlour at Thoresby? we then thought marrying would put us at once into possession of all we wanted.[1] Then came being with child, etc., and you see what comes of being with child. Though, after all, I am still of opinion, that it is extremely silly to submit to ill fortune.

(xxiii) Every thing may turn out better than you expect.

Further extracts from the letters of Mrs. Delany and Fanny Burney, Madame D'Arblay, will confirm the impressions gained from those of Lady Mary. Burke remarked in a letter to Fanny Burney that he hardly dare tell her his opinion of her place 'in an age distinguished by producing extraordinary women'.

(xxiv) then we start up, run away, and here I am, brimful of a thousand things to say to you, but have no time to write them, and that you know is a sad case. You and I perfectly agree in what you say of Sir John Stanley and my brother.

(xxv) I don't find that the troubles of the times have given any check to gay doings in this part of the world.

(xxvi) but it is something like [*inoculating for the small pox*], one does not care to *advise either for or against*;

(xxvii) I don't think there can be anything wrong in your writing to Mr. R. about poor H. Viney, if you think he will not mention the writing to anybody, but one of the crying sins of this world is the laxity of the tongue. How few people understand the perfection of silence on most occasions.

(Note again the participle *-ing* preceded by a conjunct personal pronoun.)

(xxviii) God forbid you should *stop your hand* when correction is necessary! and surely it must be so on such an occasion as that was, though I don't suppose the dear child meant the harm she did;

It is clear that the prosodies are very like those of present-day speech, and emphasis falls on *must*, *that*, and *meant*.

(xxix) To Mrs. Dewes, Bath, 28 Oct. 1760.
I have just been hunting the shops, and am not half equipped. Surely this is

---

[1] Cf. Johnson's use of *want*, p. 205 above.

the busiest idle place in the world, and yet I have not once been in the Rooms, only one morning for three minutes at Wiltshire's.

(xxx) I did not expect to hear [you lost your giddiness at once,] but [I hope in God] it will by degrees wear away; however, all means should be tried, and I hear so much from everybody of the great efficacy of the Bristol waters, that I hope you will take it into consideration; and if the doctors are not against your trying it, lose no time.

(xxxi) well taken care of,

(xxxii) Mr. Sloper . . . has been much offended that his daughter was not taken out to dance; she was the first night, and a sensible, clever woman whose daughter was taken out after her *refused* to let her dance; this put a stop to Miss Cibber's being asked again; and on Sunday night, [in the midst of the Rooms], Mr. Cibber collared poor Collet, abusing him at the same time, and asking if he had been the occasion [of the affront put upon his daughter]; he said it was '*by Mr. Nash's direction*'—the poor wretch is *now* wheeled into the Rooms;

(xxxiii) Yesterday I had a letter from Lady Weymouth, who had [but] just heard of our being at Bath: she comes here for a day or two on purpose to see me, and dines with us today.

(xxxiv) I cannot sit down in my usual place without thinking of my dear little Portia, tho' not so selfish as to wish her skipping about me, tho' *that* would be very pleasant; but her dear mama has the first claim.

The collocation *taken out to dance* could still be used, but in a different context of situation, and in a background of very different manners. The use of an emphatic *was* in *she was the first night*, is another indication of the persistence of characteristic prosodies over long periods of time. Note four further examples of the *-ing* participle, and three with preceding genitive.

(xxxv) Another of his confessions was this:

(xxxvi) 'Luckily for me,' said he, 'I have no occasion to speak till about two o'clock, when we dine, for that keeps me fresh. If I were to begin earlier, I should only be like skimmed milk the rest of the day.'

(xxxvii) Mrs. Astley, however, assured me she was pretty well.

(xxxviii) She took the time the Queen so considerately gave her for deliberation, and she consulted with some of her old friends. They all agreed there must be no refusal, and, [after many circumstances] too long [for writing], though otherwise well worth knowing, [Lady Weymouth was made the messenger of] her Majesty's offer being accepted.

(xxxix) would there be any harm in my using it to make a visit to Twickenham?

Again the prosodies are familiar, and a further example of a participial construction in *-ing -ed* preceded by a genitival nominal phrase, *her Majesty's offer*. Note the participial phrase *my using* in an entirely contemporary collocation *would there be any harm in my using it?*

Features we have already noticed appear frequently in the letters of Fanny Burney (1752–1840) from which the following extracts are selected:

MODES OF MEANING

(xl) I have for some time seen very plainly that you are [éprise,] and have been extremely uneasy at the discovery.

(xli) *Wednesday*. I broke off and an incapable unwillingness seized my pen; but I hear you are not well, and I hasten—if that be a word I can ever use again—to make personal inquiry how you are.

(xlii) I have been very ill, very little *apparently*, but with nights of [consuming] restlessness and tears. I have now called in Dr. Holland, who understands me marvellously, and am now much as usual; no, not that—still tormented with nights [without repose]—but better.

(xliii) My spirits have been dreadfully saddened of late by whole days—[nay] weeks—of helplessness [for any employment].

The letters of Horace Walpole (1717-1797) are extremely interesting from the regressive point of view—regressive, that is, in the light of common present-day usage. In the following extensive extracts there are a large number of usual collocations which must have been common in good society both in everyday talk and familiar correspondence:

(xliv) It would have been inexcusable in me, in our present circumstances, and after all I have promised you, not to have written to you for this last month, if I had been in London; but I have been at Mount Edgecumbe, and so constantly [upon] the road, that I neither received your letters, had time to write, or knew what to write. I came back last night, and found [three packets] from you, which I have no time to answer, and [but] just time to read. The confusion I have found, and the danger we are in, prevent my talking of anything else. The young Pretender, at the head of three thousand men, has got a march on General Cope, who is not eighteen hundred strong; and when the last attempts came away, was fifty miles nearer Edinburgh than Cope, and by this time is there. The clans will not rise for the Government; the Dukes of Argyll and Athol [are come post to town,] not having been able to raise a man.

Again quite modern at all levels but the social context. Note *prevent my talking of anything else* and *not having been able to raise a man*.

(xlv) that [an express] came last night with an account of their being at Edinburgh to the number of five thousand.

Note again *an account of their being at Edinburgh to the number of five thousand*.

(xlvi) But all this is not the worst!

(xlvii) Against this force we have—I don't know what——

(xlviii) I am grieved to tell you all this; but when it is so, how can I avoid telling you?

(xlix) We expect every moment to hear that . . .

(l) Lord Granville and his faction persist in persuading the King, that it is an affair of no consequence.

(li) Vernon, that simple noisy creature, has hit upon a scheme that is of great service; he had [laid Folkestone cutters] all around the coast, which are continually relieved, [and bring constant notice of everything that stirs.]

(lii) I confess my own apprehensions are not near so strong as they were; and if we get over this, I shall believe that we never can be hurt; for we never can be more exposed to danger.

(liii) the King has declared publicly to the Ministry, that he has been told of the great [civilities] which he was said to show to her at Hanover; that he protests he showed her only the common [civilities] due . . . that he never intended to take any particular notice of her; nor had, nor would let my Lady Yarmouth. In fact, my Lady Yarmouth peremptorily refused . . . and when she did go with my Lady Pomfret, the King [but just] spoke to her. She declares her intention of staying in England.

These passages contain several familiar clichés and an interesting emphatic *did*.

(liv) I forgot to tell a *bon-mot* of Leheup on her first coming over; he was asked if he would not go and see her? He replied, 'No, I never visit modest women.' Adieu! my dear child! I flatter myself you will collect hopes from this letter.

Note *on her first coming over*.

(lv) By their not advancing, I conclude that either the Boy and his council could not prevail on the Highlanders to leave their own country, or that they were not strong enough, and still wait for foreign assistance, which, in a new declaration, he intimates that he still expects.

Note *By their not advancing*.

(lvi) I don't think, considering the crisis, that the House was very full.

(lvii) With all this, I am far from thinking that they are so confident and sanguine as their friends at Rome.

(lviii) You may imagine how little I like our situation; but I don't despair.

(lix) I write you [but short letters,] considering the circumstances of the time; but I hate to send you paragraphs only to contradict them again: I still less choose to forge events; and, indeed, am glad I have so few to tell you.

(lx) though the roads are exceedingly bad and great quantities of snow have fallen.

(lxi) he insists on a declaration of our having nothing to do with the continent. He mustered his forces, but did not notify his intention;

Note *a declaration of our having nothing to do with the continent*, and common collocations.

(lxii) You have bid me for some time to send you good news—well! I think I will.

(lxiii) But what is more astonishing, Sherlock, who has much better sense,

(lxiv) If it was not too long to transcribe, I would send you an entertaining petition of the [periwigmakers] to the King, in which they complain that men *will* wear [their own hair].

An interesting sign of new manners, and a question of the emphasis on *will*.

(lxv) If he dies of it,—and how should he not?—it will sound very silly when Hercules or Theseus ask him what he died of, to reply, 'I caught my death on a damp staircase at a new club-room.'

(lxvi) Sure power must have some strange unknown charm, when it can compensate for such contempt! I see many who triumph in these bitter pills which the ministry are so often forced to swallow; I own I do not; it is more mortifying to me to reflect how great and respectable we were three years ago than satisfactory to see those insulted who have brought such shame upon us. ['Tis poor amends] to national honour to know, that if a printer is [set in the pillory,] his country wishes it was [my] Lord This, or Mr. That. They will be gathered to the Oxfords, and Bolingbrokes, and ignominious of former days; but the wound they have inflicted is perhaps indelible. That goes to *my* heart, who had felt all the Roman pride of being one of the first nations upon earth!—Good night!—I will go to bed, and dream of Kings drawn in triumph; and then I will go to Paris, and dream I am pro-consul there; [pray,] take care not to let me be awakened with an account of an invasion having taken place from Dunkirk! Yours ever,

(lxvii) Mr. Chute tells me that you have taken a new house in Squireland, and have given yourself up for two years more [to port and parsons.] I am very angry, and resign you to the works of the devil or the church, I don't care which. You will get the gout, turn Methodist, and expect to ride to heaven upon your own great toe. I was happy with your telling me how well you love me, and though I don't love loving, I could have poured out all the fulness of my heart to such an old and true friend; but what am I the better for it, if I am to see you [but] two or three days in the year?

(lxviii) Your wit and humour will be as much lost upon them, as if you talked the dialect of Chaucer; for with all the divinity of wit, it grows out of fashion [like a fardingale.] I am convinced that the young men at White's already laugh at George Selwyn's *bon mots* only by tradition. I avoid talking before the youth of the age as I would dancing before them; for if one's tongue [don't] move in the steps of the day, and thinks to please by its old graces, it is only an object of ridicule, [like Mrs. Hobart in her cotillon.] I tell you we should get together, and comfort ourselves with reflecting on the brave days that we have known—not that I think people were a jot more clever or wise in our youth than they are now; but as my system is always to live in a vision as much as I can, and as visions don't increase with years, there is nothing so natural as to think one remembers what one does not remember.

(lxix) If you are like me, you are fretting at the weather.

(lxx) My plan is to pass away calmly; cheerfully if I can; sometimes to amuse myself with the rising generation, but to take care not to fatigue them, nor weary them with old stories, which will not interest them, as their adventures do not interest me.

(lxxi) In short, they are a pleasant medicine, that one should take care not to grow fond of.

(lxxii) Good night? You see I never let our long-lived friendship drop, though you give it so few opportunities of breathing.

(lxxiii) But I seem to choose to read futurity, because I am not likely to see it: indeed I am most rational when I say to myself, What is all this to me?

(lxxiv) By the tenth article of the capitulation, Lord Cornwallis demanded that the loyal Americans in his army should not be punished. This was flatly refused, and he has left them to be hanged. [I doubt] no vote of Parliament will be able [to blanch] such a—such a—I don't know what the word is for it; he must get his uncle the Archbishop to christen it; there is no name for it in any Pagan vocabulary. I suppose it will have a patent for being called Necessity. Well! there ends another volume of the American war. It looks a little as if the history of it would be all we should have for it, except forty millions of debt.

(lxxv) These are certainly the speculations of an idle man, and the more trifling when one considers the moment.

The preceding extracts contain examples of long-standing collocations, though they also carry unmistakable marks of the social context of the eighteenth century.

Walpole died just before the turn of the century. As herald of the nineteenth I have chosen William Wilberforce. Wilberforce wrote a familiar letter to Pitt in September 1804, which provides interesting linguistic material with the highest social sanction. Stylistically, it is more contemporary than what has been shown of Walpole, perhaps less aristocratic.

(lxxvi) Fifthly, and last, not least, let me beg you, my dear Pitt, to have the proclamation issued for stopping the Guiana supply of slaves. If I felt less on that subject, I should say more; but I really do feel [on it] very deeply, and so I know you would also, if your attention were not absorbed by such a number of pressing matters: but it will not cost you half an hour I hope to settle this. I beg you will remember how much I myself am personally concerned in it, if any other excuse be necessary for my boring you so about it than the merits of the subject itself. I cannot doubt that——, and others of his set in abolition matters, will renew the attack they formerly made on me, on account of my not having endeavoured to stop this supply of slaves to the conquered settlements. I trust, however, that I need not assure you that the thing itself, far more than what any one can say on it, weighs on my mind. I repeat it, half an hour would settle the whole—the forms are at hand in the Council Office.

There is another *-ing -ed* participial phrase, *on account of my not having endeavoured to stop* . . . and there are *a number of pressing matters*, even *the forms are at hand in the Council office*. The earliest citation by the *N.E.D.* of *form* in the sense of 'a formulary document with blanks for the insertion of particulars' is dated 1855. The word as used here may bear this sense.

(lxxvii) Seventhly, I cannot help saying a word or two on a subject on which I have thought, at least daily, for many months—that I mean of the Volunteer command. Surely you will not, if there should be any landing, take your [station] as colonel of the corps, but remember that you are the mainspring of the whole machine, and there is a reason peculiar to the times or the persons [in certain high situations,] which renders it indispensable, both on grounds of duty and character, that you should be [in a station] from which you can issue general orders, applicable to all the parts of the complicated system of measures. You naturally do not hear much concerning the commander-in-chief, but I do not believe people [think of him half as well as he deserves.] Their chief reason for not being much more discontented than they are, and still more than they [avow themselves to be], is, that they believe if any thing serious really were to happen, *you* would sit in council with him, and they give him credit for a disposition to follow your advice. Let me beg you to destroy this, which I am sure you will ascribe to its true motives, regard for the public interest, and personally to yourself.

I am ever,
My dear P.,
Affectionately and sincerely yours,
W. WILBERFORCE.

Pitt is *the mainspring of the whole machine* and is responsible for the *issue of general orders, applicable to all the parts of the complicated system of measures.* These collocations must have been fairly common at the time. Wilberforce used them rather than invented them. They can still be used today.

(lxxviii) There can be no objection to his enlightening the minds of the good people of Holland on the subject of the slave trade.

Clearly set in the nineteenth-century context and familiar in all modes of meaning. Another participial phrase with genitive pronoun as part of a nominal phrase.

(lxxix) . . . you must have had a copy of it, and I hope you read it; it was a very good summary.

(lxxx) Pitt, and you yourself also, are far better judges than I can be, whether it would be proper to go the length of taking any such step as that which Brougham recommends.

(lxxxi) Do you remember my asking you, [by Brougham's desire,] whether you had any objection to his passing through Holland in his way to Vienna, Etc.?

Two participles in *-ing* preceded by genitival pronouns.

(lxxxii) Really, the idea of a war between our two countries is perfectly horrible; and I am happy to say, that I think, in this country, this most just sentiment gains ground. Like all propositions which are founded in truth and reason, it gradually sinks into the minds of men, and, though perhaps slowly and insensibly, by degrees it leavens nearly the whole mass. It will tend to produce this friendly disposition on your side of the water, if more of your countrymen would come over and live awhile among us. We are not an idle people; we are a busy people, and may not have leisure or disposition to pay all the personal attentions which politeness might prescribe; but I am persuaded that any gentleman of character and moderation, who should visit this country, would meet with such a friendly reception as would show him that the circumstance of our being the descendants [of common progenitors] is not forgotten, or rather, that it is reviving and diffusing itself with increasing force.

Much less familiar but unmistakably democratic and nearer to contemporary modes than Walpole.

(lxxxiii) and really the business of parliament has increased so much of late years, as to render it next to impossible for any man who cannot live for six or seven months, in every year, with a very small proportion of food or sleep, especially the latter, to attend at all, as he would otherwise be glad to do, to domestic or social claims.

With this last emphasis on the arrival of features of life and language well known to all of us today, I may conclude by indicating once more the main theme of this essay on linguistic description. It is an outline sketch suggesting by hints the sort of language a linguist might develop in order to describe language by making statements of meaning at a series of levels.

The presentation of the linguistic features which I have made above transcends the historical order. At the outset I illustrated as many modes of meaning as possible from the language forms themselves. Licensed to create his own diction, the poet so shapes his composition or design that a great deal of its meaning is the form he gives it. For such form, for such personal usage and style, the choice of Swinburne was for me an inevitable choice. I have made no attempt to show how Swinburne's diction is narrowly dated and determined in nineteenth-century history.

The letters bear the marks of the eighteenth century; but my purpose in presenting them was to view them regressively, noticing those linguistic features which seem to persist as normal usage over long periods.

IV

Finally, I would return to Wilde's dialogue 'The Critic as Artist' to emphasize the importance of the application of descriptive linguistics to modern, including contemporary, English by the schools of English in our universities. Writing of the Greeks and Greek, he reminds us forcibly 'that the material they criticized with most care was language'. Turning to England, he puts the case for criticism in his own idiom as follows:

England has done one thing; it has invented and established Public Opinion, which is an attempt to organise the ignorance of the community, and to elevate it to the dignity of physical force. But Wisdom has always been hidden from it.[1]

You have asked me about the influence of Criticism. I think I have answered that question already; but there is this also to be said. It is Criticism that makes us cosmopolitan. The Manchester school tried to make men realise the brotherhood of humanity, by pointing out the commercial advantages of peace. It sought to degrade the wonderful world into a common market-place for the buyer and the seller. It addressed itself to the lowest instincts, and it failed. War followed upon war, and the tradesman's creed did not prevent France and Germany from clashing together in blood-stained battle. There are others of our own day who seek to appeal to mere emotional sympathies, or to the shallow dogmas of some vague system of abstract ethics. They have their Peace Societies, so dear to the sentimentalists, and their proposals among those who have never read history. But mere emotional sympathy will not do. It is too variable, and too closely connected with the passions; and a board of arbitrators who, for the general welfare

[1] 'The Critic as Artist', from *Intentions*, by Oscar Wilde, 12th edition, p. 210.

of the race, are to be deprived of the power of putting their decisions into execution, will not be of much avail. There is only one thing worse than Injustice, and that is Justice without her sword in her hand. When Right is not Might, it is Evil.

No: the emotions will not make us cosmopolitan, any more than the greed for gain could do so. It is only by the cultivation of the habit of intellectual criticism that we shall be able to rise superior to race-prejudices.[1]

Intellectual criticism will bind Europe together in bonds far closer than those that can be forged by shopman or sentimentalist. It will give us the peace that springs from understanding.[2]

The criticism of English in English for all who use English may well prove one of the great educational forces of the age and a source of strength to all who subscribe to the ideals associated with the growth of this vast language community.

[1] Wilde, op. cit., pp. 211-12.   [2] Ibid., p. 213.

16

GENERAL LINGUISTICS AND DESCRIPTIVE GRAMMAR

I. THE GENERAL BACKGROUND

THE great languages of the older civilizations were well served by grammarians whose eminence has not been levelled or overlaid by the thousands of grammars of modern languages which have continued to flow into schools and academies since the Renaissance with the ubiquity of the printing-press. What modern linguist would wish to find serious fault with the grammatical outlines of Pāṇini for Sanskrit, of Dionysius for Greek,[1] of Donatus and Priscian for Latin,[1] or of Sībawayhi and Al Khalīl for Arabic? Three very different systems, the Ancient Indian, the Graeco-Roman, the Arabic, owe some of their excellence to their independence, to the absence of any international or universal grammatical dogma.

The voyages of discovery from the West opened our ears and our eyes to the confusion of Babel, and Latin grammar was misapplied to an ever-increasing number of languages, and with it Greek logic and metaphysics. Modern psychology of many schools has joined in and the muddle has become so embarrassing that linguists are now joining forces in attempts to clear the ground for a fresh approach. But the task is complicated by the renewed interest in problems of language of logicians, philosophers, psychologists, biologists, anthropologists, and nowadays of acousticians, engineers, and those who follow the machines of cybernetics. The old muddle hampered everybody. The present lack of mutual understanding between the various disciplines grappling with language may produce muddle with mathematics and machinery,[2] and to avoid it the heaviest responsibility rests upon the linguists.

During the last thirty years linguistics has made great advances and today may be said to be in the van of the social sciences. But scholars in other disciplines which are interested in language continue to show little understanding of the progress that has been made. In my view the findings of linguistics are basic and must be carefully studied especially by logicians and philosophers who are critics of language. There is a steady stream of books on language and logic and kindred topics. In one of them[3] Professor

---

[1] See R. H. Robins, *Ancient and Mediaeval Grammatical Theory in Europe (with special reference to modern linguistic doctrines)*, Bell, London, 1951. 101 pp.
[2] See note 1 on p. 225.
[3] A. G. N. Flew, *Logic and Language*, Blackwell, Oxford, 1951, p. 36. Cf. Sir Alan Gardiner, 'A Grammarian's Thoughts on a Recent Philosophical Work', *Trans. Phil. Society*, 1951, especially pp. 47, 51.

Gilbert Ryle says in the concluding sentence of his contribution: 'I would rather allot to philosophy a sublimer task than the detection of the sources in linguistic idioms of current misconstructions and absurd theories. But that it is at least this I cannot feel any serious doubt.' In an earlier paragraph on the same page, he had remarked, 'But this does not mean that it is a department of philology or literary criticism'. There are some linguists who should take Professor Ryle's warning to heart. There have been serious misapprehensions among linguists about modern logic, which cannot, in the nature of the case, form an integral part of linguistics of any school. There is little hope of philosophers and logicians making a serious study of the possible light linguistics might throw on some of their problems, if linguists sometimes poach unskilfully in other disciplines, showing lack of assurance in their own. The philosophers of today, especially in Britain and America, tend to make use of nineteenth-century results in linguistics and are out of touch with recent progress on the systematic and structural side of the subject. In this connexion Professor Louis Hjelmslev expresses the misgivings of linguists very clearly: 'I have pointed out certain obvious relations between the logistic language theory and the philological one. But unfortunately these relations soon come to an end. Logistic language theory has been carried out without any regard to philology, and it is obvious that logicians, while constantly talking about language, are neglecting in a somewhat indefensible way the results of the philological approach to theory. In particular the sign concept advocated by these scholars has considerable shortcomings and is unmistakably inferior to that of Saussure; it is not understood by logicians that the linguistic sign is two-sided, comprising a content and an expression, both of which can be submitted to a purely structural analysis.'[1]

Again, in a later brief article,[2] he states his dualist theory as follows:

Psychologues, philosophes et linguistes s'accordent pour reconnaître l'importance du signe. L'importance du signe est devenue plus grande encore après la découverte, établie par F. de Saussure et approfondie par la linguistique théorique de nos jours, du caractère à la fois purement *formel* (et par conséquent arbitraire, conventionnel) et *bilatéral* du signe linguistique. Le signe n'est pas un simple signifiant; il est signifié et signifiant à la fois; il est constitué par une solidarité entre une forme du contenu et une forme de l'expression. Le signe est donc une forme à deux faces, contractant un rapport conventionnel avec la substance de l'expression (substance phonique ou graphique) et avec la substance du contenu. Le rapport entre la forme du contenu et la substance qu'elle est destinée à organiser peut s'appeler *désignation*; la substance du contenu est le *designatum*; considéré au point de vue physique, c'est le monde des choses; considéré au point de vue psychique, c'est la pensée.

[1] *Studia Linguistica*, vol. i, 1948, p. 76. (I think contemporary English usage would substitute *linguistics* and *linguistic* for Professor Hjelmslev's *philology* and *philological*. In my opinion de Saussure's concept of the sign is over-valued by Professor Hjelmslev. —J. R. F.)
[2] 'Rôle structural de l'ordre des mots', *Journal de Psychologie*, Janv.-Mars 1950, pp. 54–58.

La pensée s'organise donc en s'appuyant sur le signe. Impossible dès lors d'établir une théorie de la pensée sans avoir recours au signe.

As I think I have shown in an earlier chapter,[1] English work in orthoepy and phonetics and in what would nowadays be called general linguistics goes back a long way in our cultural history. In the nineteenth century we produced Henry Sweet, whose presidential address to the Society in 1877 contains the following passage, which I continue to quote in every suitable context:

> Our tendency is not so much toward the antiquarian philology and text-criticism in which German scholars have done so much, as towards the observation *of the phenomena of living languages* ... the real strength and originality of English work lies ... in phonology and dialectology. Our aim ought clearly to be, while assimilating the methods and results of German work, to concentrate our energies mainly on what may be called 'living philology'. The vastness of our Empire, which brings us in contact with innumerable languages, alone forces us incessantly to grapple with the difficulties of spoken, often also unwritten, languages. We ought to be able to send out yearly hundreds of thoroughly and specially trained young men....

In the session 1950–1 the School of Oriental and African Studies was able *'to send out'* seven *'thoroughly and specially trained young men'* whose whole task was *'the observation of the phenomena of living languages'*, and both they and at least a score of others are *'concentrating their energies mainly on what may be called "living philology"'*. In America there is a similar history to report since the foundation of the American Philosophical Society [1838], the American Oriental Society [1842], and the Smithsonian Institution [1846]. Today there is the Linguistic Society of America which supports the annual Linguistic Institute; also the Linguistic Circle of New York, the *International Journal of American Linguistics*, and the Summer Institute of Linguistics for the training of missionaries for linguistic work in the mission fields of the world.[2]

From Switzerland and France the great formative work of de Saussure and Meillet has gone forth and shaped modern linguistics in all the principal schools.

Baudouin de Courtenay, Kruszewski, later Trubetzkoy and the Prague Circle and recently the Soviet schools joined the international forces which continue to develop the linguistic sciences of today.

All these various streams contribute in varying volume and strength to present-day schools of linguistics, each of which has well-marked characteristics and specialized interests. But in the fundamentals of descriptive grammar there is general agreement which is to some extent expressed in the recommendations of the Paris symposium which provide the occasion for this article.

[1] Chapter 8, pp. 92–120.
[2] See Chapter 12.

DESCRIPTIVE GRAMMAR

In 1921 Jespersen's book *Language* opened with the sentence: 'The distinctive feature of the science of language as conceived nowadays is its historical character.' In 1951 I think one can clearly say with Professor A. A. Hill of Virginia that 'nowadays neither linguistics nor chemistry are essentially historical disciplines'.[1] An interesting summation of one of the current trends in linguistics as a science has recently been made by Martin Joos: '... within our field we must adopt a technique of precise treatment, which is by definition a mathematics. We must make our "linguistics" a kind of mathematics within which inconsistency is by definition impossible.'[2]

'The newer linguistics takes as its aim not merely the reconstruction of ancestral forms, but the complete understanding of language activity, both in its structure and content. We can, in spite of difficulties in the way, hope that eventually we will be able to demonstrate the correspondences between the structure of language activity and the structure of all other organized activities.'[3] 'The linguist's problem', to quote Professor Joos again, 'is that the symbols of language are arranged in systems the parts of which are discrete, while the experience signified by language seems to be arranged in continuity....' 'Linguistics has had conspicuous success of late in translating continuity into discreteness, not in the sphere of semantics, but in the sphere of language sounds. Language sounds exist on two levels, one as physical and articulatory where they are mere noises, and one where they are on a linguistic level as functioning signals.'

Professor Hill and Professor Joos take a dualist view of language behaviour along with other linguists both in Europe and America. This view involves them in difficulties in the study of meaning. They find it convenient to apply behaviourist phonetics and mathematical phonemics to language events but cannot find a parallel behaviourist brand of semantics.

A much clearer presentation of the systemic characteristic of modern linguistics and of the dualism properly so-called is to be found in Professor Louis Hjelmslev's *Structural Analysis of Language*,[4] from which the following key quotations are taken:

(i) On the contrary, the real units of language are not sounds, or written characters, or meanings: the real units of language are the relata which these sounds, characters, and meanings represent. The main thing is not the sounds, characters, and meanings as such, but their mutual relations within the chain of speech and within the paradigms of grammar. These relations make up the system of a language, and it is this interior system which is characteristic of one language as opposed to other languages, whereas the representation by sounds,

---

[1] 'Towards a Literary Analysis', *Studies in Honor of J. S. Wilson*, University of Virginia, 1951, pp. 149–50.
[2] Martin Joos, 'Description of Language Design', *Journal of American Acoustical Society*, vol. xx (1950), p. 702.
[3] A. A. Hill, 'Towards a Literary Analysis', p. 158.
[4] *Studia Linguistica*, vol. i, 1948.

characters, and meanings is irrelevant to the system and may be changed without affecting the system.

(ii) This is why the structural approach to language, in the real sense of the word, conceived as a purely relational approach to the language pattern independently of the manifestation in the linguistic usage, has not been taken up by philologists before the present day.

If talking of one's own efforts would not be considered too pretentious, I should like to state, modestly but emphatically, that such a structural approach to language, considered merely as a pattern of mutual relations, has been and still will be my chief concern in all my endeavours within this field of study. In contradistinction to conventional philology, I have proposed the name *glossematics* (derived from Gk. γλῶσσα 'language') to denote this purely structural kind of linguistic research.

(iii) It is obvious that the description of a language must begin by stating relations between relevant units, and these statements cannot involve a statement about the inherent nature, essence or substance of these units themselves.

We can wind up this discussion by stating that linguistics describes the relational pattern of language without knowing what the relata are, and that phonetics and semantics do tell what those relata are but only by means of describing the relations between their parts and parts of their parts. This would mean, in logistic terms, that linguistics is a metalanguage of the first degree, whereas phonetics and semantics are metalanguages of the second degree.

Professor Hjelmslev gives five fundamental features which he considers are involved in the basic structure of any language in the conventional sense, namely the following:

(1) A language consists of a content and an expression.

(2) A language consists of a succession, or a text, and a system.

(3) Content and expression are bound up with each other through commutation.

(4) There are certain definite relations within the succession and within the system.

(5) There is not a one-to-one correspondence between content and expression, but the signs are decomposable in minor components. Such sign components are, e.g. the so-called phonemes, which I[1] should prefer to call taxemes of expression, and which in themselves have no content, but which can build up units provided with a content, e.g. words.

As I point out in Section III, I have always adopted a monistic approach with the basic postulate that all texts in modern spoken languages have what I call 'the implication of utterance' and of 'contexts of situation'. Language text must be attributed to participants in some context of situation in order that its modes of meaning may be stated at a series of levels, which taken together form a sort of linguistic spectrum. In this 'spectrum' the meaning of the whole event is dispersed and dealt with by a hierarchy of linguistic techniques descending from social contextualization to phonology.

[1] i.e. Professor Hjelmslev.

One last quotation from a review by Professor Hjelmslev which states the nature of general linguistics today in terms which all who work in the subject would be prepared to accept within the limits of the quoted words.[1]

La théorie linguistique de nos temps ne se confond pas avec la philosophie du langage de l'antiquité ni avec la grammaire générale du moyen-âge et de l'époque du rationalisme; elle en diffère par le fait d'être bâtie empiriquement sur l'observation d'un très grand nombre de langues. Elle n'est pas une théorie *a priori*. De plus, le problème qu'elle pose n'est pas celui du *quoi* ni du *pourquoi*; c'est celui du *comment*: la théorie est bâtie exprès pour fournir aux recherches la méthode et la technique nécessaires pour assurer aux résultats cette constance qui est la condition indispensable de toute comparaison.

Donc, si la linguistique structurale de nos jours peut paraître à certains esprits trop théorique, il ne faut pas oublier que la théorie est faite pour faciliter le travail pratique, et qu'elle est née d'un besoin pratique.

At this point, the occasion of the present article may now be mentioned in more detail. As a result of the initiative of Professor Alf Sommerfelt, the International Council for Philosophy and Humanistic Studies working with the Comité International Permanent de Linguistes, a commission[2] was set up and a conference was held in Paris to exchange views on the study of language structures with a view to finding possible correlations with other structures which might be set up in studies of social or mental habits.

It will be seen that a number of different schools of linguistics could be regarded as associated with the scholars of the symposium, and individually they all hold distinctive views in linguistics. Nevertheless, the result of the week's work was an agreed set of recommendations which might be submitted to other scholars specializing in various exotic languages with a view to their being invited to prepare what might be described as descriptive grammars broadly based on contemporary general linguistics.

II. REPORT OF THE COMMISSION SET UP BY THE INTERNATIONAL COUNCIL FOR PHILOSOPHY AND HUMANISTIC STUDIES, UNESCO, PARIS, 31 MAY–7 JUNE 1951

The projected linguistic investigation[3] is intended to serve as the basis for an examination of the relationships between language and the other aspects of culture, undertaken by linguists, cultural anthropologists, and

---

[1] 'La comparaison en linguistique structurale', *Acta Linguistica*, vol. iv (1944) [1948], pp. 144–7. A review of J. Vendryès: 'La comparaison en linguistique', *Bulletin de la Société de Linguistique de Paris*, vol. xlii, 1 (1946), pp. 1–16.

[2] Professors Alf Sommerfelt (Oslo, Chairman); E. Benveniste (Paris); J. R. Firth (London); J. H. Greenberg (Columbia); L. Hjelmslev (Copenhagen); Roman Jakobson (Harvard); C. Kluckhohn (Harvard); C. Lévi-Strauss (Paris); H. Vogt (Oslo). Professors R. Jakobson and C. Kluckhohn were prevented from attending the meeting in Paris.

[3] A further report on three completed descriptions is in the press. The following additional members of the Commission took part: Professors Raymond Firth (London); Harry Hoijer (California).

philosophers. The recommendations which follow are not put forward as a formal scheme of description. In each case the method of analysis and description to be employed should be synchronic in principle and appropriate to the structure of the language under examination. The intention is simply to bring out certain general and necessary requirements for the descriptions of the type desired. It may happen that certain of our recommendations cannot be followed on account of the special circumstances of each investigation. In addition, attention has been drawn to the importance of certain social factors without restricting in advance either the number or the nature of the observations in these matters.

The essential requirement is to outline a precise and complete description paying special attention to the features relevant to the object of the inquiry and keeping in mind that the phonemic description should serve primarily as a basis for the statement of the grammatical and lexical facts.

PHONEMICS

(1) The description should contain as accurate and complete an inventory as possible of all elements which have a differentiating function from the phonological point of view. Great attention should be paid to the distinction between such elements and their possible variants.

(2) Reasons should be given for the procedure followed in the analysis and for the distinctions set up. The elements which have been established should be studied with respect to their distribution, their frequency, their combinations, and the frequency of their combinations. An attempt should also be made to characterize words and analogous units in terms of syllabic structure. In describing syntactical intonation attention should be paid to its function in delimiting syntactic units, and to intonations which distinguish types of utterances.

The symbols used to represent in writing the elements which have been established should be simple in form and of a type generally accepted.

GRAMMAR AND LEXICON

(1) As a general principle, and as far as possible, the meaning of linguistic forms at the grammatical and lexical levels should be determined with reference to the system of the language and identified by linguistic context.

(2) In the description of the grammatical system the basic principle is to avoid the introduction of *a priori* classifications and to recognize only those linguistic distinctions which are formally expressed.

In the case of all formally expressed grammatical distinctions, a complete inventory of the elements should be drawn up and their distribution, function, and meaning at the grammatical level should be stated in terms of the grammatical system, as well as with reference to concrete situations.

The description of alternances (alternations) should be exhaustive both from the phonological and morphological points of view. Due attention must be given to stating as precisely as possible the range of grammatical distinctions expressed in the language. For example, for such distinctions as those of noun and verb, or noun and adjective, if these are found, it is necessary to indicate how far and by what means they are clearly shown. Morphological and syntactical criteria, that is to say formal structure and the conditions of use in utterance, should be constantly taken into account.

These distinctions should always be founded on formal, not notional criteria. The definitions and the terminology should be decided in accordance with the system of the language under examination.

If the language makes use of derivation and the formation of compounds, the degree of relative autonomy or fusion of the constituents must be defined as well as the degree to which they may be said to maintain separate function.

Specific mention should be made of those word junctions or compounds which are possible and those which involve incompatibilities imposed by the language system. If there is occasion, differences between the various norms such as the language of religion and of everyday life should be noted.

In stating the processes of formation of new words, it would be useful to bear in mind the productivity of types of derivation or compound formation and also the borrowing of foreign elements, adaptations, loan-translations, calques.

When classes or sub-classes are found, for example nominal or verbal classes, the statement of what each class comprises should include as complete a list as possible of examples with indications of the productivity of each one of the classes.

It will probably be found useful to consider the following points in the examination of numeration:—

(1) The terms used in counting.
(2) The formal bases of the numeral system (quinary, decimal, &c.).
(3) The rules relating to the distribution and order of the compound numerals.
(4) The possibility of deriving sub-categories such as ordinal, fractional, and multiplicative numerals.
(5) The presence of borrowing or calques based on foreign systems.

In the study of syntactical categories, special attention should be paid to the manner in which subordinate constituents are expressed and integrated, including the various ways in which the utterance analyses or synthesizes the aspects of a complex situation.

As much attention as possible should be paid to the social conditions of employment of these categories. For example, in a language with a highly complex verb system, one should specify the situations involved in the employment of the different categories.

In the case of those languages for which a dictionary has not as yet been written, the investigator is not, in principle, expected to compile one, but he should endeavour to classify as large a number of vocabulary elements as possible. He should specify which areas of vocabulary are the richest and the most differentiated.

In the analysis of vocabulary elements, it is important to group together those which form a series. Such series, for example, might be kinship terms, parts of the body, terms of orientation in time and space, numerals, calendrical terms, names of social units, proper names of persons as well as of places, in short all lexical elements which exhibit structure.

The same structural considerations should be applied to terms of sensory perception such as colours, sounds, smells, tastes, shapes and to terms of social and personal evaluation.

The attempt should be made to construct complete series of those terms, as well as all those which, according to linguistic or other criteria, form a system. In order to avoid difficulties of translation, the meanings of these terms should, as far as possible, be established through citations. Wherever structure can be discerned in elements with syntactic function such as those indicating interrogation, negation, conjunction, disjunction, connection, comparison, etc., the relations of these elements should be indicated by means of examples.

SOCIAL CONDITIONS OF USE

The expressive use of certain morphological and syntactical categories should be considered. For example, echo and rhyme-words, ideophones (Lautbilder, gestes vocaux), etc.

If the language contains several levels of diction (ordinary, narrative, emphatic, oratorical, poetic, ritual, etc.), the rhythmic, prosodic, and metrical features of each should be stated.

The following questions should also be considered:—

Does the society under consideration pronounce moral, aesthetic or other judgments regarding the language as such, and does it distinguish one or more norms of usage?

To what extent does the language show specializations on the basis of sex, age, occupation, social class, local, religious and ritual groupings?

Under what institutional auspices does the child learn to speak? In the family? In freely constituted groups? Or under what other conditions? Under what conditions are terms avoided or preferred? (tabu, euphemism, pejoratives, and terms of censure).

Does the society under consideration use one or more than one language and under what conditions? (Languages of contact, pidgin, lingua-franca, etc.) To what extent does this situation affect, on the one hand, the system and use of the language, and on the other hand the evaluation of the native languages and the languages of contact.

III. COMMENTARY

(i) *General*

After giving the general background in Section I, and the recommendations themselves in Section II, I now propose to add my own commentary on the subject before us, and I shall do this by suggesting how I should myself interpret and apply the recommendations. They were specifically directed towards eventual correlations with the findings of other social sciences in what may be rather vaguely referred to as studies of the meaning of culture.

Certain leading linguists, especially in America, find it possible to exclude the study of what they call 'meaning' from scientific linguistics, but only by deliberately excluding anything in the nature of mind, thought, idea, concept. 'Mentalism' is taboo. Why attempt to exclude things about which it is claimed so little can be known? To exclude them specifically is to acknowledge them and even to admit scholars in other disciplines may be able to help us by studying what is not only discarded but scouted by linguists.

My own approach in linguistics has always been based on an acceptance of the whole man in his patterns of living. The linguist has to reject most of these patterns, confining himself to the processes and patterns of life in which language 'text' is the central feature and operative force. The structure of life, or, better, of the living creature, is maintained while the changes of metabolism are constantly going on. The study of the whole man by biologists, anatomists, and physiologists, and even by neurologists and pathologists, is a commonplace of science. These disciplines select their special fields and their special data by applying their specialized framework of categories, and arrange what is caught in the net for statement by using a specialized language.

The linguist, in accepting the whole man in his culture context, must, it seems to me, assume that normal linguistic behaviour as a whole is meaningful effort, directed towards the maintenance of appropriate patterns of life. That being so, he also assumes that the events he selects for study have some of their ramifications in the nature of the human being and some in the special nurture which has given them meaning in any given society. The framework of linguistics is focused on the language events and generalizes from them. There is no need to select for exclusion 'minds', 'thoughts', and 'ideas'. You cannot *exclude* the fundamental urges, drives, needs, and desires of our animal and social nature. They are there. But the recognition of them in linguistics is indirect, and if any reference to them is made it is in terms of linguistics.

From this point of view, all branches of linguistics are concerned with 'meaning', even phonetics. The study of the sound of speech, regarded as just another sort of noise in the world, is a branch of physics.[1] The study

---

[1] Professor Norbert Wiener, who invented the word 'cybernetics' and might be described as a 'statistical mechanicist', misunderstands the linguistic theories of the sign summarized

of the systematic use of vocal sounds by a Frenchman as distinct from an Englishman recognizes a phonetic mode[1] in which a man may maintain a distinctive pattern of life or, in other words, you must use French sounds if your life has a French meaning. It is part of a Frenchman's meaning to sound like one.

This monistic approach requires that all language 'text' be attributed to participants in some context of situation.[2] Logicians are apt to think of words and propositions as having 'meaning' somehow in themselves, apart from participants in context of situation. Speakers and listeners do not seem to be necessary. I suggest that voices should not be entirely dissociated from the social complex in which they function and that therefore all texts in modern spoken languages should be regarded as having 'the implication of utterance', and be referred to typical participants in some generalized context of situation.

It is therefore entirely right from my point of view that the recommendations suggest that the elements of a language should be considered with reference to situations, and that syntactical categories may profitably be related to the 'various ways in which the utterance analyses or synthesizes the aspects of a complex situation'. Attention is drawn to the 'social conditions' and 'the situations' 'involved in the employment of the different categories'.

(ii) *Phonemics*

In Chapter 9 I have suggested the use of the terms *prosody* and *prosodies* to refer to structural features of words, pieces, and sentences as wholes or to features marking beginnings, endings, and junctions. Some scholars think that the term 'phonemics' should now be extended to cover the study of all the phonological elements and phonological systems of a language including tone, intonations, and all the features I have called prosodies. There would be a certain advantage in this use, since the term 'phonics' could then be applied to acoustic and other non-linguistic studies of human and animal noises, freeing the term 'phonetics'.

The recommendation that both 'words and analogous units' are to be studied 'in terms of syllable structure' does not imply any definition of the syllable in general terms, but does suggest that word structure can be stated in phonological terms appropriate to the particular language

---

in Section I of this article and postulates two aspects of language, the *phonetic* and the *semantic*. He even imagines we may have a *phonetic* receiving apparatus and a separate *semantic* one, which translates not 'word by word, but idea by idea, often still more generally'. See his propaganda work, *The Human Use of Human Beings*, London, 1950, especially pp. 88–90, which, from the point of view of linguistics, seem ill informed and unduly dependent on the binary opposition of two much-abused words, *phonetic* and *semantic*.

[1] See Chapter 15.
[2] See Chapter 14.

under examination.[1] Studies of word structure are particularly enlightening in dealing with loan-words.[2]

(iii) *Grammar and Lexicon*

It will be noticed that 'linguistic forms' are considered to have 'meanings' at the grammatical and lexical levels, such 'meanings' being determined by interrelations of the forms in the grammatical systems set up for the language. A nominative in a four-case system would in this sense necessarily have a different 'meaning' from a nominative in a two-case or in a fourteen-case system, for example.

A singular in a two-number system has different grammatical meaning from a singular in a three-number system or a four-number system such as in Fijian which formally distinguishes singular, dual, 'little' plural, and 'big' plural. The 'meaning' of the grammatical category *noun* in a grammatical system of, say, three word classes, noun, verb, and particle, is different from the meaning of the category *noun* in a system of five classes in which *adjective* and *pronoun* are formally distinguished from the noun, verb, and particle.

The application of the word 'meaning' to the function of an element with reference to the specific system of which it is a 'term', 'unit', or 'member' in a given language is an example of the mathematical method referred to in Section I.[3] This mode of meaning is clearly established and forms one part of what I have called the linguistic spectrum.[4] When they adopt this mathematical method of stating the function of phonological or grammatical elements, some linguists seem to think that they have left 'meaning' out. What they really imply is that 'meanings' and 'thoughts', 'ideas', 'concepts', 'intentions', or something they would deprecatingly describe as 'mentalist' are left out. My own approach to meaning in linguistics has always been independent of such dualisms as mind and body, language and thought, word and idea, *signifiant et signifié*, expression and content. These dichotomies are a quite unnecessary nuisance, and in my opinion should be dropped. Professor Hjelmslev can still pursue the glossematic method of stating certain modes of meaning at certain levels in any given set of systems which make up what we call a language. This is the main reason why the recommendations can be supported by all schools. In this connexion, Professor Hjelmslev's sentence previously quoted (p. 219), 'the main thing is not the sounds, characters, and meanings as such, but their mutual relations within the chain of speech and within the paradigms of grammar' would also suit me very well if I could be permitted to omit 'and meanings as such'. That phrase admits the dualistic principle which wrecks

---

[1] Chapter 9.
[2] Aasta Stene, 'English Loan-words in Modern Norwegian', *Philological Society of Great Britain*, 1947; and Eugénie Henderson, 'The Phonology of Loan-words in some South-East Asian Languages', *Trans. Phil. Society*, 1951.
[3] See pp. 219-20.
[4] See Chapters 14 and 15.

the empirical analysis of language material. The loose phrase 'meanings as such' is typical of our troubles. The substitution of 'words' for 'meanings' would be better. For Professor Hjelmslev's 'interior system of relations' is the basis of good grammatical description which states meanings at the grammatical level in functional terms appropriate to the language under examination. The pattern of mutual relations between the formal elements of Danish can be said to be habitually maintained by Professor Hjelmslev as part of his Danish way of life. Surely the pattern of these relations is part of the meaning of Danish as used by Danes.

Numeration was selected as a useful example of sets of grammatical categories falling into systems and also correlating with social conditions of use. It is important to distinguish between number (singular, dual, plural, &c.), numbers (45, eleventh, a dozen), numerals (one, two, three, &c.), figures (1, 2, 3, &c.), and the expressions used in counting things serially and in stating quantities of things that are countable and measurable. The grading of numerals[1] in numeral systems is also of interest.

The setting up of words in ordered series is one of the principal procedures in linguistics. Ordered series of words (o.s.w.) include, for example, paradigms, formal scatter,[2] so-called synonyms and antonyms, lexical groups by association, words grouped by common application in certain recurrent contexts of situation, and groups by phonaesthetic association.[3]

It should be borne in mind that the word 'elements' used in the recommendations covers pause, tone, intonation, stress as well as 'sounds'—in short, any phonological unit that can be abstracted from the phonic material.

Finally, there is nothing revolutionary or strikingly new in the recommendations. The important thing is that linguists of most schools would, I imagine, agree that any account of a modern spoken language which followed the recommendations would today be considered a good descriptive grammar.

[1] See S. Yoshitake, 'The Grading Method of Forming Numerals', *Trans. Phil. Society*, 1940.
[2] See Chapter 3.
[3] See Chapter 15.

BIBLIOGRAPHY OF OTHER WORKS BASED ON SIMILAR PRINCIPLES AND METHODS

CARNOCHAN, J. A Study in the Phonology of an Igbo Speaker, *B.S.O.A.S.* xii. 2, 1948.
A Study of Quantity in Hausa, ibid. xiii. 4, 1951.
Glottalization in Hausa, *T.P.S.*, 1952.
HENDERSON, Miss E. J. A. Notes on the Syllable Structure of Lushai, *B.S.O.A.S.* xii. 3 and 4, 1948.
A Phonetic Study of Western Ossetic (Digoron), ibid. xiii. 1, 1949.
Prosodies in Siamese, *Asia Major*, i. 2, 1949.
Digoron Word-List (with H. W. BAILEY), *B.S.O.A.S.* xiii. 2, 1950.
The Phonology of Loanwords in some South-East Asian Languages, *T.P.S.*, 1951.
The Main Features of Cambodian Pronunciation, *B.S.O.A.S.* xiv. 1, 1952.
MITCHELL, T. F. The Active Participle in an Arabic Dialect of Cyrenaica, ibid.
Particle-Noun Complexes in a Berber Dialect (Zuara), ibid. xv. 2, 1953.
Writing Arabic. Oxford University Press, 1953.
Introduction to Egyptian Colloquial Arabic. Oxford University Press, 1956.
PALMER, F. R. The 'Broken Plurals' of Tigrinya, *B.S.O.A.S.* xvii. 3, 1955.
'Openness' in Tigre: a Problem in Prosodic Statement, ibid. xviii. 3, 1956.
ROBINS, R. H. *Ancient and Mediaeval Grammatical Theory in Europe.* Bell & Sons, Ltd., London, 1951.
Notes on the Phonetics of the Georgian Word (with Mrs. N. WATERSON). *B.S.O.A.S.* xiv. 1, 1952.
A Problem in the Statement of Meaning, *Lingua*, iii. 2, 1952.
Noun and Verb in Universal Grammar, *Language*, vol. 28, no. 3, pt. 1, 1952.
The Phonology of the Nasalized Verbal Forms in Sundanese, *B.S.O.A.S.* xv. 1, 1953.
Formal Divisions in Sundanese, *T.P.S.*, 1953.
Five Yurok Songs: a Musical and Textual Analysis (with Miss N. MCLEOD). *B.S.O.A.S.* xviii. 3, 1956.
SCOTT, N. C. The Monosyllable in Szechuanese, ibid. xii. 1, 1947.
A Study in the Phonetics of Fijian, ibid. xii. 3 and 4, 1948.
A Dictionary of Sea Dayak. School of Oriental and African Studies, 1956.
A Phonological Analysis of the Szechuanese Monosyllable, *B.S.O.A.S.* xviii. 3, 1956.
SHARP, A. E. A Tonal Analysis of the Disyllabic Noun in the Machame Dialect of Chaga, ibid. xvi. 1, 1954.
SPRIGG, R. K. Verbal Phrases in Lhasa Tibetan. I, ibid; II, ibid. 2, 1954; III, ibid. 3, 1954.
The Tonal System of Tibetan (Lhasa Dialect) and the Nominal Phrase, ibid. xvii. 1, 1955.

WATERSON, Mrs. N. Notes on the Phonetics of the Georgian Word (with Mr. R. H. ROBINS), *B.S.O.A.S.* xiv. 1, 1952.
Some Aspects of the Phonology of the Nominal Forms of the Turkish Word, ibid. xviii. 3, 1956.

See also the work of the following:
ALLEN, Prof. W. S. The Indo-European Primary Affix *-b[h]-, *T.P.S.*, 1950.
Notes on the Phonetics of an Eastern Armenian Speaker, ibid.
Phonetics and Comparative Linguistics, *Archivum Linguisticum*, iii, fasc. ii.
A Study in the Analysis of Hindi Sentence Structure, *Acta Linguistica*, vi. 2–3, 1950–1.
Some Prosodic Aspects of Retroflexion and Aspiration in Sanskrit, *B.S.O.A.S.* xiii. 4, 1951.
Phonetics in Ancient India. London Oriental Series, 1, 1953 (Geoffrey Cumberlege, Oxford University Press).
Relationship in Comparative Linguistics, *T.P.S.*, 1953.
Retroflexion in Sanskrit: Prosodic Technique and its Relevance to Comparative Statement, *B.S.O.A.S.* xvi. 3, 1954.
Structure and System in the Abaza Verbal Complex, *T.P.S.*, 1956.
HAAS, W. On Defining Linguistic Units, *T.P.S.*, 1954.
HALLIDAY, Dr. M. A. K. 'A Study of the Language of the Chinese Version of the "Secret History of the Mongols".' Thesis presented for the Degree of Ph.D., University of Cambridge, 1955.
Grammatical Categories in Modern Chinese, *T.P.S.*, 1956.
MACFARLANE, J. Modes of Translation, *Durham University Journal*, 1953.

Abbreviations used:

B.S.O.A.S. Bulletin of the School of Oriental and African Studies, University of London.
T.P.S. Transactions of the Philological Society.

INDEX

Aelfric, 100-1.
Alliteration, 194, 198, 203.
Alphabetum anglicum, 106-7.
Alternances, 1-2, 3-5, 36-37, 38, 47-52, 71-74, 80-91, 222-3.
American Indian languages, 162, 163-4, 167, 172.
American language, the, 157 et seq.
American Oriental Society, the, 161-2, 164, 166.
American Philosophical Society, the, 160, 161, 163, 164,
Arabic alphabet, 111-12.
Aspiration, 59, 63, 64.

Bedeutungslehre, 8.
Beligatti, C., 59-60.
Bell, Alexander Graham, 95, 96, 110, 119, 166.
Bell, Alexander Melville, 94, 95, 96, 102, 110, 111, 113, 116-19, 166.
Bloomfield, L., 15-16, 167-8, 179.
Bréal, 8, 11-12, 13, 15, 16, 17.
Bright, Timothy, 102-3, 104-6.
Bullokar, W. (1586), 98-99, 107.
Butler, Charles (1633), 108.

Cardinalization, 146, 148-55.
Carpani, M., 62-66.
Categories, 145, 223, 225, 226, 228.
Chambers, R. W., 97.
Character:
    (i) Chinese, 103, 104, 105.
    (ii) real, 103.
    (iii) universal, 102-3.
    (iv) general, 103, 106.
Chiming, 194.
Citation, 212, 224.
Coles, Elisha (1674), 101-2.
Collocation, 194-214.
Consonant, 145-6.
Constructs, 190.
Contextualization, 3, 4, 5, 6, 7, 10, 13, 14, 18, 19, 20, 21, 24, 25-28, 29-33, 35-46, 71-74, 122, 192-4, 195, 197, 199, 201, 203, 205, 222, 226, 228.
Conversation, 31-32.

Dalgarno, 104, 106, 109-10.
Darmesteter, 8, 9, 11, 15.
de Courtenay, Baudouin, 1, 17, 71, 167, 218.
de Saussure, F., 2, 8, 16, 17, 71, 121, 144, 167, 179-81, 183, 190-1, 217.
Devanagari, 110, 111, 112, 125.
Diacritica:
    (i) phonetic, 80.

    (ii) prosodic, 79, 91, 127.
    (iii) syllabic, 76, 80, 86.
    (iv) general, 127.
Difference, differentiation, 3, 5, 6, 25, 39, 48, 49, 50, 51; differential, 52, 80, 85-86, 87, 88, 89, 91, 133.
Digraphs, 59.
Distribution, 10, 20, 37, 42, 45, 49, 127, 131, 195, 206, 222.
Dualism, 19, 217, 219, 227.
du Ponceau, P. S., 162, 163.
Duration, 174.

Edgerton, Franklin, 165.
Elements, 20, 21, 24, 76, 82, 83, 84, 89, 90, 133, 134, 222, 223, 224, 227, 228.
Ellis, A. J., 94, 109, 110-11, 113, 115, 116, 166.
Etymology, 8-9, 14, 15.

Facts (statement of), 140, 144, 145.
Formal conditions, 24, 223.
Franklin, Benjamin, 158, 160, 161.
Function, 19, 20-21, 24, 26-27, 31, 33, 71, 72, 143, 222, 224, 227.

Gardiner, A., 7, 18, 24, 181.
Gemination, 174.
General linguistics, 7, 143, 156, 170-1, 190.
Grammar (descriptive), 3, 5-6, 7, 16.
Grammar (universal), 140.
Grammatical designation, 7, 11, 14, 192.

Haldeman, S., 114-16, 125, 166.
Hart, John (1569), 98, 99-100, 101, 111.
Historical principle, 7-8, 12, 16, 17.
Hjelmslev, Louis, 140, 217-18, 219-20, 221, 227-8.
Holder, William (1669), 108-9, 110, 111, 116.
Hume, Alexander (1617), 95-96, 97.

Instances, 127, 137, 173.
Institutions (linguistic), 122, 191, 192.
International Phonetic Association, 93-94, 145, 167, 169.
Isolate, 122, 147, 190, 192, 198.

Jakobson, Roman, 167.
Jespersen, Otto, 2, 24, 169, 179, 219.
Johnson, Samuel, 7, 9, 11, 12-13, 17, 142, 183.
Jones, Daniel, 2, 93, 94, 95, 97, 146, 159, 167, 169, 170.

INDEX

Jones, Sir William, 17, 106, 107, 110, 111–14, 116, 125–6, 161, 165.
Junction, 49, 123.

King's English, the, 157–8.
Kruschevski, 1–2, 218.

Labio-velarization, 80, 86, 88; see also w-features.
Language community, 186.
Lear, Edward, 194, 195.
Lepsius, 114, 115, 165.
Letters, 22.
Level, levels, 24, 25, 26, 144, 145, 170–1, 182, 183, 192, 193, 194, 195, 197, 198, 201, 202, 205, 206, 214, 222, 224, 227.
Lexicography, lexicographical, lexical, 7, 19, 20, 26, 36, 37, 41, 42, 46, 49, 120, 192, 227.
Linearity, 147.
Linguistic analysis, 70, 144, 190.

Malinowski, B., 30, 143, 169, 170, 181, 182.
Meaning, meanings:
    (i) applied, 9, 10, 12;
    (ii) central, 9;
    (iii) change of, 8, 9, 11, 12, 13, 14, 15, 16;
    (iv) component of, 7, 10, 14, 18, 19, 20, 24, 26, 33, 192;
    (v) domain of, 9;
    (vi) essential, 10;
    (vii) general, 7, 32, 33, 190, 214, 227, 228;
    (viii) grammatical, 11, 24, 197;
    (ix) mode of, 191, 193, 194, 197, 198, 200, 213;
    (x) original, 9, 10, 12;
    (xi) primary [denotation], 11, 12;
    (xii) secondary [connotation], 11;
    (xiii) specialized, 12.
Meillet, A., 9–10, 12, 14, 121, 179, 180–1, 218.
Morphology, 14, 15, 18, 19, 23, 24, 37, 38, 41, 45, 50.
Multiple definition, 10–11.
Multiple statements, 192.
Murray, Lindley, 100, 110, 127–8, 158–60.

Nasalization, 51, 59, 62, 71, 80, 84, 85, 88, 89, 134.
New English Dictionary (Oxford), 7, 8, 9, 11, 13, 14, 15, 16, 17, 28.
Nomenclature, 140–1.
Notation, 3, 47–8, 49, 79, 85, 91, 123, 124, 125–7, 133, 136, 141, 146.

Ogden, C. K., 10, 16, 19, 168–9.
Onomatopoeia, 192, 194.

Paradigm, 121, 219, 227.
Passy, Paul, 93–94.
Peanius, C., 60–62.
Person, personality, 141, 142, 143, 144, 171, 181, 182, 183–5, 186, 187, 188, 189.
Philological Society, the, 7, 8, 92, 102, 116, 119, 120.
Phonaesthetic, 39, 41, 44, 45, 73, 194, 196, 197, 198, 199, 201, 228.
Phonematic, 122, 123, 127, 128, 130, 131, 132, 133, 134, 135, 136, 137, 138, 146, 192, 193.
Phoneme (first use in English), 21.
Phoneme, 1–2, 3–4, 5, 21, 38, 45, 48, 51, 71, 122, 123, 125, 128, 145, 167.
Phonemics, 145, 167, 219, 222, 226.
Phones, 4, 145, 146, 147.
Phonetics, 21–25, 34, 35, 37, 47–48.
Phonetic sequence, 73.
Phonetic transcription, 148.
Phonic, 226, 228.
Phonology, 34–35, 192; see also Phoneme, Phonemics, Phonetics, Phonematic, Prosody.
Pickering, John, 161, 162–3.
Pitman, I., 102, 106, 108, 109.
Place, 35, 76–77, 80, 91.
Prosody, prosodies, prosodic, 79, 121, 122, 123, 124, 125, 126, 127, 128, 129, 130, 131, 132, 133, 134, 135, 136, 137, 138, 146, 192, 193, 194, 196, 197, 198, 199, 200, 201, 207, 208, 224, 226.
Punctuation, 6.

Quantity, 127, 128, 129, 130, 174.

Relations, 19, 21, 127, 128, 130, 137, 182, 219, 220, 221.
Relations (contextual), 19, 20, 21.
Relations (statement of), 220, 228.
Retroflex consonants, 49, 59, 61, 150–1.
Richards, I. A., 10, 16, 19, 168–9.
Ritual (social), 28, 31–32.
Robins, R. H., 216.
Roget, S., 106.
Roles, 28, 29.
Royal Society, the, 160.

Sapir, 24, 167, 172.
Scatter, formal, 13, 26.
Segments, 127, 137, 147.
Semantic, 7, 15.
Semantics, 7, 8, 13, 15–16, 17, 18, 19, 21, 23, 25.
Series, 71, 72, 73, 228.
Shorthand, 102, 103, 104, 106.
Situation, 3, 25–32, 33, 35, 37, 39, 42, 45, 75, 144, 181–3, 192, 197, 199, 203, 205, 208, 223, 224, 226, 228.
Skeat, 8.

INDEX

Smith, Sir Thomas (1568), 98, 106–7, 108, 111, 157.
Smithsonian Institution, the, 162, 163.
Sommerfelt, A., 221.
Speech fellowship, 186, 187.
Sperber, H., 10, 12, 13.
Statement, 140, 141, 145, 146, 147.
Straumann, H., 18, 19, 38.
Structuralism, 219, 220.
Structure, 36, 121, 122, 123, 125, 126, 128, 130, 131, 132, 136, 142, 143, 146, 222, 223, 224, 226, 227.
Stylistics, 190, 194, 196, 198, 202, 204, 206, 212.
Substitution, 5, 20–21, 22, 24, 25, 26, 27, 37, 39, 40, 42, 45, 48, 50, 71.
Sweet, 2, 92, 94, 95, 102, 110, 111, 119, 120, 141, 146, 159, 166–7, 169, 183, 218.
Swinburne, 196-203.
Syllabic features, 80.
Syllable, 37, 48, 63, 64, 76, 77, 78, 80, 81, 82, 83, 84, 85, 86, 88, 90, 91, 122, 125, 126, 127, 128, 129, 130, 131, 132, 133, 134, 135, 146, 222, 226.
Syntax, 192.
System, 40, 43, 47, 73, 74, 122, 123, 128, 130, 132, 133, 134, 135, 136, 137, 139, 143, 144, 145, 147.
Systematic, 73, 139, 187.
Systemic, 35, 36, 143, 144, 145, 147, 187.
  (i) Monosystemic, 121, 123, 137.
  (ii) Polysystemic, 121, 137.

Terminology, 140-1.
Terms, *see* Units.

Texts, 75, 145, 192, 225.
Theory, 140, 141, 143, 144.
Time-track, 147.
Tongues of Men, 106, 160.
Transcription, 47, 51, 53, 146, 147.
Translation, 32, 193, 198, 224.
Trench, 9, 15.
Troubetzkoy, 167, 169, 179, 218.

Units (or terms), 37, 39, 40, 43, 47, 48, 51, 71, 72, 73, 74, 86, 89, 90, 91, 222.
Utterance, 145, 146, 147, 226.

Values, 35, 72.
Vowel, 145–6.
Vowel harmony, 5, 130, 134.

Wallis, Dr. John, 102, 108, 109, 115, 116.
Webster, Noah, 157-8, 160.
w-features, 133.
Wegener, P., 181-2.
Whitney, W. D., 111, 158, 165–6.
Wilkins, J. (1668), 103, 104, 105, 106.
Word (theory of), 5.
Words (focal, pivotal), 10, 13.
Words, pieces and phrases as wholes, 91, 121, 122, 130, 134, 137, 149, 150, 155, 173, 201, 204.
Wright, J., 93, 95, 120.

y-features, yotization, 60, 80, 81, 82, 84, 85, 86, 89, 90, 91, 133.

Zipf, 11.

SET IN
GREAT BRITAIN
AT THE
UNIVERSITY PRESS
OXFORD
AND REPRINTED
LITHOGRAPHICALLY BY
HALSTAN AND CO. LTD.